Lady Nugent's
Journal
of Her Residence in Jamaica
from 1801 to 1805

MARIA NUGENT
From a pencil and wash drawing by John Downman

Lady Nugent's
Journal

of Her Residence in Jamaica from 1801 to 1805

EDITED BY

PHILIP WRIGHT

WITH A FOREWORD BY VERENE A. SHEPHERD

THE UNIVERSITY OF THE WEST INDIES PRESS

Barbados • Jamaica • Trinidad and Tobago

University of the West Indies Press
1A Aqueduct Flats Mona
Kingston 7 Jamaica

©2002 by The University of the West Indies Press
All rights reserved. Published 2002

06   5 4 3 2

CATALOGUING IN PUBLICATION DATA

Nugent, Maria, Lady, 1771?–1834.
Lady Nugent's journal of her residence in Jamaica from
1801 to 1805 / Lady Maria Nugent; edited by Philip Wright
with a foreword by Verene A. Shepherd.
p. cm.
Previously published: Kingston: Institute of Jamaica, 1966.

ISBN: 976-640-128-4

1. Nugent, Maria, Lady, 1771?–1834. 2. Jamaica –
Description and travel. I. Wright, Philip.

F1871.N95 2002   917.202

Cover design by Robert Harris.
Printed in the United States of America.

CONTENTS

LIST OF ILLUSTRATIONS

PREFACE

A Journal of a voyage to, and residence in, the island of Jamaica, from 1801 to 1805, and of subsequent events in England from 1805 to 1811, by Maria, Lady Nugent, was first printed in 1839, for private circulation only, five years after the death of its author. A separate journal dealing with her residence in India from 1811 to 1815 was printed at the same time. The Jamaica journal was edited, together with extracts from the India journal, by Frank Cundall and published in 1907 with the title *Lady Nugent's Journal*; subsequent editions appeared in 1934 and 1939.

Cundall's treatment of the text of the Jamaica journal has been generally followed in the present edition; that is to say, in the part dealing with Jamaica nothing has been omitted except some trivialities and repetitions, but the part dealing with life in England is considerably abridged. A few entries omitted by Cundall have, however, been restored to the text, while extracts from the India journal are altogether excluded. The title of previous editions, *Lady Nugent's Journal*, is retained, but in the introduction and notes the author is referred to as *Mrs.* Nugent, the style by which she was known throughout her stay in Jamaica, while writing the journal.

Identifications of people mentioned in the journal, and biographical notes, are incorporated in the index of persons at the end of the book; in a few cases only, biographical information is repeated for convenience in the footnotes. The introduction attempts to fill in some of the background of the diary mainly by reference to General Nugent's official correspondence. The results of his labours, so often alluded to by his wife, are preserved in several collections. Many of his despatches among the Colonial Office papers at the Public Record Office, London (C.O.), are duplicated in the Nugent MSS at the Institute of Jamaica. All quotations in this edition from Nugent's letters to Admiral Duckworth are from the MS collection of Nugent-Duckworth correspondence in the Library of Rhodes House, Oxford. I am grateful to the Curators of the Bodleian Library for allowing use to be made of this collection, and for permitting reproduction of part of one of the two letters in it written by Maria Nugent. I also wish to thank the Librarian of the Royal United Service Institution for allowing me to consult the collection of General Nugent's papers in his care (mostly dealing with military business), and the Earl of Crawford and Balcarres and the Keeper of Manuscripts at the John Rylands Library, Manchester, for allowing me to examine the Crawford MSS, relating to Lord Balcarres' governorship, on loan to that library.

I am grateful to the Hon. Mrs. Christopher Fremantle and the Oxford University Press for permission to quote from the *Wynne diaries*; to Sir Guy Nugent, Bart., for permission to reproduce the family group by Downman; to the West India Committee, for permission to reproduce two paintings by Wickstead; and to the Trustees of the British Museum, for permission to reproduce the portraits of Gen. and Maria Nugent by Downman, and sections of Robertson's maps of Jamaica. Finally I would like to thank Dr. Elsa Goveia and Mr. H. P. Jacobs for reading a draft typescript of the introduction and notes, and for making a number of helpful suggestions; Mons. Raphael Bogat and Professor Gabriel Debien, for information derived from French archives; and Miss Glory Robertson, for much help in checking points of detail in the West India Reference Library of the Institute of Jamaica, after I had left the island. Anyone who has resorted to that indispensable library as much as I have must feel indebted to the late Frank Cundall who did so much to build it up: and who, perhaps, performed not the least of his many services to readers interested in Jamaica, when he introduced them to Maria Nugent's Journal.

P.W.

INTRODUCTION

Maria Nugent

Maria Nugent's Journal is mainly concerned with life in the household of the Governor of Jamaica during a period of about four years, from August 1801 to June 1805. As the Governor's wife, the writer found herself at the centre of a slave-owning society, with a part to play there and no mere onlooker, yet observing its manners with the curiosity of a stranger. She met everyone of importance in the colony, for sooner or later everyone was to be seen at the Governor's mansion in Spanish Town, either calling on business or sitting down to the huge suffocating dinners which were routine during sessions of the Assembly. Mrs. Nugent also accompanied her husband on a tour round the island, encountering the local bigwigs on their home ground and sampling the hospitality of planters' houses in every parish. Her diary has been recognised as one of the most interesting of the contemporary accounts of colonial life in the West Indies, and a distinguished American scholar has described it as giving "an utterly inimitable and imperishable picture of planter society."[1]

In one respect the Journal is tantalising. Its writer had a close-up view of the business of administering the greatest of the British West Indian colonies during a critical period of the Napoleonic war. The diary faithfully tracks the Governor on his everlasting round of official duties, and reflects his worries and vexations about island politics and military defence. But although Mrs. Nugent copies out confidential despatches and knows about everything that goes on, she is markedly reticent about matters of state in her Journal, confining herself for the most part to brief allusions and rather evasive hints. More than once she promises to say more at a later date, but never does. It may be that in the heat and the social hustle she could not be bothered to explain situations which did not greatly interest her, except in so far as they affected her husband's

[1] Lowell J. Ragatz, *The fall of the planter class in the British Caribbean*, New York, 1928.

digestion. She wrote for her own amusement and the future interest of her children, not with a view to publication. The lists of guests and visitors, which she scribbled down daily, perhaps had the practical function of aiding her social memory.

Maria Nugent was born in 1771, probably at Perth Amboy in New Jersey, of American parents whose ancestry was Scottish, Irish and Dutch. Her paternal grandfather, the Reverend William Skinner, came from Scotland. He belonged to the clan MacGregor; as a young man he had taken arms for the Stuart cause in 1715, and probably stood in the MacGregor contingent at the battle of Sherrifmuir. When the rebellion collapsed, and the rebels were hunted, he went into hiding in the house of a friend called Skinner, whose name he prudently adopted; and thus camouflaged, got out of the country and eventually made his way to North America. Such, at any rate, was the family tradition. What is certain is that in 1718 William Skinner began teaching school in Philadelphia; he was sponsored by the Bishop of London, and a few years later, on the Bishop's advice, he returned to England to take holy orders, and went out to America again under the auspices of the Society for the Propagation of the Gospel; in 1724 he became the first Rector of St. Peter's Episcopal Church at Perth Amboy. He was twice married, firstly to the widow of a fellow missionary, and secondly to the daughter of a famous Dutch-American family: Elizabeth Van Cortlandt, whose father, Stephen Van Cortlandt, was some time Mayor and Chief Justice of New York. The eldest son of this marriage was Cortlandt (or Courtlandt) Skinner, who became a lawyer, practising first at Newark and later at Perth Amboy. In 1752 he married Elizabeth Kearney, whose father was also a New Jersey lawyer and whose grandfather had emigrated from Ireland. Courtlandt and Elizabeth Skinner had five sons and seven daughters, the fifth of whom was Maria, the future Mrs. Nugent.

Almost nothing is known of Maria Skinner's early life. Her father was a prominent citizen of New Jersey, being Attorney General and Speaker of the Assembly for more than ten years. When the War of Independence came, the New Jersey Congress offered him command of the provincial troops, but Skinner chose the loyalist side; he fled to the British headquarters on Staten Island, and his wife and family received orders to quit their home. Sir William Howe commissioned him Brigadier-General of all troops to be raised for the Crown in New Jersey, and he succeeded in raising four battalions of Volunteers – "Skinner's Greens", or "The Tory

Brigade of New Jersey" – which he commanded in several minor engagements. He was able to supply the British command with useful military
intelligence, and Lord Cornwallis afterwards deposed "that he had from
him once a week a perfect account of the real state of Washington's army."
After the war the Skinner family removed to the British Isles, where
Courtlandt received compensation for his forfeited American property,
and a Brigadier-General's half pay until his death in 1799. Most of his
twelve children entered, or married into, the British armed forces or other
branches of Government service. At the time of his death he was resident
in Bristol, but the Skinners also had property in Ireland, and it may be
that Maria was living in that country before her marriage, which took
place in Belfast in 1797.

Her husband, also, was of Irish descent. His grandfather was Robert,
Earl Nugent, a genial Irish peer who sat in the House of Commons for
forty years, held minor office in several Governments, and acquired a
small fame and a great fortune by successively marrying two very rich
widows. Earl Nugent was predeceased by his only son, Edmund, a
Lt.-Col. of the Foot Guards, who died unmarried in 1771, leaving two
natural sons: George, the future Governor of Jamaica, and Charles Edmund, a future Admiral.[1] George, who was born in 1757, entered the
army at the age of sixteen and saw active service in the American war.
After taking part in Clinton's expedition up the Hudson he served chiefly
in New York and may well have met the Skinner family at that time.

George Nugent and his brother inherited their grandfather's personal
estate of £200,000, and benefited in other ways from the family connection. Their father's half-sister – Earl Nugent's daughter by his third wife –
had married George Grenville, who later became the first Marquess of
Buckingham (and eventually inherited Earl Nugent's title and real estate).
The Grenvilles were a lordly family, rich and influential. Lord Buckingham was the eldest surviving son of the George Grenville who, as Chancellor of the Exchequer, had imposed the Stamp Act on the American
colonies in 1765. Buckingham's aunt had married William Pitt, first Earl

---

[1] Claud Nugent, in his *Memoir of Robert, Earl Nugent*, 1898, says that Edmund Nugent
was alleged to have married a Miss Elizabeth Vernon in 1755, but that after the birth
of George and Charles Edmund and a daughter who died young, the marriage, which
had been opposed by Earl Nugent, was set aside (possibly having failed to comply
with the forms laid down by the Marriage Act of 1753 to put a stop to clandestine
marriages); whereupon Elizabeth Vernon left her supposed husband and returned
to her family, but later married a Count Du Pont. However this may be, it seems
likely that she is the Madame Du Pont mentioned in the later part of this Journal.

Chatham; his younger brother, Thomas Grenville, interested himself in politics and diplomacy, was a close friend of Charles Fox, and bequeathed a library of 20,000 volumes to the British Museum; and the third brother, William Wyndham, Lord Grenville, was Foreign Secretary from 1791 to 1801 and Prime Minister in 1806-7. Lord Buckingham himself had twice been Lord Lieutenant of Ireland, and had a reputation for arrogant manners and an overweening family pride. In middle age he retired from the forefront of politics, to preside over the family interest from his mansion of Stowe, in Buckinghamshire, of which county he was Lord Lieutenant.

The Grenville influence was brought to bear on George Nugent's career. He was ADC to Lord Buckingham in Ireland. For ten years he was Member of Parliament for Buckingham, a "rotten borough" where voting was controlled by the Marquess. When war broke out with France, he raised a corps of Buckinghamshire Volunteers, later known as the 85th Light Infantry, and became Colonel of the regiment; a very remunerative position owing to the valuable perquisites attached to it. After a period of service with his regiment in the Netherlands, he was appointed to the staff in Ireland, and promoted Major-General. In 1797, at the age of forty, he married. During the rebellion which broke out the following year he commanded the Northern District of Ireland, and after the rebellion was Adjutant General until March 1801, when he resigned.

In December 1800 the Nugents were staying with the Buckinghams at Stowe, presumably on Christmas leave from Ireland, and we get a glimpse of Mrs. Nugent through the eyes of a fellow guest and diarist, the twenty-one-year-old wife of Captain Thomas Fremantle, RN, another protégé of the Marquess. Her first impression was unfavourable:

Lady Temple has very engaging gentle manners and I like her excessively as she is perfectly unaffected, but Mrs. Nugent is the most conceited little woman I ever saw, she is very pretty though shorter than myself, she has the smallest head that can be, very thin and little. She is an amazing dresser, never appears twice in the same gown.

Ten days later, the ladies go on a shopping expedition in Buckingham:

Mrs. Nugent bought a great deal of lace, she seems not to care how much money she spends in dress, but she truly improves upon acquaintance and is a pleasant, even-tempered little woman.[1]

Mrs. Nugent says that her husband was surprised by his appointment as Lieutenant-Governor and Commander-in-Chief of Jamaica; which,

[1] Anne Fremantle, ed., *The Wynne diaries*, 1935-40.

however, he had applied for directly he reached London from Ireland and learned that the Governor designate, Major-General Knox, had been drowned at sea on his way out to take up the appointment. The island was still referred to as the Crown's most important colony, and its governorship was among the most highly prized.[1] The Nugents landed in Jamaica at the end of July 1801. Within the next thirty months their two eldest children were born, and the later part of the diary shows Mrs. Nugent becoming more and more preoccupied with the infants' health and the chances of getting them out of the country alive. She sailed for England with them in June 1805, but her husband remained in his command until the following February, when he handed over to Sir Eyre Coote. Soon after reaching England, Mrs. Nugent makes for Stowe, where she has "a long and very interesting conversation with Lord Buckingham, on the subject of General Nugent's affairs."

General Nugent was hoping for a Knighthood of the Bath, but he had to be content with being made a Baronet. After his return he commanded successively the Western and Kent Military Districts of England, and in 1811 was appointed Commander-in-Chief of the army in India. Lady Nugent (as she had now become) went with him, leaving her children in the care of her friends at Stowe.[2] She began a new journal, which tells of Sir George endlessly reviewing the troops, as of old, and overburdened with paper work in the heat of Calcutta. But the Indian Journal, with its rather studied descriptions of scenery and excursions into Indian history, has very few flashes of the gaiety which enlivens the Jamaican one. Possibly the ex-Governor and his amiable consort (as the Jamaican newspapers used to call her) found it difficult to be quite satisfied with a secondary position. Sir George felt himself slighted by Lord Moira, the new Governor-General, and in 1813 he resigned his command. This was the end of his active career.

The Nugents returned to Buckinghamshire and settled down to pass the rest of their days at Westhorpe, their house near Marlow. From 1818

[1] "The office of governor, or lieutenant-governor, of Jamaica is a very lucrative and important one." (J. Stewart, *Account of Jamaica*, Edinburgh, 1808). In a later edition, this is expanded into: "The Government of Jamaica is the most lucrative in the gift of the Crown, next to the Lord-Lieutenancy of Ireland and the Governor-Generalship of India. Including emoluments, it is computed to yield about £10,000 per annum." Nugent himself put the total emoluments at about £8500 per annum on the average in peace time and almost double that amount during a war with Spain (when the Governor received fees from the granting of trading licences to Spanish ships, as well as a percentage of the value of ships seized and goods confiscated).

[2] She gave birth to her younger son, Charles Edmund, five weeks before she sailed.

to 1832 Sir George again represented the borough of Buckingham in Parliament. His lady resumed her good works in the parish, but otherwise we know as little of the last twenty years of her life as we do of the first twenty-five. She died in 1834; the printing of her Journals five years later was perhaps by way of a tribute from her family. Sir George survived her by fifteen years, was promoted Field-Marshal, and died at the age of ninety-one, leaving four children. He was buried beside his wife in the church at Little Marlow, a small village which still has an air of rural seclusion. Her memorial tablet reads:

Sacred to the memory of Maria the much lamented wife of Gen. Sir George Nugent Bart. of Westhorpe House Bucks. and daughter of Brigadier-Gen. Cortland Skinner who died Oct. 24 1834 leaving her husband and children in the deepest affliction for the loss of one whose strictly religious principles, angelic temper and endearing qualities rendered her sincerely and universally beloved. She will long be mourned by the poor of the parish of whom she was for many years the devoted benefactress and friend.[1]

And the last of her benefactions is recorded on a wooden plaque, also in the church:

£600
Bequeathed to the Parish
of Little Marlow by MARIA
LADY NUGENT and placed in
the Hands of the Proprietor of Westhorpe
Estate and the Vicar for the Time being
as Trustees, the Interest of which Sum is to be applied
as follows for the Benefit of the Poor –
£10 per Annum to provide 12 Loaves of Bread for as
many in Number of the most helpless & impoverished Persons
on every alternate Sunday in the Year –
£10 per Annum to provide Salaries for the Master and Mistress
of the Sunday School. £5 each – The remaining
Interest of the Bequest is to provide
Bibles, Testaments, Common Prayer Books,
Slates and any other Articles
considered most useful for the
School
1834.

The small income from this bequest still serves to provide some books for the school and a Christmas present for some old people of the parish.

---

[1] The church also contains memorials to her younger son Charles Edmund (1811-1890), her sister Catherine Robinson and her brother-in-law Admiral Sir Charles Edmund Nugent.

MARIA NUGENT'S RELATIONS

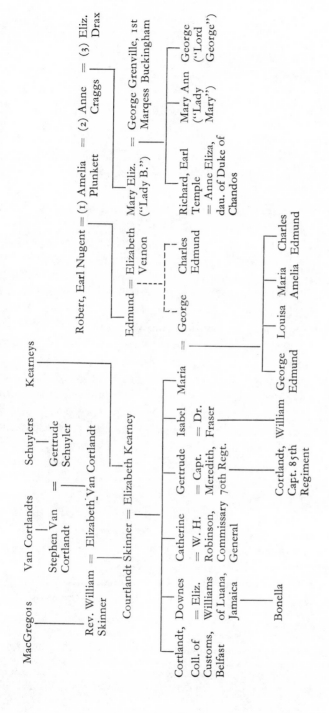

Brothers and sisters of Maria not mentioned in the Journal are omitted.

The Shadow of Saint-Domingue

When the Nugents arrived in Jamaica, Britain had been at war with France for eight years, and for four years with France's allies or satellites, Spain and the Netherlands. The struggle was economic as well as military, and both sides attached great importance to the commerce of their West Indian colonies. It was the opinion of Henry Dundas, the British Secretary for War, that the landing of 15,000 French from a superior fleet in Jamaica would be a greater disaster than their landing in the British Isles; "the loss of Jamaica would be complete ruin to our credit."[1] There was fighting in the Eastern Caribbean, where, as in previous wars, several islands changed hands; but the British generally had superiority at sea, and by 1801 they were in occupation of Martinique, Trinidad, the Dutch settlements in Guiana and Curaçao, and other enemy possessions; all of which, except Trinidad, were restored under the Treaty of Amiens in March 1802, but retaken after the war was resumed in 1803. Only once did Jamaica seem in immediate danger of attack. This was in the early part of 1805, when, at one stage of the transatlantic chase which preceded the battle of Trafalgar, the French for some weeks had a superior force in the Caribbean. Mrs. Nugent was still in Jamaica, and describes the flurry of defence preparations and a tense period of waiting for the attack which never came.

Nevertheless, for some years there was a danger-point very close to Jamaica, which needed careful watching: the French colony of Saint-Domingue, little more than a hundred miles to windward.[2] Up to the time of the French Revolution, Saint-Domingue had been the most richly

[1] In a letter dated 24th August 1796, quoted in *Cambridge History of the British Empire*, v. 2, p. 66.
[2] The western part of the island which Columbus had called La Isla Española (anglicised Hispaniola) was occupied by the French colony of Saint-Domingue, now Haiti, and the eastern part by the Spanish colony of Santo Domingo, now the Dominican Republic. The British applied the name St. Domingo to the whole island.

productive of all Caribbean colonies; more productive, it was said, than all the British islands put together. But how could a slave colony continue in business under the banner of Liberty and Equality? In the early stages of the revolution, while the National Assembly in Paris debated the rights of free mulattoes, there was skirmishing in Saint-Domingue between whites and mulattoes and between royalist and republican whites, and some knowledge of what was going on inevitably permeated among the slaves. In May 1791 the French Assembly declared for political equality between freeborn coloured men and whites. But soon after the news of this decree reached Saint-Domingue, all other hostilities were merged in the much greater upheaval of a slave rebellion.

The kind of nightmare which haunted every colonial planter now became sickeningly real in Saint-Domingue. Plantations flamed, towns were looted, murders were avenged by massacres with the desperate atrocity of racial fear and hatred. After twelve months of havoc, the Jacobin Government in France sent out a Commission, backed by military force, to restore order in the colony. But the troops proved ineffective; to crush the resistance of royalist-minded colonists, the Commission enlisted the support of the revolted slaves, and proclaimed the abolition of slavery. White colonists fled for refuge to the United States, to Cuba or Jamaica or Puerto Rico, and a deputation of them went to England where they offered the allegiance of the rebellious French colony to the British Crown and urged its occupation by British troops.

In September 1793 a small British force from Jamaica landed in the southwest of Saint-Domingue, where the French planters had retained some control over their slaves, and occupied the principal points on the west coast without much resistance. But this was the limit of their success. Their numbers were drastically reduced by yellow fever, and the reinforcements which they badly needed had to be used elsewhere, partly to deal with trouble in the Eastern Caribbean, where the French recaptured Guadeloupe, and partly to contain a serious rising of the Maroons in Jamaica. The British in Saint-Domingue hung on miserably for five years, but in 1798, worn down by their losses from disease and the skilful opposition of the Negro General Toussaint, they evacuated the island. Their commander, General Maitland, signed a convention with Toussaint which provided for mutual non-aggression and a carefully regulated commerce between Saint-Domingue and Jamaica.

During his first months in Jamaica, General Nugent was much occupied by the problem of relations with Toussaint. This former slave had emerged as the dominant leader in Saint-Domingue. He had crushed the opposition of the mulattoes and by the middle of 1801 was master of the whole island, having overrun the eastern or Spanish part, which had been formally ceded to France in 1795 though the actual transfer of power had been postponed. Ostensibly Toussaint administered Saint-Domingue in the name of the French Government, but in 1801 he seemed ready to throw off this allegiance and caused himself to be proclaimed Governor for life of the whole island. Would he, and could he, in fact remain independent of France? The arrangements which he had agreed upon with Maitland for the importation of arms and supplies to Saint-Domingue were not working smoothly, and needed to be re-defined and extended so as to apply to the increased territory which he now controlled. There was prolonged discussion of the terms of a new convention, which was finally signed by Toussaint's emissary in Jamaica in November 1801.

It was too late to take effect. For the whole position was altered by the news that Britain was no longer at war with France; the peace preliminaries had been signed in London in October. Soon afterwards, Napoleon informed the British Government that he proposed to send an armament of thirteen ships of the line and 25,000 men to Saint-Domingue "for the purpose of re-establishing the authority of the Mother Country in that colony." Lord Hobart, the British Secretary for War and Colonies,[1] instructed Nugent to preserve strict neutrality as between the French forces and Toussaint. And in a confidential letter, he stated his frank opinion: "Toussaint's Black Empire is one, amongst many evils, that has grown out of the War, and it is by no means our Interest to prevent its Annihilation." As a precaution, the naval and military forces in Jamaica were to be increased. Nevertheless, Nugent later confided to Admiral Duckworth that he had "always thought it very impolitic of the Minister" (i.e. of the British Government) "to permit so considerable an Armament to proceed to St. Domingo, previous to the Conclusion of a Peace." A strong French force to windward might well be a more dangerous neighbour than Toussaint, who had no navy.

In January 1802 the French troops commanded by General Leclerc began landing in Saint-Domingue. Napoleon had provided the General, who was his brother-in-law, with a brisk plan for the recovery of the colony in three stages, and for a time it seemed almost as if this might be carried out. Within a few months, Toussaint and his principal lieutenants

[1] From 1801 to 1854, a single Secretary of State was in charge of both War and Colonial Departments.

had ceased resistance. Toussaint was later trapped into letting himself be arrested, and was shipped off to France where, after a year in prison, he died. But yellow fever had begun to destroy the French army, and the news that the French had re-imposed slavery in Guadeloupe stirred the Negroes of Saint-Domingue to renewed resistance. The French were short of supplies, and Leclerc's officers periodically turned up in Kingston seeking credit from the Jamaica merchants. Dining at King's House, they gave Mrs. Nugent more and more lamentable accounts of the situation in Saint-Domingue.

The final blow for the French expedition was the renewal of war with Britain in May 1803. Warships from Port Royal blockaded the ports of Saint-Domingue, cutting off the French from supplies and reinforcements, and compelling them to choose between surrendering to the British Navy or being overrun by the armies of Toussaint's successor, Dessalines. Eight thousand French prisoners were shipped to Jamaica, where the officers were placed on parole in Kingston and Spanish Town, and the other ranks confined aboard prison ships in the harbour.

Their presence only aggravated the security problem. Kingston, wrote Nugent, was "the Resort of all the disorderly and mischievous Part of the Community, both Natives and Foreigners", and the city magistrates were very nervous about this alien population, with its large admixture of French-speaking refugees. They mistrusted the allure of the Frenchified brown ladies ("the People of Colour . . . are principally Females, and have great Influence there"). But most of all they feared the slaves whom many of the refugees had brought with them from Saint-Domingue, for these could be carriers of the dreaded revolutionary infection. In Spanish Town, Mrs. Nugent was agitated by the rumours of conspiracy among the "alien blacks". The Assembly legislated "to prevent any intercourse or communication, between slaves of this Island and foreign slaves of a certain description," and it gave the Governor powers to round up all dangerous aliens into prison ships, in which they would await deportation. A proclamation of 25th November 1803 called upon all alien white persons "to embark themselves and their slaves upon certain vessels provided by the Government of this Island to transport and convey them, free of expense, to New Orleans."[1] Nugent wrote a letter to the Governor in Chief of Saint-Domingue, whom he referred to in less diplomatic moments as "that horrible brute, Dessalines":

[1] A number of French refugees of royalist sympathies had been permitted to settle in Jamaica and were formally naturalised, therefore not "alien".

Jamaica, November 27th, 1803.

Sir,

Conformably to the Desire expressed in Your Excellency's Letter to me of the 6th Instant, which I have just received, I have in Concert with the Admiral upon this Station, given Directions for the Departure of all Foreign Blacks and Persons of Colour who happen to be in this Island and who are free to be landed in St. Domingo as soon as possible. Many of those who had been in Confinement were previously to the Receipt of Your Excellency's Letter embarked for that Destination, the Admiral and I having taken for granted they would be an acceptable Present to you.

Those Foreign Blacks and Persons of Colour who have emigrated from St. Domingo at different Periods with white French Emigrants are now embarking with them for North America so that in a short Time there will remain none of these Descriptions in Jamaica. Should any however, be discovered in future here, they shall be immediately taken up and transmitted to St. Domingo for Your Excellency's Disposal, as I wish to prove how much it is my Desire to pay every possible Attention to your Requests. Although the Subsistence of those Persons who have been confined here, during the last six or eight month, has been a considerable Expence to this Government, I shall not think that I should make any Charge for that Service, and I trust that the Admiral will also give them a Passage on board the Ships of War free of any Expence, as a Mark of the Consideration with which I have the Honour to be,

Sir,
Your Excellency's most obedient and faithful Servant,

G. Nugent.

His Excellency,
General Dessalines.[1]

Nugent was hoping to conclude a convention with Dessalines on the lines formerly agreed with Toussaint, and early in 1804 he sent the former British Agent in Saint-Domingue, Edward Corbet, back to Haiti (as it was now renamed) to negotiate. But nothing came of it. Nearly two years later Nugent summed up in a despatch to London:

It does not appear probable . . . that Dessalines will make any Advances to this Government for the Renewal of Intercourse between the two Islands. The Americans have fully supplied his Wants from the earliest Period of his Command in St. Domingo, upon better terms than he could expect to receive from Jamaica, and he never showed any Inclination to follow the Policy of his Predecessor Toussaint, by favoring us in any Respect whatever . . .

The People of this Island are now perfectly convinced that they have nothing to apprehend from the Vicinity of a Black Empire, so long as every Impediment is thrown in the Way by us to their Navigation, and the Island of St. Domingo is no more talked of here, than if it was in the East Indian Seas.[2]

[1] C.O. 137/110.
[2] Nugent to Sullivan, 27 Dec. 1805, C.O. 137/114

Tribulations of a Lieutenant-Governor

Every colonial Governor had the task of inducing the local legislature to vote the measures which he recommended to them in accordance with his instructions from London. When Nugent wrote a memorandum on the Governor's duties for the benefit of his successor, he rather airily described this part of his functions as "meeting the Assembly for about two Months at the latter end of each Year, when they grant the usual Supplies." But meeting the Assembly was rarely the painless formality which this implies.

The forty-three members of the House of Assembly were elected by the freeholders in the island's twenty parishes; that is to say, by the votes of a few thousand white landowners. Most of the elected members were themselves planters and "attornies" managing the estates of absentee proprietors, and their state of mind was apt to be closely related to the state of the market for colonial produce. During the war the price of sugar in England fluctuated considerably, while the duty on colonial sugar entering that country was progressively raised to increase revenue. In 1802, the Nugents' second year in Jamaica, the price of sugar sank to its lowest for the past ten years, and rumours of an impending increase in the duty led Simon Taylor, the largest proprietor in Jamaica, to draw up a protest which spoke of the imminent ruin of the colony.

Another unpopular feature of British economic policy was the restriction on trade between the West Indian colonies and the United States, which were their cheapest source for the supply of lumber and shingles, of staves for making hogsheads, of flour, beef and pork, and of pickled fish and other provisions for the slaves. Imposed at the time of American independence, these restrictions had been suspended for considerable periods out of sheer necessity, but in November 1804 an Order in Council from London gave notice to colonial Governors that the trade was to terminate at the end of six months from that date. Merchants and planters in Jamaica protested strongly, and appealed to Nugent to postpone the effective date of the order another six months, on grounds of dire emergency. When he refused, claiming that he had no authority to do so, they complained that he was taking far too narrow a view of his discretionary powers. This was one reason why the Assembly's farewell address to him was markedly lacking in the fulsome congratulations usually offered to a departing Governor. But the issue which caused most trouble in his dealings with the Assembly was not, primarily, an economic one. It concerned the "black corps", the employment in Jamaica of a Negro regiment.

Because of the high mortality from disease of European troops in the Caribbean, the British had taken to recruiting Negro units. The first "black corps" were raised in the Windward Islands in 1795, from free Negroes and purchased slaves. They fought well, and presently there were eight West India Regiments, as they were called. But the proposal to station one of them in Jamaica outraged the planters; it was "incompatible with our safety and pregnant with the most fatal calamities." True enough, they had just had serious trouble with the Maroons, and black rebellion was loose in Saint-Domingue. It was customary for the Assembly, not without grumbling, to vote funds for the subsistence of British regiments stationed in the island. Now, on condition of being spared the presence of armed Negroes, they undertook further to find full pay and subsistence for a permanent garrison of 2000 European troops. This was agreed to: but notwithstanding, a few months before Nugent's arrival, the 2nd West India Regiment, consisting of some 500 Negroes under white officers, was sent to Jamaica as a part of the garrison. The Assembly regarded this as a breach of faith which absolved them from their previous undertaking.

So Nugent found them in obstinate mood. At a special session in June 1802, he laid before them the latest proposals from Lord Hobart at the War Department: the Negro regiment would be withdrawn, on condition that the Island would provide for an increased total of up to 5000 European troops, since additional reinforcements were now considered necessary on account of the French expedition to Saint-Domingue. The Assembly refused; whereupon the West India Regiment, which had actually been embarked at Port Royal for shipment to Barbados, was disembarked again and returned to its quarters at Fort Augusta. Eighteen months later the War office tried again, modifying its demands; but to no avail. Nugent disgustedly began to talk of resigning . . .

Nugent's predecessor, Lord Balcarres, in handing over the government, advised him: "Where you must act with a strong hand and a strong mind the great Relief I should look to is to consult the Council." The Honourable the Council served both as an Advisory Board to the Governor, and as the Upper House of the Legislature. Its twelve members were appointed by the Crown from among "the most opulent and respectable" of the island's inhabitants, with the result that most of them were either what Nugent called "superannuated", or else unavailable; since there was a tendency for opulent and respectable Jamaicans to linger indefinitely in the Mother Country. Writing to the Secretary for the Colonies in 1804, Nugent felt obliged to point out "the urgent Necessity of superseding Nathaniel Beckford, Esq., who has been so many Years absent from his Duty here (I believe 7 or 8)." Mr. Beckford, a senior member of the Council, returned to Jamaica and his duty the following year.

Absenteeism could also make serious holes in the civil service. Nearly all the more profitable places were granted by royal patent to persons who remained in England and appointed deputies to do the work in Jamaica and remit them a proportion of the fees; for fees, rather than salary, formed the chief part of the emoluments. It was reckoned that deputies holding patent offices in Jamaica remitted not less £30,000 sterling annually to their principals in England. Over such deputies the Governor had little or no control. One of them was Mr. Carthew, whom Mrs. Nugent mentions as breakfasting at Government Pen one morning in 1802, before being sworn in as Collector of Customs. Two years later Nugent was writing to England;

I must observe that the Collector of the Port of Kingston, Mr. Carthew, did not remain above three Months in the Island, that he has obtained Leave of Absence for two Years and a half, that a Merchant acts for him nominally without attending to the Duty (independent of a Merchant's not being a proper Person to act in that Capacity), that a Clerk really does the Business of the Office, who is bribed right and left, and that unless Mr. Carthew returns to Jamaica or some proper Person in his Place, it will be wholly impossible for me to control the illicit Traffic which has been practiced so long in the principal Port of the Island in particular.

The merchant referred to was Matthew Atkinson, who also held the offices of Commissary General and Island Secretary. The firm of Atkinsons, Mure and Bogle had purchased the lease of the Island Secretaryship from the patentee, the Hon. Charles Wyndham, son of the Earl of Egremont, to whom the Crown had granted the reversion of the patent for his lifetime in 1763, when he was three years old.

It was a common complaint among Governors that a Governor himself had the power of bestowing only minor appointments. How, asked Balcarres, could he be expected to win support without any Loaves and

Fishes to distribute? "I make use of every Means in my Power of attaching Members" (of the Assembly), wrote Nugent, "by keeping open House, & by applying the little Patronage in my Gift to that Object, but it is too trifling to influence in any great degree." The social round had its political undertones, and in the Journal the Governor's lady is found indefatigably winning friends and influencing people by endlessly "making the agreeable", and occasionally by cruder methods.

In Nugent's time, although the Governor of Jamaica was usually a professional soldier, it was part of his duty to preside over the Court of Chancery and other courts of law. The anomaly had been noted by Edward Long in his *History of Jamaica*,[1] where he indulges in a caustic review of the shortcomings of a typical Governor:

From the commander of a brigade of foot, a gentleman is metamorphosed, on a sudden, into a grave judge of courts, to discuss cases in equity, solve knotty points of law, or expound the doctrines of last wills, devise, and inheritance. What is to be expected of such judges?

Nugent described these judicial functions as "a most irksome and unprofitable Office", and the ever responsive Mrs. Nugent finds the Chancery sessions "odious."

A great part of Nugent's time was, indeed, taken up with military affairs. He was Commander-in-Chief of the regular forces in the colony, numbering anything from 3000 to 6000 men, and of the local militia. The regular forces were constantly being depleted by disease, drink and desertion. The medical staff was under strength, and the temporary barracks at Up Park near Kingston had inadequate buildings and a deficient water supply. Nugent drew up plans for new and better barracks. He prevailed upon the British Treasury to sanction the building of a hospital at Up Park, and eventually, after three years of nagging, of a permanent barracks for 1000 men at the same place. The Jamaica Assembly voted £20,000 local currency for barracks to be built on high ground in the interior of the island, with improved amenities (blankets and iron cooking pots); but there were endless difficulties about getting the work started. "The Embarrassments which a Military Man labours under upon this Establishment are very great", Nugent growled, "as he cannot, under the present System, direct the driving of a Nail, without the Consent of the Board of Works, let the Exigency of the Service be ever so great." In spite of his efforts, he had to report an unusually high rate of mortality among the troops during the last eight months of his command.

[1] Published in 1774. Referred to hereinafter as Long.

Much depended on the relations between the Commander-in-Chief and the Admiral on the Jamaica Station. Nugent sometimes had trouble in keeping the Navy in step with his policy regarding Saint-Domingue. At all times he was embarrassingly dependent on their assistance. Owing to the difficulties of land communication in Jamaica, local troop movements were made by sea, and the General had to be perpetually applying to the Admiral to ferry detachments and supplies between Port Royal and the out-stations such as Montego Bay and Port Antonio; in addition to asking numerous passages for officers returning to Europe. Fortunately Admiral Duckworth was a personal friend, whose son became Nugent's ADC and a member of the favoured King's House "family", and relations between the two men – sweetened, no doubt, by the amiable Mrs. Nugent – were generally harmonious.

In their farewell address to Nugent at the end of his term, the Assembly complimented him upon one thing, and one thing only; his improvement of the militia. This was elaborated by James Stewart, a member of the Assembly, in the *Account of Jamaica* which he published in 1808:

> Lieutenant-General Nugent . . . is much to be thanked and commended for his zealous attention to the militia of this island. He certainly took more personal pains to improve it in discipline than any of his predecessors had ever done. Few of them had taken the trouble of making periodical tours through the island, for the purpose of seeing, *with their own eyes*, the state of discipline of the respective corps. Even the simple circumstance of his thus reviewing them in person had the effect of inspiring a spirit of emulation, and a wish to excel. He also, no doubt, added something to the *esprit du corps* of the militia martinets, by giving them a handsome uniform (scarlet with blue and gold) and a hat (*chapeau bras*) and feather quite *à la militaire*. Perhaps, however, a round hat would have suited the climate better; and as a proof that this was his excellency's *private* opinion, he always wore one.

Every free male between the ages of sixteen and sixty was liable to service in the militia, which normally paraded once a month. Each infantry regiment included a company of mulattoes and one or two companies of free Negroes; in the Kingston and St. Catherine regiments, Jews also served in separate units. On paper the militia was about 10,000 strong, with a majority of white men; but perhaps only on paper, for in 1802 the Jamaica Agent in London told Lord Hobart that it was "a subject of most serious regret that white men compose a very small proportion of the effective militia."

On his arrival, Nugent found the militia "by no means upon that respectable Footing, which the Gentlemen of Property wish to lead a Stranger to imagine"; and at first, certainly, Mrs. Nugent witnesses some laughably inefficient manoeuvres. But a year later, things were going more smoothly. In January 1803 the Governor, attended by Mrs. Nugent and high-ranking officers, watched the following display by the 1st Battalion of the St. Catherine's Militia and Troop of Horse, and expressed his approbation of what he saw:

> By day light the Battalion, and its Artillery on its right flank, were drawn up in line, at Open Order, to await the arrival of His Excellency the Commander-in-Chief, and received him with a discharge of 21 guns, and a General Salute; the Battalion then marched past him in Review Order, formed in line, and performed the Manual and Platoon Exercises.
> The battalion advanced in line and fired.
> Threw back its left by the file movement, and fired.
> Took ground to the right by the open column movement.
> Brought forward its left by the Echellon movement, and fired.
> Changed its front to the rear by the Counter march of divisions, by files, and fired.
> Reversed its front, by the counter march of divisions to the centre, and fired.
> Advanced in line, and fired.
> Advanced in open columns, formed behind the two centre divisions.
> Formed a hollow square, and fired.
> Advanced in a square, and fired.
> Formed line on the centre by the Echellon movement, and fired.
> Advanced in line at open order. – a general salute.

Alas, when Nugent's successor took over he was far from satisfied with the militia. On his first tour of inspection Sir Eyre Coote found "several corps in the country parishes in a state so imperfect that their best exertions could be of very little utility." It is only fair to add that Sir Eyre Coote was an inveterate critic and complainer.

Notes on a Planter Society

The population of Jamaica in Mrs. Nugent's time was composed of three classes of person, each with a distinct legal status; slaves, whites, and "free coloured".[1] The free coloured were second class citizens with limited civil rights. In order to put an individual coloured person on the same legal footing as the child of English parents, a special Act of the Assembly was required; most of the persons benefiting from such Acts were the natural children of well-to-do white men, like the group of coloured ladies whom Mrs. Nugent meets on her tour("they are all daughters of Members of Assembly, officers, &c. &c."). Coloured people were barred from government office and the professions. When an Ensign in the 60th Regt. was found to be a mulatto, the natural son of an old soldier, the War Office had to be advised of "the Propriety of removing him from the Service, or to a Station where his Pedigree will become a Secret, as People of Color are not considered eligible to fill any Situation in the West Indies."[2] Consequently they were not to be met with in official society in Spanish Town. It is very doubtful whether a coloured person ever sat down to dinner with Mrs. Nugent. When staying at planters' houses, she receives the coloured ladies apart from the rest of the company, usually in her bedroom. According to the missionary historian Gardner, it was not until some thirty years after her time, when Lord Mulgrave was Governor (and more significantly, perhaps, when the free coloured had achieved full citizenship), that coloured guests were invited to functions at King's House.[3]

Viewed in their relation to the coloured and black, all white people could be thought of as equal, and members one of another. Once when there was a question of supplying wives for European ex-soldiers to be

[1] Their numbers cannot be known for certain; contemporary guesses tended to approximate to some such figure as: 300,000 slaves, 20,000 to 30,000 whites, and perhaps twice that number of free coloured.
[2] Nugent to Clinton, 20 March 1804, Royal United Service Institution, Nugent papers.
[3] W. J. Gardner, *History of Jamaica*, 1872.

settled in Jamaica, the Colonial Department proposed to send out a shipload of young women released from British gaols, and Nugent had to explain that this would not be good enough: "the Description of Females which you mention would not be well received here. Every white Person is upon the same Footing in Jamaica."[1] But this of course did not mean social equality. A British woman who visited the West Indies in the 1820's was told by an ancient resident that in his young days "the only distinction of ranks consisted in white, coloured and negro persons. Tradesmen of every description, *if white*, were admitted and invited to the best society." But, adds the writer reassuringly, "it is needless to add that these days are long gone by, and that there is a sufficient number of a secondary rank among the white people, to form a society of themselves."[2] Mrs. Nugent's day-to-day visitors, so far as she records them in the Journal, are almost exclusively of the proprietor and professional classes, and it was only at the annual ball on the King's birthday that "everyone that can afford a dress is allowed to come to it."[3] She herself was perfectly well versed in class distinctions (for how could it be otherwise?) and quick to notice the slightest irregularity; shopping in Montego Bay and again in Kingston, she remarks on the easy familiarity of the shop people with the wives of the local gentry. Her natural habitat was among the Anglo-Irish aristocracy into which she had married, and the Journal gives no reason to think that she disagreed with her husband's opinion of white society in Jamaica. "There is but little Society of any kind in Spanish Town or the Neighbourhood", he wrote. He described one member of the Assembly as "a gentlemanly Character, which is no trifling Merit in Jamaica", and another as "decent in his Conduct but of low Origin in common with the great Majority of the Inhabitants." It was difficult to find suitable men to fill the position of Custos, or chief magistrate of a parish – "in some of the Parishes, the white Population is so ill composed and so trifling in Numbers." (Especially in the numbers of white women. Mrs. Nugent travels through the country for a week, and stays each night at a different house, without meeting a single one).

[1] Nugent to Sullivan, 30 Apr. 1803, C.O. 137/110.
[2] Mrs Carmichael, *Domestic manners and social condition of the white, coloured and negro population of the West Indies*, 1833.
[3] Some Jews, perhaps, were in a special position. Like the free coloured they still lacked full citizen rights, but as white people, and men of considerable property, enjoyed a higher social prestige. Alexandre Lindo, an important man of business, is seen at breakfast at Government Pen. Dr. Jacob Adophus (of Jewish birth, apparently not a practising Jew) becomes one of Mrs. Nugent's many medical advisers and a frequent guest.

But what troubled her more than the low origins of the planters was their ungodliness. This was a commonplace, remarked by all who had written about them. The clergy of the Established Church (and to all intents and purposes there was no other) were notoriously lax and unspiritual, even by the standards of eighteenth-century England. Nugent seems quite charitable when he describes as many as five of the twenty parish rectors as "very fit for their Situations. The other Parish Rectors, altho' some of them are good, moral sort of Men, are but indifferent Clergymen." His wife records some strange incidents in church. She took an active interest in church affairs, and seems to have been responsible for the appointment of more than one rector. After a few months in Jamaica, Nugent wrote to the Bishop of London, who controlled the licensing of priests for the colonies, asking him to send out some well qualified clergy. The Bishop, Beilby Porteous, had already made a valiant but unsuccessful effort to encourage missionary work in the West Indies. He promised Nugent to do what he could, but pointed out the difficulties: "Clergymen of Character here, especially if they have the smallest Prospect of Preferment in this Country, can scarce be tempted by any Advantage to go to the West Indies where they are in dread of the Climate."

As yet there was only a handful of Dissenting missionaries in the island, who, however, unlike the Established clergy, were eager for an opportunity to preach to the Negroes. They met with strong opposition from the planters. In December 1802 the Assembly passed a violently worded Act imposing severe penalties on persons convicted of preaching without a licence from the local magistrates. It was signed by Nugent but subsequently disallowed by the Crown. Dissenters did not frequent planter society, and Mrs. Nugent does not seem to have met any.

Had she done so, she might have found them more sympathetic than the Established clergy to her thoughts about slavery. The anti-Slave Trade agitation in England had brought the condition of slaves on the plantations into question, and the whole system was coming under scrutiny as never before. Wilberforce's campaign for abolition of the trade had temporarily been set back by the British Government's preoccupation with the war, and the fears generated by revolution in France and the outbreak in Saint-Domingue. But its final triumph was only a few years off, and the planters foresaw that once the trade was abolished, the days of slavery itself would be numbered. Though naturally curious about the effect of slavery on its victims, Mrs. Nugent does not say much about it in the Journal. A Governor's wife could know little at first hand of how the slaves lived, apart from the relatively favoured category of domestic servants. After discussions with her slave-owning acquaintances she is prepared to accept the claim that "generally speaking . . . the slaves are extremely well used", and like other visitors, she compares their material conditions favourably with those of Irish peasants. She was writing at a time when English labourers could be sentenced to transportation for poaching, and when flogging was a common punishment in the armed forces. For her, the slaves' cruelest misfortune was to be deprived of religion, and she directed her efforts to the rescue of souls. In preparing her own servants for baptism, she was doing something which, though generally disregarded, was actually enjoined upon slave-owners as a duty by the Slave Code. After this, it was only logical to advocate Christian marriage among slaves, but this was a step which most planter opinion emphatically rejected; in her eagerness to disarm their opposition, we shall find Mrs. Nugent advancing onto dubious ground.

Chronology of the Nugents' Residence in Jamaica

1801	July 29	Nugents land at Port Henderson and take up residence in Spanish Town.
	Sept. 12	Death of Admiral Lord Hugh Seymour.
	Sept. 28–Oct. 2	Nugents visit Liguanea and Kingston.
	Oct. 9	Admiral Montagu arrives.
	Oct. 20–Dec. 12	The Assembly in session.
	Nov. 20	News of peace preliminaries signed with France.
1802	Jan. 26	Admiral Duckworth arrives.
	Jan. 29	*French force commanded by Gen. Leclerc reaches Saint-Domingue.*
	Feb. 10–13	Nugents visit Parishes of Clarendon and Vere.
	Mar. 5–Apr. 24	Nugents tour the island:

Mar.	5	Liguanea
	6–7	Parish of St. David
	8–12	Parish of St. Thomas in the East
	12–15	Parish of Portland
	16–21	Parish of St. George
	21–25	Parish of St. Mary
	26–30	Parish of St. Ann
Mar.	31–Apr. 8	Parish of Trelawny
Apr.	9–13	Parish of St. James
	14	Parish of Hanover
	15–16	Parish of Westmoreland
	16–22	Parish of St. Elizabeth
	23	Parish of Vere

	Mar. 27	*Treaty of Amiens signed with France.*
	Apr. 27	Leclerc's ADC on mission from Saint-Domingue.

June 15–23	The Assembly in session. Trouble over the "black corps".
July 12–22	Nugents visit The Decoy, in St. Mary
Sept. 15	Leclerc's ADC reports distress of the French in Saint-Domingue.
Oct. 12	Birth of the Nugents' son, George Edmund.
Oct. 19–Dec. 18	The Assembly in session.
Dec. 25	Vicomte de Noailles on mission from Saint-Domingue.
1803 Mar. 14–Apr. 22	Mrs. Nugent at The Decoy and The Ramble.
May 12	French officers on mission from Saint-Domingue.
June 22	News of the outbreak of war with France and Holland.
July 9	First French prisoners arrive.
Sept. 8	Birth of the Nugents' daughter, Louisa.
Oct. 25–Dec. 18	The Assembly in session.
December	More French prisoners. Alarms about internal security.
1804 Jan. 9–Feb. 13	Nugents at Apostles' Battery.
Apr. 4	Admiral Dacres arrives.
June 9–July 6	Nugents at Stony Hill.
July 7-Sept. 9	Mrs. Nugent at Mount Salus.
Oct. 23–Dec. 18	The Assembly in session.
1805 Feb. 19	Admiral Duckworth leaves Jamaica.
Mar. 8	French fleet reported at Dominica.
Mar. 10–Apr. 13	Mrs. Nugent at Port Henderson.
Mar. 30	French fleet reported at Saint-Domingue.
Apr. 1–19	Martial law in force.
Apr. 15–20	The Assembly in session.
May 2–23	Nugents at Port Henderson.
May 23	French combined fleet reported in Caribbean.
May 24-June 22	Martial law in force.
June 28	Mrs. Nugent and children embark for England at Old Harbour.
July 3	The convoy sails from Negril.
1806 Feb. 20	General Nugent leaves Jamaica.

FOREWORD

The historiography of the former Taino territory of Jamaica, ruled by Spain from 1494 to 1655 and by England from 1655 to 1962, especially that of its slavery history, is now quite extensive. Historians have been able to reconstruct the island's history from a wide range of sources, mostly archival, though the oral tradition has not been ignored, particularly in works set in the post-1900 period. Personal journals have formed part of this rich repository of sources. Arguably the two best known are those kept by Thomas Thistlewood (1750–1786) and Maria Nugent (1801–1805). Both were more than casual visitors to the island. They were white residents who had become "creolized" into the local culture in many respects. As such, they had ample opportunity to observe Jamaican society under the slavery regime and to provide an insider's view of one of Britain's most prosperous sugar colonies, one from the perspective of a working-class overseer and later small property-owner, the other from the perspective of an upper-middle-class governor's wife. From her position, Maria Nugent was able to observe Jamaican society from the private sphere of her household as manager of domestics, enslaved black and free white; as hostess at King's House to a seemingly endless stream of white visitors (mostly French and British); and as visitor herself to other great houses around the island as she accompanied her husband to social engagements or visited on her own account. While Thistlewood died before slavery ended, Lady Nugent died at age sixty-three in 1834, the first year of the implementation of the Emancipation Act in the British-colonized Caribbean. Her "blackies" had finally received their liberation, a liberation that went beyond the spiritual liberation that was her hope for them and which she, as a deeply spiritual woman, tried to secure for them through her proselytizing efforts. Admittedly, she was constantly preoccupied with slavery, but she exposed no deep anti-slavery feelings. Indeed, she seemed to have believed that, in general, the enslaved were "extremely well-used".[1]

[1] Philip Wright, ed., *Lady Nugent's Journal of Her Residence in Jamaica from 1801 to 1805* (Kingston: Institute of Jamaica, 1966), 81.

Both journals were published after their authors died: Thistlewood's, edited by Douglas Hall, in 1989,[2] almost two centuries after his death in 1786, and Nugent's, decades earlier. Maria Nugent in fact kept two journals, one in Jamaica from 1801 to June 1805 and one in India from 1811 to 1815. Both sets of journals were printed five years later in 1839 for private circulation. The Jamaica journal (along with extracts from the India journal) was edited by Frank Cundall and published in 1907. Three subsequent editions were published, the last one, in 1966, being revised and edited by Philip Wright. Wright (who followed Cundall's version to a large extent) indeed must be thanked for his detailed introduction, genealogical table, quick chronology, appendices, index of persons and biographical notes on the Nugents and others, all of which give much needed background and contributed to the contextualization of the Jamaica journal. Maria Nugent was not writing a history of Jamaica, so she felt no particular compulsion to include biographical details on the many characters she mentioned or to explain the complicated political history of England's colonies. Wright's introduction provides the needed clues. We now have plausible explanations for her principal concerns and are able to understand better the rationale for her choice of subjects to record, for example, her preoccupation with Haiti and her constant entertainment of French officers.

Thirty-six years after its last publication and 163 years after its first printing, *Lady Nugent's Journal of Her Residence in Jamaica from 1801 to 1805* remains a rich source of information on nineteenth-century Jamaica. The journal represents a fairly continuous record (with only occasional breaks) of life and activities in Jamaica, and in England from 1805 to 1811, after which the Nugents were relocated to India and sheds valuable light on the local and regional political context of the early nineteenth century; Jamaica's social, economic, military and political history; the foreign affairs concerns of Governor Nugent as well as a chronology of his governorship; and the island's social structure, class and gender relations. Through Maria Nugent's eyes, we get a glimpse of the lives and culture

[2] See Douglas Hall, ed., *In Miserable Slavery: Thomas Thistlewood in Jamaica, 1750–1786* (London: Macmillan, 1989).

of the enslaved as well as access to their (albeit ventriloquized) opinions on a variety of issues, including pre-natal and birthing customs. The journal reinforces the diversified nature of the Jamaican economy during slavery and the variety of contexts in which the enslaved lived and worked. It is clear from Maria Nugent's journal entries that while the pro-slavery ideology of white supremacy united the white settlers, their differential class origins represented a distinguishing element. She exposes her elitist views about Creole white men and women, for example, the women's parochialism and creolization into African culture, and the men's tendency towards sex with blacks and coloureds (a habit she detested) and their excessive consumption of food and drink. Though of Irish descent, she articulates no "Irish cause" and obviously prefers England as a place of abode, but she is aware of inter-ethnic rivalries and makes occasional comments (some disparaging) about the Scottish settlers and property-owners in the island.

Lady Nugent's Journal also has implications for women's history and gender analysis. Since the emergence of "women's history" as a definable field in the 1970s, interest in sources written by and/or about women has intensified. Therefore, because it represents the literary production of a woman, within a long tradition of contemporary writings by men (for example, Sir Hans Sloane, Thomas Thistlewood, Edward Long, Simon Taylor, Charles Leslie, Bryan Edwards, M.G. Lewis and Cynric Williams),[3] the journal has acquired a new significance for feminist historians keen to access the voices of women in the pre-emancipation Caribbean, be they from the subaltern black or white elite classes. Indeed, the journal is now part of a growing list of sources generated by women –

[3] Sir Hans Sloane, *A Voyage to the Islands* (London: British Museum, 1707–25); Journals of Thomas Thistlewood, Lincolnshire Record Office, 1750–1786 and Hall, *In Miserable Slavery*; Edward Long, *History of Jamaica*, 2 vols. (London: J. Lowndes, 1774); Simon Taylor's Correspondence, Vanneck Papers, Cambridge University Library; Charles Leslie, *A New History of Jamaica* (London: J. Hodges, 1740); Bryan Edwards, *The History, Civil and Commercial of the British Colonies* (London: John Stockdale, 1807); M.G. Lewis, *Journal of a West Indian Proprietor* (London: Murray, 1834); Cynric Williams, *A Tour Through the Island of Jamaica* (London: Hunt and Clarke, 1826).

others being those of Mary Prince, A.C. Carmichael and Mary Seacole[4] – and can be used comparatively to examine the intersecting roles of race, class, gender, colour and ethnicity in Jamaican and wider Caribbean society. Maria Nugent's journal allows us an intimate look into the mind of a woman: her fears (especially for the health, safety and well-being of her husband and their Jamaican-born children George and Louisa), hopes, emotions and intellectual ideas. She was obviously deeply in love with her husband, having been married for only four years when they arrived to take up duties in Jamaica. Although she was not enthusiastic about living in Jamaica and "playing the Governor's Lady to the blackies"[5] when the idea was first presented, she made the best of it for her husband's sake, for he had chosen a life of public, political service. She quickly understood the local culture and what was expected of the governor's wife and was aware of "political correctness" before the term came into vogue, always dancing her "political dances" at dinner parties and balls. Her one *faux pax* seemed to have been her dancing with an elderly black man at one of her parties. One suspects, though, that Mrs Nugent enjoyed the stir her action created. She had previously flouted social convention by sitting next to her husband and engaging him in conversation at a dinner party.[6]

The way the journal is written and flows, with diverse topics blending into each other on a daily basis, brings into sharp question the public/private dichotomy traditionally used to compartmentalize women's lives. The description of a dinner party or a second breakfast was often juxtaposed alongside a comment on the island's politics in which she showed a marginal interest out of regard for her husband.

On the other hand, one cannot help but marvel at how normal life seemed in Jamaica for the elites and the Jamaican socialites – a constant round of church-going, breakfasts and second breakfasts, lunches, dinner

---

[4] Moira Ferguson, ed., *The Narrative of Mary Prince, 1834* (London: Pandora, 1987); A.C. Carmichael, *Domestic Manners and Social Conditions of the White, Coloured and Negro Population of the West Indies* (New York: Negro Universities Press, 1969); Mary Seacole, *Wonderful Adventures of Mrs Seacole in Many Lands* (New York: Oxford University Press, 1988).

[5] Wright, *Lady Nugent's Journal*, 2

[6] Ibid., 24.

parties and balls; of gift-giving and sending; of being pampered by
enslaved people. It was a life spoilt only by the threat of insect bites and
death by diseases that forever depressed Maria Nugent. (Good health in
nineteenth-century Jamaica seemed to have been the exception rather
than the rule.) That the brutal slavery regime existed at the same time and
fed the social lifestyle of the elite remains understated. Maria Nugent
seems amazingly able to shift her focus from the impending hanging of
an enslaved young man to expressing sympathy for her St Domingue
cook, Baptiste, who had become flustered by having to serve more dinner guests than the number for which he had catered.[7]

Finally, the question of the accuracy of the entries in the journal has to
be confronted, and this is a question that has to be asked of any historical
source. It is clear that, from the outset, Mrs Nugent fully expected that
others would read her journal, even if she did not expect it to be published. She may, therefore, have taken particular care to construct its contents carefully. She wanted her children to read the account of her life in
Jamaica and left the Jamaica journal where they could find it in the event
that she and her husband did not make it back from India to England
alive. The entry of 30 December 1802 is a case in point. She wrote: "for the
benefit of posterity I will describe my dress on this grand occasion" (a ball
given in her honour by the House of Assembly). However, since crucial
aspects of the life she described can be corroborated from other sources,
the journal appears to be a fairly accurate (if at times exaggeratedly dressed
up) account of life in early-nineteenth-century Jamaica.

Lady Nugent's Journal has been long out of print, and many will welcome the republication of Wright's edited version by the University of the
West Indies Press. This reissue is particularly timely, coming as it does on
the fortieth anniversary of Jamaica's independence from Britain, as historical issues such as slavery, reparation and the nature of colonial power
have been framing and contextualizing public debates.

Verene A. Shepherd
University of the West Indies, Mona
October 2002

7 Ibid., 51–52.

MARIA NUGENT'S JOURNAL

PLATE I

GEORGE NUGENT
From a pencil and wash drawing by John Downman

MARIA NUGENT'S JOURNAL

CHAPTER I

I MUST preface my intended Journal by saying, that it commences immediately after we had terminated a residence of some years in Ireland, of which we were both heartily sick, tired, and disgusted; having witnessed during the Rebellion, which broke out in 1798, all the horrors of a civil war, during which my dear husband had the command in the north; so that he was not only obliged to meet the poor, infatuated, misguided people in the open field, but, after defeating them there, had also the distressing task of holding courts martial, and signing the death warrants of very many, which was indeed heart-breaking to us both.

After the suppression of the Rebellion, we wished to refresh ourselves and recruit our spirits, by returning to England; but Lord Cornwallis so earnestly desired that General Nugent would remain, and act as his Adjutant-General, that we took up our residence in Dublin, where we were aiding and abetting in all the odious *tracasseries* of the union between the two countries, till that point was carried. A change of Ministry then enabled General N. to resign his situation, and, to our great joy, on the 5th of April, 1801, we arrived once more in dear England.

A few days after our return, General Nugent was surprised by his appointment as Lt.-Governor and Commander-in-Chief of the Island of Jamaica. We were neither of us over well pleased; but, like good soldiers, we made up our minds to obey.

As I had a cough, and was otherwise unwell from the anxieties of our Irish campaign, the doctors advised that I should not sleep in town. General N. accordingly took a little place at Hampstead, where we spent a most agreeable time, till the first week in May, when we took up our abode at Reddish's Hotel in St. James's Street. Our little home at Hampstead was so nice, that we regretted it very much. We had there dear Miss Acheson, and many visitors that I loved; and, in short, I enjoyed my little abode so much, I should greatly have preferred remaining, instead of playing the Governor's lady to the *blackies:* but *we* are soldiers, and must have no will of our own.

May 22nd. All things being ready for our departure, came the painful task of taking leave of our dear friends. – Could not sleep all night, and were glad when the bustle of the day began. – Had, soon after breakfast, a curious scene, with a despairing confession, about my friend Miss A., from Sir James Blackwood. Could do or say nothing to lessen his *misery*, but left him, poor man! to her *mercy*. – Then dear Lady Buckingham, Lady Temple, little Lady Mary, and Lord G. Grenville, came to our hotel, and we took a most affectionate leave of each other. I promised to send accounts of the Western World to my young friends, and dear little Lord George mounted the hotel steps at parting, and just as I was about to get into the carriage, seized me round the neck, and gave me a *great* hug, and a most *sounding* kiss, before all the *beau monde* assembled in St. James's Street. This did me a great deal of good, as, in spite of all our grief, we could not help laughing heartily. We then drove to Grosvenor Street, to take leave of my poor dear mother, and many dear friends and relations; and, at 4 o'clock, started for Winchester, where we were most comfortably seated at supper by 11. – A servant was off some time before us, and had all the horses ready, so we made famous good speed, and, after we had dried our tears, we amused ourselves with reading the placards and advertisements, pasted on the walls, as we passed, and General Nugent was so ludicrous, with the discoveries he made on his side of the carriage, that he made me quite merry, in spite of myself.

23rd. Breakfasted in the cloisters with the Comtesse Du Paet. – Mrs. Wm. Mackinnon, Fred. Mash, and Tiny, were of the party. – Bade adieu to all, and arrived at Portsmouth about 3 o'clock. – Crowded immediately with visitors; among them were the Naval Commander, &c. &c.; and General Whitelocke and his lady (he is Commandant), and we are to dine with them to-morrow. Then came Sir Charles and Lady Saxton, and she was my most amusing visitor; she called me "your Excellency" five hundred times, I believe. At first I was rather frightened, and thought she was mad, but found her visit afterwards the most entertaining possible. – Had a little quiet dinner, and went to bed at eleven.

24*th*. Captain and Mrs. Colville, with many officers and their wives, of both army and navy, came to pay their compliments after church. – Captain Colville commands *our ship*, the *Ambuscade*. He is the eldest son of Lord Colville, an old acquaintance of mine, and appears to be one of the most polite and agreeable of men. – Dined with General and Mrs. Whitelocke, and returned home at 9 o'clock to our inn. – I gave the gentlemen of our party *a fright*, which ended in discovering Billy Fitzroy and Mr. Dyke, who were in the next room. They joined our supper party, and were very merry, poor fellows. To-morrow they start for Egypt, and we expect to sail for the island of Jamaica. God grant us all a safe return to our native land.

25*th*. Embarked on board the *Ambuscade* frigate, of 36 guns. The yards were manned, and we were received on the quarter-deck by Captain Colville, all his officers, and many other gentlemen. Mrs. Colville accompanied us on board, and I felt for her in parting with her husband; but they seemed to me to take leave with more good breeding and politeness than affection; so my commiseration was quite thrown away. – A salute, &c. and off we sailed from Spithead, towards the afternoon. – What little wind there is they say is against us, but the weather is so fine, and the ship so quiet, I don't much care about it. My maid Johnson, and our valuable Margaret Clifford, and the General's man Forbes, with William Hallam, were our only attendants. – All seem happy and comfortable; only the poor maids don't like their bedroom, it is so open to the inspection of the ship's company, &c. who are constantly peeping at them.

26*th* and 27*th*. Calm, and what little wind we have is contrary. – Sit on deck all the day, and amuse myself very well, talking to General N. about the future, and really enjoying the beautiful scene around us, as we move slowly on.

28*th*. The wind was boisterous all night, and we were obliged to put into Torbay in the course of the morning. – Saw a poor little wherry, loaded with stones, founder; there were only two men on board, and they, I am afraid, perished. – I went down to my cabin, and could not help feeling very melancholy, though the gentlemen comforted me with the idea that the boatmen perhaps had saved themselves by swimming.

29*th*. Fired a salute for the Restoration; told little Brooke the story of Charles the First, &c. after all the noise was over. – The ship shook dreadfully, and so did I, for it was a frightful sensation altogether, though Captain Dunn told me, that Lady Horatia Seymour could fire off a gun herself. I can only say, that she has more courage, or better nerves, than I have. – Captain Talbot, R.N. and other naval visitors. Captain T.'s ship had lost a mast, which obliged him to put into Torbay. – Wind still very high, and the sea extremely rough. I don't feel in the smallest degree deranged by the motion of the ship; on the contrary, I continue to walk about, with General N.'s arm, though, as night comes on, I can't help being a little anxious. – We eat gingerbread all the morning, and yet I am always ready for my dinner at 3 o'clock. I now begin to eat meat, and have a large glass of Hock every day, so I shall soon be a Hercules.

30th. The wind fair. – Left Torbay soon after 8, and passed Plymouth before dinner. – In the evening fired at a vessel, and brought her to. She turned out to be only an English merchantman, from America. The sailors seemed disappointed; they had hoped for a battle, and a prize, I suppose. I was satisfied.

31st. General N. and I read our prayers soon after breakfast; then, as usual, sat on the deck, where I am allowed a chair and small work-table, but the gentlemen could only sit on the guns. – Saw several merchantmen; one from Jamaica, in little more than a month.

June 1st. Passed the Wolf Rock. – In the evening it rained; and blew rather hard. Not at all sick, but a little afraid when we went to bed.

2nd. Came in sight of some Irish mountains; but there is so little wind, that we can scarcely get on at all.

3rd. Got into Cove Harbour. Lord Gardner sent to us immediately. He is ill, but he lent us his yacht, and we went up the beautiful river to Cork. There General Myers received us, and we were paid the greatest attention to, being such *great* people as we are.

4th. Poor dear old King George's birthday! Parades, *feux-de-joie*, &c. &c. – Invited to dinner by General Myers, but declined, as we gave a *grand* dinner, at one of the principal inns, to Captain Colville, his officers, &c. In the evening I had all the ladies, headed by Mrs. Myers, to tea and coffee. It is wonderful how much a *high station* embellishes! – I heard it whispered on the parade this morning, that General Nugent was one of *the finest men* that ever was seen, and Mrs. Nugent, although small, *a perfect beauty!*

Speaking of my size, reminds me of some anonymous verses, left in Grosvenor Street for me, by a smart footman, who would give no name. I will insert them here.

ANONYMOUS VERSES

How many charms are there combin'd
  Within that little frame!
You seem by Nature's self design'd
  All Nature's love to claim.

How can so small a space contain
  So wondrous large a heart?
I fear this riddle to explain
  Would baffle every art.

'Twas thus I reason'd, till, at last,
  Made by experience wise,
'Twas only at my folly past
  I felt the least surprise.

Kind Nature's wisdom I confest,
  Who, with delightful art,
Whate'er she borrowed from the rest,
  Has added to the heart.

Your sincere Friend and Admirer,

ALDIBORONTIPHOSCOPHORNIO.

5th. Did not leave Cork till this evening. – Received visits all day, and went to shops. General N. laid in a stock of wines for the voyage, those on board being very so so. I bought forty-five Bibles, and as many Prayer Books, for the poor sailors. They were all I could collect in Cork.

6th. Sailed this morning; a nice breeze. I felt a little melancholy, at losing sight of land again; but I was soon cheered, for have I not my own little world with me, in my devoted husband and best of friends.

7th. The Captain very cross; he cannot collect the convoy as he likes, there are so many slow sailers. Colonel Noble, too, out of humour with his dinner, and his only consolation is the good wines that General N. brought from Cork. I cannot help laughing at their wry faces, and Captain Dunn tells me all their distresses for my amusement. General N. and I read in our cabin this evening, and then sat on deck till 10 o'clock.

8th. Still very wry faces, and some salt tripe for dinner, that increased Colonel Noble's misery beyond anything. He wishes me to complain; my answer is, we are at sea, we cannot remedy it now, and besides, the biscuit and gingerbread are still very plentiful and good. How lucky it is that General N. laid in such a stock of gingerbread at Portsmouth.

9th. The Bay of Biscay! The weather fine, and we are getting on prosperously.

10*th*. The ships so close together all night, that drums were beaten, &c. to enable them to keep clear of each other; there being such a fog, that they could not well see.

11*th*. The fog still continues, but the sailors say it will rain soon.

12*th*. The wind blew hard, with rain, all night, but no fog. Taken aback during the night, which they say was a great risk for us all, but, thank God, we are safe. We are now going six knots an hour, but must soon slacken sail for the dull sailing ships.

13*th*. High wind all night. I quaked a little, but put as good a face on the matter as I could. – The day as usual – some cross, some merry. – General N. and I read and talk, and amuse ourselves very well.

16*th*. Keep our course, though the wind is not quite what Captain Colville likes, as I can see by his visage.

17*th*. The wind fair towards evening, though not a great deal of it, and this I cannot say I regret.

19*th*. Saw the Island of Madeira, about 3 o'clock, but not near enough to see what it was like; only it appears very high. – A turtle feast in prospect, and Colonel Noble happy.

20*th*. Beautiful weather. – To-morrow we are to have our turtle feast.

22*nd*. I have not been able to write since the 20th. We have had a dreadful shock. Poor Colonel Noble is no more! – On Saturday, he sat the greatest part of the day, as usual, talking to me on the deck. Captain Twysden, of the *Revolutionnaire*, part of our convoy, sent us a turtle on Friday, and said, as our cook was better than his, he would dine with us on Sunday, and partake of the feast. Poor Colonel Noble said repeatedly, on Saturday, that he was sure some contretemps would occur, and that we should be disappointed of our turtle. I made a joke of this. In the evening he was as well as ever; we played at whist, and all went on as usual till 10 o'clock, when he went on deck, while General N. and I were preparing for bed. Just before 11 o'clock, he came down to the cabin and was whistling in a low tone all the time he was undressing. As there was only a curtain between his cot and ours, I could hear him distinctly. The instant he put the extinguisher on his candle, he called out that he was a dead man, and should die without assistance. – General N. was so sound asleep, that I could not wake him, and therefore ran myself to poor Colonel Noble's cot. The scene was frightful! All was done for his relief that possibly could be done, but by 2 o'clock he breathed his last. I have felt completely miserable ever since; the shock was dreadful, and, alas! I fear so unexpected and so unprepared! But God rest his soul in peace! On Sunday the 21st he was buried in the sea, and a most awful ceremony it is. The Captain read the Funeral Service. Young Noble knelt by my side the whole time. He is a fine young man, and General N. appointed him one of his Aides-de-Camp. I am sorry to say, that he shewed very little feeling; however, he is very young, and had not, perhaps, been much with his father.

23*rd*. The day calm, and the weather altogether delightful; but I cannot shake off the recollection of poor Colonel Noble, and had a dreadful dream about him last night.

24*th*. The weather still fine. – I am anxious about poor M. Clifford, who is very unwell. However, she is better this evening.

25*th*. Came into the trade wind. – Beautiful weather. – Flying fish, &c. – Every thing is so new and so gay around me, that I find my spirits much better; but I hate the cabin now, and live entirely upon deck. – My nightcaps are so smart, that I have tied up all my hair under them, and so sit on deck in the most comfortable manner; for I found it impossible to keep my hair at all tidy and in good order. To tell the truth, I really think I look better in my nightcap than in my bonnet, or quite as well, and, as I am surrounded by men who do not know a nightcap from a day-cap, it is no matter what I do, so I please myself.

26*th*. A sailor sent me a flying-fish for my breakfast. We all tasted it, but I cannot say I admire this food, pretty as it looks in the water. Feel less nervous the two last nights.

27*th*. All well. – A nice breeze, and Captain C. less cross to his officers than usual.

28*th*. Read Prayers in the cabin of Captain C.; all the Service but the Litany, which I read. One little brig has lost a mast, and several vessels have left our convoy. These are the only events of to-day, excepting that I was rather disgusted with an unfeeling trait of young Noble, but I do not like to think about it.

29*th*. Pass the Tropic. Neptune and Amphitrite came on board, and there was a masquerade throughout the fleet, which lasted almost the whole day. General N. and I were unmolested, and allowed to see all the sport without any annoyance. Some poor men were sadly pulled about, and shaved in the roughest manner, though all was done in perfect good humour.

July 1*st*, 2*nd*, 3*rd*, 4*th*, 5*th*, 6*th*, and so on to Wednesday the 15*th*. No variety; but sometimes squalls and occasional showers. – I have learnt to box the compass, and General N. marks our daily progress on the map. One thing I must mention, I have gone on, very regularly, with the education of my little pupil Brooke, who is a sad pickle. I have turned the greatest part of the History of England into verse for him, to assist his memory, as to principal events, &c.

16*th*. Came in sight of Barbadoes. The first appearance of the island quite beautiful. It put me in mind of the scenes in Cook's Voyages.

17*th*. Early in the morning anchored in Carlisle Bay. We were immediately surrounded by boats, with naked men and women covered with beads, and bringing us all sorts of tropical fruits. – The pretty Bridgetown, the hills behind it, the palms of all sorts – in short, the whole – was most picturesque, and altogether enchanting. Landed with the usual fuss and bustle attending *Great People*. – Lord Seaforth's Aide-de-camp, to tell us that he was too ill to receive us, owing to the explosion of an air-gun. – Found excellent accommodation at the inn; much amused with the natives; in short, we were all delighted to be on shore again, and were as merry as possible. – Gave a grand dinner to Captain Colville and all the officers of the frigate, our own suite, &c. &c. A turtle at the head of the table, and all sorts of odd dishes covering it. – Had my own two maids, to prepare my room for the night, intending to have a nice quiet sleep, without rocking; but, alas! my repose was not a little disturbed, by the large beetles and centipedes, that were discovered about the bed – General N. killed a huge centipede, by dropping wax upon him, just as we were going to put out the candles.

18*th*. General N. and I up early, to the great astonishment of the natives, parading the town, exploring the market, &c.; a carriage followed us, but we only made use of it to go a mile out of the town, to procure money from the Agent, from whose windows we saw a cart load of pigs and poultry, all dead from the heat of the sun, and no doubt to the great disappointment of the poor sailors, for whose refreshment they were intended. – I ought to remark that they were covered with large plantain leaves, so only imagine how great the heat of the sun must be. – Some officers came to visit us, with running footmen, holding by their horses' tails, and the whole scene was new and amusing in the extreme. – I was sorry to embark again, which we did in the evening, and sailed for Jamaica. – I must not omit to say, that General N. was surprised at his bill, which was sixty odd pounds, but our landlady remarked, that it was nothing for the great Governor of Jamaica.

19*th*. Little wind, and scarcely making any way, but enjoy looking at the beautiful Barbadoes.

20*th*. See St. Vincent's, St. Lucia, and other islands, and in the evening we anchored in Port Royal Bay, Martinique.[1] Captain Dunn, young Duckworth, English, &c. all landed, and I lost my little friend Brooke, who is gone on board Admiral Duckworth's Flag-ship, as a Mid.[2] The Diamond Rock is very curious, it stands out so far into the sea, and is so high.[3] – Captain Colville very cross, not having been well received by the Admiral, on account of his incivility to Captain Dunn, his Flag Captain, whom he wished to leave at Portsmouth, and, after all, left a great deal of baggage for the Admiral there.

21*st*. We received all sorts of civilities from the shore, but soon weighed anchor again, and took our leave, passing the beautiful town of St. Pierre. I must say that Martinique has altogether the appearance of a little paradise. – The porpoises all to-day were innumerable.

22*nd*. A poor seaman died last night, and was buried to-day in the sea. It was very melancholy, and reminded me of poor Colonel Noble; but I cannot say that his son seemed to feel it at all.

23*rd*. Heavy squalls of rain and wind all night, and about 12, almost a tempest for a short time.

24*th*. One of the ships in distress, having suffered from the heavy squalls, the *Midsummer Blossom* was ordered to take her in tow. We were obliged to lie to a long time, and the *Ambuscade* rolled dreadfully, as the wind was still very boisterous.

25*th*. Getting on fast to our destination; the wind more moderate.

26*th*. In sight of St. Domingo; the land high, but too distant to make any further observation. – The lightning in the evening was very vivid, but there was no thunder.

27*th*. In chase of a Spanish vessel early this morning, but found she had a pass from the Governor of Jamaica, so could not detain her. The sailors again very much disappointed.[4]

[1] Port Royal is a mistake for Fort Royal (now Fort de France). Martinique was held by the British from 1794 to 1802.

[2] According to his Admiralty record, Henry Brooke seems to have been only nine years old in July 1801 when he joined the flagship *Leviathan* as a Volunteer 1st Class (equivalent to the status earlier known as Captain's Servant). Officially the minimum age for entry was eleven, and the Volunteer must serve two years at sea before rating as a midshipman, which Brooke duly became in 1805.

[3] The Diamond Rock is an islet rising sheer from the sea to a height of about 600 feet, near the entrance to Fort Royal bay. For eighteen months it was commanded as a sloop of the Royal Navy, being held from January 1804 to June 1805 by a party of 120 men from HMS *Centaur* under the command of Lt. James Wilkes Maurice, who landed some of the ship's guns and used them to harass French shipping.

[4] Although Britain was at war with Spain, Governors of British West Indian colonies

28*th*. Come in sight of Jamaica. We were all up, and on the look-out by 6 o'clock. It appears beautiful. – Such hills, such mountains, such verdure; every thing so bright and gay, it is delightful! – Not much wind; it is now 7 o'clock in the evening, and we have only just anchored in Port Royal Harbour. – Thank God for all his mercies. – An express is just sent off to the Governor, in Spanish Town. – Colonel Ramsay of the Artillery, and Captain Coates of the 69th regiment, with a Navy officer from Lord Hugh Seymour, came on board immediately. – I am disappointed – I hoped to have landed instantly, but there is so much etiquette about it, that it is settled we are not to stir till to-morrow morning.

29*th*. General N. landed at 6 o'clock, under salutes from the forts and all the ships of war in the harbour. The *Ambuscade* fired on his leaving the deck, and I lay down in my cot, with a pillow over my ears, the noise was so stunning. Major of Brigade, Gould, with numerous carriages, was waiting at Port Henderson, to escort us to Spanish Town. General N. accordingly proceeded with the Major of Brigade, and one of his own Aides-de-camp, leaving all the rest of the cavalcade to accompany me. This escort was a party of the 20th Light Dragoons, and he was received by Lord Balcarres, with all the garrison under arms, &c. &c. To avoid this bustle, and the noise of salutes, I remained on board till near 10 o'clock. I then landed, and found a chariot and four waiting for me, with kittareens, &c.[1] for my maids and the other domestics. I was received, at the entrance of the King's House, by Lord Balcarres, some of the Members of the Council and Assembly, and the gentlemen of his own family,[2] all with yellow wrinkled faces. – Dined with this party at 5, had tea and coffee at 7, and was glad to retreat to my own apartment at nine.

30*th*. Up at 6 o'clock, and much amused till 8 (when we breakfasted) at seeing the black population, and the odd appearance of every thing from my windows. – The King's House, which is now our residence, is a large brick building, of two stories high, forming one side of a square; opposite is the House of Assembly; the two other sides are formed by a

---

were authorised to issue licences for Spanish ships to trade at specified free ports, of which there were at this time four in Jamaica: Kingston, Port Antonio, Montego Bay and Savanna-la-Mar. British merchants valued this "vent" for their manufactured goods, and the silver coin received in payment did something to meet the chronic shortage of currency in Jamaica.

[1] A kittareen, or catherine, was a kind of one-horse chaise with an umbrella or raised awning over the seat.

[2] i.e. the officers of his staff. Balcarres' wife did not accompany him to Jamaica.

PLATE 2

KING'S HOUSE, SPANISH TOWN

From Adolphe Duperly, *Daguerian excursions in Jamaica*, 1844

Guard House and Public Buildings.[1] Our apartments are very spacious, but very dirty. Immediately after breakfast, Margaret Clifford set the black ladies to work, that our rooms may be a little less filthy before we go to bed again.

Lord Balcarres, and a large party of gentlemen, at breakfast. – I then retired to make my little arrangements, and Lord B. and General N. began their discussions, which lasted the greatest part of the morning. – At 5 o'clock we found a numerous party assembled in the drawing-room. There were only two ladies, Mrs. Rodon and Mrs. Drew, the first old and plain, the other the reverse. Lord Hugh Seymour came for about half an hour, but could not remain for dinner. – All the gentlemen, civil and military, were introduced to me before we sat down; I scarcely recollect the name or visage of any of them, only they all looked very bilious and very warm. One gentleman seemed to suffer exceedingly: for, in spite of his constant mopping, the perspiration stood like drops of crystal on his face the whole time we were at dinner. All took their leave soon after nine. No suppers are given in this country, and I am glad of it, for I have neither strength nor inclination for late hours.

31st. I could not help laughing at a reply of Lord Balcarres, when I went down to breakfast. I remarked to him that it was a very fine day; to which he answered, "Yes, it is, but I assure you, Mrs. Nugent, you will be tired of saying this before many weeks are over." Captain Halkett and Captain Loring, of the Navy, at breakfast, in addition to the staff. – I wish Lord B. would wash his hands, and use a nail-brush, for the black edges of his nails really make me sick. He has, besides, an extraordinary propensity to dip his fingers into every dish. Yesterday he absolutely helped himself to some fricassée with his dirty finger and thumb. – Lord B. and General N. were discussing affairs all the morning. – Another

---

[1] King's House was completed about 1762 under the direction of the Island Engineer, Thomas Craskell. Earlier British Governors lived in whatever house they chose or could find available. King's House continued to be the Governor's residence until the seat of government was moved to Kingston in 1872. In 1925 much of it was destroyed by fire, only the façade being preserved. The recent establishment of a Folk Museum in the reconditioned stables of the old King's House is part of a larger project for the use of this site as a cultural centre.

The plan of the square is due to the Spaniards, but no Spanish building remains. In Mrs. Nugent's time the lay-out was much as it is now, except that the Courthouse occupying the south side was not yet built. It is curious that she does not mention Admiral Rodney's monument on the north side, which was set up in 1793. During her residence, iron railings were imported to enclose the monument and the centre of the square, and in 1804 a firm of local contractors submitted a bill for £1801. 10s. 6½d. (local currency) for erecting these railings on a dwarf wall.

large dinner party at 6. Mrs. Rodon again, and Mrs. W. Bullock. The
ladies told me strange stories of the influence of the black and yellow
women, and Mrs. Bullock called them serpents. – The table to-day was
loaded with large joints of meat, turtle, turkeys, hams, &c. – I must not
omit to mention here an extraordinary pet of Lord B.'s, which makes its
appearance every day in the dining-room. It is a little black pig, that goes
grunting about to every one for a tit-bit. The first day his staff appeared
very much shocked; but, seeing me rather amused with the novelty of it,
they seemed reconciled.

August 1*st*. It rains quite a torrent, and I have had a great triumph over
Lord B., in varying my remark; and I exclaimed, "What a sad rainy
morning, my lord." – Only a staff dinner to-day. I sat between Lord B.
and Colonel MacMurdo, the latter actually dripping with perspiration.
He saw me looking at the drops as they fell from his forehead, poor man!
and this increased them almost to a cascade.

2*nd*. Read in our own room, for we cannot go to church to-day. –
Another tropical shower, and we had no close carriage landed yet, and
that which Lord B. sent for me, to Port Henderson, was borrowed.
Lord B. and General N. had a very long conversation, which lasted almost the whole day. – Many new gentlemen at dinner, myself the only
lady. – Leave them early, and go to bed at 10. – To-morrow Lord B.
leaves the Government House, and then we mean to have a thorough
cleaning of this Augean stable.

3*rd*. Up at 6. – A grand breakfast at 8, and a council at 10. – Lord B.
set off immediately for his country-house, called the Penn.[1] A salute was
fired, and all due honours paid to him, as he drove off. General Nugent
then walked in procession to the House of Assembly, and was sworn in
as Lieut.-Governor and Commander-in-Chief. Then another salute was
fired, and he came back and held a levee. I remained above stairs until
4 o'clock, seeing all the proceedings from my windows, or the gallery
round the Egyptian Hall. I then went to the drawing-room, and received
all the ladies of Spanish Town, &c. the principal officers of the Navy and
Army, the Members of Council, and a number of the gentlemen of the
House of Assembly, who had come to compliment the new Governor
and his Lady; bowing, curtseying, and making speeches, till 6 o'clock.
The ladies then dined with me in the Ball-room, and the gentlemen with

---

[1] The use of the word *penn*, or *pen*, in Jamaica to mean a farm or property with
livestock dates from the seventeenth century, when the first British settlers found
the cattle left by the Spaniards running wild.

PLATE 3

THE GREAT SALOON AT KING'S HOUSE
From an oil painting by Philip Wickstead

General N. in the Egyptian Hall.[1] My guests were forty in number, with
ten gentlemen to carve for us. General N. had three or four times that
number with him; but we should not call them *our* guests, as these dinners
were given to us by the public.[2] – I must remark the loads of turtle, turkeys, hams, and whole kids, that crowded my table, and increased the
heat of the climate. The room, too, was filled with black servants; and
all the population, I believe, both white and black, were admitted to walk
round the table, and stare at me after dinner. They did General N. the
same favour, being, I suppose, very curious to see what sort of looking
people we were; but their curiosity added most exceedingly to the heat,
and, indeed, I never felt anything like it in all my life. At 12 o'clock all
the ladies took their leave, and some of the gentlemen; but General N.
left those that remained to enjoy their bottle, and he and I retired to
our own apartment, but not to rest, for the garrison gave us a grand sere-
nade, and the house was a scene of dancing, singing, and merriment
almost the whole night.

4th. This day we have kept to ourselves, and the house is put into as
good order as we could prevail upon the poor blackies to do it. They are
all so good-humoured, and seem so merry, that it is quite comfortable
to look at them. I wish, however, they would be a little more alert in
clearing away the filth of this otherwise nice and fine house. – Only our
own staff at dinner, and as we were up at 6, and very busy all day, we
took the liberty of going to bed at 9.

[1] The Egyptian Hall must be the "great saloon", shown in Plates 3 and 5, which
Long describes as being used for public audiences, balls, and the Court of Chancery.
The ball-room mentioned by Mrs. Nugent, and later referred to as the gallery, was
probably the ground-floor gallery in the other half of the building. Egyptian Hall was
a term applied in the eighteenth century to various large rooms, such as the dining
room in the Mansion House, London, which supposedly conformed to Vitruvius'
description of an Egyptian saloon, the characteristic feature being a giant order of
columns along the side of the room, with a gallery above. The painting by Wickstead,
who died before 1790, shows members of the Governor's Council assembling for a
meeting in the Council Chamber at the far end. The pictures are a pair of those
official portraits of George III and Queen Charlotte which were turned out in large
numbers by the studio of the King's Portrait Painter. The bust between them is perhaps one of those playfully alluded to by Long in his description of the room as "the
busts of several ancient and modern philosophers and poets, large as life; which being
in bronze, the darkness of their complexion naturally suggests the idea of so many
Negroe Caboceros, exalted to this honourable distinction for some peculiar services
rendered to the country."
[2] On 5 December 1801 the Council directed the Receiver General to pay out £1400
(local currency) for the entertainment given to His Honour on assuming the government, and the ball given to Mrs. Nugent. This was one of several disbursements under
the same head.

5th. Up at 6. – Saunter from room to room, trying to persuade the blackies to follow Margaret Clifford's advice; and make the house clean as soon as possible. – General N. poring over papers all day. – Dine in the Council Chamber, but decide never to make that our dining-room again, the heat was so dreadful.

6th. Reflect all night upon slavery, and make up my mind, that the want of exertion in the blackies must proceed from that cause. Assemble them together after breakfast, and talk to them a great deal, promising every kindness and indulgence. We parted excellent friends, and I think they have been rather more active in cleaning the house ever since. – Mean to give my first Assembly to-morrow, and am therefore in a great hurry to get all things into proper order. Doctor Lind and Captain Fraser, in addition to our staff party, at dinner.

7th. General N. attended by some of his staff, went over to Kingston early this norning. A mulatto man, named Rogers, engaged as his valet de chambre. I rejoice that my dear N. will be much more comfortable with this man, I hope, as he is higly recommended. He has not been at all so with Mr. Forbes, who now leaves him. – Only the gentlemen of the family at dinner. Soon after 7, the ladies began to arrive, also many gentlemen. – Find a sad want of local matter, or, indeed, any subject for conversation with them; so, after answering many questions about how I liked the country, &c. and being thoroughly examined by the eyes of them all, I sent for fiddlers, and we had a very merry dance till 11 'oclock, and before 12 they all took their leave. I mean in future not to attempt anything like a conversazione, but to have Friday dances.

8th. Begin letters to England at 6 o'clock, but find that, at the request of the merchants, General N. had ordered the packet to be delayed, till the 17th. I rejoice at this, as we shall now be less hurried. – Various strange fruits and curiosities sent me to look at to-day. – Mr. Matthews at dinner.

9th. Could not go to church, as it is under repair, and putting in order.[1]

---

[1] Refers to the St. Catherine's parish church in Spanish Town, which since 1843 has been the cathedral of the Jamaica Diocese. Plate 6 shows it at some time before 1790, without the tower which was added in 1817. After the completion of the structural repairs referred to, there was trouble with the organ. The parish vestry at their meeting on September 11 heard "an adverse report on the state of the organ and violence offered to it . . . it appeared that the door opening on the keys had been forced open split and totally destroyed merely because Mr. Scott [the organist] had left the key at home . . . a great number of pipes taken down and left lying about the organ loft . . . it was represented that for some Sundays past the organ could scarce afford the usual

– Read prayers in our own room, and then I marked places in several good books, for my own maids. – Some new gentlemen at dinner. Mrs. Rodon called, and I took a short airing with her. – Mrs. Pye, &c. in the evening.

10*th*. General N. and I went out before breakfast, for the first time. – We drove to Lord B.'s Penn. Never was there such a scene of dirt and discomfort. Lord B. was in a sad fright, thinking that we should expect a breakfast. However, upon his Secretary's whispering me, that there was but one whole tea-cup and saucer and a half, we declared our intention of returning to the King's House, where a party was waiting for us to breakfast. – The road to the Penn is most exceedingly pretty. Penguin hedges, which are like gigantic pine-apples, with beautiful red, blue, and white convolvuluses running all over them. There was also a variety of curious trees. – Only Captain Wright, in addition to our staff party, at dinner to-day.

11*th*. The house appears now quite a paradise, so clean and nice after Lord B.'s dirty Penn. Some gentlemen, from Kingston, to breakfast, and remain all day. Mr. Hanbury, who was a sugar merchant, talked technically; and, in speaking of some one, who was fond of good living, said, he always liked to have his keg well filled! Lord H. Seymour came in the morning, but could not stay to dinner.

12*th*. General N. attended by Lieut.-Colonel Irvine, &c. drove over to Kingston, and returned in the heat of the day. Feel quite unhappy for fear my dear Nugent should suffer by his imprudence; but he has promised to be more careful in future. – General Churchill, and his Aide-de-camp, &c. at dinner.

13*th*. After breakfast, General N. walked out, to my great annoyance and alarm, and to the surprise of every one. – He says he forgot all about the climate, and does not feel the worse for it. However, Dr. Lind has made him promise not to go out again in the heat of the day; at least not on foot.

14*th*. The morning as usual. – Major and Mrs. Pye at dinner: she flattered me so much, that I was quite sick, and glad to dance off my ill humour in the evening.

15*th*. Poor young Noble taken very ill. General N. sent off for the

music, that the two upper rows of keys had for a considerable time been useless." The organist was suspended from duty and the repair of the organ, at a cost of £120, was entrusted to Sergt. Christian Scholl of the 4th Battn., 60th Regiment (which was largely composed of Germans).

doctor, who pronounces it to be the yellow fever.[1] I trust, however, it will be but slight, as he has not a tinge of bile in his complexion. But, alas! he has been very imprudent in drinking punch and sangaree, &c.[2] The doctor said, in the evening, he could give no decided opinion, and we passed the night in much anxiety.

16*th*. Poor Noble much worse. Feel sincerely for him. – Spend the day in our own apartment, as we have no church yet to go to. – Mr. and Mrs. Woodham, the Spanish Town clergyman and his wife, dined with us. – Poor M. Clifford taken ill in the evening. Dr. Lind says, however, it is merely a bilious attack. Quite low, and feel really ill, with seeing and hearing of others being so.

17*th*. General N. rose before 5, to review some troops. While he was dressing, a severe shock of an earthquake occurred. The doors flew open and shut again with a violent noise, and there was, at the same time, a great rumbling in the air. I leaped out of bed, for it shook dreadfully. – General N. had called out to the servants not to disturb me by opening the door so violently: but he soon found what was the case, and stayed with me till I got a little composed, for indeed the visitation was most awful. – Poor Noble much worse, and General N. sent for another doctor. – The Attorney-General, &c. at dinner. Very uncomfortable, and thinking of poor Noble the whole time; but here no one appears to think of or feel for those who are suffering from these frightful attacks. – A party in the evening. – Heartily glad when they were all gone. – Noble stationary, which they say is a good omen.

18*th*. Noble better. – A large party at dinner; Lord Hugh Seymour and his Flag Captain (Penrose), the Rev. E. Ward, Mr. Mitchell, Colonels Gillespie and Wale, &c. &c. Mrs. Pye the only lady. – Poor Noble's fate, they say, will be decided to-morrow. My anxiety is inexpressible.

19*th*. Noble so much better that there are great hopes of his ultimate recovery. – Quite in spirits to receive my morning visitors, as well as my dinner company. – Lord Hugh Seymour, the Marquis de la Jaille, &c. &c. and a large party at dinner.

20*th*. Noble out of danger, and taking bark. – Some new military people at dinner. – My mind quite relieved, and I went to bed comfortable.

[1] Yellow fever, a great killer of Europeans in the West Indies, was brought under control after 1900, when the U.S. Army's Yellow Fever Commission headed by Major Walter G. Reed established that the disease was caused by a virus transmitted by the mosquito *Aedes aegypti*.

[2] sangaree: Madeira wine, diluted and sweetened.

22nd. Drove out at 5. – All our baggage from England arrived safe this morning.

23rd. Go to church in state for the first time. All the world staring, and the church crowded to excess. – A prayer against earthquakes, in which I joined most heartily. Received the Sacrament at our own desire, as it is only administered here three times a year. Several gentlemen visitors before dinner. – At dinner the Rev. Mr. Woodham and his wife, Mr. and Mrs. Rodon, Colonel Wale, Captain O'Brien, &c. &c. and the Misses Rennalls. – Young Noble out of his room for the first time.

24th. Lord Balcarres and a large party at breakfast. I behaved very ill, having placed an Aide-de-camp between me and his lordship; for really his hands, &c. were so dirty, I could not have eaten any thing had he been nearer.

25th. Drove out at 5, towards Port Henderson, our usual road. – Major Cookson, Mr. Matthews, Major and Mrs. Pye, Mrs. Rossington, &c. dined with us.

26th. Drove out a new road. All the country is flat, but very pretty. The farms are of various descriptions, and the orange trees, &c. lovely. I am told that the scenery of the interior is quite beautiful, and this I can well imagine, from the lilac-coloured mountains, and the variety of ground and tints, that I see from my window. General N. had a council at 9. – A large dinner party to-day, and very pleasant. – When I went to bed at 9, I found my maid Johnson ill, which lowered my spirits.

28th. More of our English baggage arrived, and the morning was spent in seeing it unpacked. – A Mr. Rothey in addition to our staff dinner party. – A large party in the evening; danced only two dances, as I can't help being a little afraid of the yellow fever.

29th. General N. galloped to Port Henderson, and back again, to the great dismay of Colonel Irvine, &c. &c. who attended him. They complained sadly of fatigue. – After breakfast, had a great deal of conversation with Mr. Woodham, on the subject of the black domestics, whom I am instructing, previously to their being christened. – Captain Manby, &c. &c. at dinner. – Drive out in the evening. – Desire the maids to take the carriage in the morning, as I don't mean to make the exertion myself. I cannot tell what it is, but this climate has a most extraordinary effect upon me; I am not ill, but every object is, at times, not only uninteresting, but even disgusting. I feel a sort of inward discontent and restlessness, that are perfectly unnatural to me. – At moments, when I exert myself, I go even beyond my usual spirits; but the instant I give way, a sort of despondency takes possession of my mind. I argue with myself against it, but all in vain. I acknowledge that I am ungrateful to that Providence, that has bestowed so many and such great blessings upon me, in the best and most indulgent of husbands, with the power and the inclination to serve my fellow creatures; but till the malady of the spirits has taken its departure, all these considerations, and even religion, are of no avail. As for poor General N. he feels it in a different manner. He is so over-worked in the writing way, and the different interests he has to attend to, that he suffers in mind, though, thank God, not yet in body.

30th. Rise at 6, and was told, at breakfast, that the usual occurrence of a death had taken place. Poor Mr. Sandford had died at 4 o'clock this morning. My dear N. and I feel it very much, but all around us appeared to be quite callous. – Go to church at 10; uncomfortable, and absorbed in melancholy the whole service. – After church, studied an Exposition of the Catechism, that I might be able to explain more fully to the black servants, what they undertake in becoming Christians. – At 3 o'clock a large dinner party. – Captain and Mrs. Lomax the only new faces. – Poor Mr. Sandford was buried this evening; some of our staff attended.

The people here are so uncongenial to us, that I am often reminded of the complaint of the poor French émigré, that I met with in some late publication – "Toutes les pages du livre de ma vie semblent effacées: il " faut recommencer à me faire connaitre, à me faire estimer. – Je me dis " souvent, je n'interesse aucun de ceux que je vois. – Je puisse vivre, " souffrir, mourir, sans exciter un sentiment. – Mon cœur est surchargé " de son propre poids; il voudrait se répandre, mais non, il ne peut pas ici." – But, as long as we have each other, we are much happier than the poor emigrant, and have no right to complain.

31st. We drove to Port Henderson at 5, and walked on the sea shore, which did our spirits good. – General N. unusually busy all the morning. – Lord Balcarres, Major Alston, Mr. Douglas, and in short a large dinner party. – Feel much better in spirits from a determination to do my duty.

September 1st. General N. much engaged with letters and papers all day. – Read, and try to regulate my feelings, till dinner time. – At dinner every thing in the best order. Our English china, &c. &c. all very nice.

2nd. Take a delightful drive on the Kingston road. – I am determined not to lament, as I am too apt to do, for the illness and deaths I hear of daily, among various parts of our society. Our own immediate family all well, excepting little bilious attacks from their own imprudence. Thank

God, the climate appears to agree perfectly with my dear husband. – A very large dinner party. – Colonels Gillespie, Ainslie, &c. &c. with a few of the usual ladies. – Poor M. Clifford very ill indeed this evening; ordered to take calomel, &c.

3rd. Drove to Port Henderson. Saw crabs innumerable crossing the road. – Lord Hugh Seymour and a large party at breakfast. He stayed and talked to me till 2 o'clock, General N. being engaged. I then stole away to rest a little, before dressing for our 3 o'clock dinner. – Talk again incessantly with Lord Hugh till half-past 6, when he took his leave, as we could not prevail upon him to take a bed, that he might avoid the dangerous atmosphere of the Lagoon, between Spanish Town and Kingston. – This has, indeed, been a fatiguing day, and not a moment have I had to myself, for reading, writing, or any occupation, but have gossiped from five in the morning till nine at night.

5th. Dine at 3 : our new guests were Mr. Batteley, Mr. Bissett, and Mr. Carey. Leave the gentlemen, and drive out at 6. See Mr. March's Penn, called Belle Vue.[1] – Disappointed at not finding Mr. Johnstone at home, as we are told there is a great variety of shrubs and plants in his garden, worth seeing, and of course novel to us.

6th. Colonel Wale and a military party at breakfast. – A large dinner party at 5. – The Custos and Mrs. Rodon, Mr. and Mrs. W. Bullock, Mr. and Mrs. E. Bullock, Mr. Smith, King Mitchell, Mr. Cuthbert, Dr. Brodbelt, the Attorney-General, the President of the Council, Mr. Douglas, and several new military people. – Colonel Irvine unwell.

7th. Drive to Port Henderson at 5. – See a curious cold bath there. – It is under the rocks, quite separate from the sea, and yet the water is salt. It is said to be very dangerous, from the extreme cold, and several midshipmen have lost their lives by bathing in it.[2] Return home at 7. Find Colonel Irvine still ill; but the doctors say not in danger. – Had a nice

---

[1] About three miles northwest of Spanish Town, on the road to Point Hill.

[2] In 1776 John Henderson, advised that the stream from a cold saline spring on his property was medicinal, "cut through the hill and made a bathing-place for sickly persons", and applied to the Assembly for aid in erecting a public bath house. The Assembly consulted five local doctors who concurred in the opinion that "cold bathing is peculiarly beneficial in many disorders of a tropical climate", and at some time the bathing-pool was enclosed in a building known as the Spa. The main flow from the spring ceased after a seismic disturbance in 1957. At the end of the eighteenth century the mouth of the Rio Cobre silted up and Passage Fort was superseded by Port Henderson as the embarkation point for Spanish Town. Port Henderson became a popular holiday resort, and remained so within living memory. The Spa and other buildings of the eighteenth and early nineteenth centuries have recently been restored by the Jamaica National Trust Commission.

morning with my dear N. talking over many interesting subjects. – At dinner, Major Mosheim, Mr. McHarg,[1] 67th regiment, in addition to our usual party. – In the evening Colonel Irvine worse, and I am indeed very uneasy about him. The complaints in this country are, in fact, so rapid and so mysterious, that one cannot feel a moment's security.

8th. General N. drove to Kingston this morning, in spite of my persuasion. The heat is so dreadful, that I cannot help feeling sadly afraid, but God will, I trust, be merciful to me, and protect him. – Lord H. Seymour is ill from the same imprudence. – The Speaker, &c. called during General N.'s absence, and I made the agreeable to him. – General N. returned a little after 4. – Lord Hugh so unwell, that he has gone on board ship, to try what sea air will do for him.

9th. Colonel Irvine a great deal better. – Some new guests at breakfast. – About 2 o'clock a dreadful thunder-storm. It was indee dfrightful, but it has cleared the air, and we breathe more freely in consequence. As the rainy season is approaching, we shall soon have plenty of these dreadfully refreshing showers, they say.

10th. A bright and very hot morning, – Some gentlemen at breakfast. – By one o'clock, black clouds over the mountains, and rumbling thunder till 3; but, alas! no rain. – Major and Mrs. Pye, Major Alston, &c. at dinner. – Leave our guests, and intend to drive to Mr. Lewis's Coffee Mountain. After much wandering and fatigue, find our servants, by mistake, had taken us to a Mr. Reid's. My dear N. not well and much heated. Feel very uneasy about him, and pray for him in secret the whole time. – Return to the King's House, and our guests, with red eyes.

11th. General N. went out early on horseback. I read and amused myself in my own room, till breakfast time. – At one, dreadful thunder and lightning, and a little rain. – A few gentlemen at dinner, and a very large evening party. – Major and Mrs. Heslop were of the party; the lady talked to me a great deal about my family – The gentleman, it seems, was formerly in my father's regiment, and the lady's sister nursed one of my brothers. – N.B. When I write to my mother, ask her all about them.

12th. Drive at 5 to Mr. Lewis's Penn. – Enjoyed the morning air in the mountains very much, and did not return till after 8. – The weather most exceedingly oppressive, till a dreadful thunder-storm, with torrents of rain, cleared the atmosphere. – At 4 o'clock the sun shone again, and we

---

[1] The text has 'Carge'. Mrs. Nugent writes names as she hears them pronounced, e.g. Quarle for Quarrell, Rounie for Rannie, etc. Being a General's wife, she rarely makes a mistake about an officer's rank or regiment.

sat down to dinner. – Soon after, an express from Port Royal announced the awful and melancholy tidings of poor Lord Hugh Seymour's death. – We were indeed greatly shocked. I could not help thinking of the risk my dear Nugent ran, harassed as he is both in body and mind, in this horrid country. – The sudden departure, too, of a person I had seen so short a time ago, in the fullest health, and looking forward to a long career of worldly enjoyment, was too much for my spirits, and I was obliged to leave the table. – Oh, my God, while scenes of this sort shew us more than ever the uncertainty of this life, let them also teach us to make the best use of our time; that we may be found, in some degree, prepared for that moment, in which we may so suddenly be called upon. – Keep this sad news from poor Colonel Irvine, who is still in such a weak state, that any shock may be fatal to him. – General N. sent off an express to Port Royal, with orders for all the proper arrangements to be made, and has announced his intention of going himself to Kingston to-morrow, with all his household, &c. &c. to attend the melancholy ceremony. I wish it was possible to prevail upon him to remain at home, and not expose himself to such risks at this unhealthy season; but I know persuasion is of no use, and I am therefore silent on the subject.

13th. Had a dreadful night; was restless, and had frightful dreams. – General N. was up at 3, and was just stepping into the carriage, when another express arrived from Captain Bayntun, R.N. at Port Royal, saying, that as a ship must be sent immediately to England, to announce the death of poor Lord Hugh, it was thought advisable to send the body home in a leaden coffin. This is, indeed, a relief to my mind, as my dear N. will not be exposed to the risk, which I had apprehended he would have to encounter to-day.

Poor Lord Hugh sailed in the *Tisiphone* only on Thursday morning, and died before 8 on Friday. It seems that, just as the ship got under way on Thursday, he received a great shock, on hearing of the arrival of the *Topaze*, with the loss of Captain Church, and twenty or thirty of his crew, by the yellow fever. It is sad, too, to think, that poor Lord Hugh had not the smallest idea of his approaching end, but was almost in the act of arranging business when he expired. The last day he dined with us, he and I had much conversation; he spoke of the chance of Lady Horatia Seymour's recovery, with almost sanguine expectation; but, alas! I fear by this time, she, too, must be no more, and his poor children orphans indeed. Of his own strength he boasted much, and shewed me his giant hand; but in this deceitful dreadful climate what does strength avail? –

Major and Mrs. Pye and our usual staff dinner. – Found in the evening, that Colonel Irvine had been told of poor Lord Hugh's death, and bore it better than, in his weak state, could have been expected.

14*th*. Drove to Bellevue very early. Return to breakfast, and employ the morning in my own room. – Write to Lord W. &c. &c. an account of poor Lord Hugh's illness and death. – My dear N. is now, in his character of Chancellor, sitting in the Egyptian Hall all day, surrounded by lawyers. I have been to peep at him from the gallery several times. – The heat is intolerable. Not a breath of air, and the thermometer from 90 to 95. I wish it would rain, but, alas! there is only distant thunder and lightning, and all the rain falls provokingly on the mountains, – Received several visitors in my dressing-room – Some officers of the 67th regiment, &c. &c. – Dine at 6 in the library. – A party of lawyers, in addition to the staff. Poor Colonel Irvine crawled to see me for the first time. He is sadly low, and looks wretchedly.

15*th*. Don't drive out, but order chocolate in my dressing-room, that I may have leisure to make my arrangements to go into the country, which I hope to do to-day. All our attendants were sent off at 12. Received Mr. Douglas, &c. in my own apartment. He took leave on going to Curaçoa. – The Chancery Court over to-day at 4 o'clock. Set out for Bellevue soon after. – A snug, comfortable, and cooler dinner than we have enjoyed for a long time. – Explored the rocks round us, admired the immense bamboos, and spent a delightful evening till 9, when we went to bed to avoid the innumerable insects, that put out our candles, in spite of the large glass shades. – Here I must mention, among the agrémens of this climate, the innumerable musquitoes, that have almost eaten us up, and certainly spoilt our beauty. My face, neck, hands and arms, have been martyrs.

16*th*. Our landlord, Mr. March, and Captain Taylor, were of the party. – General N. off on horseback, before 8 o'clock, for the King's House, to perform the duties of Chancellor. – Wrote to dearest Lady Buckingham, &c. &c. to go by the *Sting* tender, that conveys poor Hugh's body to England. – General N. returned at 4 o'clock – Skerrett, and another officer of the 83rd regiment, and two of the staff, attended him. They left us soon after 8, and we went to bed. – This day General N. decided Mr. Irving's cause[1] in his favour, to the great satisfaction of the public, and was particularly happy himself in seeing others so.

[1] James Irving, MD, 1713–1775, came to Jamaica from South Carolina and acquired three north-shore properties, Ironshore and Hartfield near Montego Bay, and Irving

17*th*. The musquitoes tormented us all night, and the morning was more than usually sultry. – Soon after 7, General N. rode to Spanish Town. I begged to remain in the country to avoid the great dinner to be given to the lawyers to-day. – At 12 o'clock, a sudden and frightful high wind, and the house shook dreadfully. This was succeeded by tremendous thunder and lightning, and torrents of rain. – Towards 5, a dead calm, very sultry, exactly like a vapour-bath, and not a breath of air. – Poor Colonel Irvine drove out to avoid the crowded dinner, and dined *tête-à-tête* with me. Drank tea at 7, and before 10 my dear N. returned, having had an immense and broiling party. We have only now to rejoice that it is over.

18*th*. Major Alston, Captain Johnson, &c. at breakfast. Soon after, all rode into town, with General N. – Pass the morning quietly; read and compose for the blackies. – Dress for dinner at 3. Then walk with Cupid and my umbrella towards Spanish Town, in hopes of meeting General N. Dreadfully sultry; only distant thunder and no rain to-day – Obliged to return. – Wait till 5, when General N. &c. &c. arrived to dinner. – All left us at 8, and we were in bed at 9. – Received a letter from Captain Penrose, R.N. requesting that I would keep the French books, lent me by Lord Hugh Seymour.

19*th*. Some gentlemen at breakfast, chiefly Scotch. A long discussion on Burns' Poems. – Prevail on General N. not to go into town to-day. Spend a most comfortable and social morning. – At dinner Mr. March, Major Maxwell of the Dragoons, Captain Taylor, &c. &c. In the evening made melancholy, by hearing of the death of Captain Macnamara, R.N. and several other officers.

21*st*. Dinner at 4, Major Gould, &c. came with General N. The weather too hot to move.

22*nd*. Very frightful thunder and heavy rain during the night. – General N. and Colonel I. drove to town, in the curricle, before 8. – The air is cooler – The thermometer is at 83. – Spend a comfortable morning; read and think a great deal. Religion is now my greatest source of happiness. – I thank God for the blessings I enjoy, and I pray ever to be resigned to his will. – General Churchill and ten guests at dinner to-day.

23*rd*. General N. off early , as usual, for Spanish Town. – My prayer has been to-day, that we may have grace to do our duty in this foreign

Tower near Martha Brae, which he left to four sons. The two sons surviving in 1801, John B. and Jacob Aemilius, were both defendants in the lawsuit referred to, which concerned these properties.

land, and be allowed to return to our native country, there to shew our gratitude, by devoting ourselves to the welfare of our fellow creatures. – General N. and only two of his staff came out to dinner, and we felt very comfortable in being so quiet.

24*th*. Mr. Douglas and several gentlemen at breakfast; I thought he was at Curaçoa long since. – General N.'s second great dinner to the lawyers to-day. – Margaret Clifford and the blackies with me till 4, when I was glad to see Colonel Irvine, as the thunder and lightning have been very dreadful the greater part of the day. The house shook, and there is scarcely a dry place in it, for the torrents of rain have burst in, in every direction. – A beautiful calm moonlight night at 9, when my dear N. came home, having run away from his lawyers as soon as possible after dinner.

25*th*. Leave my little quiet abode, and breakfast at the King's House, with a crowd, at 8 this morning. – Saw Mr. March, and invited him for the evening, and have a handsome present ready to send him to-day. – All the morning, my poor dear N. harassed with business. – In the midst of his Chancery, he is called upon for some military and then some commercial affairs, and then must turn his attention to the French and St. Domingo; and all this hurry and occupation increases the heat of the climate most exceedingly. Poor fellow! I am sure I feel it all equally with him. – Mr. and Mrs. Batteley, General Churchill, and in short a very large party, at dinner. – My visitors this evening very numerous. Open the ball with General Churchill, and finish it with Mr. Affleck. – To the great astonishment of some of the company, General N. and I sat together, and conversed the greatest part of the evening. – In fact, he has many and great vexations, and we have but little time to talk them over. I only pray his health may not seriously suffer.

26*th*. Breakfast in my own room for a wonder. – My spirits are worn out with my poor dear N.'s worries and vexations. – Put on great spirits, however, and pretend to be gayer than usual. – After the Court of Chancery had broken up, we set off to Bellevue, with only two of the staff, and enjoyed a quiet dinner, rejoicing to be so snug after the bustle of the week.

27*th*. We spent the morning all alone, which was delightful. – After our duties, General N. wrote some despatches of moment. I read, wrote, and sketched by his side. – We agreed that we had scarcely ever read our prayers with more fervour, than we did this day – I am sure it was from our very hearts. – Drove in the curricle to Spanish Town, at 5. – Found the dinner party assembling. – Dressed immediately, and dined at 6. – Mr. and Mrs. Woodham, Major and Mrs. Pye, Captain Taylor, 67th, Mr. George Cuthbert, Messrs. Nixon, Parkinson, and Vidal, 20th Dragoons, dined with us, in addition to our staff.

28*th*. Set off before 5 for Mr. Cuthbert's in Liguanea. – General N.'s man Rogers, and my maid Johnson, with various blackies, in attendance upon us. Some of the staff were of the party, and one of Mr. Cuthbert's servants as a guide. The road beautiful and romantic, overhung with bamboos, and different picturesque trees and shrubs. Then, again, opening to a great width, and the soil like the bed of a river, owing to the torrents that occasionally pour down from the mountains. The palms and cotton trees on each side of it were quite majestic. It was all singularly beautiful, and my delight was increased upon arriving at Clifton (Mr. Cuthbert's seat), which is indeed indescribably lovely. The views from it are quite enchanting. We found some of our staff there before us, and Mr. Cuthbert and his son waiting breakfast for us.[1]

As soon as I could get away from the party, I went to my own room, the better to enjoy the landscape, as from my windows it is enchanting indeed. Imagine an immense amphitheatre of mountains, irregular in their shape and various in their verdure; some steep and rugged, others sloping gently, and presenting the thickest foliage, and the most varied tints of green, interspersed with the gardens of little settlements, some of which are tottering on the very brinks of precipices, others just peep out from the midst of cocoa-nut trees and bamboos, the latter looking really like large plumes of green feathers. The buildings are like little Chinese pavilions, and have a most picturesque effect. In front is a view of the sea, and the harbours of Kingston, Port Royal, Port Henderson, &c. full of ships of war and vessels great and small; the whole affording an exceedingly busy and interesting scene. The plain, from the Liguanea mountains, covered with sugar estates, *penns*, negro settlements, &c. and then the city of Kingston, the town of Port Royal, all so mixed with trees of different sorts, and all so new to an European eye, that it seemed like a paradise; and Clifton, where I stood, the centre of the blissful garden. Clifton stands upon a small mountain, and the plain in front, to the sea side, is about four miles in extent. The way to the house winds up the

[1] Clifton lay within the triangular area bounded by the present Constant Spring and Manning's Hill Roads, a part of which was later known as Streadwick's Hill Gardens. About this time George Cuthbert acquired the neighbouring Constant Spring estate.

mountain by a rugged road; the house itself is in the midst of a garden. Its form is the usual one, of one story with a piazza, &c. The garden contains a great variety of flowering shrubs and fruit trees, and the hedge round it is of lime trees, kept constantly cut, which makes it thick and bushy. The limes were ripe, and the yellow tint mixed with the bright green had a beautiful effect. Here and there the logwood was seen, which is something like our hawthorn. In other places are seen rows of orange trees, the fruit just turning yellow; mangoes, red and purple; forbidden and grape fruit, in clusters; the acqui, a tree that bears a large scarlet fruit, the inside of which, they say, when dressed is like a sweetbread; and the avocado pear, or real vegetable marrow, which poor Lord Hugh told me he ate for his breakfast on his toast, instead of butter.[1] There were also pomegranates, shaddocks, &c. in abundance, and a tree, that looks like the cherry at a distance, but is redder and much larger. Coffee, too, is a very pretty shrub, bearing a bright red berry. Besides these, there are several trees from which perfumes are made, but I forget their names. One had a narrow long very green leaf, and a very bright pink flower, which looks at a distance like a large full blown rose. Another tree has small dark green leaves, and tufts of scarlet flowers, something like the geranium. But it is quite impossible to describe the great variety of beautiful plants, trees and shrubs, that at this moment delight my eyes, and regale my nose. General N. and I spent the whole morning, looking about and admiring every thing, as far as the scorching sun would permit. – Only a Mr. Stimpson added to our dinner party, when the table groaned, as usual, with piles of food, and not an inch of the table-cloth was to be seen.

29th. At 4 o'clock, General N. &c. set off to review the troops at Stony Hill. – I took a walk in the garden till the heat drove me in. Tête-à-tête with mine host at breakfast. Had a learned conversation on the cultivation of sugar-canes, the population of the negroes, &c. Mr. C. told me he gave two dollars to every woman who produced a healthy child; but no marriages were thought of!![2] After I had got all the information I wished from Mr. C. I went to my own room and amused myself very well till

---

[1] "Avocado, or Alligator pears, alias midshipman's butter." (Charles Kingsley, *At last*, 1871). Captain Marryat, in his novel *Frank Mildmay, or The Naval Officer* (1829), speaks of "Abbogada pears (better known by the name of subaltern's butter)."
[2] Spanish and Portuguese coins were current in Jamaica, a Spanish silver dollar, or piece of eight, being equivalent to 6s. 8d. Jamaica currency, or about 4s. 9d. sterling. Faced with the threat of abolition of the slave trade from Africa, the planters were

dear N. returned; when we met with as much joy as if we had parted for months. He took some tamarind drink, and slept till dressing time. – An immense party, from Kingston and Up-Park Camp, at dinner, but no ladies, to my great joy; so I did as I pleased, ordered tea in my own room, and went to bed at ten.

30*th*. General N. started at 4 this morning to review the troops at Up-Park Camp. – I had a nice early walk in the sweet garden, and conversed a great deal with Mr. Cuthbert, at our *tête-à-tête* breakfast, on the state of slaves in this country, &c. &c. He is a sensible man; but we are creatures of habit, his mind is prejudiced, and I fear his heart is hard. – My dear N. returned at 3, and, while he refreshed himself with a nap, I read and kept off the musquitoes from him. Several gentlemen at dinner, in addition to our party, whose names I don't recollect. No ladies; so I have had my tea, and now am enjoying the cool breeze from the mountains, until my dear N. comes from the dinner party. In the mean time I shall take a review of the week, as far as it has hitherto passed. It has been quiet and comfortable. I have heard much of slaves, plantations, and counting-houses, but these subjects are new, and I have curiosity. For the principal part of my comfort, I have seen my dear N. composed and cool. He has had what for him is moderate exercise, and he has had relaxation of mind; his countenance is quite changed, it is now placid, cheerful and serene; he has no more that hurried heated manner, that has too often made me miserable. Oh, my God! grant to him health of mind as well as of body, and enable me, as far as may depend upon my conduct and ability, to contribute to his welfare and happiness. Grant that I may conquer every propensity that may occasion him the smallest uneasiness, or make me less worthy of the blessings thou hast bestowed upon me. Teach me to suppress all sinful repinings, and to become entirely resigned to thy Divine will. With this prayer I shall go happy to bed, though it has thundered and lightened dreadfully, and the rain is now pouring in torrents.

October 1st. Up at 4, and dress by candle-light. The fire-flies looked beautifully in the hall, as we passed through to our carriages. The walls were quite illuminated.

Drove to Mr. Hutchinson's place, called the Papine estate. A large party

---

interested in encouraging their slaves to breed, and the Slave Law of 1792 offered incentives to the proprietor and overseer of any estate which could show a natural increase in its slave population during the year. For Mrs. Nugent's views on slave marriages, see p. 86–7 of gentlemen, and a grand cavalcade of all descriptions. All sorts of meats and fruits at breakfast. See a fine bamboo walk afterwards, reaching from one end of the garden to the other. Every ten or twelve feet there is a cocoa-nut tree, as a pillar to support the feathering bamboo. Nothing could well be more beautiful. The bread-fruit tree is here in great perfection. The jackfruit tree is like an enormous pumpkin, growing on the trunk, as it is too heavy for the boughs. There is also an infinite variety of beautiful flowers; in short, the garden is the best and most curious I have yet seen. – The situation of the house is bad; it lies low, and it is shut out from the sea breeze, by what is called the Long Mountain, and from the land breeze, by a range of mountains, under which the house is placed. Mr. Hutchinson is a quiet, awkward Scotchman, and so overcome by the honour we have done him, that it is quite distressing to see the poor man.

About 10 we drove to the Hope estate. We took a cross road, through a sugar plantation, or rather cane-piece, as it is called; a negro man running before the carriage, to open the gates. The Hope estate is very interesting for me, as belonging to dearest Lady Temple, and I examined every thing very particularly.[1] It is situated at the bottom of a mountain, and as the Hope river runs through it, the produce is more certain than on estates in general, which often suffer from the great droughts in this part of the world. A severe hurricane alone can affect it. It is said to be an old estate, and not further improveable than yielding, as it does now, 320 hogsheads of sugar.[2] – They say that, though it is incapable of yielding more, it is better, as being a sure produce, than most estates in the island, which are liable to great vicissitudes. – As you enter the gates, there is a long range of negro houses, like thatched cottages, and a row of cocoa-nut trees and clumps of cotton trees. The sugar-house, and all the buildings, are thought to be more than usually good, and well taken care

[1] Hope estate was settled by Major Richard Hope, an officer of the English army of 1655, and passed to the Elletson family by the marriage of his daughter to Roger Elletson, Chief Justice, whose grandson Roger Hope Elletson was Lt.-Governor, 1766–8. Roger Hope Elletson's widow married the third Duke of Buckingham and Chandos, and their daughter Anne Eliza, Mrs. Nugent's friend, married Lord Temple, elder son of Lord Buckingham. In 1871 the Government acquired part of the estate to establish the Hope botanic gardens.

[2] A hogshead was reckoned to contain about 16 cwt. of muscovado sugar on an average. Bryan Edwards (*History . . . of the British colonies in the West Indies*, 1793) estimated that an estate producing 200 hogsheads of sugar and 130 puncheons of rum of 110 gallons each per annum required a capital outlay of £30,000 sterling, and that any estate producing less that this was not an economic proposition. A few Jamaica estates produced 600 hogsheads in a good year.

of. The overseer, a civil, vulgar, Scotch officer, on half-pay, did the honours to us; but, when we got to the door of the distillery, the smell of the rum was so intolerable, that, after a little peep at the process, I left the gentlemen, and went to the overseer's house, about a hundred yards off. I talked to the black women, who told me all their histories. The overseer's *chère amie*, and no man here is without one, is a tall black woman, well made, with a very flat nose, thick lips, and a skin of ebony, highly polished and shining. She shewed me her three yellow children, and said, with some ostentation, she should soon have another. The marked attention of the other women, plainly proved her to be the favourite Sultana of this vulgar, ugly, Scotch Sultan, who is about fifty, clumsy, ill made, and dirty. He had a dingy, sallow-brown complexion, and only two yellow discoloured tusks, by way of teeth. However, they say he is a good overseer; so at least his brother Scotchman told me, and there is no one here to contradict him, as almost all the agents, attornies, merchants and shopkeepers, are of that country, and really do deserve to thrive in this, they are so industrious. I should mention that there is an excellent hospital on this estate, which is called a hot-house, where the blackies appear particularly comfortable, and well taken care of.

Return to Clifton to dinner; some dreadful peals of thunder this evening; for we are so near the mountains, it is quite terrific, and the house seems shaken to its very foundation; but, after our fright, we shall have a nice clear and cooler air to comfort us.

2nd. Dress by candle-light, and off at 4 o'clock. – The morning darker than usual, and the fire-flies more brilliant; all the walls seem covered with gold spangles. We drove first to Kingston, and I was left at Mr. Atkinson's, while General N. reviewed the 69th regiment, quartered in the town. Mr. A. made grand efforts to amuse me during his absence. The mountain wind, the sea breeze, slaves, plantations, and the prices of different articles, were the edifying topics, till a little after 7, when breakfast made its appearance, and Mr. A.'s spirits were relieved by the appearance of Mrs. Pye, who came to offer her services, hearing that I was in Kingston. Poor man, he seemed very happy, so was I. Some officers came soon after, and we sat down to the usually profuse breakfast. Afterwards, Mrs. Pye took her leave, Mr. A. and Mr. Bogle (his partner) went to their counting-house, and the officers to their camp. General N. brought General Churchill and some other officers with him. Admiral Smith and several officers of the Navy called. – At one, General N. and I drove about town, and then to General Churchill's Penn, to see his monkey and other curiosities. – Back to Mr. Atkinson's; dress and dine with a large party, at 6. General C., Mr. Simon Taylor, Mr. Cuthbert, &c. &c. &c. officers of the Army and Navy, and, in short, half Kingston and Port Royal, but no lady; so I did not meet the gentlemen after dinner, but went to bed at half-past nine, to be off early next morning for home.

3rd. Up at 4, and drive to the Admiral's Penn.[1] Admiral Smith and a party met us. See the house, grounds, and stables, and select what furniture we wished to have, as all was to be sold. Feel truly melancholy, in thinking of the sad fate of its late possessor, and was glad to return to the carriage. Arrived at the King's House, and breakfasted at 8, with the sun broiling over our heads, and the heat tremendous. Hear a great deal of gossip from some of our staff about favouritism; for I am such a great lady, that all I say and do is remarked upon. Mrs. Pye, &c. are spoken of as in my confidence, and likely to guide me in my conduct towards others. What ninnies! But to avoid cabals, I determine not to go to Port Royal on Monday, and so I shall not have that lady in my train, and shall prevent at least some remarks. I mean, as much as possible, to live alone at my private hours, and so put an end to all these silly jealousies. – After breakfast, General N. held a Court of Ordinary in the Egyptian Hall, which lasted till 4 o'clock.[2] We had only our usual staff dinner, and slept at dear little quiet Bellevue.

4th. Breakfast at 7, read our prayers, then walk about the gallery, and have a snug conversation, which we enjoyed very much. – General N. made memorandums for the business of to-morrow, and I wrote French verses, and translated them for his amusement. They were very bad, but very affectionate, and he wishes me to keep them; but some future day they may make me blush for their want of merit; so I shall give them to the winds. – Drove to the King's House before 5; some clouds obscure the sun, and make the heat more supportable. – Dined at 6; the clergyman and his wife, Major and Mrs. Pye, Captain Taylor, &c. &c. with our usual staff dinner.

5th. General N. &c. off to review the troops at Port Henderson. – As soon as I had breakfasted, made arrangements for his comfort, and mean to surprise him with a cool writing room, when he returns. Saw Monsieur

---

[1] The property was purchased in 1774 for an official residence for the Admiral on the Jamaica Station, and was used as such until the 1820's. The site is now occupied by the Kingston and St. Andrew poorhouse.
[2] The Court of Ordinary dealt with the probate of wills and the granting of letters of administration.

Grandjean d'Aubancourt in my dressing-room, and settle for his break-fasting here every morning, and reading French to me for an hour. He thinks my verses very good, but, query, does he speak the truth? – Read Mrs. Haverdon's papers with real interest and attention; write and tell her, that all that can be done in her case shall be done. – General N. returned at 3, and was delighted with his new apartment, to my great joy. – Set off after dinner for Bellevue, much against the advice of Dr. Lind, as it was quite dark.

6th. Have not suffered at all for our great imprudence, and, though the musquitoes were in myriads about our beds, we had a tolerable night, and went, at gun-fire, to see Mrs. Pennington's Mountain. – Don't like it half as well as Bellevue, which I mean to try and persuade Mr. March to let to us. – After our breakfast, Captain Fraser, &c. about barracks. A good deal of jobbing going on, but General N. is determined not to countenance it. – Much rain, with thunder and lightning, the greatest part of to-day.

7th. General N. gave audience to Monsieur Bunel, &c. from St. Domingo.[1] – Wrote to Mr. March, and sent him a present, of porter, hams, &c. all just arrived from England, and a great treat here. – General Bell, &c. dined with us. – Hear of the arrival of our carriages from England. – Drive with General N. in the curricle, as usual, to Bellevue, and enjoy sleeping once more in the fresher and purer air of that place.

8th. A sad head-ache all this evening. – Some of the staff at breakfast, and some Kingston gentlemen on business with General N. – Rain, thunder and lightning, at intervals, all day. – Dine at the King's House, at 5; Colonel Maclean, Monsieur Grandjean, &c. at dinner. Carriages ordered for the navy officers to-morrow evening at Port Henderson.

9th. The carriages went at 4, but returned empty, as Admiral Montagu's arrival at Port Royal has kept all our navy friends there. Am not very sorry, for I still have a head-ache, and am not very equal to any great gaiety. – Read and converse with Monsieur Grandjean, for an hour after breakfast, and have begun to write an Abridgement of French History. – At dinner, General Bell, Mr. Rose, Mr. Minott, Colonel Gillespie, Captain Macdonald (just from England), Mr. H., Colonel MacMurdo, Mr. Matthews, Admiral Smith, and the eternal Major and Mrs. Pye, in addition to our staff. – In the evening an immense party, but not so many ladies as usual, on account of the torrents of rain.

[1] Joseph Bunel, a Frenchman in the service of Toussaint, was in Jamaica to negotiate a new trade convention (see Introduction p. xx).

10*th*. Was present at the review of the troops in this garrison, at 5 o'clock. – Colonel Gillespie, &c. breakfasted with us afterwards.

13*th*. Drive to the Government Penn at 6; the works there going on slowly, and Jones, the head workman, says, that, although Lord Balcarres said he would lay out £700 in repairs, he had limited him to £55!¹

14*th*. General N. surprised us by walking off at 6, to see a penn, or rather a mountain, belonging to Mr. March, two miles off. He did not seem to be the worse for it, and I trust will not suffer; but such walks are very imprudent. – The Secretary, &c. with papers to sign, and, after breakfast, we were left to ourselves; when General N. wrote his speech. We actually now feel the cold quite uncomfortable. The heavy rains have so saturated the walls with damp, and the squalls of wind are so powerful, that they pervade everything, and we live in almost a bath; so I fear we must soon leave this dear pretty quiet retreat.

15*th*. A pain in my head and shoulders from the damp air last night; but drive into town to breakfast. Find Lord Balcarres and a large party. – After breakfast, read and go through my usual avocations with Monsieur Grandjean. Dr. and Mrs. Ludford arrived at 10 – Conversed with them till 2. – Very unwell; and I mean, as symptoms arise of any illness, always to mention it; because, if I should die in this country, it will be a satisfaction to those who are interested about me, to know the rise and progress of my illness, &c.

16*th*. Still unwell, but carriages are gone for the Navy, and I must do my best to be gay. At half-past seven, Captains Bayntun, Cathcart, and Loring, Dr. and Mrs. Ludford, &c. &c. – Then Lord Balcarres, Captain Woolley, Mr. Carthew, Mons. Le Vaillant, Major and Mrs. Pye at dinner. – A large evening party of ladies, and crowds of gentlemen, both civil and military. All in high spirits, and, in spite of my illness, I danced, and was as gay apparently as any of them; though the enquiries of my people shewed, that I did not disguise quite so well as I thought.

¹ Government Pen is three miles southeast of Spanish Town, and is now a part of the United Fruit Company's estates. The house was severely damaged in the hurricane of 1951, and is now demolished. It was built in 1777 for the use of the Governor, who was also provided with a mountain provision ground or "polinck", with a villa on it. But in 1797, at the request of Lord Balcarres, both these properties were sold at auction and in lieu of them the Governor's salary was increased by £2000 per annum. It seems, however, that Balcarres later acquired the same Pen for himself, since in May 1801 the St. Catherine's parish vestry "ordered that the Rt. Hon. Earl Balcarres be taxed for his Pen (formerly the Government Pen)", and in Robertson's map of 1804 (see endpapers), the site of Government Pen is marked "Earl of Balcarres". The Nugents' rent for the Pen was paid to Balcarres in Britain.

PLATE 4

(b) A WEST INDIA REGIMENT PRIVATE
From an aquatint by J. C. Stadler

(a) GENERAL TOUSSAINT
From Marcus Rainsford, *An historical account of the black empire of Haiti*, 1805

17*th*. Get our English letters. – All well, thank God! General N. all the morning reading his despatches. Dr. and Mrs. Ludford at Kingston all day, so we were left to ourselves. – Only our usual dinner party, with Monsieur Grandjean, our eternal guest now, poor man!

18*th*. Drive out with General N. at 6 o'clock, and go to church at 10. – Our English carriage and four horses for the first time. – A large party at dinner. – Still unwell, and glad to go to bed at nine.

19*th*. Drive out at 6. – The Marquis de la Jaille in addition to our breakfast party. Then the Attorney-General, to consult with General N. about his speech, and some few alterations were made. – Read as usual with Monsieur Grandjean. – Mr. Warren, our chaplain, made his appearance for the first time. – All the morning interrupted by visitors, that I am obliged to receive. – General N. held a privy council at 5, to whom his speech was read. – At 6 a dinner in the Great Hall; about forty or fifty guests. I dined in my dressing-room, with Mrs. Pye and Mrs. Ludford.

20*th*. At 4, the House of Assembly met, and came over to the King's House, in grand procession. General N. read his speech, and they departed to discuss it.

21*st*. Send out cards for my balls, and distributed to the black women, gowns, petticoats, &c. and various presents for my wedding day. Dr. and Mrs. Ludford took their leave at 3. – Messrs. Bogle, Atkinson, Forbes, B——, Donaldson, &c. at dinner, with Mr. Corbet, the St. Domingo agent. After dinner had a great deal of conversation with Mr. Corbet, about General Toussaint l'Ouverture, which was particularly interesting. He must be a wonderful man, and I really do believe intended for very good purposes.[1]

22*nd*. – The actual rainy season, they say, set in last night; and I believe it, for we were so uncommonly chilly, that we kept the counterpane on all night, and this morning it rains torrents. – We could not drive out, and I amused myself till 8, in translating General N.'s speech into French, for Monsieur Grandjean's edification. – At breakfast, Mr. Corbet, &c. – Drove, with some of the staff, to Lord Balcarres's auction. – Every article

[1] Edward Corbet, the British representative in Saint-Domingue, was a public servant of unusual zeal and integrity in whom Nugent placed great confidence. His reports from Saint-Domingue were sympathetic to Toussaint, the Negro generalissimo.

Rainsford's portrait of Toussaint (Plate 4) may be regarded as an idealised expression of admiration and gratitude by a somewhat indifferent artist. Capt. Rainsford of the 3rd West India Regiment met Toussaint unofficially in 1799 at Cap François, where his ship had been forced to put in for repairs. Later he was arrested and condemned to death as a spy, but reprieved by Toussaint's intervention.

had its price put upon it, by Lord B. himself, who was present the whole
time, and had his emissaries to bid for him, till all was sold at his own
price, which was always more than their worth; consequently most of the
things remain on his hands. – Returned and read French with Monsieur
Grandjean, for a couple of hours; then gave audience to the old superannuated President of the Council, who wanted me to patronize a de-
cayed milliner of bad character. Altogether it was an unpleasant business,
and I got rid of it civilly, but decidedly. – A very flattering answer to
General N.'s speech came over from the House of Assembly. – The
Members of the Council sent one equally so, and General N. replied to
all at half-past four. – We went to dinner at 6. – Mr. Corbet, Colonel
Skerrett, Mr. MacCluny of the 87th, &c. dined with us, and all departed
at nine.

23rd. General N. rode out at 6; I had not had a good night, and did not
accompany him. – Read and converse, after breakfast, with Monsieur
[Grandjean] d'Aubancourt, in my dressing-room, till 12. – Afterwards
received a few visitors in my own room. – General N. and I then had a
tête-à-tête, and conversed a good deal upon the subject of his situation,
&c. and he sent several messages to the House of Assembly. He has
strange people to deal with. The trade of this island has been for a long
time much injured, and several merchants almost ruined, by the constant
depredations of small privateers and feluccas, which infest the coast;
while the Navy are engaged in distant pursuits. Admiral Montagu, who
succeeds to the naval command, *pro tempore*, has offered, at the represen-
tation of General N. of the necessity of keeping cruisers to guard the
coast, that he will station his ships, so as to intercept these mischievous
privateers; this offer was very handsomely made in a letter to General N.,
who shewed it to the gentlemen in Council, when it was drily received,
as a matter of perfect indifference; although not many weeks since, the
remissness of the Navy, in this respect, was not only complained of by
them, but was a cause of general complaint. Many very severe philippics
appeared in the newspapers against poor Lord Hugh Seymour, on account of the cruisers not doing their duty in guarding the trade.[1] But

---

[1] The *St. Jago de la Vega Gazette* (Spanish Town) of 8–15 August 1801 printed the
following message dated Falmouth, August 12: "At no period in the war have the
coasts of this island been so daringly insulted, or such depredations committed, as
during the last six months. Not a day passes, from the East to the West-end, that
picaroons are not seen making captures and absolutely blockading our ports; of this
description one was hovering off Montego Bay and this port last week, and on Satur-

such are these people, and such is their littleness, that because they suppose that General N. has the order of Ministers to employ black corps[1] in the island, they seem determined to do every thing to make his situation uncomfortable, and to discourage every arrangement, though for their own good and advantage. He must, however, do his duty, and it is to be hoped that time will bring all things right. – Dined at 5 – The two Mr. Cuthberts, Colonel de Charmilly, Mr. Warren, Captain Taylor, Mr. Matthews, Monsieur Grandjean, &c. in addition to the staff. – In the evening a very large party, and much dancing. – We had three hours to-day of the heaviest rain I ever saw: it came down like a torrent.

24th. Drive out. – Admiral Montagu, and some of the Navy, at breakfast, at 8. – At 10 received several visitors. – I forgot to say, that although Dr. and Mrs. Ludford did take their leave, they returned, and were still our guests. – Found time before dinner to translate one of Sappho's Odes from the French. It is addressed to the Rose, and is very pretty.

25th. Drove to the Penn at 6. – Went with Lord Balcarres to see the garden, or rather where the garden has been, for not a plant of any kind is there existing at present. – A party at breakfast, and go to church at 10. – After church, visit Mrs. Bailey and Mrs. Ramsay. – Find at the King's House all Lord B.'s poor negroes, to solicit favours. Make them all as happy as I can, by promising kindness.[2] – At dinner, Monsieur and Madame Grandjean and Mademoiselle Robert, Mr., Mrs. and the Misses Warren, Mr. and Mrs. Woodham, Major and Mrs. Pye, and some officers of the Navy and Army. A strange mixture of people altogether, and a most laughable party.

---

day captured a drogger bringing up flour for the troops stationed here, a loss much to be lamented at this period . . . The successes of these marauders has encouraged an immense trade of privateering out of the ports of Cuba, which, if not corrected by a suitable description of cruisers, must be productive of incalculable mischief to the trade of this country.

"The privateer which captured the shallop with flour, the day before, off Runaway Bay, made a prize of a very fine copper-bottomed sloop, supposed to belong to a gentleman of St. Ann's Bay; she also boarded and plundered a ship from New York bound to Lucea."

[1] The 2nd West India Regiment. See Introduction p. xxiv.

[2] On October 26 Nugent's secretary wrote to Balcarres' secretary: "Gen. Nugent will send a person on Saturday to the Penn to value on his part the small stock. He does not wish to have any of the pigs or goats – he would wish to have Quaco and Jenny – he also consents to the exchange of Betty (a woman belonging to the King's House) for Phoebe; and he has no objection to take old Nelly, as she has no relations here, altho' she will be an incumbrance. His object is merely to restore relations to each other . . ."

26th. After breakfast, drive to the Penn. The sun extremely oppressive. Lord B. very civil, but, I am sure, very much annoyed. Dr. Ludford, who was of the party, taken ill of *the* fever, in consequence of the heat; and, indeed, it is very unsafe to go out so late in the day. We all felt the heat very much. – Poor Mrs. Ludford was very uneasy, but the fever is not thought serious. – Mr. Corbet, &c. at dinner.

27th. Dr. L. better this morning. – General N. and I drove towards Kingston at 6. – Read, &c. with Monsieur G. after breakfast; then received a visit from the Attorney-General, with his niece, in my dressing-room. – Only Grandjean and our staff at dinner. – Dr. L. getting well.

28th. At 5, drive on a new road, by the river side, and enjoy it much. – After breakfast read with Grandjean, as usual. – The Attorney-General many hours in conference with General N. on the subject of black corps, &c. Employ myself and the maids in decorating the ball-room. – Send off Baptiste (our French cook) to Kingston, with orders for ornamental cakes, &c. – A grand dinner given to-day to General N. by *King* Mitchell. – Mrs. Pye and Mrs. Ludford with me. – To bed early.

29th. Drive out at half-past five. – The Attorney-General again at breakfast this morning. – A long conference, and all about General N.'s message, respecting black corps, &c. – I feel very anxious myself for the issue, as it is all such a source of vexation to my dear N. – Read with Grandjean, write English letters, dine at 5, and the eternal Major and Mrs. Pye of our party.

30th. Up at gun-fire.[1] – Did not drive out, but General N. rode. I was glad of the excuse to be quiet till breakfast time, as I was kept awake by the band of the 20th dragoons, that regiment having given a parting dinner to the 67th. – Dr. and Mrs. L. took leave, on account of their child's illness. Do all I can to comfort them before they left us, as we feel a particular interest for them, on account of Colonel and Mrs. M. Murray, and Sir J. and Lady M. Murray. – Dress for dinner at 6. – My evening party full of ladies, but not so many gentlemen as usual; owing, I imagine, to the dinner and serenading last night. General N. did not make his appearance, but left me to do the honours, as he had so many letters to write, and so much business of various kinds on his hands. Poor fellow, he works hard, and I do indeed pity him!

November 1st. Hear of the death of George the Second, who was assassinated, and King Stephen proclaimed as Regent. The Commander-

[1] "In all the islands of the West Indies a gun is fired at the hours of five in the morning, and eight in the evening." (F. W. N. Bayley, *Four years' residence in the West Indies*, 1830).

PLATE 5

A GRAND JAMAICA BALL!
or the Creolean Hop à la Muftee, as exhibited
in Spanish Town.

Graciously dedicated to the Honble Mrs R . . . n, Custodi morum &c. &c.

From a print by William Holland after a drawing by A. James

in-Chief sent the intelligence from the Musquito Shore, with his mark by way of signature.[1] – An immense dinner party of gentlemen at 6. – Dined in my dressing-room. Wrote and read, and waited for General N. till near 12, whose party found it so agreeable, he could not get rid of them before that hour.

2nd. General N. inspected the 20th dragoons at 6. – The morning as usual. – I gave each of the white servants a present for our wedding day. – Captain Taylor came to take leave for England. – Gave him some medicines, &c. for his voyage. – Hear of the arrival of a packet from England.

3rd. Give Colonel MacMurdo a present of comforts for his voyage to dear England. – Pass part of the morning in inspecting the decorations of the ball-room. – Dress soon after 7, and at 8 all the company were assembled. – General N. and I then went down to the Great Hall, at the door of which all the staff were paraded, and we marched up to the sophas, at the upper end, to the tune of "God save the King." General N. then went round the room, attended by most of the staff, and spoke to all. The ladies were then handed up to me, one after the other, and made their curtsies. After all this ceremony was over, I opened the ball, with a Member of Council, then danced with a Member of the Assembly, then with a military man; and, having performed all these agreeable duties, seated myself in state till supper time. – Handed to supper at 12 o'clock by Mr. Scott the Member of Council, with whom I opened the ball; but after supper, I forgot all my dignity, and with all my heart joined in a Scotch reel. – Many followed my example and the ball concluded most merrily.[2]

4th. So tired I could not get up till 7. A large breakfast party. – After reading with Grandjean, lounged away the morning in my dressing-room.

[1] George the Second, etc., were chiefs of the anglophile Indians of the Mosquito Shore, on the eastern coast of what is now Nicaragua. A letter dated February 1802, among Nugent's papers in the Royal United Service Institution Library, seems to be a later version of the letter referred to here (see Appendix A).

[2] The caricature of a King's House ball reproduced in Plate 5 probably dates from Balcarres' time; the artist's name is given on the companion print (Plate 10) as A. J. (i.e. Ensign A. James), 67th Regiment, which was stationed in Jamaica from 1798 to 1801. The dedication is to Mrs. Rodon, wife of the Custos of St. Catherine's parish; she is styled *Custos morum*, or guardian of morals, to match her husband's title of *Custos rotulorum*, or guardian of the rolls. Whether this lady ever tried to ban the military as dancing partners I do not know. From the title of the print, and the verses beginning:

> Farewell, ye girls! and still alas!
> As Mama bids sad Red Coats shun!,

it might seem so.

5*th*. General N., &c. went with old Grandjean to the Penn, early this morning, to arrange about the garden. – After the usual breakfast, gave my last lecture to the blackies, and finished my Christian story. I consider them now so well acquainted with their expected duties, that I have appointed the Rev. Mr. Warren to be here to-morrow, at 12, for the purpose of baptizing them. Saw the Rev. Mr. Woodham, also, upon the same subject, and he approved, as well as Mr. Warren, of the little Catechism I have arranged for their use, and the progress of their instruction. – Major Drummond, just arrived from Turkey, and Mr. Davis, our only new guests at dinner to-day.

6*th*. Drive to the Penn at gun-fire. – Settled all about the apartments we are to inhabit, their being painted, &c. – Return to a large party at breakfast. – Captain Parker came; he is newly arrived. – At 12, Messrs. Warren and Woodham, with their families, came; all the servants were assembled in the chapel, and the gentlemen of the staff as witnesses. – Twenty-five of our black domestics were made Christians, and I trust will be so indeed.[1] After the ceremony, cake and wine, in large pieces and glasses, for the newly made Christians. – Captain Parker, Major Drummond, &c. &c. at dinner; and a large party in the evening, and we danced till the usual hour, eleven o'clock.

7*th*. General N. went to Kingston, with part of the staff, at. 6. The rest breakfasted with me at 8. Captain Parker went to Port Royal, immediately after. – Left alone part of the morning, with Major Gould, who entertained me with an account of Lord B.'s *domestic* conduct, and his ménage here altogether. Never was there a more profligate and disgusting scene, and I really think he must have been more than half mad. I was glad to get to my own room, and employ my time more profitably than in listening to such horrid details. – Found Major and Mrs. Pye in the drawing room, with the family assembled, at 6. General N. came soon afterwards, and we went to dinner. He brought me a very nice wedding present from Kingston, as our anniversary is to-morrow week.

8*th*. Don't drive out, but read till breakfast. After church, shut myself up for some hours, composing instructions for the new made Christians. – At dinner, Mr. Warren and family, Mr. and Mrs. Woodham, Major Cookson, Colonels Ainslie and Skerrett, Mr. Nixon, &c.

---

[1] In 1803 there were 33 servants provided by Government at King's House, and Nugent asked the Assembly to sanction the purchase of ten more. Long tells us that the room over the entrance lobby at King's House, "being somewhat darkened by the pediment of the portico, was converted by Governor Lyttelton into a chapel."

9*th*. General N. rode to Mr. Hanson's Penn at 6, and has ordered sheep, &c. for our Penn, in a most farmer-like manner. – Major Cookson, &c. at breakfast.

10*th*. Drove, at half-past five, to Major Cookson's Penn. The morning delightfully cool. – The Attorney-General, &c. at breakfast. – General N. full of business, and really nearly hurried and worried to death, the whole day. – I employed my morning, translating all the family, but especially kitchen, regulations into French, for the benefit of Baptiste, who is a St. Domingo *gentleman*, and scarcely understands a word of English; so now I hope the cuisine will go on more prosperously.

11*th*. Had a pleasant drive. – The horses were much quieter than they have hitherto been, and the black postilions understand them better. – Saw the Penn, and settled many important affairs with Jones. – Had a long conversation with Mr. Warren, about the blacks. I don't think he is much interested about their spiritual welfare, but he is a well-meaning man.

15*th*. This is our fourth Wedding Day. God bless and preserve my dear husband, and continue to us our present happiness. – General N. much better, but stayed at home, while I went to Church with the staff. Delighted to see the black servants look so well, so orderly, and behave so properly during the Service. – Assembled them all afterwards, and gave them each a dollar for a wedding present. – Their wish was, that General N. and I might live happy together, till our hair was as white as their gowns. They don't know what snow is, or I suppose they would have said snow, rather than gowns; but their muslin was very clean and white. – Dined at 5, with a very large party. – Poor General N.'s looks shew how ill he has been the last two days; it is really astonishing, to see so robust and florid a man so soon changed; but he has much fatigue both of body and mind, and this, added to the climate, keeps me in constant alarm. – God preserve him!

16*th*. Thank God! N. is much better, but we did not drive out. – A note in the evening from General Churchill, telling us of the death of his mother, Lady Mary Churchill.

17*th*. Drive to the Penn at 6. After breakfast very busy, with Johnson. M. Clifford, &c. &c. decorating the ball room. – Dine at 3 with General N. in my dressing room. – Try to get rid of my headache by a little sleep. – Dress at 7, and enter the ball-room with General N. &c. in great state, A very large party was assembled, and all the benches were full. Open the ball with the Attorney-General. Then dance with a Member of the

Assembly. Begin the ball after supper again, with the Commanding Officer of the Military, and then, having done my duty, steal away to bed, and leave General N. to do the honours.

19th. General N. drove me to the Penn at 6. – I don't think any year of my life I ever read half as much as I have done since I came to this country; in spite of the musquitoes, that constantly annoy every one who is sitting at any quiet occupation. – Don't dine till half-past 7, on account of the House of Assembly sitting so late. The Speaker, the Attorney-General, and eleven Members, at dinner, besides our own party; only two ladies.

20th. Drive to Port Henderson, and bring Captain Colville and several of his officers. Mr. Creyke, Mr. Becker, and Mr. Henry, also came to breakfast, and stayed all day. – A larger assembly than usual in the evening. Dance down twenty-three couples, to begin the ball, and half kill poor Captain C. who, being an Honourable, was obliged to be my partner. – Heard the delightful news of peace,[1] and the evening ended very merrily.

Till the Session is over I can only speak of events, and make no remarks, for I have no time. I ought to have mentioned, that, after the two first dinners were given to General N. and me, there was a demur about what the third entertainment should be. I was referred to, and named a ball. This pleased all parties, and it is soon to take place.

21st. Don't drive out, but, after breakfast, send off Captain C. and his party, in the sociable, to Port Henderson. – The rest of the day much as usual, every one talking of and delighted with the idea of peace; though there are some who don't seem as well pleased with it as we are ourselves.

22nd. General N. and I passed a comfortable morning together afterwards, anticipating the delights of home, and talking over our prospects of returning to dear England soon. Fourteen people in addition to our staff party, at dinner. – Very much shocked in the evening, by a sad account of the massacre of three hundred and seventy white persons in St. Domingo. How dreadful, and what an example to this island.

23rd. Drive to the Penn. – All the gentlemen of our family, excepting Major Drummond, gone to dine with Captain Colville, on board the *Ambuscade*. – The Marquis de la Jaille, Monsieur Bunel, and Monsieur Grandjean, our only party at breakfast. – General N. held a Court of Appeal at 10, which lasted till 3. He then gave audience till 5 to Monsieur

[1] The peace preliminaries, signed 1 October 1801, which led to the Treaty of Amiens in March 1802.

Bunel, on the subject of St. Domingo; and, as dinner was ordered at that hour, it was so late that he did not change his Chancery dress, but sat down in black. – After dinner, as there were only Major and Mrs. Pye in addition, Major Drummond and I had a long conversation on the subject of religion. He appeared to be particularly well informed, and had read much upon serious subjects. I have lately devoted much of my time to Mr. Wilberforce's works; therefore his conversation was very interesting to me. He is a young man, and has been running a great deal about the world, which makes his thinking so seriously the more extraordinary.

25*th*. The carriages were sent to Port Henderson for some Navy men. We had twenty at breakfast and at dinner, in addition to our party. – Much talk about peace; some pleased, some the reverse. I am of the contented party; and went to dress in great spirits for the grand ball, given me to-night by the Council, &c.: put on my smartest dress, with a gold tiara, and white feathers, and made myself look as magnificent as I could. At 8, was received at the entrance of the House of Records by the Members of Council, some of the Assembly, and some military. Was conducted to a sort of throne, covered with pink silk and draperies festooned with flowers. The decorations of the room were beautiful, and the supper was superb: one dish I shall never forget; it was a roasted peacock, placed before me, with all the feathers of the tail stuck in, and spread so naturally, that I expected every minute to see him strut out of the dish. Danced myself almost to death, to please both civil and military, Army and Navy, and stayed till 1 o'clock.

26*th*. A party of Navy officers to breakfast, and Monsieur Pechon. The breakfast was crowded with visitors, before I could make my escape. Very much fatigued, and lie down afterwards till 3. – My dear N. had prepared a little luncheon for me, of a couple of snipes, which we enjoyed very much, talking over England, &c. and the peace. – Twenty-four guests added to our dinner party; only six ladies of the number. Retire at ten.

27*th*. General N. rode out at 6. – I was so tired I rested a little longer than usual. – Send the carriages for Navy officers. – Eighteen new people at dinner. – The Speaker and Mr. Scott were the only civilians; the rest were of the Navy and Army. – A very large party in the evening, and the Navy men skipped away famously.

28*th*. Don't drive out, but send the carriages for more Navy friends, Captain Fremantle, &c. &c. &c. and we had an immense party all day.

General Churchill, and Captain Coatquelvin, came to dinner also.[1] After the party broke up, kept my eyes open half an hour later than usual, to talk to Captain F. of England, and of English friends. He hates this country, and is most dreadfully alarmed at the climate.[2]

29*th*. Send Captain F. in the sociable to Port Henderson, with several other officers. – Mr. Colin Donaldson, the new clergyman, at dinner, with Mrs. Warren and Mrs. Woodham, General Churchill, Captain Coatquelvin, Mr. W. Bullock, &c. – Heard of the arrival of an English packet, just as we were going to bed, and longed for the news of the morning.

30*th*. Before 6, large despatches, but very few letters, though those were comfortable. – General N.'s regiment (the 85th) is at Madeira.

December 1*st*. A more than usually warm morning. See the bills of fare for dinner and supper, and pity poor Baptiste, &c. &c. who, they say, have sat up all night preparing them. – Send carriages for Captains Penrose, Essington, Foley, Fremantle, &c. – General N. had to hold a Court of Appeal, and then a Privy Council, after breakfast, so that I was obliged to entertain the gentlemen all the morning. However, the task was easy, as the novelty of all things was quite enough for them, and they took particular interest in the decorations of the supper room, &c. – In the evening, I danced with all my Navy friends, and I thought they would have twisted my arms off, and broken my neck, in their wild spirits; and this was shockingly indecorous, after our stately and solemn entry into the ball-room, which astonished them very much, as they told me afterwards. – One of the black women produced two boys, this morning. Went to see them, and they were exactly like two little monkeys.

---

[1] Capt. Coatquelvin, ADC to Gen. Churchill, served in the Dutch Artillery, two companies of which had been taken into British service when the Netherlands was overrun by the French in 1795. In Jamaica the Dutch were "in general stationed at the most unhealthy spots . . ., their habits being more sober than the British."

[2] Capt. (afterwards Vice-Admiral) Thomas Fremantle was a personal friend of Lord Nelson with whom he had served in the Mediterranean and at Copenhagen, and was still suffering from a wound received in Nelson's unsuccessful assault on Teneriffe in 1797. His ship *Ganges*, with four others, had been detached from the Channel fleet and sent to Jamaica on account of the French armada expected at Saint-Domingue. Fremantle, like Nugent, was a protégé of Lord Buckingham. His eldest son Thomas (afterwards Lord Cottesloe) married the Nugents' elder daughter, Louisa; and a younger son, Charles, who also became an Admiral, gave his name to Fremantle in Western Australia when he hoisted the British flag there in 1829.

2nd. Give orders to have all the remains of the supper distributed. Send the old Custos some rich cake, as he is as fond of such things as a child. To the shopkeepers, &c. in Spanish Town, cake, &c. also. The rest was given to the blackies, which made them all very happy. – General N. was engaged in Court, till 3. We then drove with the Navy captains to the Penn.

3rd. General N. accompanied our Navy guests to Port Henderson. He and the staff on horseback, and they in the sociable, drawn by four fine new horses. Each of them, one of the Aides-de-camp told me, cost General N. £200, and the horse the servant rode was of the same price. Good animals of the sort are of course very dear in this country. – A small dinner party to-day, and a nice little conversation, in the evening, on the subject of religion, which here is quite a treat to me; Major Drummond and Dr. Lind are both very good men.

4th. Mrs. Pye called to say, that she and Major Pye were going on a cruise with Captain Penrose. Invite them and some Navy men to dinner. – The poor Chief Justice is just dead, and the house is beset with applicants for the situation. However, General N. has made up his mind on the subject, and it is to be made known to the happy man to-morrow. The Chief Justice's illness lasted only two days; but he was a worn out looking skeleton, poor man, and had not stamina, I am sure, to withstand any illness. – At 7, a very large party in the evening, and the candidates for the Chief Justice's situation particularly smiling and attentive. Some of them danced merrily on the occasion, and particularly when they were my partners.

5th. Drove to Port Henderson, at 6. – Only the Speaker at breakfast, who attended General N. and the staff to the funeral of poor Mr. Henckell. – On returning to the King's House, Mr. Kirby, (one of the barristers), was immediately declared the new Chief Justice. – The Judges of the Court, (none of whom are lawyers), were expecting this appointment, so I suppose it will be rather an unpopular act. However, they all expressed their approbation, on account of Mr. Kirby's character, and many because he was a lawyer, which the late Chief Justice was not. Besides, the deceased had the superintendence of so many estates, that it was impossible for him to attend properly to the duties of his office. He had charge of Lord Balcarres' property, who, the scandalous "Chronicle" said, received a douceur of a thousand guineas for giving him the appointment. General N. has made it a point with Mr. Kirby, that he should hold no second situation, but devote himself solely to his duties as Chief Justice; it is therefore to be hoped, that all will go well.[1] – Although we dined late to-day, on account of finishing despatches for the *Ambuscade*, General N. went to his room immediately after dinner, and I joined him, to take copies, or make duplicates, of many papers going to England, that he does not wish others to see.

6th. Drive to Port Henderson, soon after 5; all the staff with us. Baptiste and his myrmidons had gone on some hours before. At breakfast, omelettes, fricassees, &c. all prepared. Captains Colville, Foley, Essington, Penrose, Fremantle, &c. landed from Port Royal, just as we came to the inn door. – Breakfast at 7. – Talk over dear home, and our English friends. Gave Captain Fremantle a hundred messages and commissions. Then took leave of all at 9 o'clock, half laughing and half crying, but putting the best face upon it that I could; and we arrived at the church door, just in time not to keep the Service waiting. Mr. Supple read the prayers, and Mr. Donaldson preached before us for the first time. They are both young men, candidates for livings; and General N. is determined not to give one away, without being well acquainted with the character and talents of the gentleman whom he appoints. Mr. Supple read very well, only he has rather a discordant voice and Irish accent. Mr. Donaldson does not appear to have a sufficiently powerful voice; but he was so nervous to-day, that it was impossible to judge fairly. His discourse shewed more knowledge of the narrative part of Scripture, than talent to draw sound inferences from his text; *mais nous verrons.* – In addition to the clergymen who read and preached, the Rector and his wife, Mr. and Mrs. Clement, Doctors Walker and Gallagher, Mr. Blake, 20th dragoons, and Mr. Handfield of the Navy, formed our dinner party.

7th. Read a shorter time than usual with Grandjean this morning; he talks so much, and stays so long, that he teases my poor dear N. Admitted Mr. Ward, poor Lord H. Seymour's Chaplain, and had a long conversation with him, in my dressing-room. He is a most sincere Christian,

---

[1] John Henckell was the last Chief Justice to hold that office without having legal qualifications. All except one of the barristers senior to Mr. Kirby had declined the office, having "a much more lucrative employment as advocates." The Chief Justice received a salary of £120 (Jamaica currency) and about £3000 a year in fees, but an Act passed in 1804 increased the salary to £4000, in lieu of fees, and laid down that any candidate for the office must have practised at the Jamaican bar for at least three years.

If the "scandalous Chronicle" refers to a local publication, it may have been the *Cornwall Chronicle*, published weekly in Montego Bay from 1773. Balcarres' properties were Martin's Hill, in St. Elizabeth, and Balcarres, in St. George; in 1810 they were registered as having respectively 242 slaves and 663 head of stock, and 204 slaves and 26 head of stock. See also p. 32 n. above.

and a most excellent man, and truly interested in the cause of religion, particularly in the instruction of the poor negroes. Our dinner would have been very comfortable, if Grandjean had not made his appearance, and bored General N. sadly.

8th. It is not 6 o'clock, and the thermometer is at summer heat. I am writing *en chemise*, and don't find it at all too cool. The rains have ceased for ten days, and they say we shall have no more showers till May. During the rainy season, there were not above two or three days on which we could not take an early drive in the morning, or have a nice one in the evening. – However, when it does rain, it comes down like a torrent, and converts the streets into rivers; but the sun and the heat of the earth absorb all moisture almost immediately, so that, if we have no rain before May, we shall indeed be burnt up. – Poor N. still so unwell, that Dr. Lind ordered quiet, and some medicine. Remain with him all the morning, but he was obliged to see several persons on business. – One of the little twins, born last week, died to-day. – Send for Mr. Woodham, and had the other christened Philip King. Margaret, one of the black maids, and two of the footmen, lately christened, stood sponsors. They appeared much flattered at being selected for the office, and promised to do the duties of it, poor things!

9th. I would give any thing for a little rest and quiet, but must exert myself at dinner, to make the agreeable to the big wigs. – Went to the drawing room at 6, though the House of Assembly did not break up till much later. – At dinner, Mr. Speaker (Osborne), Mr. Scott, and the other Members of Council, Messrs. Edwards, Lewis, Murphy, Thorpe, &c. &c. all Members of Assembly; Colonel Gillespie, and several military men. No ladies, so I got to bed early.

10th. General N. full of business all the morning, but he is so much better he does not mind it. – Feel quite subdued, but don't complain, and anticipate a quiet evening, as General N. and his whole staff dine with *King* Mitchell. – Took my dinner in my dressing room, and read till a little after 9, when General N. came home, and gave me an account of his party. – A loaded dinner, as usual in this country, but better served, and more *recherché*, than is generally met with. Mr. Mitchell is a coarse looking man, but humane, and treats his negroes most kindly. He disgusted me very much the other day, by making a joke of poor Lord Hugh's death; but it is a common custom here.

11th. General N. wrote his take-leave speech, and the House, thank God! is to be prorogued to-morrow. Bathe at 3 o'clock; then dress for dinner. Eight or ten people, in addition to our staff. – While we were at table, the Speaker came to say, that the House did not wish to break up till 9 to-morrow morning. Agreed to by General N., and the Session will conclude; and they say it has been the quietest and most peaceable ever known here. A large party, and much merry dancing, in the evening.

12*th*. Colonel de Charmilly, &c. &c. at breakfast. – At 9, the House met. At 11, General N. made his speech, and prorogued the meeting, according to the usual forms. As soon as possible after, the greatest part of the Members set off for their homes, as happy, I dare say, to depart as we were to see them go away. – Monsieur Grandjean, Madlle. Robert, Major and Mrs. Pye, &c. at dinner. Some singing afterwards. – At 8, all took their leave, and we went to bed. General N. delighted to have a respite from such continual tiresome business, and I equally so, from a constant round of company.

13*th*. General N. rode out early. After church, a despatch from St. Domingo. Toussaint is determined to keep his command. This reminds me of a conversation General N. had with Colonel de Charmilly, who said that General Toussaint, he was sure, would negotiate with France, and for a compensation resign his command. General N. thought differently, and that he would retain his power as long as he possibly could; that he would probably call upon the whites to join him, and, in case of their refusal, a general massacre of those unfortunate people would be the consequence, that is, if he found himself at all pressed by the French force sent to St. Domingo. General N. thought, also, that he would be likely to burn the towns, and retire to the mountains. The sequel of the disastrous history of that wretched country, will prove which is the right opinion. At present, General Toussaint having declared exactly what General N. thought he would do with respect to his government, had sent secret advice to all the white inhabitants, to come over to this island as soon as possible, with what property they could collect.[1]

14*th*. General N., after writing a few despatches, began to read a novel, called The Infernal Quixote.[2] I rejoice to see him so much disengaged and at his ease already, as to mix amusement and light reading with his worrying and serious occupations. – Major and Mrs. Pye set

[1] She means that Nugent had sent this advice to British residents in Saint-Domingue. Not all seem to have taken it, for a year later James Grant Forbes, a Kingston merchant, was still writing from Port-au-Prince where he was "C.O. the Company of Foreigners."

[2] *The Infernal Quixote; a tale of the day*, 4 vols., 1801, by the Rev. Charles Lucas, curate of Avebury, Wilts., who also published volumes of sermons and religious verse.

off to the country to-morrow, with Mr. Herring; all took their leave, and I can't say that I am sorry.

15*th*. Drive to the Penn. Lord Balcarres' cattle have ruined our garden; but I cannot help laughing at the rueful faces of our blackies. – Write English letters all the morning after breakfast.

16*th*. Drive again to the Penn, with Clifford in our *suite*, driven by old Grandjean; she set the black women to work, and I hope now that the house will be clean. – Write English letters all the morning. – Poor Johnson was more than usually cross. – Mr. Hall, Grandjean, and two friends of Captain Johnson's, that were at the Charterhouse School with him, all left us at eight.

17*th*. The gentlemen of the family, except Colonel Irvine, set off for Kingston, where General Churchill and Colonel Gillespie give a ball to some French ladies. We sent excuses. General N. had a great deal of St. Domingo business, and sat writing the whole day in my dressing room. – Very comfortable indeed.

18*th*. At 6, Colonel Irvine went in the sociable to bring a cargo of Navy officers, who all arrived for breakfast. – Hear of the arrival of a packet. – General N.'s despatches all he could wish (thank God!). All his applications attended to. Poor Irvine confirmed Deputy Adjutant-General, with the rank of Major in the Army, and, in short, nothing could be more comfortable in every respect. My letters were from my brother, Lady Temple, Lady Mary, and Lord George Grenville, all of whom write in the greatest spirits, and give the most delightful accounts possible. – At 5, Captains Lobb, Stephens, Meades, &c. exceedingly lively and pleasant; as indeed every thing has appeared to me since the good tidings from England. My English letters always put me in a state of happy fuss for a day or two after their arrival. – A nice dance this evening. – The Navy men very happy, and all was gaiety.

19*th*. Have a more than usually fine *déjeuner à la fourchette* for our Navy friends, who started immediately after for their ships.

20*th*. General N. rode out early. – To church at 10. – The rest of the morning, my dear N. and I passed in reading and writing, and interesting talk. Confess my misery, that the dear name of mother will never greet my ear probably. – My mind relieved, and promise never to be so ungrateful to Providence any more; but to be resigned to His will, who knows what is best for us, and above all to be grateful for the many blessings I enjoy. – Mr. and Mrs. Woodham, Captain Cross, Messrs. Hiatt, Hylton and Lewis, Mr. Nixon of the 20th dragoons, at dinner. –

Grandjean and Baptiste bring in their *projets* for family arrangements, to our great amusement. – General N. gave Mr. Nixon, to-day, the appointment of Assistant Deputy Quarter-Master General, and he dined with us the first time, as a member of the family.

21st. All the morning my dear N. writting in my dressing room, while I drew, read and wrote by his side.

23rd. Drive to the Penn at 6. All getting in beautiful order. Busy making my arrangements.

24th. Some vulgar Messrs. Gallagher, from Ireland, of our party. – General N.'s business and worries decrease rapidly, and we shall now, I trust, be very comfortable. – Dine at 5. – Only the Irish gentlemen at dinner.

25th. Christmas Day! All night heard the music of tom-toms, &c. Rise early, and the whole town and house bore the appearance of a masquerade. After Church, amuse myself very much with the strange processions, and figures called Johnny Canoes. All dance, leap and play a thousand antics. Then there are groups of dancing men and women. They had a sort of leader or superior at their head, who sang a sort of recitative, and seemed to regulate all their proceedings; the rest joining at intervals in the air and the chorus. The instrument to accompany the song was a rude sort of drum, made of bark leaves, on this they beat time with two sticks, while the singers do the same with their feet. Then there was a party of actors. – Then a little child was introduced, supposed to be a king, who stabbed all the rest. They told me that some of the children who appeared were to represent Tippoo Saib's children, and the man was Henry the 4th of France. – What a *mélange!* All were dressed very finely, and many of the blacks had really gold and silver fringe on their robes. After the tragedy, they all began dancing with the greatest glee.[1] We dined in the Council Chamber, but went to bed early, but not to rest, for the noise of singing and dancing was incessant during the night. – I must not omit to say, that Mr. Ward called. I gave him one of my catechisms for the blackies, and one to send to Mr. Wilberforce.

26th. The same wild scenes acting over and over again.

27th. The town very quiet. – To church at 10. – A particularly full

---

1 "John Canoe" dancing, of a sort, can be seen at Christmas time at the present day. The name is probably corrupted from an African language, but the etymology has never been satisfactorily explained (see F. G. Cassidy, *Jamaica talk*, 1961). Tippoo Sultan of Mysore, whom Napoleon encouraged to oppose the British in India, was killed at the storming of Seringapatam, his capital, in 1799.

congregation, and the heat excessive. – Colonel Gillespie, &c. and young Lake arrived; the latter so like all his family! Not more than twenty-one, and yet he looks thirty-one, so thin, pale, and wrinkled. – Dined at 5. Warwick Lake, the clergyman and his wife, &c. of our party.

28th. The Christmas sports recommenced, and we don't like to drive out, or employ our servants in any way, for fear of interfering with their amusements. Poor things, we would not deprive them of one atom of their short-lived and baby-like pleasure. – The whole day, nothing but singing, dancing, and noise. – Dined in the ball-room, every thing in confusion. A bad dinner; no servants to attend; and I am sorry to say, more than half our family tipsy. Major Mosheim and young Lake did not seem quite so lenient about it as we were; the former seemed to think that German discipline would be useful, and the latter that of the quarter-deck.[1]

29th. Sent young Lake back to Port Royal.

30th. Drive to the Penn. Very busy all the morning after we returned. – Read Wilberforce, and have Cowper's Poems sent me by the Rev. Mr. Ward.

31st. I packed up papers and books for the Penn, where we hope to dine to-day. This is the last day of the year, and I rejoice, as time passes, to think, that every day, now, will bring us, please God we live, nearer to dear England, and our domestic comfort there. I will endeavour to deserve that blessing from Heaven, by being more vigilant and active in my duties here. I will begin the new year, at the Penn, by instructing the poor negroes, and if I do but succeed in making them the better understand their duties as Christians, I shall be happy indeed; and I pray for a blessing on my efforts for that purpose. – Drive to the Penn, all the staff attending, at 2 o'clock.

[1] Major Lewis von Mosheim was an officer in the 60th Regiment (afterwards the King's Royal Rifle Corps), in which there were many Germans. Originally called the Royal Americans, the regiment had been raised in 1755–6 for service in the French and Indian War, chiefly from American colonists of German and Swiss origin. After the War of Independence, it was stationed more or less continuously in the West Indies. Capt. Warwick Lake, RN, was a son of Lt.-Gen. Viscount Lake, Commander-in-Chief in India. His interpretation of quarter-deck discipline was later to prove disastrous; in 1810 he was dismissed from the Navy for having punished a seaman by marooning him on an uninhabited Caribbean islet.

CHAPTER II

January 1*st*. At 6 a party of singing men and women at our door, and all our servants, &c. dancing mad, I think. Give them a holiday. – Some of the staff come to breakfast, and another party to dinner, but left us early, and we went to bed at 8. – We have had no rain since the last week in November, but the heat is very supportable. The north wind blows furiously from 12 till 4 o'clock, and then dies away into a perfect calm, before the sun sets. The mornings and evenings are delightfully cool, and the nights so much so that we can bear a counterpane as well as a sheet upon our bed; but in the middle of the day it is very warm indeed, and if it were not for the sea breeze, would be almost intolerable. The sun is never under a cloud, but shines unremittingly, from half-past six in the morning till the same hour at night; but almost the instant the sun sets, the night comes on. No twilight, either in the morning or evening. – Received many compliments to-day, upon the new year, particularly from French people. Answer all in the best manner I can.

2*nd*. A headache. General N. rode out, and then went to town, with the staff gentlemen that came to breakfast. – Spent the morning alone. – Some pan sugar also, from Mrs. Lewis. The new sugar is excellent, drank in cold water; and I like the pan sugar of all things. – Sent, in return, a purse to Mrs. Jones, and some wreaths of flowers to Mrs. Lewis's daughters. In short, all sorts of civilities have passed between us. – Our staff came to dine, and two of them remained to sleep at the Penn.

3*rd*. Send the servants and all the family to church. – General N. detained by business, and I stayed with him. – Write to Lord George Grenville, and send him some sketches of Christmas gambols, and a view of our Penn. Read with dearest N. till dinner time.

4*th*. Only two of the staff at breakfast, and they went to town soon

PLATE 6

(a) GOVERNMENT PEN
From the 1839 edition of the Journal, probably
after a drawing by Maria Nugent

(b) THE PARISH CHURCH OF ST. CATHERINE, SPANISH TOWN
From an oil painting by Philip Wickstead

after. – Enjoyed looking over our little farm. Two lambs born. They were the sixth since we took the Penn. How prolific! – Many negroes came to make complaints of their masters. It will be all investigated fairly, so I shall make no remarks at present; but it is a difficult situation for a Governor. – Are invited by the Custos and his lady for Twelfth Night. – Only a family party to-day. Major Drummond, for the first time since his illness, and means to remain. – Play cassino in the evening till 8. The gentlemen then go to town. – This day has been quite comfortable and rural, and I have enjoyed it beyond measure. General N. and I walked out, and looked at our ducks, chickens, &c. in the evening.

5*th.* Our stud not arrived from Spanish Town, so we walked in the veranda only till breakfast time. – Teach Cupid (now George) part of his catechism. – Only Major Codd in addition to our staff party.

7*th.* Mr. Sandford Peacocke introduced at breakfast by Mr. Cuthbert.

9*th.* Find all the gentlemen in the breakfast-room, when I make my appearance. – Afterwards hear Cupid and Bristol their catechism. – Three of the staff stayed to sleep.

10*th* To church at half-past nine. A good sermon, but the bats made such a loud chirping noise all the time, that I could hardly hear any thing. – The heat was excessive. – In the morning a carpenter, from Spanish Town, applied to General N. to respite a slave, sentenced to be hanged to-morrow. The law of the land is, it seems, that three magistrates may condemn a slave to death. This case was, that two slaves, one, an old offender, the other, a boy of sixteen, robbed a man of his watch, &c. The old man shewed the boy how to get in at the window, and gave him all his instructions, while he remained on the outside, and received the things stolen. The old man has been condemned to hard labour, and the boy to be hanged. General N. made every exertion, but in vain, to save the life of the boy, and send him out of the country; but it appears that it could not be done, without exercising his prerogative very far, and giving great offence and alarm to the white population.[1] – This law of the three magistrates appears to me abominable, but I am too little versed in such matters to do more than feel for the poor sufferer. – Found to-day that we had fourteen people at dinner, when the cook only expected a very small party: poor man! – Mr. and Mrs. Woodham, Mr. Corbet, Mr. Wakefield, Mr. Smith, Mr. Williams, Mr. Parkinson, &c. were of the party. – Walked on the lawn with Mrs. Woodham after dinner.

[1] The Governor had the power of pardoning in criminal cases except murder and treason, and in these he could grant a reprieve during the King's pleasure.

11*th*. Cupid and Bristol are almost perfect in their catechism. Finish Addison on the Christian Religion, and have been much gratified with the perusal. – Dine at 3; Colonel Ainslie, Captain Maclean, and the staff, at dinner. – Settled that Boisdabert's poor little negroes shall be sent to the black corps, at Fort Augusta. I rejoice at this, for they would be starved if they returned to their impoverished master.

13*th*. Study Wilberforce till breakfast time. – Colonel Cookson, Captain Perkins, R.N. at breakfast, and remain all day.

14*th*. A present from Mr. Hanson, of a peacock and two hens.

15*th*. My dear N. went at 4 to review the militia at Kingston. All the staff, excepting Major Drummond, with him. – Write, &c. till breakfast; then Major and Mrs. Cookson, their two daughters, and a little boy, a black maid, and two men, came on a West India visit, to spend the day. Mrs. C. is a perfect Creole,[1] says little, and drawls out that little, and has not an idea beyond her own Penn. Had fruit for the children at 10; then second breakfast a little after 11. – Dined at 3, and the hopeful family took their leave at 6. – General N., &c. returned at 12, and had evidently taken too much wine, but appeared perfectly well.

16*th*. General N. complains a little of headache, but is not ill. – Plant some balsams. – Dine with our family party, at 3.

17*th*. Send off a carriage to Port Henderson, for Captain Parker, R.N. – Go to church at 10. A good sermon, and the church less warm than usual. Spend an hour at the King's House; then return, and meet a party at the Penn, at 3; Mr. and Mrs. Woodham, Messrs. Blake and Vidal of the 20th dragoons, Captain Parker, &c. Not a breath of air, and very warm indeed. All went away at eight. Dearest N. and I enjoyed the moonlight before going to bed, and never was there a more lovely night; quite like a soft beautiful day.

19*th*. Despatches sent off to England, conveyed by Capt. Milne. – Drive out after dinner in the sociable; Captain Parker with us. Visited Messrs. March and Hanson at their Penns. – Then tea, coffee and cards, and to bed at nine.

Just as we were taking leave for the night, came despatches from Lord Hobart, brought by the *Racoon* sloop of war. They were delightful; and General N. has the satisfaction of finding that he has in every respect

---

[1] i.e. a white West Indian; properly speaking, a person born in the West Indies of white parents. Major Cookson was one of those Royal Artillery officers whom Nugent described as useless, chiefly as a result of "their long residence in the country, and the connections they have formed."

anticipated the wishes and orders of Government, on the subject of St. Domingo, even to the expressions to be made use of to General Toussaint, respecting the neutrality of England, &c. A large naval force is ordered out here, and General N.'s regiment (the 85th), is coming from Madeira, as well as some artillery, to reinforce us. So now we go to bed contented and happy in our minds. Mine, however, is merely a reflected happiness, in seeing my dear husband pleased; otherwise, these warlike preparations make me tremble.

20*th*. General N. drove Captain Parker, in the curricle, to Port Henderson, at 5. – The Speaker, Mr. Edwards, &c. in the piazza, when I came out to breakfast. – Expect Sir J. T. Duckworth in a few days.

21*st*. A cloudy morning, and an appearance of rain on the mountains. – Receive a present of an immense quantity of peacock's feathers. – At dinner, a larger party than usual; Messrs. Cross, Hanson, March, O'Farrell, &c. – Have coffee, cards, &c. till 8. Only Captain Cross, of the 20th dragoons, remained.

22*nd*. Begin sketches in my Green Book. – A letter from Admiral Montagu, announcing the certainty of Sir J. Duckworth's coming to succeed him in the command.

23*rd*. General N. off at 5, to fix upon the site for a new barrack at Stony Hill, and to arrange the quarters for the 85th regiment. I did not get up, but found a note on my dressing table, from my dear N. with his good wishes, &c. as he expects to be absent the whole day. – Set all the blackies to scrape and clean all round the house, the lawn, &c. Treated them with beef and punch, and never was there a happier set of people than they appear to be. All day they have been singing odd songs, only interrupted by peals of laughter; and indeed I must say, they have reason to be content, for they have many comforts and enjoyments. I only wish the poor Irish were half as well off. Had a visit and a good long conversation with Mr. Ward to-day.

24*th*. My dear N. being obliged to go to Fort Augusta to-day, we did not go to church. Had prayers in the dining room for all the servants. They behaved very devoutly. – Mr. Jennings and Mr. Bailey, from Fort Augusta, and old Grandjean, at dinner.

25*th*. An English packet, and letters by Major Cameron at breakfast. – The Court of Chancery begins to-day. – Read, write, draw, and teach the blackies their catechism, from the time General N. went, till he sent a dragoon with my letters, at 2 o'clock – At 4 my poor N. came home, much exhausted, by attending to the long causes and the fatigues of Chancery.

26th. General N. walked out with his gun at 6. I sat in the piazza, and saw the sun rise most beautifully from behind the mountains. Nothing, certainly, can exceed the beauty and enchanting scenery of this country. Immense mountains, covered with the thickest wood, of the most lively green; others, rocky, and looking quite blue. Then, here and there, tufts of green upon their craggy and tremendous looking sides. Then, the fertile plains and plantations and penns, all mixed. When the sun first rises, all this is particularly beautiful, for the mist is cleared away gently, like a large transparent curtain, through which we see the *silver* hills, and bright green woods, &c. The dew is very heavy, and all the animals about the house seem to enjoy the coolness of the ground in consequence, in the early morning, though they are panting and appear miserable with the heat, during the middle of the day, their mouths open, and the poultry with their wings distended, all seeking the shade. – General N. in Chancery again. – On returning to dinner, he presented Mr. Supple with the living of St. Dorothy's, and means to name Mr. Ward for St. Ann's, a much better living, vacant by the death of poor Mr. Holmes, a young man, only a few months in the island. – Heard of the arrival of Sir J. T. Duckworth. A salute fired, &c.

27th. A modest request from Mr. Peacocke, that General N. would endorse a bill to the amount of more than £3000! His plea is, that, his brother having been General N.'s Aide-de-camp in Ireland, he takes the liberty of a friend. *Decline his proof of friendship.*

28th. Have a correspondence to-day with the Rev. Mr. Ward, on the subject of St. Ann's living, by General N.'s desire. He is an excellent man, and, if possible, too conscientious.[1] – Mr. Hinchliffe, Mr. Affleck, &c. at dinner.

29th. The Court of Chancery as usual, and every day for a fortnight. – My day as usual, driving out, reading, writing, and teaching the blackies.

30th. I now bathe in cold water, and then write, &c. some times *en chemise*, and this makes me cool and comfortable for the rest of the day. – It is quite wonderful how time flies in this monotonous life, and I have scarcely hours enough for my occupations.

February 1st. Dress by candle-light, and set off for the race-course.

---

[1] Why, then, on receiving his appointment as Rector of St. Ann, did he write to the parish vestry requesting a year's leave of absence? On February 17, and again on May 3, we shall find him preparing to leave for England. Later he wrote to the vestry recommending a curate to act for him, but he never returned to Jamaica himself. Instead, he became perpetual curate of Iver, Bucks., and kept a school there to which, in 1810, Mrs. Nugent sent her son.

General N., &c. on horseback; myself in the sociable. Took up three Spanish Town ladies on my way, Mrs. Hughes, and the Misses Rennalls; and asked others to breakfast. – General N. reviewed the Spanish Town militia, who performed exceedingly well. though it was ridiculous to hear the negroes, who were spectators, laugh at the Jew company when it fired, which it did very badly – "Now Massa Jew! Dat right! dat well, Massa Jew!" &c.[1] All the officers of the militia breakfasted with General N. at the King's House, and a party of ladies with me at the Penn, and never was there any thing so completely stupid. All I could get out of them was, "Yes, ma'am – no, ma'am," with now and then a simper or a giggle. At last, I set them to work stringing beads, which is now one of my occupations; and was heartily glad when their carriages came at 2 o'clock. I also drove to the King's House, and sat listening to a cause in the Court of Chancery, between two slave merchants, and was not a little disgusted with some details that came out in evidence. – At half-past five all concluded, and we got home to dinner soon after 6. – Mr. Wilkie, recommended by General Grenville to General N., dined with us. He is exactly like a man who has been buried and dug up again; so pale, lean, and miserable looking. Went to bed very tired.

2nd. Captains Penrose and Walker, R.N. at breakfast. They stayed almost the whole morning. Then came Mr. Spires, and Mr. Hardy with letters from Lord Longueville.

3rd. General N. &c. went to Port Henderson, and brought Sir J. T. Duckworth, Captain Dunn, &c. to the Penn, to breakfast, a little after 7 o'clock. – General N. had much business about barracks, &c. with Captain Fraser, the Island Engineer, so that I am left to amuse the Navy men. Admiral Duckworth is as fond of early hours as we are, so we went to bed at 9 o'clock.

4th. Dress by candle-light, at half-past five. – The Admiral, &c. set off for Port Henderson, and we for Bushy Park estate, Mr. Mitchell's, where we breakfasted in the Creole style. – Cassada[2] cakes, chocolate, coffee, tea, fruits of all sorts, pigeon pies, hams, tongues, rounds of beef, &c. I only wonder there was no turtle. Mr. M.'s delight is to stuff his guests, and I should think it would be quite a triumph to him, to hear of a fever or apoplexy, in consequence of his good cheer. He is immensely rich, and

---

[1] The principal Jewish communities were in Kingston and Spanish Town. In the infantry regiment of the Kingston militia, three of the twelve companies were composed of Jews.
[2] i.e. cassava.

told me he paid £30,000 per annum for duties to Government.[1] His
house is truly Creole. The wood-work mahogany – galleries, piazzas,
porticoes, &c. In front a cane-piece, and sugar works, with plenty of
cocoa-nut trees and tamarind trees, &c. He seems particularly indulgent
to his negroes, and is, I believe, although a very vulgar, yet a very humane
man.

After breakfast, set off to Spring Gardens, to review the militia of St.
John's Parish and St. Dorothy's. Spring Gardens was formerly a fine
place, but its owner now lives in England, and the house and every thing
are neglected. The situation is beautiful. I saw an immense fig-tree, with
a palm growing out of the top; it had a most singular appearance, but
how the palm was engrafted, no one could tell me. The house has carved
mahogany doors, &c. and many remains of its former magnificence.

On the lawn we found the regiments assembled, and spectators of all
colours crowding the place. Kittareens, horses, and mules, in abundance,
attending. – The whole review, in fact, was most funny. Not one of the
officers, nor their men, knew at all what they were about, and each had
displayed his own taste, in the ornamental part of his dress. They were
indeed a motley crew, and the Colonel whispered me – "Ah, ma'am, if
the General did but know half the trouble I have had to draw up the
men as you see them, he would not ask me to change their position; for
what they will do next I don't know. You see I have drawn a line with
my cane for them to stand by, and it is a pity to remove them from it."
Poor man! I did pity him, for at the first word of command they stared,
and then moved in every direction, and such a scene of confusion at
any review I believe was never beheld. – A magnificent second breakfast,
which succeeded this display, proved that, at Spring Gardens, the business
of ménage, or eating and drinking, was better understood than military
tactics.

After their repast, Colonel Ogilvy wished me to receive the thanks of
the corps, for attending the review; but I begged leave to decline the
display, and as soon as possible we all returned to Bushy Park, where

---

[1] Presumably this refers to the duty paid on sugar entering England. The duty in
1802 was 20s. per cwt., so that reckoning 15 cwts. per hogshead a payment of £30,000
sterling would imply a shipment of 2000 hogsheads, the produce of four or five large
estates. Apart from his own properties, William Mitchell was attorney for others; in
1807 he told a House of Commons committee that during his forty years in Jamaica
he had sometimes had sixteen or eighteen estates in his care at a time. According to
his own statement to another committee, he derived about £3000 annually from his
office of Receiver General.

we arrived to rest ourselves about 4. Had a profuse dinner at 5. – Sick of so much eating and fatigue, and get rid of the remembrance of it all by going soundly to sleep at 9 o'clock.

I don't wonder now at the fever the people suffer from here – such eating and drinking I never saw! Such loads of all sorts of high, rich, and seasoned things, and really gallons of wine and mixed liquors as they drink! I observed some of the party, to-day, eat of late breakfasts, as if they had never eaten before – a dish of tea, another of coffee, a bumper of claret, another large one of hock-negus; then Madeira, sangaree, hot and cold meat, stews and fries, hot and cold fish pickled and plain, peppers, ginger sweetmeats, acid fruit, sweet jellies – in short, it was all as astonishing as it was disgusting.

5*th*. Do not feel the least fatigued to-day. Write my journal, &c. before breakfast. Soon after, some gentlemen of the *Sanspareil*, Mr. Lutwidge, and Mr. Ward arrive. – Write, and endeavour to console Mrs. Heslop, for her husband's dismissal from the army, and promise General N.'s assistance to herself, &c.

6*th*. Not quite well early this morning, but meet Mr. Ward, &c. at breakfast, and at one we all set off to visit Sir John Duckworth on board the *Leviathan*. Find the boats waiting for us, and we were received with due honours. Before dinner, were shewn every part of the ship, and were delighted with the neatness and wonderful economy of the whole. A large party of Navy officers, &c. at dinner. Bring young Brooke home with us in the evening. The poor child was rejoiced to see me.

7*th*. Made some visits in Spanish Town, and, when we returned to the Penn, found Capt. Campbell and Mr. Browne, just arrived from England. The latter brought letters from dear Lady Buckingham and Lady Temple, with some beautiful millinery as presents from Lord Buckingham, and from dear, kind Lady Temple. Our two new visitors, and the clergyman and his wife, the Rev. Mr. Harrison, &c. at dinner.

8*th*. General N. off to review the militia of St. Thomas's Parish, at a very early hour. – Had no visitor this morning, but Mr. Sinclair, of the *Santa Margaretta*. Tried to make young Brooke read, and employ himself usefully. He is a sad pickle, and keeps me in a constant fright, he is so mischievous and daring. Scold and laugh at him by turns. He seems affectionate, and I hope to lead him right at last.

10*th*. Set off to-day for the parish of Clarendon. A large company was assembled at Mr. Israell's, to meet us. The house is a long low building, with outside and inside very like a barn. A loaded table, and Mrs. Israell

continually walking about the room, pressing every one to eat. There
was a new fish, the mountain mullet, very small, but excellent, and having
expressed my approbation, it was with great difficulty I escaped Mrs.
Israell's intention to make me sick, by devouring the whole dish, or
rather dishes, of marrow-like little fish. The conversation of the hostess
was not very interesting, but rather curious. The extent of Mrs. Israell's
travels has been to Kingston, and she is always saying, "When I was in
town;" she says too, that frost and snow must be prodigious odd things.
The daughter has been brought up at the *Queen Square Boarding School*,[1]
and is much looked up to by her mamma; and she, in return, is in constant anxiety, for fear they should be guilty of some mistake, &c. This
difference of education is, I think, a real and mutual misfortune. – About
8 began dancing. Broke the fiddle-strings. Poor Blackie was in despair,
and so were some of the ladies. I rejoiced secretly, and we got to bed
soon after nine.

11*th*. Set off very early, to review the militia, at Walker's Inn. Mrs.
Israell, her daughter, &c. with me, in the sociable. Mr. Israell, in his full
uniform, with General N.; and Mrs. Israell talking of her husband as a
great hero. – A large party of ladies, &c. at the Inn to receive me. Get to
Mr. Osborne's (the Speaker), in Vere Parish, at 3 o'clock. – Mr. Ashley
and Mr. Schaw the only strangers; but a large party in the house. Woods
is the name of the place. Like all West India houses, it is neglected, and the
grounds are wild. An excellent, but profuse dinner, as usual. – Heard
such frightful stories of scorpions, that I lay awake half the night in
terror of them.

12*th*. Set off early for Pusey Hall, the estate of Mr. Edwards, and to
review the Vere militia. The house is neat and comfortable, but the sugar
works are so near, that, as this is crop time, we were much annoyed by
the noise. After the review, had a profuse breakfast, and at 4, sat down
to an immense dinner, with all the gentlemen of the militia, &c. – We
then proceeded to Mrs. Sympson's estate, called Money Musk. Mrs.
Sympson is a widow for the second time, and has an estate of ten or
twelve thousand a year, which she manages entirely herself. They say she
is an excellent planter, and understands the making of sugar, &c. to
perfection. She has had many proposals, but finding all her admirers
interested, she has wisely declined taking a third husband. The widows
Henckell and Bailey were staying with Mrs. Sympson. Alas! how often

[1] A fashionable girls' school, known as the ladies' Eton, in Queen Square, Blooms-
bury, London.

in this country do we see these unfortunate beings! Women rarely lose their health, but men as rarely keep theirs. May God protect my dear, dear husband! Returned with our cavalcade to Woods, in the evening. – Annoyed sadly by musquitoes, and my little protégé Brooke's face is terribly disfigured by them. Captain Parker says his tough skin is proof against their attacks, and, if so, it must be tough indeed.

13th. Dress almost in the dark, intending to set off for home, without disturbing the family; but find them all up, and a fine breakfast prepared. Set off, as soon as possible after, for Spanish Town. Arrived at 11 at Old Harbour Inn, and have a second breakfast. We left our horses to be led on, and proceeded with those provided for us, and arrived at home a little after 4. Began dressing immediately, for Mr. Cuthbert's dinner to Admiral Duckworth. Fortunately, the Admiral sent to say, that the sailing of the packet on Monday would prevent his coming, so we sent our excuses, and dined with only the staff, and got to bed at 9. Heard this evening of the arrival of the 85th regiment from Madeira.

14th. Captain Parker took leave, for Port Royal, after church. – Some officers of the 85th. – All the day, hurry and bustle. – Poor General N. overwhelmed with business of all sorts, and he must make a report on all subjects by the packet that sails to-morrow. Feel for him, and make myself useful when I can; but alas! it is but little I can do to assist him. Sent off the despatches by a dragoon at 6, and then to dinner with some of the 85th, in addition to our usual and Sunday dinner party.

15th. General N. rode into Spanish Town before breakfast. – Sent a carriage to Port Henderson, for Colonel Gordon, Colonel Roberts, and some gentlemen of the Assembly, and I had to talk all day, as General N. was much engaged with business. – After dinner all went away, and we to bed at eight.

16th. Began to teach French to young Brooke. At dinner Colonel Gordon, Colonel Brisbane, Mr. Oliver Herring, Mr. Dobbin, and Captain Maclean. They all went at 8; and about 10 our repose was disturbed by a dragoon, with General N.'s letter-bag, as a packet had arrived.

17th. Send carriages for the Admiral, &c. to Port Henderson. We had a very pleasant party at breakfast, both civil and military. – Mr. Ward called to take leave for England. – Major Aston, &c. – After dinner, General N. and I drove out with little Brooke, leaving the rest of the party to take their coffee: called upon Dr. Lind, to consult him about my health, which has of late been a little deranged, and I have lost my appetite; we were afraid that the climate had seized upon me, but Dr.

Lind says, that I shall probably be quite well in time, and that I had better take no medicines, but leave myself to nature. The moon shone delightfully as we returned. Nothing could be more beautiful than the evening.

18th. General N. off before day, to review the troops in Kingston and St. Andrew's. – Not well all day. – Only a small dinner party. – Despatches from St. Domingo, at 7. – General N. returned at 9, and opened them. The French have landed 20,000 men, and the consequence is just what General N. predicted. The whites have all been taken into the mountains. Many of them were dragged there, bound hand and foot. – Cape François, &c. have been burnt; in short, it seems Toussaint's plan to distress the French as much as possible, by burning the towns, and harassing them from the woods and mountains, where the blacks have already taken refuge. How dreadful a business it is altogether; and, indeed, it makes one shudder, to think of the horrible bloodshed and misery that must take place, before any thing can be at all settled in that wretched island. Poor dear N. was sadly hurt at all this news, and was also greatly fatigued, having, in addition to reviewing the Kingston and St. Andrew's regiments, seen his own corps, the 85th, at Stony Hill. The staff are not only astonished at the fatigue he undergoes, but those who attend him are not a little alarmed for themselves; though many of them go in kittareens, &c. when he rides.

19th. Mr. Carthew, once Secretary to Mr. Pitt, and Mr. Bogle, came to breakfast. General N. went with them to the King's House, and swore in Mr. Carthew as Collector of the Customs at Kingston. Major Drummond and I copied the French despatches, and General N. made his Report to-day, upon the subject of St. Domingo; all of which is to go by the *Raven* sloop-of-war to England tomorrow. – Mr. Sherriff, Mr. V., Mr. Bogle, and Mr. Carthew, all at dinner. – A large party.

20th. For a wonder only ourselves at breakfast. – General N. then settled barrack business with Captain Fraser. – He had next the disagreeable task of announcing to Colonel Ainslie and Major Forsyth, the Duke of York's commands, that they should leave the service. He feels this disagreeable and painful business very much. However, by every account it appears that they have merited the severity shewn them, and so he must endeavour not to think of it. At dinner Mr. and Mrs. Herring, Doctor, Mrs. and the three Misses Rennalls, Miss Hanson, Mr. and Mrs. Rodon, Mrs. and the three Misses Lewis, Colonel Brisbane, and Colonel Roberts, which, with our own family, amounted to nearly thirty.

21st. Not well. Have the Psalms and Prayers read at home. – General

N. not at all comfortable, and very anxious about St. Domingo, &c. –
Mr. Corbet, &c. on business the greatest part of the day. – At 3, Mr. and
Mrs. Woodham, Mr. Corbet, &c. at dinner, and we were glad to get rid
of all, and to bed at eight.

   22nd. Alone with little Brooke. – General N. off at 4, to review the
Port Royal militia, to consult with the Admiral, &c. – Poorly all day. –
Gave French and English lessons to Brooke. – General N. came home,
thank God, quite well, notwithstanding all the fatigues of the morning;
for he went to Fort Augusta and saw a detachment of the 85th there. –
At dinner we were shocked to hear of a mutiny on board the *Seine*
frigate, and ten mutineers to be tried immediately. What a dreadful thing
to think that these poor creatures may so soon be sent out of this world,
with all their sins upon their heads! I thank God that I am not a man, to
run either the risk of such offences against society, or the being obliged
to pass sentence upon them.

   23rd. The carriages sent to bring the Admiral, young Baker, Colonel
Brisbane, and Major Otway, 85th, to dinner.

   24th. Dress by candle-light, and set off, with an immense party and
cavalcade, for the Walks,[1] and New Hall (Mr. Mitchell's) four miles
beyond Spanish Town. We entered the Walks, which is really the most
romantic, beautiful, and picturesque road I ever saw or could imagine.
The road winds along the side of a mountain, very narrow, and, excepting in a few places, excavated in the rock; only room for a carriage. There
is a precipice on one side, and the rocky mountain hanging over your
head as you pass on. At the bottom of the precipice is a clear, beautiful,
and rapid river, and, on the other side, another high mountain rises
almost perpendicular, covered with trees and shrubs. In some places
the road was really awfully beautiful; the height of the mountains, on
each side, throwing a very dark shade, and entirely excluding the sun,
and almost the light. Then the roar of the river beneath, which was quite
sublime. In some places, large fragments of rock, which had rolled down
the precipice with the trees and shrubs upon them, looked like islands.
We were all in curricles, gigs, or kittareens, or I don't know how we
should have got on, the road was so narrow in many places.

   About half way through the walk, which is six miles long, there is a
most beautiful but tremendous bridge to pass, composed of logs and earth,
without railings or defence of any sort. Just after you cross the bridge,

---

[1] Now called Bog Walk.

the mountains take a different form. They are exactly perpendicular, with the trees growing as it were out of the rock, for you scarcely see a vestige of earth. The road then runs down close to the roaring river, winding most beautifully, and the rocks, &c. projecting at different intervals, that I almost fancied the horses' heads would come against a rock, and we should find ourselves quite shut in.

We arrived at Mr. Mitchell's Penn before 9, and, after eating an abundant *creole* breakfast, set off for the sugar works. Sir J. Duckworth, Mr. Mitchell and myself, were in a carriage. General N. and suite on horseback. – We then examined the whole process of sugar making, which is indeed very curious and entertaining. The mill is turned by water, and the cane, being put in on one side, comes out in a moment on the other, quite like a dry pith, so rapidly is all the sweet juice expressed, passing between two cylinders, turning round contrary ways. You then see the juice running through a great gutter, which conveys it to the boiling-house. There are always four negroes stuffing in the canes, while others are employed continually in bringing great bundles of them. – Then after the juice is expressed, the pithy stuff, which is called trash, is conveyed to a place below the boiling-house, to keep the fire going constantly. In the boiling-house there are nine cauldrons; three of them merely simmer the sugar. This throws up all scum and useless particles to the top of the cauldron. The pure liquor then runs into the first boiling cauldron, and so is conveyed to another, till it granulates. After that, it is carried by a large gutter into a large trough, called a cooler, from whence the negroes take it in pails-full, and put it into the hogsheads, and so ends the process. Those casks, however, have holes bored at the bottom, and, being on stands, the coarsest part, called molasses, runs through, and is used in the distilling of the rum. Four negroes attend the mill; two put in the cane, one receives the dry cane, and throws it into the trash house, and there is always one attending to see that all is right and done well. At each cauldron in the boiling-house was a man, with a large skimmer upon a long pole, constantly stirring the sugar, and throwing it from one cauldron to another. The man at the last cauldron called continually to those below, attending the fire, to throw on more trash, &c.; for if the heat relaxes in the least, all the sugar in the cauldron is spoiled. Then there were several negroes employed in putting the sugar into the hogsheads. I asked the overseer how often his people were relieved. He said every twelve hours; but how dreadful to think of their standing twelve hours over a boiling cauldron, and doing the same thing; and he owned to me that sometimes they did fall asleep, and get their poor fingers into the mill; and he shewed me a hatchet, that was always ready to sever the whole limb, as the only means of saving the poor sufferer's life! I would not have a sugar estate for the world!

After this, we went to the distillery, but this I cannot so well describe; but it seems that the molasses and dirty part of the sugar ferments, and, after passing through fire and under water, in a long tube, it becomes a strong spirit. They have a sort of glass bead, by which they try the strength of the spirit, but I could not comprehend that part of it; and the smell of the dunder, as it is called, made me so sick, I could not stay to make a minute enquiry.

Returned to New Hall about 2 o'clock, drank the juice of a common orange and a Seville orange mixed, which is very refreshing, and then laid down to rest till dressing time. Find after all, that I have only half-an-hour, and therefore merely make a little change, and join the gentlemen at dinner. It is wonderful the attention that is paid me, and the care that is taken of me; all I say and do is perfection, for I am the only woman! Not well at dinner, and the loads of hot meats, &c. were disgusting. Every man was on the alert to serve me; laugh it all off, and get into the carriage with great glee that is to carry us home to-night, upon a perilous journey back, through the beautiful Six Miles Walk. – Invited to a Jew's wedding, but, after a little debate, agree that it is better to drive through Spanish Town to the Penn, and promise ourselves to attend the next.

25th. Admiral Duckworth, young Baker, &c. off at 6. On parting, the Admiral made very fine speeches, and said this was a Paradise, and General N. and I were the Adam and Eve of it, we were so happy and so much in love with each other!! At dinner, Colonel Ramsay, R.A., Major Stehelin, Major Cookson, Captain Hardy, Mr. Supple, and Mr. Bruce, who has come on a visit of a few days. – Walk after dinner, with the *boys* of the party, and play cassino with them after the visitors go away.

26th. General N. in town, immediately after breakfast. Sick, and lie on the sopha, pretending to the boys to read all the morning – Meredith, Browne, and Brooke.[1]

27th. General N. and I on horseback soon after 5. In the hedges we

[1] Lt. Cortlandt Skinner Meredith, 85th Regt., was Mrs. Nugent's nephew. 2nd Lt. Thomas Gore Browne, Royal Artillery, aged 17, had brought messages and gifts from Stowe (see above, Feb. 7). His name suggests that he may have been related to the Marquess of Sligo. Nugent later wrote to Lord Buckingham: "Browne of the Artillery has been with us ever since our return, and is considered as one of the family."

saw clusters of the red (liquorice) beads, sold in the jewellers' shops in England. They grow on a sort of vine, and are in pods like peas, and spread over the trees in great clusters, looking beautiful. General N., to please me, plucked them as we passed through the lanes, and filled his pockets with them; but when we came home, he was covered with black ants, and really tortured with them, and obliged to change every thing before breakfast.

March 1st. Captain Garth of the *Tartar*, with despatches, from the Governor of Cuba, for General N. – To-day I made the boys string beads, instead of teaching them any thing, I was so very poorly.

2nd. General N. in town early, to swear in Custom House officers, &c. – Send away all our young friends, preparatory to our tour. – Send the carriage for Sir J. Duckworth, Captains Dunn, Walker, and Garth. Have also Captain and Mrs. Elrington, and Captain and Mrs. Davis, 69th regiment, the Attorney-General, Mr. Bullock, Mr. Campbell, &c. at dinner. – Walked in the garden with the two ladies, and all took their leave at 8 o'clock. Then came Mr. Douglas; have refreshments for him, and hear all his St. Domingo news, &c.

3rd. Mr. Douglas left us after breakfast. – Employed all the morning in giving orders for our tour round the island. – Captains Maitland and Munro of the 85th regiment, with Major and Mrs. Pye, at dinner.

4th. Don't feel well, but see Baptiste, Hallam the butler, &c. and make all proper arrangements, previous to leaving home. – Mr. Drummond, of the second West India regiment, at dinner. Retire early, for to-morrow we begin our grand tour. Only sorry I am so very complaining, and feel so unequal to all exertion; but I will do my best, and be as merry as I can.

5th. After an immense fuss, hurry, and bustle, we started from the Penn at half-past two o'clock, with an enormous cavalcade; carriages, horses, sumpter mules, &c. &c. Detained by business at the King's House, for an hour. Then, delayed by various difficulties, on the road; but we arrived all safe, and in high preservation, at Mr. Simon Taylor's in Liguanea.[1] As there were merely gentlemen of the party, I only brushed the dust off, and went down to dinner at 7 o'clock, they no doubt thinking me very smart. A most profuse and overloaded table, and a shoulder of wild boar stewed, with forced meat, &c. as an ornament

I have stationed him in Spanish Town, giving him a room at the King's House, and have procured leave for him to be a member of the mess of the 69th regiment. He is really a sensible fine boy." For Brooke, see p. 9 n. above.

[1] Prospect Pen, later known as Vale Royal, and at present the official residence of the Acting Premier.

PLATE 7

THE TAYLOR FAMILY
From a photograph of a pastel by Daniel Gardner
Simon Taylor (seated), with his brother, Sir John Taylor, Bart., and the latter's wife
(Elizabeth Haughton) and children

to the centre of the table. Sick as it all made me, I laughed like a ninny, and all the party thought me the most gay and agreeable lady they had ever met with, and Mr. Simon Taylor and I became the greatest friends. When I left the gentlemen, I took tea in my own room, surrounded by the black, brown and yellow ladies of the house, and heard a great deal of its private history. Mr. Taylor is the richest man in the island, and piques himself upon making his nephew, Sir Simon Taylor, who is now in Germany, the richest Commoner in England, which he says he shall be, at *his* death. – Did not return to the gentlemen, but went to bed as soon as my coloured friends left me.

6th. Breakfast at 6, and start for Albion, another place of Mr. S. Taylor's. Leave my dear N. at Rock Fort, to review the Yallahs and Bull Bay companies of militia, as well as to view the Fort. At Albion I found a large party of gentlemen assembled. – General N. came about 3. We dined at 5. I tried to taste the brawn, but it made me sicker than ever. – The road this day was beautiful, but tremendous. Steep rocky roads, rivers to ford, high rocky hills to pass over, thick woods for the carriage to be dragged through, aloes and a variety of beautiful plants and shrubs in full bloom, and innumerable parties of negroes, laughing, dancing, and singing, and dressing their food on the roadside, and all hurrying to get to Kingston; for, alas! Sunday is the great market day. It is a sad custom, but I fear difficult to reform or alter in any way. After giving audience to the coloured ladies, went to bed at nine.

7th. Reading our books, and dearest N. with me. – Then set off at 7 for the Speaker's. First go to Cow Harbour, and see a small fort there; then, after a most delightful drive, something the same as yesterday, only more majestic and awful, fording large rivers, &c. we arrived at Montpellier, where there was a large party assembled. – Mr. Robinson and Mr. Milner were the only two gentlemen new to me.

The house is most delightfully situated, on a little mountain, and in front is the sea. Behind are mountains rising above mountains, and the famous Blue Mountains in the distance. Beautiful trees and shrubs round the house. In short, it is altogether indescribably beautiful.

I went to my own room, and lay down to read, as usual. My favourite book just now is Dodd's Reflections upon Death.[1] On asking Johnson

---

[1] *Reflections upon death*, by the Rev. William Dodd, a fashionable London preacher, was first published in 1763 and frequently reprinted. In 1777 the author was executed for forgery, in spite of petitions on his behalf by Dr. Samuel Johnson and other distinguished persons.

(who is deaf), for it, she said, "Pink or blue to-day, ma'am," thinking of my shoes, as always being the colour of my dress. – Dinner, Creole-French, and very good; but I was very sick, and wished myself in bed, where I soon was, after giving audience, as usual, to the coloured ladies, while I took my tea, and leaving the gentlemen to their cigars, &c. for which, I am sure, they were much obliged to me.

8*th*. Write my journal before we breakfasted; set out to review the St. Thomas in the East, Yallahs and Morant companies of militia, at Belvidere. The Speaker drove me in his curricle – The rest of the party were on horseback. After the review, we all went to a place called Licence,[1] another estate of Mr. Taylor's. – The situation is high, and the view magnificent. – The musquitoes tormenting! – An immense party at dinner. – My usual levee of coloured ladies. One told me she was twenty-four years old, and shewed me her grand-child. I found afterwards that she was fifty-four; but they have no idea of time or distance. They reckon the one by the number of Christmas masquerades they can recollect, and for the other have no scale. If you ask how far to such a place, they will say, "two or tree mile," if it should be twelve or fourteen. If it exceeds that, they say, "far enough, massa," or "too far, massa."

9*th*. Devoured by musquitoes all night. – Set off for Bath immediately after breakfast, with an immense cavalcade of gentlemen on horseback, or in kittareens, sulkies,[2] &c. &c. in addition to our own party. Stopped at Mr. Baillie's Penn,[3] just above Morant Bay. General N. &c. crossed over to see a fort and block-house, and I proceeded, with the rest of the party, to Bath. A most beautiful and romantic drive over mountains, on the ledges of precipices, through fertile vallies, &c. – Bath is truly a lovely village, at the bottom of an immense mountain. The houses are surrounded with gardens and cocoa-nut trees, and there is an immense row of cotton trees in front, most magnificent, and like our finest oaks. General N. came at 4. – Dined at 6. – Mr. Cuthbert and Mr. Chief Justice are here, for drinking the waters. They joined our party, and drank punch made of the Bath stream. I tasted it, and it is sickly, nauseous stuff. – To bed before ten.

10*th*. Up at 5. – Set off on horseback, in my night-cap, dressing gown,

---

[1] or Lyssons; named after Nicholas Lycence, Member of Assembly for St. Thomas in the Vale, 1671–2. Simon Taylor and his brother, Sir John Taylor, Bart., are buried there.

[2] Sulky: a light chaise seating one person only; in contrast to the kind of family carriage known as a "sociable".

[3] The site of the present Courthouse.

and pokey bonnet, with General N. and a party of gentlemen. The road is the most beautiful thing I ever saw, narrow, and winding for two or three miles up a mountain. A dreadful precipice is on one side, at the bottom of which runs a river; but bamboos, &c. growing thickly up the sides of the mountain, lessened one's fears for the narrowness and height of the road.

The bathing-house is a low West India building, containing four small rooms, in each of which there is a marble bath. Then there is another house for infirm negroes, &c. In fact, a kind of public hospital with baths, and they tell you of wonderful cures performed by the waters.[1] I drank a glass of it first, which was really so warm, that it almost scalded my throat. I then went in for twenty minutes, and had the heat increased till I got familiarized to the bath, which I really found most delightful and refreshing. I must, however, mention an adventure of the Governor's Lady. The old woman attending the bath was very anxious to see her, but her pokey bonnet covered her face, and her dressing-gown concealed her person; but as the lady was stepping out of the bath, in a perfectly undisguised state, she heard a voice near her, and perceived, under the door, a pair of black eyes, and indeed a whole black face, looking earnestly at her; for the door was half a yard too short, and the old woman's petticoat had been applied to the breach; this she had slyly removed, and laid herself down on her stomach to peep. The Governor's Lady gave a great squall, and away ran the old woman.

After I came out of the bath, I drank another glass, and then proceeded down the mountain, at the bottom of which is a botanical garden. We rode, and were really much gratified, in seeing the variety of plants, shrubs, and trees, all so new to an European eye. The bread-fruit, cabbage tree, jack-fruit, cinnamon, &c. were in great perfection; as likewise were the sago, and in short a number of beautiful shrubs I can't describe, and some of them as curious and extraordinary as they are beautiful. – The leaf of the star-apple tree is like gold on one side, and bright green on the other. Another tree, the name of which I can't recollect, was purple on one side, and also green on the other. The Otaheite apple is a beautiful tree, bearing a bright pink blossom, like a tassel; but it is impossible for

---

[1] The thermal spring was acquired by the Government in 1699, and administered by a corporation, the Directors of the Bath of St. Thomas the Apostle. Dr. Thomas Dancer's *Short Dissertation on the Jamaica Bath Waters*, 1784, contains a Catalogue of the Diseases in which the Bath Waters were found useful, and the list includes cancer, convulsions in general, elephantiasis, hysterics, sterility and tetanus.

me to describe all the beautiful plants I saw. Besides, we were obliged
to hurry home, a shower of rain coming on, which prevented our beginning our journey till 10 o'clock, when we proceeded to Golden Grove,
another estate of Mr. Simon Taylor's. I cannot here avoid mentioning,
that Mr. Taylor is an old bachelor, and detests the society of women,
but I have worked a reform, for he never leaves me an instant, and attends
to all my wants and wishes. He recollects what I have once commended,
and is sure to have it for me again. Every one of the party is astonished
at this change; but I believe he takes me for a boy, as I constantly wear
a habit, and have a short cropped head.

The road to-day was bad and intricate, so that we were obliged to
have a guide to Golden Grove. After fording Sulphur and the Devil's
River, we arrived safe there. It is an excellent house, surrounded by sugar
works, cocoa-nut trees, &c. We drove up just at the dinner hour of the
negroes. Never in my life did I see such a number of black faces together.
We went into the sugar works, ate sugar, talked to the negroes, &c.;
but another shower of rain coming on, obliged us to go to our own apartments. I put on my dressing-gown, and attempted to rest, but was every
instant interrupted by mulatto ladies, with one curiosity or another in
the eating way. A conch was first brought to me. It was a delicate white
on the outside, and a beautiful pink in the inside. It was just caught, and
the women told me that they put a little fire to the shell, and it instantly
left its dwelling, poor little fish. A turtle, and several curious fish were
also introduced for my inspection. So, as I found I could get no rest, and
was uncommonly well after bathing this morning, I dressed, and walked
about the house till dinner time. A little mulatto girl was sent into the
drawing-room to amuse me. She was a sickly delicate child, with straight
light-brown hair, and very black eyes. Mr. T. appeared very anxious for
me to dismiss her, and in the evening, the housekeeper told me she was
his own daughter, and that he had a numerous family, some almost on
every one of his estates. The housekeeper's name was Nelly Nugent. She
told me that her father was a Mr. Nugent, from Ireland, who had been
some years ago upon that estate. She of course considers herself a connection of ours, and we were consequently well acquainted in a short
time. – Our dinner, at 5, was even more profuse than usual. A great
variety of fish, barbecued hog, fried conchs, &c.; in short, I can't
recollect half the strange dishes – but I tasted of a great many, and particularly of the black crab pepper-pod [pepper-pot], which was very good
indeed.

According to usual custom, when I went to my bed-room, I was surrounded by all the mulatto ladies the neighbourhood afforded. One little black girl came to beg that I would take her with me. She was a remarkably thick-lipped and ugly, but intelligent child. She could say the Lord's Prayer perfectly, but could not tell how she had learnt it; both her father and mother are field negroes, and neither of them can say their prayers. – This led me to talk of the field negroes, with my friend Nelly Nugent, who told me that Saturday and Sunday were allowed them to work in their own gardens, and to raise provisions for themselves. The smallest children are employed in the field, weeding and picking the canes; for which purpose they are taken from their mothers at a very early age. Women with child work in the fields till the last six weeks, and are at work there again in a fortnight after their confinement. Three weeks in very particular cases are allowed, but this is the very longest time. Nelly Nugent remarked, however, that it was astonishing how fast these black women bred, what healthy children they had, and how soon they recovered after lying-in. She said it was totally different with mulatto women, who were constantly liable to miscarry, and subject to a thousand little complaints, colds, coughs, &c. Indeed, I have heard medical men make the same observation. – Soon after 9, the gentlemen began to smoke. General N. left them, and we went to bed.

11*th*. General N. &c. &c. set off at 5, for Rocky Point. I wrote and amused myself till 9, when they all returned to breakfast. – The Speaker is quite ill to-day. I don't wonder at it, for he eats so enormously, that it is impossible he should escape indigestion. – Soon after breakfast we went to another estate of Mr. Taylor's, a few miles from Golden Grove, called Holland, where we found a profuse second breakfast prepared for us. Visited the sugar works, &c. The house is a good one, but the situation is low and damp, and I should think not healthy. The negro-houses are extremely pretty. All neatly built on the borders of Plantain Garden River, and innumerable cocoa-nut trees are mixed with the gardens and houses.

Return to Golden Grove at 3, and half-an-hour after set out for the Moro, Mr. Scott's, of the Privy Council. I went in Mr. Taylor's carriage to the bottom of the hill. We then all mounted our horses, and for two or three miles clambered up a steep road, with a precipice on one side, really frightful, which almost terrified me out of my little wits; but I made up my mind there was no danger, being mounted on an old quiet horse of Mr. Scott's, that travelled up and down the hill every day, and was perfectly acquainted with all the difficulties of the road. The Moro[1] is a good house, situated on the pinnacle of a mountain. You can't go ten yards from the door, without descending; but the view is really charming. In front you see a rich vale, full of sugar estates, the works of which look like so many little villages, and the soft bright green of the canes, from this height, seems like velvet. The guinea-corn fields make a variety in the green, and the canes that are cut are of a brownish hue; which, with the cocoa-nut and other trees, make a delightfully varied carpet. Plantain-Garden River runs through the whole, and loses itself in the sea, at the bottom of the vale. On the other side of the vale, hills rise over hills, some clothed in wood, some in canes, and all have small settlements here and there. Then, the rest of the view, as far as the eye can reach, is all sea; and as there are many shoals and rocks, on this part of the coast, you see it constantly foaming over them. There is, however, a good harbour, at Rocky Point, for vessels to come up and take the sugars from the several estates, which are carried down Plantain-Garden River in boats.

Our dinner, at 6, was really so profuse, that it is worth describing. The first course was entirely of fish, excepting jerked hog, in the centre, which is the way of dressing it by the Maroons.[2] There was also a black crab pepper-pot, for which I asked the receipt. – It is as follows; a capon stewed down, a large piece of beef and another of ham, also stewed to a jelly; then six dozen of land crabs, picked fine, with their eggs and fat, onions, peppers, ochra, sweet herbs, and other vegetables of the country, cut small; and this, well stewed, makes black crab pepper-pot. – The second course was of turtle, mutton, beef, turkey, goose, ducks, chickens, capons, ham, tongue, crab patties, &c. &c. &c. – The third course was composed of sweets and fruits of all kinds. – I was really sicker than usual, at seeing such a profusion of eatables, and rejoiced to get to my own room, and, after my usual levee of black and brown ladies, to go to bed. – I pitied poor Mr. Osborne, he was in the situation of Tantalus, and obliged, among all the good and savoury things, to dine merely on the wing of a boiled turkey.

[1] Moro formed part of Hordley Estate.
[2] Cassidy, *op. cit.*, says that "jerk" is the English form of a Spanish word of Indian origin, meaning to prepare pork in the manner of the Quichua Indians. "Maroon" and "buccaneer" had once been alternative descriptions of the men who hunted wild hog in the islands and sold the cured meat to passing ships; in 1803 Dallas, in his *History of the Maroons*, described them as "fugitive negroes, now designated by the appellation of Maroons, or hog-hunters."

12*th*. Up at 6 – Wrote my journal, and soon after breakfast the whole party set off on horseback for Amity Hall, our carriages were sent round to meet us, by a different road. After ascending a very high hill, the view was lovely; but, as it was only a more clear and full one than that from the Moro, I shall not describe it. Stayed half-an-hour at Amity Hall, then joined our carriages at the bottom of Featherbed Hill, where we took leave of our good friend, Mr. S. Taylor, and of Mr. Scott; the rest of the party proceeding with us to Merton, the estate of Mr. Bryan. When I expressed my regret at parting with Mr. Simon Taylor, he said, "I am very sorry, too, Ma'am, but good Almighty God, I must go home and cool coppers." I thought really he was going home, to have all the large brass pans emptied to cool, that I had seen the sugar boiling in, and that it was part of the process of sugar making; but I found he meant that he must go home, and be abstemious, after so much feasting.

The road to-day was beautifully romantic. but tremendous. Merton is an excellent house, and delightfully situated, having a fine view of the sea, and Manchioneal Harbour. It does not stand above ten yards from the edge of a precipice. Mr. Bryan is in England, but his agent, Mr. Milner, received us. Salutes were fired from the block-house, and the ships in the harbour. – I walked about the lawn, and talked to the negro children, who were weeding, superintended by an old woman. I gave them a little money, and this brought almost all the negroes of the estate about us; for I found that the works were stopped, and the negroes had been given a holiday in consequence of our arrival. Poor creatures, they seemed much pleased, and talked a great deal, but I could scarcely understand a word they said. General N. returned, and we sat down to dinner, profuse as usual, at half-past six. I was glad to get to bed as soon as possible after.

13*th*. Breakfast before 8, and then set off for Castle Comfort, the estate of Mr. Jones. Mr. Orr received us, with a large party of gentlemen of the country, and the Members for the parish, as usual. The road frightfully beautiful! – Had a sumptuous second breakfast, and walked about after, till the carriages were ready. Saw a most beautiful tree, called the scarlet bean. It is like a large coquelicot-geranium: for the leaves fall off as soon as the flowers make their appearance. The floor of one of the rooms in the house particularly struck me. It was of zebra wood, the ground like satin wood, the stripes mahogany colour, and all so polished that it was quite dangerous to walk upon.

At 3 set off for the senior Mr. Bryan's estate, called the Bog, a mile beyond Port Antonio. The road was very hilly and rocky, but, as usual, extremely picturesque. I counted thirteen gentlemen on horseback, who had joined our party. These, with our former friends, servants, sumpter mules, &c. formed an immense cavalcade. At Port Antonio, the whole neighbourhood was assembled to stare at us. A salute was fired from the ships in the harbour, and the Fort saluted also as soon as we entered the town; where we were met by several officers of the 60th regiment, quartered there. The guns happened to be particularly near, which put our horses in a fright. Off they set, the rest of the party, sumpter mules, &c. joined in the scamper, and we went through the place as if we were mad; turning over the old women's baskets, and knocking down every thing in our way. I felt in a sad fuss, but, fortunately, our horses were stopped a short distance from the town, and all arrived safe at Mr. Bryan's at half-past six. We were received by him, and a Mr. and Mrs. Cosens. Mrs. Cosens is the first white woman, except my maid, that I have seen since we began our journey. – At 8 we had a dinner, in the usual style of plenty, and we went to bed as early as we could, heartily fatigued with the day's journey.

14th. General N. set off at 4, to see a settlement of the Maroons, called Moortown. – I breakfasted at 8, with the family here, and a small party. After breakfast, converse a good deal with Mrs. Cosens, who appears a very pleasing young woman.

The situation of this house is beautiful, but it is very odd and looks dark and gloomy. All the others we have been at were painted and newly done up, for our reception, while this is dirty and comfortless; but, as they have taken great pains to mend our roads, and seem particularly anxious for our accommodation, we ought not to complain of slight inconvenience. Every one appeared here in a bustle, nothing but running in and out; the old gentleman himself, I believe, intended to dress the dinner, for I have seen him constantly going into the kitchen, or cookroom, as it is called in this country. The idea of making so much fuss, and giving so much trouble, disturbs my repose.

Feel uncomfortable about poor little Cupid, who was sadly hurt yesterday by a vicious mule; he is, however, better to-day. – General N. did not return till near 8 o'clock. – A feast had been given him by the Maroons, of jerked and barbecued hog, plantains, yams, &c. After that there was one dance, and then their war exercise concluded the fête. We sat down an immense party, between 8 and 9. To bed at twelve.

15th. At 5, General N. went to review the battalion of the 60th regiment, at Port Antonio, to inspect their barracks, &c. A second edition of salutes and firing. – I breakfasted with the party here, and, immediately after, we all set off on horseback, to see the review of the Portland militia, a little beyond Port Antonio, where we were joined by General N. and his cavalcade. A tent was prepared for us, with fruit, wine, &c. I had my saddle changed, and put on a beautiful grey horse, belonging to an officer of the 60th regiment; and, after the review, I rode it back to Mr. Bryan's, to which we were attended by an immense number of gentlemen on horseback, and sat down, a large party, to a second breakfast at 2 o'clock. I liked my little horse so well, that General N. paid a hundred pounds for him, and sent him to the stable immediately.

Notwithstanding the fatigues of the morning, my dear N. was obliged to go, at 4 o'clock, to dine at Port Antonio, with the officers of the militia. I dined with a small party of about twenty-two people. – After dinner, had a conversation upon religion. Some of the opinions of the gentlemen were shocking. Not one professed to have the least religion, and some said it was all a farce. I took courage, and expressed my disapprobation. This brought some awkward apologies, and so ended the conversation.

16th. Breakfast at 8; a very large party. – Mr Sherriff, Member for St. George's, and some gentlemen of that parish, came to advise us to proceed immediately on our journey, as much rain had fallen in the mountains, and there was a prospect of more; which, in all probability, would render the rivers impassable before the next morning. We therefore sent our excuses to the 60th regiment, with whom we were to have dined, and set off, at about 11, for the parish of St. George. The Speaker and Mr. Edwards, &c. took their leave, and we proceeded, with almost an entire new party, to an estate of Mr. Shirley's, called Spring Gardens. – My little attendant, Cupid, much better, and able to attend us.

I rode the first four or five miles, the roads being very bad, and remarkably narrow, and winding on the edge of a frightful precipice; but, to the astonishment of all, General N. drove the curricle the whole way. At the River Grande I was obliged to get into the carriage, and we forded it extremely well; but it was very deep, and I trembled the whole time. Then we had hills to mount, and the sea shore to encounter, with the waves dashing against our horses' feet, till we arrived at Swift River, which was so deep, that boats were in waiting for us; but General N. preferred fording it, so we sent a black man on, to wade through before us, and we got over safe; though, as everything was wet through, my gingerbread nuts were spoiled. They were a *delicate* attention of Mr.

Simon Taylor's, and the only thing that relieved my sickness. – Again
we had sea shore, mountains, precipices, and sloughs, till we came to
Spanish River. After that the road improved, till we got to Spring Gardens, though it was still very hilly and rocky. It seems the roads being so
very bad was owing to our being a few days sooner than we were expected; though there were hundreds of negroes at work, they could not
clear away or mend half the bad places. Got to Spring Gardens about 6;
my maid did not arrive till near 7, which alarmed me very much. Went to
dinner about 8, very, very sick, and more so than usual, from the fright
and fatigue of the day. – Had a light all night, and was so unwell that I
could not sleep at all.

17th. Did not get up till 7. – Mr. Fitzgerald, and Mr. Murphy and
Mr. C. Grant, the two Members for St. Mary's, came to join our party. –
General N. full of business till 2. He and I then took a walk in the garden,
which is an excellent one, and kept in very good order. Saw a great
number of curious trees and plants, amongst which were the chocolate-
tree, &c. &c. I found five or six strawberries, some roses, and a variety
of beautiful flowers. – Dined at 6, with a very large party.

This house is a very good one, placed at the top of a hill, at the bottom
of which, on one side, are the negro houses, neatly laid out into a street,
with a stream running through the vale, plenty of cocoa-nut trees and
plantations. The vale, on the other side, contains the garden, which is
also well watered by a river, that comes from the mountains; and the
gardener told us that alligators often appeared on its banks, which rendered it dangerous for bathing. In front is the sea, sugar works, cane
pieces, &c. While we were in the garden this morning, two poor negroes,
who had been in chains nearly a year, came to General N., to ask him
to intercede for them, and they were accordingly released in the evening.

18th. Up at 6. – A large party at breakfast, and set off immediately
after for Kildare, the estate of Mrs. Fitzgerald. The road tremendous.
First, under a frightful rock, the sea beating against our horses' feet;
and then over a still more frightful mountain; but General N. drove
the carriage the whole way, a thing never attempted before. We proceeded a few miles beyond Kildare, to review the St. George's militia, after
which we all rode on to Charlestown, a Maroon town. – The Maroons
are composed of the descendants of those who made their escape during
the Spanish dominion, and were established on lands by the British
Government, after the conquest of the island. Many of them, however,
were runaways from estates of British planters, at a later period, and

PLATE 8

(a) HOLLAND ESTATE, ST. THOMAS IN THE EAST
From James Hakewill, *A picturesque tour in the island of Jamaica*, 1825
Book-keepers' barrack on the left, with still-house and boiling-
house beyond; overseer's house on the right

(b) SPRING GARDEN ESTATE, ST. GEORGE'S
From James Hakewill, *A picturesque tour in the island of Jamaica*, 1825
Showing from left to right, the Great House, part of the slave village, the sugar
works, and wharf storehouse

before their treatment was so lenient as it is at present, and before the treaty made with all the Maroon towns by Governor Trelawny.[1]

The Maroons received us as if they were much pleased with our visit; the women danced, and the men went through their war exercise for us. The dancing was exactly like that of the negroes at Christmas, and their military manœuvres seemed to consist entirely of ambuscade; taking aim at their enemy from behind trees, leaping up, and rolling about, to avoid being wounded themselves. Altogether it was so savage and frightful, that I could not help feeling a little panic, by merely looking at them.

The women were all dressed with a variety of trinkets and finery, and many not unbecomingly, though very fantastically. Their band was composed of all sorts of rude instruments, neither very musical, nor with much variety of cadence. The Coromantee flute is a long black reed, has a plaintive and melancholy sound, and is played with the nose.[2] – Charlestown is situated between two high hills, with cocoa-nut trees, &c. up to the very tops, with little huts up the sides of the hills, each having a piazza in front, and a little garden, looking really picturesque. – The Maroon clergyman preached for us, as he called it, which was merely repeating a part of our Morning Service, and murdering the sense of it most completely.

At 4, General N. went to dine with the militia gentlemen; and at 6, I sat down with Mrs. F. and a party here. – This day I have suffered more than usual from sickness, and find in Mrs. F. a very pleasing, sensible, motherly woman, and like her much.

19*th.* General N. off early, to see a situation in the mountains for a barrack. – I breakfasted with a large party here. – My dear N. came

[1] The treaty of 1739, which terminated years of guerilla warfare, provided that the Maroons should be "in a perfect state of freedom and liberty", and should possess "for ever" certain reserves in the mountains, in return for which they undertook to help the Government in repelling invaders, and to return any runaway slaves. In 1795 the Maroons of one settlement, Trelawny Town, took up arms against the Government; eventually forced to surrender, they were deported to Nova Scotia and thence to Sierra Leone, and their reserve was abolished (but the place is still known as Maroon Town, in St. James). In 1805 a total of 822 Maroons were registered in the four settlements of Charles Town and Moor Town, in Portland, Scot's Hall, in St. Mary, and Accompong, in St. Elizabeth.

[2] Coromantee, the name of a town on the Gold Coast (now Ghana), was applied to all Gold Coast Negroes. No other visitor to the Maroons seems to have mentioned a nose flute, nor have I traced any mention of one in the Gold Coast area. S. Chauvet, *Musique nègre*, Paris, 1929, describes a nose flute used by the Bahuana of the Belgian Congo, and capable of producing two distinct sounds.

back at 12, quite wet through, and all splashed with mud; for, though it is dry here, there has been much rain in the mountains. Poor fellow, he has indeed a great deal of fatigue, but he does not seem to mind it! He changed his dress, had a second breakfast, and then we began our journey again, along the sea shore, through rivers, over rocks and stony roads, till we arrived at Mr. Sherriff's coffee estate. Passed Alligator Pond, which they say abounds with those monsters, but we did not see any of them.[1]

We found Mrs. Sherriff, her mother Mrs. Strachan, and a Miss Cumming, dressed ready to receive us, all in their best. Mrs. S. is a fat, good-humoured Creole woman, saying dis, dat, and toder; her mother a vulgar old Scotch dame; and Miss C. a clumsy awkward girl. The house is a good one, quite new, and every thing neat about it. It is situated in the midst of mountains, out of which issue abundant streams of water; all up the sides of the mountains are plantain and cocoa-nut trees, and coffee bushes. The coffee is a beautiful shrub, bearing a white flower on the stalk, and the leaf is a most brilliant green.

We dined at 6. A large party. In the evening the house was very damp and cold, owing to the numerous streams that run about it, and the great quantity of rain that generally falls in the mountains, at this season of the year. We had a wood fire, which I found extremely comfortable, as I am still very unwell, and susceptible of the smallest change in the atmosphere. This house is perfectly in the Creole style. A number of negroes, men, women, and children, running and lying about, in all parts of it. Never in my life did I smell so many.

20th. Did not breakfast till 9. – Saw a flight of parrots this morning, all chattering as they flew. They are said to be very destructive to cocoa-nut and plantain trees. The negroes eat them, and some people make soup of them. – Went to the coffee works, and saw the process of preparing coffee, &c. – Mrs. Sherriff had a cabbage tree dissected for me. It is really very curious and beautiful. They grow wild in the woods, are eighty years coming to perfection, and for a dish of cabbage you cut down the whole tree, as the top of it is the only part eaten, and the tree dies when that is taken off.

At dinner a large party of men. – In the evening a fire again, and we all agreed it was very comfortable. – When the gentlemen joined our party,

---

[1] In Robertson's map of the County of Middlesex (1804), Alligator Pond is marked in a morass lying inland of Palmetto Point, between Buff Bay and Annotto Bay.

there was a vulgar Mr. Murdoch so drunk, that I called for my maid, and went to bed. – I think nothing so hideous and disgusting as a drunken man, and how happy am I that my husband joins with me in this opinion, and I never have seen him in the least intoxicated.

21*st*. We took our leave a little after 7, and proceeded towards Annotto Bay. The firing from Fort Brunswick frightened the horses, and terrified me not a little. General N. examined the fort, &c. We then sent our servants forward to Agualta Vale, and proceeded ourselves six or seven miles farther up the country, to look for a situation for a barrack, on Mr. C. Ellis's estate, called Fort George. The situation is pretty, but the house is merely one fitted up for the overseer. There was wine, biscuit, &c. prepared for us, and I could not help observing, although the gentlemen of our party had all eaten and drank at Fort Brunswick, they did the same here, and I am sure so much eating injures the health of many of them. General N. and I touched nothing at either place.

We now returned to Annotto Bay, where we were saluted again, on our way to Agualta Vale. At 6 we pursued our journey again, to Mr. Grant's, in St. Mary's. We were benighted, and, after a tedious, doubtful, and frightful drive, we arrived at his estate, called Hopewell, at about 10. I forgot to mention, that we had a profuse second breakfast at Agualta Vale, which was in every respect an immense dinner, though otherwise denominated. A large dinner was prepared for us at Mr. Grant's, but a little soup was the only thing any of us could take, except one gentleman, who declared it was only the fifth time he had eaten in the course of the day, and he stuffed of every thing, even to mince pies, the first I have seen in this country.

My maid did not arrive till after 11. The mules had taken it into their heads to lie down two or three times in their way. Poor creature, I pity her very much; she has no associates, and no equals; she is left to the care of a parcel of blacks, and every thing is new and strange to her. However, she bears it extremely well, and makes no complaints. We went to bed as soon as possible; and did indeed sleep most profoundly, being all much fatigued.

22*nd*. All well, except the gentleman who ate so much yesterday. – A dragoon with despatches. – No English mail yet, but a packet expected every hour. – This house is a very good one, every thing neat about it, and it commands a view of a very beautiful country. The estate is just now worth clear £18,000 per annum. It is wonderful the immense sums of money realized by sugar in this country, and yet all the estates are in debt.[1] – Read, &c. in my own room all the morning. A large party of gentlemen at dinner, at 6. – Get to my room at 9. – Dismiss my mulatto friends as soon as possible, and go to bed. Several of them gave me their histories. They are all daughters of Members of the Assembly, officers, &c. &c.

23rd. Leave Hopewell at 12. – Arrive at the house of the late Mr. Bryan Edwards, called Nonsuch, about 2. The road very rough, but the country pretty. Miss Murphy and Miss Spencer there to meet me, and several gentlemen. The place is pretty, surrounded by cocoa-nut trees, with a magnificent cotton tree in front of the house; but every thing wears the appearance of age and neglect. All the doors, wainscots, &c. are of mahogany. At 6 the usual profuse dinner.

In the evening, the conversation fell upon hurricanes, when many frightful stories were told. This reminds me of a strange circumstance, that was related to me by Mr. Shaw, Member for Kingston, when we were at Spring Gardens. Messrs. Grant and Murphy also attested the fact, therefore I will relate it. About six or seven months ago, Mr. Shaw saw from his window dark clouds arise from opposite points, accompanied by sudden and violent wind. They seemed at first to have a conflict; at last they united together, and came towards the house, in a great black column. The house was situated upon an eminence, in the parish of St. George, and fronting the sea; but, as there were deep ravines on both sides, Mr Shaw hoped the wind would be attracted by one of them. However, it made directly towards the house, and he and his servants had just time to escape with their lives, when the whole was carried away, scattered, and sunk in the sea, and now not a vestige remains. These columns of wind I have observed several times, but had no idea they were ever so serious in their effects. However, this is a most uncommon instance, and affords much matter for wonder and conversation. – Did not get to bed till eleven. These are sad hours in this climate, but it can't be helped. – Less sick to-day than usual.

24th. Awoke at 6 by English letters. Every thing pleasant. – N.'s public letters delightful. – Breakfast, and set off at 9, for the review of the St. Mary's militia. The two young ladies and myself in a phaeton; General N. and Mr. Murphy in another; the rest of the party on horse-

---

[1] £18,000 seems an extraordinarily high figure. In 1807 a House of Commons committee, after hearing evidence from several Jamaican planters (who probably exaggerated their troubles), came to the conclusion that in the years after 1800 planters had not been able to expect a return of more than $2\frac{1}{2}\%$ or $1\frac{1}{2}\%$ on their capital. More than a hundred Jamaica estates are said to have gone into chancery during that period.

back. Our servants, mules, &c. were sent on to the Ramble, Mr. Murphy's estate. After the review a sumptuous second breakfast, consisting of hot fish, all sorts of cold meats, pies, &c. abundance of cakes, confectionary, fruit, &c. and the greatest variety of wines. – Mrs. Edwards, Mrs. Cruikshanks, and Miss Bigsby, were introduced to me. – Set off a little before 4, for the Ramble, with an immense cavalcade of horsemen, &c. – Mrs. Murphy, Mrs. Mason, Mrs. Cox, Miss Hicks, three Misses Murphy, and Miss Spencer, composed the lady-party; the men in crowds. – Dined a little before 7. – Began dancing at 10. – I steal away before 12. N. soon followed my example, for we were both heartily fatigued with our journey, society, &c.

25th. Breakfast at 8. – General N. &c. set off immediately after, to see the fort at Port Maria, &c. &c. – I walked with the ladies in the garden, to the bath, and about the grounds, till our horses were ready, when we all mounted, attended by a few gentlemen, and went to a cottage, a mile or two off, which belongs to Mr. Murphy. From that went to Mrs. Mason's; from both of which places we had fine views of the country, the sea, &c. Mrs. M. joined our party, and we all returned to the Ramble about 2, and sat down to a second breakfast.

I now found the reason that the ladies here eat so little dinner. I could not help remarking Mrs. Cox, who sat next to me at the second breakfast. She began with fish, of which she ate plentifully, all swimming in oil. Then cold veal, with the same sauce!! Then tarts, cakes, and fruit. All the other ladies did the same, changing their plates, drinking wine, &c. as if it were dinner. I got away to my own room as soon as possible, lay down and slept for an hour; and then read till 6. – Soon after, General N. returned, and we went to dinner at 7. – Began dancing a little after 10. – We got away, and to bed before one.

26th. Up at 6. – Breakfast before 8, and then walk through the sugar works, &c. &c. At 10, began our journey. Very bad roads. Did not get to Mr. Shaw's till near 2. An immense second breakfast was prepared. Mrs. Shaw, Mrs. Lewis, Miss Shaw, and Miss Henry, were the ladies. – At 5, we all mounted our horses, and proceeded to St. Ann's Bay. The road was frightful; so narrow and rocky, and the precipices dreadful. Arrived at General Rose's at about 7. The family were General and Mrs. Rose, Miss Chambers, Miss Whitewood, Captain and Mrs. Carr. A profuse dinner, and to bed at ten.

27th. A large party at breakfast; and, immediately after, we all started for the review of the St. Ann's militia. The ground was crowded, and I was introduced to a hundred people. The heat was excessive. After the review, General N., escorted by the cavalry, and attended by all the gentlemen of the country, and I by a number of women, returned to Seville. A tedious introduction and conversation then took place; the men drank all the sangaree, and then the party dispersed. Immediately, sets of singing women sent me word of their approach. They danced, and sung several songs; some made in honour of General N. and some of me, till we were heartily tired of them. General N. then dressed, and went to dine with the military, and I sat down, at 6, with a party of ladies and a few gentlemen, to dinner. More ladies in the evening, and the gentlemen joined us at ten.

This is really a most uncomfortable house; the servants awkward and dirty, the children spoiled, and screaming the whole day. As for the ladies, they appear to me perfect viragos; they never speak but in the most imperious manner to their servants, and are constantly finding fault. West India houses are so thin, that one hears every word, and it is laughable, in the midst of the clamour, to walk out of my room, and see nothing but smiles and good humour, restored to every countenance in an instant. The old gentleman and lady are really diverting. They never agree upon any point; but she generally gets the better, from her extreme volubility; and always, when she stops to catch breath, she exclaims, "But now, Mr. Rose, let me speak;" then off she sets again with as much vivacity as ever. The daughter seems perfectly worthy of such a mother; but I am ungrateful to make these remarks, for they are very kind and friendly to us, though I heartily wish it was over.

28th. At breakfast General N. received an express, and set off for Spanish Town, at 12; as it was necessary he should call a Council, and decide upon some measures respecting St. Domingo, as well as give notice, for the assembling of the Legislature, to take into consideration communications which he has received from Ministers. I am really unhappy at this, for various reasons; the fatigue he must undergo, and the risk he must run, from mountainous bad roads, in crossing the island, as well as from the great heat of the climate. Another reason is, my being left alone in such a house, so really unwell as I am. He said he would be back on Tuesday night, but that is impossible, without his suffering dreadful fatigue.

Passed the greatest part of the day in my own room, crying and reading, till 6 o'clock, when I joined a large party at dinner. I ate little, and talked less. The chattering Mr. Whitehorne was on one side of me, and really wore down my spirits, and put me out of patience, by speaking with his mouth full, and obliging me constantly to change my plate. I am not astonished at the general ill health of the men in this country; for they really eat like cormorants and drink like porpoises. But to-day I am out of humour, and see every thing *en noir*. – Almost every man of the party was drunk, even to a boy fifteen or sixteen, who was obliged to be carried home. His father was very angry, but he had no right to be so, as he set the example to him. – Went to my own room at 12, but not to sleep, as they kept up their jollity much later. This, with the absence of my dear N., and my anxiety on his account, kept me awake almost the whole night.

29th. Thank God, in good health this morning. Ask for blessing for my dear husband. – If I were the Queen of Sheba, I could not be made more fuss with than I am here. It is really overpowering. A word from me decides every thing with the ladies, and a look sets all the gentlemen flying to anticipate my commands. The ball they are to give me occupies every one. – A hundred messages from the stewards in the course of the morning. – What hour shall the ball begin? what door shall I enter? &c. &c. Please the ladies, by making my maid arrange their dresses for the evening. – My little attendant, Cupid, is ill; the complaint announced to be repletion. – Only gentlemen at dinner. – Start for the ball at 8, with a grand cavalcade. Received at the door with great ceremony; led in by two stewards, and followed by a large party of gentlemen, the music playing God save the King. Immediately on my being seated on the state sopha, all the company came up, and paid their compliments. I then opened the ball with Mr. Henry, one of the Members for the parish, and really a gentleman-like man. After dancing a little, the carriages were ordered; but first I walked about the room with my suite, and after curtseying and making fine speeches, took my leave, with the same ceremonies with which I entered; and got home at 2 o'clock. – I slept soundly. – I could not help laughing, as we entered the hall at Seville, to see a dozen black heads popped up, for the negroes in the Creole houses sleep always on the floors, in the passages, galleries, &c. Got to bed about three.

30th. Rise early, and was in the breakfast room before any of the party. Dr. Weston in addition to our number. – This day, in spite of my fatigues, I felt particularly well and comfortable, as I expect my dear good N., and to-morrow we shall be able again to continue our journey. – A great many gentlemen called in the morning, to make enquiries after

the ball. Steal away to my own room as soon as possible, for, towards
the middle of the day, I began to feel a good deal tired, with talking, the
bustle of people coming and going, and the incessant noise of the children, not to mention the continual scolding at the servants, which is to
me the most distressing thing in the world. – Am the first in the drawing-
room at 5 o'clock. – Wait dinner till 6. All the company assembled, except
General N., who had not arrived. Endeavour to be reconciled to his
absence till to-morrow, when, to my great joy, just as we were going to
place ourselves at table, he made his appearance. He did not leave
Spanish Town till 12, being obliged to hold a Council this morning. This
is really a great fatigue, and more than he ought to risk. – Major Gould
seems to feel it infinitely more than General N., however; the latter
looking as perfectly well and in good spirits as usual, while the poor
Major appeared at least twenty years older. Unfortunately, soon after
they came in, the horse, which drew the gig the whole way, died of the
complaint they call the *pant*, which is very common with horses not
bred in the West Indies; and this was an American horse, therefore
not accustomed to the climate. He was really a fine animal, and cost
General N., three or four months ago, two hundred pounds. What a
mercy that the horse was the only sufferer! To bed by twelve.

31st. Breakfast at 8, and take leave of the family, &c. &c. at Seville,
and set off at eleven for Arcadia. After a pleasant, though rather a hilly
and rocky drive, reach Riobueno, where we met the members of Trelawny Parish, and other gentlemen; Mr. McAnuff, agent for Mr. Barnett,
who is the proprietor of Arcadia estate, came to invite us there, accompanied by a Mr. Galloway and a Captain Sherry. Mr. Barnett is
married to a Miss Markham, daughter of the Archbishop of York, and
they have lately left this country. Found a profuse second breakfast
prepared for us, at the inn, and, after General N. had inspected the forts,
&c. we proceeded to Arcadia, where we arrived at 6. Found a party
ready to receive us, and sat down to dinner before 7. To bed early. –
Every thing here is so quiet, clean and comfortable, that we feel ourselves
in Arcadia indeed.

April 1st. This day year we left Ireland. What would I not give, if we
had now so short a voyage to make to England; but I won't think of it. –
Much refreshed by our comfortable night's rest. My dear N. quite cool
and well to-day. Yesterday he complained much of headache, which
alarmed me a good deal, as it is always the forerunner of evil in this coun-
tyr.

This house is not large, but it is very neat and convenient. It stands on a high hill, overlooking the sea, and a great extent of beautiful country; it is surrounded with very fine orange trees, &c. The ladies, who spent the day with me, were Mrs. Galloway, Miss Howorth, and Mrs. Littlejohn; and at dinner we had a fresh relay, Mr. and Mrs. Easson, Dr. Littlejohn; and in short, a large party. – Get to my own room before ten, but obliged to give audience to all the black and brown ladies in the parish, while I was undressing.

2nd. Up early. – General N. made arrangements for expediting our tour, on account of the situation of St. Domingo, and the private intelligence he had received from Lord Hobart, about the treaty with France. – As soon as breakfast was over, a party of gentlemen, headed by General Bell and Mr. Cunningham, arrived to attend us to Falmouth and Montego Bay. General N. then left us for Mahogany Hall, and to-morrow he is to proceed on, and view the Black Grounds, Quashie and Mouth rivers, to fix on situations for barracks.

At 4, General Bell and myself, in his phaeton, and the rest of the gentlemen in kittareens, and on horseback, went to Bryan Hall, to dine with Mr. and Mrs. Galloway. The Hall was the seat of the late Bryan Edwards, where he wrote the greatest part of his History of the West Indies. It is really a beautiful place; the house is a good one, and tolerably well furnished, and has a Turkey carpet in the drawing room – an extraordinary sight in this country. The house stands rather higher than Arcadia, and is surrounded by pimento (allspice) groves, so laid out, as to make the prospect of the sea and the country more picturesque, through vistas. The pimento is a large fine tree, with the brightest green foliage imaginable. The process of preparing the allspice is merely picking it and laying it in the sun to dry, and then thoroughly cleaning it by taking off the rough husks, &c. About eighteen or twenty years ago, this was a very valuable and productive article to the island; but, latterly, there has been little or no demand for it, on account of the great supply of spices from the East Indies.[1] – A large party of gentlemen, but only three ladies besides myself. Felt more than usually sick during dinner time, and was glad to get back to Arcadia. Took leave of all my gentlemen as soon as I arrived. – I then went to bed, but not to sleep, being very ill all night.

---

[1] Bryan Castle estate, which Mrs. Nugent calls Bryan Hall, was advertised for sale in 1803 as having 1402 acres, of which about 300 were in sugar canes, 400 in grass and pimento, and 700 in provisions and wood. There were 167 slaves, and the crop taken off in 1802–3 was 255 hogsheads of sugar of 18 cwt. each and 165 puncheons of rum.

3rd. Called my maid, and had some tea at 6. Then sent my excuses
to the gentlemen, and remained in bed. Miss Howorth and Mr. Miller
came to attend me to Mahogany Hall, to meet General N. on his return
there. – Found myself too unwell to rise. Miss Howorth sat by my bed-
side till one; I dozed till four, but was so unwell, notwithstanding, that
I could scarcely dress for dinner; but looking most impatiently for the
return of my dear N. to comfort me. – At half-past five, went to the
drawing room, to receive the *'grand monde.'* Looking out for General N.
till near 7, when a message arrived to tell me that he could not come back
till later in the evening. Soon after 9, he made his appearance with his
party. They had had a most fatiguing day; thirty miles of shocking bad
roads, or rather no roads at all, through the woods; the trees and bushes
so thick, that they were obliged to have negroes going on before to clear
the way, and they themselves leaping their horses over stumps at almost
every step. Thank God, my dear N. does not appear to have suffered in
the smallest degree, nor does he complain of fatigue.

4th. Full of business, and writing letters, to go by the express to Spanish
Town. Leave Arcadia about 12, and arrive at Falmouth to dinner. The
streets crowded with people, and a negro market held in front of General
Bell's house. The negroes seemed very happy, selling their yams, cocoa-
nuts, plantains, &c. and salt fish. When we shewed ourselves in the piazza,
they laughed, danced, bowed, curtesied, and grinned, and used every
possible grimace to express their happiness in seeing us. I took a fancy to
an immense water-melon, which my maid secured for me, and I devoured
it all, while I was dressing for dinner. – A very large party. – General and
Mrs. Bell are very comfortable people. Their house, and every thing
about them, is in the best order, and there is a white woman for a housekeeper. They have no children, but have adopted a niece (a Miss Virgo),
who lives with them. – Several ladies at dinner, and more in the evening;
but we were all in bed by eleven.

I must not forget to record a funny adventure of my poor deaf maid
Johnson. General N.'s Military Secretary has the same name, and he
had driven her out to-day in his kittareen; consequently the servants
supposed they must be man and wife, and therefore they only prepared
one apartment for them. As soon as I was undressed, she retired to her
bed-room, where she was not a little surprised to see a military coat,
boots, &c. When the servants answered to her questions, "Only the
Captain's, Ma'am," she, not liking to acknowledge she was deaf, nodded
her head as usual, and said, "Very well, very well." – The musquito net

was comfortably tucked round her, and she was enjoying her first sleep, when the Captain was shewn in, who, in his turn, was not a little surprised to find that he was only to have half a bed, and that his questions were answered with "Only Missis, Sir." The light awoke Johnson, who began to vociferate most loudly, and it was some time before good order was restored, by the Captain retiring to the pallet prepared for the *femme de chambre*.

5th. General N. off to review the detachment of the 60th regiment, quartered here, and to breakfast with the officers. – Nothing but guns firing, drums beating, and all sorts of noise. I breakfasted with the ladies here, people crowding in upon us continually, till 11, when we all set off for the review, and were attended back by an immense party to second breakfast; after which we retired to our own room, to rest a little. At 5, General N. went to dine with the officers of the Trelawny militia, which he had also reviewed in the morning. – I sat down to dinner with no less than ten ladies. – About 8, a number of gentlemen came to attend us to a ball, given at a Mr. Baillie's. Danced only three dances, and got away at 12, rather sick, and much fatigued.[1]

6th. Very unwell, but a great crowd of people at breakfast. However, we contrived to pass part of this morning in our own room. – Dined at half-past five. A large party; Navy officers, &c. I forgot to mention Admiral Duckworth's attention, in sending Captain Loring, with a small squadron in command, to attend us round the coast. The Navy men have been great acquisitions to our society on our tour; but, from the state of the roads, we have not been obliged to accept of their services at sea. Indeed, General N. is determined not to quit terra firma, if he can possibly avoid it. At 9, we all went to a public ball, given to us by the gentlemen of the parish. I opened the ball, and danced a few dances.

---

[1] In "Philo Scotus" (P. B. Ainslie), *Reminiscences of a Scottish gentleman*, Edinburgh, 1861, there is an account of festivities during the Governor's visit, when the author as a young man newly arrived in Jamaica was staying with Mr. Baillie, whose house was "nearly the largest and handsomest in Falmouth." Mr. Baillie was Collecting Constable of the parish and also captain of the fort, and his preparations to fire a salute on the Governor's arrival "occasioned much alarm to Miss Baillie for the safety of the windows in her brother's house, several of which were glazed – a very unusual comfort at that time in Jamaica, except in Kingston." The account seems to refer to Nugent's visit of the following year, when Mrs. Nugent did not accompany him, but events followed the same course, including a ball at Mr. Baillie's. "French cotillons had gone out, and the quadrille, the waltz, and the polka were still in the womb of time. The good old country dances, therefore, were the order of the evening diversified occasionally by highland reels . . ."

Supper at 12, and got home before 2. – The ladies all very fine, and the gentlemen particularly civil and attentive.

7th. General N. &c. off for the Maroon Town at 5, to view the place, and to inspect the 2nd battalion of the 85th regiment, just arrived from England. – For a wonder, a *tête-à-tête* breakfast with Miss Virgo. Mrs. Bell was in her bed with a headache, and all the gentlemen were gone with General N. A Mr. Heywood called, and kept me an hour talking of Southampton, and my old friends there. Got to my own room to rest. At 2 the *white* housekeeper came and said, "Ma'am, shall I have the honour to offer you your breakfast," luncheon being always called so. – Mine consisted of chicken soup, ham, oysters swimming in oil, &c. – The *sight* of the oysters and oil was sufficient for me; but I have observed that the ladies here eat a great deal of it. – Went at 4, with the ladies, to dine with a Mrs. Mitchell, three miles out of town. Tired to death, making the agreeable till after 6, when we went to dinner. The Navy officers, and a large party as usual. – Got away before ten.

8th. Only ladies at breakfast. – Immediately after, Captains Loring, Johnstone, and Barrie, of the Navy, Captain Carr, 83rd regiment, Mr. Hiatt, a planter, &c. At 1, General and Mrs. Rose, Mrs. Carr, Mr. and Mrs. S. Rose, &c. Soon as the party dispersed, went to my own room, looking out for my dear N. We had frequent showers this morning.

Amused myself with reading the Evidence before the House of Commons, on the part of the petitioners for the Abolition of the Slave Trade.[1] As far as I at present see and can hear of the ill treatment of the slaves, I think what they say upon the subject is very greatly exaggerated. Individuals, I make no doubt, occasionally abuse the power they possess; but, generally speaking, I believe the slaves are extremely well used. Yet it appears to me, there would be certainly no necessity for the Slave Trade, if religion, decency, and good order, were established among the negroes; if they could be prevailed upon to marry; and if our white men would but set them a little better example. Mrs. Bell told me to-day, that a negro man and woman of theirs, who are married, have fourteen grown up children, all healthy field negroes. This is only one instance out of many, which proves, that, the climate of this country being more congenial to their constitutions, they would increase and render the necessity of

---

[1] Printed in 1791. The prospect of abolition had receded during the war with France, but in 1804 Wilberforce returned to the charge and for the first time won a majority for his Bill in the House of Commons. The Act abolishing the slave trade was passed by Parliament in 1807.

the Slave Trade out of the question, provided their masters were attentive to their morals, and established matrimony among them; but white men of all descriptions, married or single, live in a state of licentiousness with their female slaves; and until a great reformation takes place on their part, neither religion, decency nor morality, can be established among the negroes.[1] An answer that was made to Mr. Shirley, a Member of the Assembly (and a profligate character, as far as I can understand), who advised one of his slaves to marry, is a strong proof of this – "Hi, Massa, you telly me marry one wife, which is no good! You no tinky I see you buckra no content wid one, two, tree, or four wifes; no more poor negro." The overseers, &c. too, are in general needy adventurers, without either principle, religion, or morality. Of course, their example must be the worst possible to these poor creatures.

General N. came home a little after 5, extremely well, and in excellent spirits, thank God; but wet through, as a great deal of rain had fallen in the mountains. Dressed, and went to dine at Mr. Galloway's at 6. – Got home as soon as we could, and to bed at twelve.

9th. During breakfast, a crowd to take leave of us. About 12, we left Trelawny Parish, and started from Falmouth for Montego Bay. About six miles on our journey, Mr. Cunningham's chaise and four met us. Proceed in it to Iron Shore, the estate of Mr. Irving;[2] found an immense party, and a great second breakfast ready. A large old house, and the situation beautiful. – Proceed on our journey to Montego Bay. Arrived at Mr. Cunningham's at 6 o'clock. Found fifty people assembled to meet us, was introduced to the crowd, and then hurried to our rooms to dress. Sat down to dinner at 7. – An additional company; altogether sixty or seventy people. Every face perfectly new to us, for the glare of the sun

---

[1] Mrs. Nugent backs her plea for marriage, on religious and moral grounds, with an argument addressed to the slave-owners' material interest. The proposition that marriage would lead to an increase in the number of slave children seems to be a corollary of the planters' cherished theory that the chief cause of infertility among slave women was their promiscuity, as stated e.g. by Bryan Edwards (*op. cit.*): "They hold chastity in so little estimation, that barrenness and frequent abortions, the usual effect of promiscuous intercourse, are very generally prevalent amongst them." But Edwards, like others, emphatically denied that this could be remedied by introducing formal marriage among slaves; anyone who thought of doing so must be "utterly ignorant of their manners, propensities, and superstitions." Perhaps the chief reason for the planters' opposition to marriage was that it would make the sale of slaves more difficult. The cost of marriage registration on a large scale may also have been a consideration.

[2] cf. p. 22 n. Ironshore remained in the possession of an American branch of the Irving family until 1952.

had so dazzled us, on our first arrival and introduction, that it was quite impossible to distinguish a feature, or hardly black from white. – The dinner was in the usual abundance, and consisted of every Jamaica delicacy; and we were pressed to taste of so many things that it was scarcely possible to avoid being stuffed into a fever. – Began dancing at 10 or 11. Danced with various partners till 1, and then got to my own room at last, where I found General N. who had stolen away half an hour before.

This house is as comfortable as possible. The rooms are good, and well furnished, and the situation is delightful. The town of Montego Bay is situated in an amphitheatre of very high hills. In front a most beautiful bay, full of vessels, and open to the sea. On the hills are all the gentlemen's houses, or those not immediately shopkeepers. These are interpersed with gardens, palms of all sorts, &c. So that, from the town, quite up to the tops of the hills, you see nothing but villas peeping out from among the foliage. Mr. C.'s house overlooks the whole town, bay, &c. &c. and altogether the prospect is lovely. Nothing can exceed the hospitality of our host and his wife. They have a numerous family, and a crowd of relations, constantly with them. Every thing wears the appearance of content and cheerfulness; the children are well managed, and not young enough to disturb one with their noise. The heat, however, is great, and we suffer a good deal from occupying the state apartments; which here, as well as at Falmouth, are, from 12 o'clock in the day, entirely exposed to the sun.

10th. General N. set off with his *suite* at 4 o'clock this morning, on board the *Syren* frigate, Captain Loring, for Lucea. Here we had an immense dinner party, as well as breakfast and second breakfast, and crowds of visitors all day. Among the ladies that came to dinner was a Mrs. Russell, an English woman, and the wife of an officer in the artillery – a very pleasing person. As the Navy officers were of our party, we had a dance in the evening; and, having rested so much during the day, I rather enjoyed the gaiety. – To bed at 12 o'clock.

11th. An immense breakfast party at 8, and at 10 we all went to church. The congregation very respectable, and a number of the military. The prayers were read by a Mr. Barnet, and Mr. Rickard preached. Before the service began, I was surprised, and not a little shocked, at Mr. Rikard's proposing to me to dismiss all the congregation for an hour or two, as *his Excellency* would probably land by that time! Of course I declined. After the service, when I remarked the number that had attended, Mr.

Rickard very coolly told me, that was on account of our being here, for that he had in general scarcely any congregation, and the military had not been in church for nearly three years! – A splendid second breakfast was given me by Mrs. Grey, a sister of Mr. Cunningham, and at 3 o'clock we all returned home, to meet General N. who had just landed. Guns firing, and a great crowd, as usual; the whole place being in the greatest bustle. – An immense dinner party – *all* the Navy officers, a number of the military, and gentlemen of the country; four ladies, besides those of the family, Mrs. Evans, Mrs. Coward, Mrs. Landsdown, and Mrs. –, I forget her name. – To bed at 12 o'clock.

12*th*. A large breakfast party, and we all started for the review ground at 10; Mrs. and Miss Cunningham and myself in a chaise and four, and all the rest in kittareens and phaetons, and on horseback. – After the review went a-shopping with the ladies. – All the shopkeepers' wives shook hands with the ladies of my party, and appeared perfectly on a footing with them, talking of the review, the ball to be given to-morrow, &c. A more than usually large second breakfast at Mr. Cunningham's to-day, on account of the review. – Soon after 5, General N. went to the public dinner, and I sat down to mine at 6, with a number of ladies, and a few *civil* gentlemen, as all the military were with General N. In the evening, many more ladies and gentlemen, and about 10, several from the grand dinner, with General N., who took his leave of the company almost immediately. – I danced till a little after 12, and then, when supper was announced, pleaded fatigue, and got to bed as soon as I could, having scarcely an atom of strength left.

13*th*. This is to be a grand day, and all the house was in a bustle very early. – Soon after breakfast, held a *council* with the ladies, to decide upon the dresses for the evening. Get my maid to work for the young people, to make them smart for the ball, and *advise* also with Mrs. Cunningham, upon the subject of her cap, &c. – My dearest N. full of business, settling disputes between the military and civilians, and harassed with their complaints and nonsense till after 6. – Then hurried to dress, and dine, about two miles out of the town, with the Custos and his lady, a Mr. and Mrs. Mowat. – Find sixty-two people assembled, and the clergyman ready to make Christians of three of their children, the eldest of whom was about four years old, and the youngest as many months, and for this last we were sponsors. – The heat was dreadful, and the crowd so great at dinner, that there was scarcely room for the servants to change the plates. The smell, added to the intense heat, altogether was very near overcoming me, but I tried to support it as well as I could, and re-joiced when an express arrived from the town, to say the ball-room was full, and all the world waiting for us. The few moments of fresh air between the dinner and the ball-rooms were a real treat; but when we arrived at the latter, the crowd was so great, that the heat if possible surpassed the former. However, the smell of the blackies and of the hot meats was absent, and that was some comfort. But never shall I forget the combination of a crowd of Creoles, and a mob of blackies, with turtle-soup, pepper-pot, and callipash and callipee,[1] at Mr. Mowat's, as long as I live in this world! – General N. and I both began the ball. He at the head of one set, and I at the head of another, and my partner was so anxious to exhibit me, that I was obliged to jig to the very bottom of the dance, which consisted of no less than thirty-one couples! – Supper at 2 o'clock, and we felt ourselves bound to remain for it, as such prepara-tions had been made, that it would have been a *sin* to disappoint the steward, &c. – but conceive our fatigue! Poor dear Nugent had a rest-less night, and so had I, and he complained sadly of heat.

14*th*. We can scarcely say that we have been in bed, for we did not lie down till past 4, and were up again at 6, hoping to get away from the kindness of the crowd here at an early hour. Both of us half dead with the heat, and with aching heads from the fatigue and want of sleep. – A large party to breakfast, at 8. – Constant visitors till 12, when we set off for the parish of Hanover, a party of gentlemen, civil and military, accompanying us. – Met by Colonel Malcolm and his friends, on the road. – General N. inspected a barrack as we passed on to Knock-Alva, the estate of Mr. Malcolm the Colonel's elder brother.

The country beautiful, and the roads tolerably good. Arrive about half-past four, and intend to keep my room, and recruit my strength and spirits a little, as I am the only lady, and this is a bachelor's house; but my dear N. is so unwell, that the doctor says he must go to his bed imme-diately, and, in consequence, I am doomed to go to dinner; for as our host has been at much trouble and expense, to prepare for our reception, it would be the *acme* of cruelty not to look at the dinner at least. – Cry and lament myself all the time I am dressing, not only on account of my own fatigue, but from alarm and apprehension about my dear, dear husband! Sit down soon after 6, with twenty gentlemen, to a loaded table, extend-ing all the length of the piazza. Three courses were served with the

---

[1] The flesh of the turtle's back and belly.

greatest bustle and confusion, the servants nearly knocking each other
down in their hurry and awkwardness; for I suppose it is an age since
they have had such fine doings. The dinner was so tedious, and I felt so
really unwell, that I begged leave to retire before the cloth was removed,
and then it was near 11 o'clock. – Take a little tea with my dear Nugent,
who is, thank God, much better, and get to bed as soon as I can. He has
had a refreshing sleep, and the doctor's prescriptions appear to have
done him a great deal of good.

15*th*. Up at half-past four, and hope to make our escape before Colonel
Malcolm is stirring, but find the house lit up, and a profuse breakfast
prepared. Take some tea only, but feel much better than yesterday. God
be praised, dearest N. quite well again. Set off for Paradise, the estate of
Mr. Wedderburn. A large party, breakfast ready. A good house, and
lovely situation altogether. As soon as breakfast was over, we proceeded
to the review ground, near Savannah la Mar. Meet a number of ladies,
and Major and Mrs. Dunbar gave us a grand second breakfast, after the
review of the 83rd, which succeeded the militia review; and this was
rather hard work for poor General N. who had also to inspect the barracks, hospital, &c.

Drove to the Custos, Mr. Murray's, in his carriage, which I rejoiced
to find waiting for us, on the review ground. Mr. and Mrs. M. are a
comfortable old couple, and made us welcome in a plain manner, and
with less fuss than we have been used to, and so we promise ourselves
a little rest and quiet here. We were allowed to remain without interrup-
tion, in our own apartment, till near 6, when General N. went to dine
with the militia, and I sat down to a profuse dinner, with many ladies,
but very few gentlemen. The dinner very dull indeed; the ladies almost
mute, and staring at me, which obliged me to keep up the conversation
as well as I could, the whole time, with Mr. Stewart, clergyman of the
parish. He appeared rather an illiterate person, though a well meaning
man; but much cannot be expected, when it is known, that, only a few
years since, he was an overseer, on Mr. Wedderburn's estate of Paradise.
It seems Mr. Wedderburn, to reward his services as an overseer, purchased the living of Savannah la Mar, and the Bishop of Man ordained
him![1] – In the evening, more ladies and gentlemen, in crowds, many of

---

[1] Wedderburn through his friend William Ricketts had procured the Governor's
recommendation of Stewart to the Bishop of London, who licensed him as a priest in
the normal way. "Purchased the living" implies a bargain with the Governor to
appoint Stewart, or with the previous incumbent to vacate the living.

whom came with General N. from the dinner. – A dance as usual. At 12, we got away to our rooms, but I could not rest or be satisfied, till I got a little piece of salt ham, that I saw on the supper table, as we passed near where it was laid. This seemed to cure my sickness, and I slept most comfortably after it.

Good Friday, 16*th*. Make early reflections, and explain the meaning of the day to the black servants that are with us. – Breakfast at 7 o'clock; a number of gentlemen, who, with Mr. Murray, attended us, to look at the church. It is better fitted up than usual, and altogether looks very nice and respectable.[1] I only regretted we could not remain for the service of the day, though it seemed doubtful whether there was to be any: but I dare say, if we had stayed, Mr. Stewart would have put on his canonicals. We then visited the court-house, which is a very good building; and after driving all over the town, went down to the Bay, where, while General N. was inspecting a small work for the protection of the harbour, I heard a full account of the dreadful hurricane in the year 1780, from a gentleman who was present at the time. He showed me where the sea had rushed in, and carried all before it, and then retreated, bearing away with it to the deep many houses with their hapless inhabitants, almost in a moment. Our landlord and landlady had only time to get out of their house, when it was blown down, and their only place of shelter was in the body of an old carriage, taken off its wheels, and placed on the ground.

At 10, began our journey again; the heat excessive. A beautiful road along the coast. Arrived at the farm, Mr. Wilkie's estate, soon after 2 o'clock. – Two Mr. Jones's, and a Mr. McFarlane, with Mrs. Wilkie, to receive us. Our own party, however, was sufficiently large to fill his house, which, although the situation is pretty, looks miserable, and is very low, as well as most intolerably hot. The master of it is a wretched looking man, and all the household are equally meagre, and indeed appearing as if they were half starved; but we had a coarse greasy feast, and were glad to pursue our journey as soon as possible, which we enjoyed particularly, for it was a lovely moonlight night, and the roads were uncommonly good, having been prepared on our account. – Arrived at the parsonage, Mr. Warren's, in St. Elizabeth's, a little before

[1] Mr. Murray, as Custos, had laid the foundation stone of the church a few years previously, in 1797. The present church contains a brass tablet commemorating this event, which was found on the old foundation stone in 1904 when a new church was being built.

12 o'clock. A large party was assembled to receive us, but we begged only to take tea, and go to our rooms, as soon as all the bows and curtsies were over.

17*th*. Up at 6. – Poor D.'s wife, with her pretty little girl, came to spend the day with me.[1] I was rather pleased with her appearance and manner, and delighted with the child, it is such a dear little thing. – General N. went to Black River, to review the St. Elizabeth's militia, while I spent a most fatiguing morning, talking to a dozen women. Mrs. and the Misses Shakespeare, Mr. and Mrs. Vassal, Mrs. and Miss Hylton, and Miss Williams, in addition to the party already in the house. – In the evening a large assembly chiefly of gentlemen, who accompanied General N. from Black River. A dance, and to bed soon after 12 o'clock. – Mr. Warren's two sons sad objects – they have St. Vitus' dance, and are both quite deformed, and poor General N. was quite uneasy at their handing me about, and shewing me so much civility; but I tried to look at them as little as possible.

18*th*. Up at 6. Explain the day to the servants, and gave them the same present that I did on Good Friday. – I am, at this moment, admiring from my window one of the largest and most beautiful acacia trees I ever saw. It is in full bloom, and quite lovely, My maid tells me that the negroes say that they make a very good aperient medicine from it.

At 10, go to Black River, about five miles off, to church. The building is shabby and much neglected. All the congregation, excepting our party and nine other persons, were either black or brown. I cannot help here remarking, that the clergyman's wife, Mrs. Warren, excused herself from attending, on account of the service being so long to-day. Her married daughter, too, who is the widow of the late Chief Justice, did the same. At the Communion, there were only one old white man and woman and one *brown* lady, besides ourselves, for the clergyman's two daughters, who came with us, left the church with the rest of the congregation; and yet they are certainly of an age to join in the service, being nearer to thirty than twenty years old. But, altogether, it was a most extraordinary scene; for, just before the service began, and when I thought the church doors were to be closed, in walked a strange gentleman, and took his seat in our pew, and began making fine speeches, about going to his house to-morrow. This invitation General N. very

---

[1] "Poor D." is Mrs. Nugent's brother, Downes Skinner, recently appointed Collector of Customs at Savanna-la-Mar. His wife was Elizabeth Williams, of Luana, near Black River, and their child's name was Bonella.

civilly declined, while I kept my eyes upon my book, and said nothing. General N. opened his, but the gentleman still talked on. The clergyman went to the altar, and every thing appeared quite ready to begin the service. General N. then said, "Pray, Sir, do you stay for the Communion?" "Oh, no," was the answer, and then after a few bows, and a few more speeches, off he walked. It is scarcely necessary to say, how much we were disgusted at this conduct; but I am sure that the poor man had not the smallest idea of the impropriety, to say the least of it. When we went up to the altar, the clergyman began *his civilities* – first asking whether we would prefer having the bread and wine brought to our pew; then hoping the heat was not too great; and, in the midst of the service, stopping to enquire whether I would like a window opened that was over the altar. I said not a word, and General N. shook his head, saying, "Please to go on, Sir, I beg!" All this time, the young ladies were talking and laughing, loud enough to be heard, as they sat in the carriage at the church door; and, in short, it was altogether shocking. – We drove afterwards to Luana, where Mrs. Williams gave us a grand second breakfast. – Little B. very pretty and very engaging. She came with her mamma to the parsonage. – Miss Williams, Miss Hylton, &c. all remained till 9 o'clock, when they took their leave, and we were glad to get to bed early.

19*th.* Set off soon after breakfast for Lacovia, the estate of our host, the Rev. Mr. Warren. The two Misses Warren accompanied us, and the two sons would hand me to the carriage, to General N.'s great annoyance. – Captain and Miss Owen there, and another breakfast ready, though it was only 10 o'clock. The house and the place altogether very ugly. But there were some remarkably fine mango trees, loaded half with fruit and half with blossoms, which had a very extraordinary effect. – At one o'clock a third breakfast of fish, hot stews of all sorts, &c. and at 3 we pursued our journey to Windsor. – The road lovely. Arrive soon after 5. Received by a Mr. Armstrong (a Scotch overseer) and his friends. The proprietor of the estate is a Kingston merchant, and rarely comes here. – The house is old, and much out of repair, but the place is famous for an excellent garden. While dinner was preparing, General N. and the gentlemen walked to see it, but I begged to rest a little, feeling much fatigued. – A very coarse dinner, but the poor man had done his best, and no doubt thought it very fine; and so it was, if abundance of beef and pork could make it so. – To bed before 10, and all glad to rest ourselves.

20*th.* General N., &c. off at 4, for the town of the Accompong Maroons. – At 7, sat down in the piazza to a complete overseer's breakfast of salt fish, salt beef, Irish butter, &c. &c. As my poor maid was the only white person in the house besides myself, I sent for her, intending she should make the tea, and take her breakfast with me. But she was so very mincing and miserable, that, as I had no appetite myself, I took one cup of tea, and then left her to enjoy the delicate fare alone. I had a nice walk in the garden, which amused me extremely, till the excessive heat drove me in. The trees and plants very curious, and in great variety; not only natives of this country, but also from Otaheite, the Cape of Good Hope, &c. The gardener is an intelligent Scotchman, and seems perfectly well acquainted with his business. He made me remark the Otaheite plum particularly; it bears a bright pink blossom, like a tassel, and although some of the branches were covered with them, others were loaded with fruit, some of the fruit quite green, others quite ripe; and all round the tree the ground was covered with the blossoms that had fallen, to make way for the fruit, and was really like a bright pink carpet. The camphor, cinnamon, sago, &c. &c. in great perfection. There was the largest jack-fruit tree I ever saw, and the most abundant mango and bread-fruit trees. A very good bath and fish pond in the garden, but the late dry weather has destroyed all the fish. However, the gardener told me as soon as the rainy season began, he would fill the pond immediately, by sending negroes to the mountains in the night, with lanterns, and they could fetch abundance. – General N. returned about 3 o'clock; he had been very much gratified by his visit to Accompong. – A Mr. Vernon and Mr. Griffiths were added to the party. Dinner at 6, and to bed at ten.

21st. General N. off early to see Hector's River, &c. Mr. Vernon, Major Drummond, and Captain Johnson breakfasted with me, and we then proceeded to Derry, Mr. White's estate. Nothing could well be more frightful than the road – hills and precipices continually, and one hill extended six miles, with a narrow road full of stumps and rocks. The views were beautiful between the openings of the mountains; fine vales, covered with sugar estates, penns, &c. One place that we passed was called Paradise, and a Mr. Angel was the inhabitant. At 2, reached Derry. It is a lovely romantic situation; and, as we passed through the woods to the house, we saw several flights of parrots, and various curious birds. A fine second breakfast prepared for me, by Mr. White, who, with his nephew, was waiting to receive us. – I have taken some soup, and am now going to rest myself a little, if the black and brown ladies will allow me. – At 6, General N., &c., and all wet through, the mountain showers were so heavy. – To bed at 11 o'clock. – I can't sleep all night, thinking of our host, who is certainly the ugliest man I ever saw – but so civil!

22nd. The morning much cooler than usual, owing to the height of the situation. – Soon after breakfast set off for Porus, an estate of Mr. Conolly's, an Irish lawyer, who, I believe, never visits this country. The drive lay through woods; the trees fine, and a variety of beautiful shrubs. The wild pine is particularly curious; it shoots out from the branches of trees, and has the oddest effect. – Reach Grove Place at 1. A superb second breakfast ready; but, as there was no cover for our horses, and the clouds seemed to threaten rain, we were persuaded by another Mr. Vernon, who had joined our party, to proceed on without delay to Porus, where we arrived at 3 o'clock. Mr Grey and Mr. Lafnan, Mr. Conolly's agents, received us.

Porus is very pretty – surrounded by woody mountains. The house stands in the midst of a garden, and you enter it under a bower of granadillas, the blossom of which is exactly like large passion-flowers. The trees in the garden are loaded with fruit, and the mango trees, in particular, are quite bowed down by the weight of theirs. – Try to lie down, and read a little, by way of resting myself; but the heat is excessive, although my room is all doors and windows, and quite open to the garden. – Have a great deal of talk with some of the black women of the house. There is an old negro man here, who was coachman to Lord Portland, when he was Governor of this island in 1721.[1] He is still healthy and active, and this reminds me of an old woman, who died while we were in St. Mary's, who was so old that no one could tell her exact age; but, from known circumstances, she had certainly seen her 140th year! Does not this prove how congenial the climate is to their colour?[2]

23rd. Up at 6, and set off, as soon as we had taken our breakfast, for Woods, the estate of Mr. Osborne, Speaker of the House of Assembly. Stop a few moments at Parnassus. The road unusually good. Before we reached our destination, General N. and I had a most extraordinary vision. He was driving me in the curricle, and we were some distance before our party, who drove slower that we might avoid the dust. We came to the top of a hill, and just as we were about to descend, General N. drew up with astonishment at the prospect before us, and we both

---

[1] 1722–6. Portland parish was named after him.

[2] The Kingston *Royal Gazette* periodically reported the death of Jamaican ladies of advanced age. A Mrs. Rebecca Mills of St. Elizabeth, who died in February 1805, was said to have been aged 113 and to have left 295 living descendants, 61 of whom, all having the family name of Ebanks, formed a company of foot in the militia.

thought we must have mistaken our road most strangely. We knew that our journey was quite inland, and that, on the road to Woods, it was quite impossible we should see the harbour of Port Royal, or any place on the coast; and yet before us appeared an expanse of water, a headland with ships lying at anchor, some with their sails half exposed to the sun, as if to dry, and others with their sails close furled; in short, it was a perfect view of a harbour with its accompaniments. Soon, however, it began to change, and as we moved gently forward, descending the hill, nothing but a plain with sugar estates was before us, and no water or ships to be seen. I have read of these things, but never before saw the effects of vapour.

We found a large party and second breakfast at Mr. Osborne's, about 2 o'clock. Mr. and Mrs. Ashley, Mrs. Rossington, and Miss Faro, were the only new people, but Mrs. Rossington I had seen before, and I must, at the conclusion of this day, tell an adventure, in consequence of her advice. – After dinner, we had a dance, in which I joined, though I was so unwell with a cold, that I had much rather have gone to bed. Mrs. R. said she had a receipt that would certainly cure me, and my maid was sent for it, as soon as I was in bed. It tasted very sweet and nice, and I never slept better in my life. When I awoke in the morning, however, I felt a little giddy, and when I thanked Mrs. Rossington for her medicine I told her so. She asked how much water I had put to it? I said none at all. She exclaimed, "Why, it was only the ingredients of very strong punch, and you should have put at least half a pint of hot water to it!" So I was certainly very tipsy, but I slept so sound that I knew nothing of it.

24*th*. We could not begin our journey home till near 10. Stop at the inn, at Old Harbour, for two or three hours, as some of the mules were ill. Then sent all the baggage and stuff on before us, and drove the back way to our Penn; avoiding all the fuss and bustle of going with a great caval-cade through Spanish Town. Several gentlemen, however, came to greet us on our return home, and stayed dinner. – To bed before 10, however, and feel delighted to think that we have no journey to make to-morrow, and I thank God sincerely for all his goodness and mercy.

I will conclude my tour through the island with a few remarks. In this country it appears as if every thing were bought and sold. Clergymen make no secret of making a traffic of their livings; but General N. has set his face against such proceedings, and has refused many applications for the purpose. He is determined to do all he can towards the reformation of the church, and thus rendering it respectable. It is indeed melancholy, to see the general disregard of both religion and morality, throughout the whole island. Every one seems solicitous to make money, and no one appears to regard the mode of acquiring it. It is extraordinary to witness the immediate effect that the climate and habit of living in this country have upon the minds and manners of Europeans, particularly of the lower orders. In the upper ranks, they become indolent and inactive, regardless of every thing but eating, drinking, and indulging themselves, and are almost entirely under the dominion of their mulatto favourites. In the lower orders, they are the same, with the addition of conceit and tyranny; considering the negroes as creatures formed merely to administer to their ease, and to be subject to their caprice; and I have found much difficulty to persuade those great people and superior beings, our white domestics, that the blacks are human beings, or have souls. I allude more particularly to our German and our other upper men-servants. – It was curious to observe, when we were entering any town, the number of trunks, band-boxes, &c. that were hurrying to the different houses, and the same at our departure, all going back to the country again, and all on negroes' heads; for whenever the ladies go to town, or are to appear in society, their black maids and other attendants start off with their finery in cases, or tin boxes, on their heads. Trunks of any size are carried in the same manner. In short, every thing is put upon the head, from the largest to the smallest thing; even a smelling-bottle, I believe, would be carried in the same way. I have often, on our tour, seen twelve or fourteen negroes in one line of march, each bearing some article for the toilette on his head. – The Creole language is not confined to the negroes. Many of the ladies, who have not been educated in England, speak a sort of broken English, with an indolent drawling out of their words, that is very tiresome if not disgusting. I stood next to a lady one night, near a window, and, by way of saying something, remarked that the air was much cooler than usual; to which she answered, "Yes, ma-am, *him rail-ly too fra-ish.*"

25*th*. My dearest N. very unwell, and kept his bed till 2 o'clock. – The staff and Mr. Scott of the Council breakfasted with me. Had a long conversation with the latter, on political subjects; and, as his was a visit of business, General N. saw him in his bed-room afterwards. Mr. G. Cuthbert, also, about a place in the Custom House, for a friend of his, as one of the officers is dead. – Give the servants an entertainment in the evening, and a dollar each. Poor creatures, they seemed the happiest of the happy, dancing and singing almost the whole night.

26th. Colonel Roberts and Major Mackenzie of the 85th, Dr. Lind, Major Pye, and Captain Fraser, &c. at breakfast. – My dear N. better, but so harassed with business, that he has hardly a moment to himself, and we can scarcely speak to each other. Made a present to the white servants to-day. – Dine between 5 and 6. General Churchill and his Aide-de-camp, Mr. Scott, the gentlemen of the 85th, and Mr. Hanbury, in addition to our party.

27th. Soon after 6, sent off carriages for General Le Clerc's Aide-de-camp, Colonel Bourke, and the other French officer, who have just arrived from St. Domingo. They came to breakfast about 8. General Churchill, &c. and about thirty people, at breakfast. Wore my new Neapolitan mantle, sent me by dear Lady Buckingham. – The gentlemen seemed to be bragging republicans, and General Churchill and I had a great deal of fun, in questioning them about their adventures in St. Domingo, and were indiscreet enough to make our remarks to each other in English, thinking that they did not understand us; but we found, afterwards, that they had only pretended to be ignorant of English, for when General N. sent an Aide-de-camp with them to do the honours of the King's House, &c. to them, as he could not speak French, they were quite fluent in English. So poor General C. and I are in a sad scrape. – Admiral Duckworth and his son added to our party at dinner. – The Frenchmen all went to Kingston, and the Admiral remained for the night.

28th. Sir John Duckworth set off at 5. – The late Attorney-General of St. Domingo, for our Government, was at breakfast, – strongly recommended to General N. by the Duke of Portland. Also Mr. Cuthbert, Mr. Lindo, and Major Mosheim, with some of the staff. Soon after, Captain Hogg and his son came. – General N. full of St. Domingo and other business, and sadly bored by insignificant people. Got rid of them all in the evening, and go to bed at 9 o'clock.

29th. Soon after 7, Dr. Lind, Mr. Corbet, Mr. Hanbury; and Mr. Heslop, to be sworn in for his appointment in the Custom House. Then Colonel Lethbridge, of the 60th regiment, just arrived from England. After a great deal of talk, get away to write our English letters. Only Mr. Corbet and Mr. Hanbury remain for dinner. General N. had a great deal of business to transact with Mr. Corbet, about St. Domingo.

May 1st. Send carriages at 1, for Sir J. Duckworth and the Navy men, and at four for the French gentlemen. – General N. busy all the morning with his English despatches. – Twenty-eight people at dinner. Sir J.

Duckworth was obliged by business to leave us early, and the rest all took their leave by ten.

2nd. The horses were galled and tired by their frequent journies during the last week, so we said our prayers at home. Kemble went to Kingston, to take possession of the appointment given to him by General N.[1] – Only Duckworth remained at the Penn for the night.

3rd. A dreadfully hot morning. – Mr. and Mrs. and Mr. W. M. Murphy, Mr. and Mrs. Woodham, Mrs. and the Misses Rennalls, Mrs. and the Misses Lewis, Captain Penrose, and Mr. Ward – the two latter gentlemen to take leave for England. All left us by 1, and we wrote English letters till dinner time, and then despatched them by a dragoon to Port Henderson.

4th. Drive to Port Henderson at 5, and bring young Meredith, Browne, and Rogers, to the Penn. – Mr. and Mrs. Hibbert, Mr. and Mrs. Hughes, the Rev. Mr. Scott, and Mr. Cuthbert, at dinner.

5th. General N. off at 4, to review the 69th regiment. Find Captains Ross and Hatley, R.N., in the breakfast-room. – My dear N. back at one, not the worse for the excessive heat, thank God. The Navy men, and Mr. Drummond of the 60th regiment, in addition to our staff party.

6th. Set off at 5 for Stony Hill.[2] – General N. drove me in the curricle. My maid was driven by Mr. Duckworth in a gig. General N.'s man Rogers with various blackies on horseback, and our own horses, were sent on before. The staff joined us near Spanish Town. Arrive about 9, at the bottom of Stony Hill. Major Gould and our horses already there. Mount and ascend the hill. At the barracks we were received by Colonel Gordon and the officers of the 85th regiment, and a large party, assembled for breakfast. After which the regiment was reviewed, the barrack was inspected, and we saw the men at dinner. – The band played for me all the morning, stationed in front of my window. Highly gratified in every respect. General N. complimented the regiment, and we took our leave, all parties thoroughly well pleased.

At the bottom of the hill find our carriages ready; but then it was near four o'clock, and the sun broiling over our heads furiously, and the dust intolerable. – A large party assembled at the Admiral's Penn. The dinner

---

[1] Kemble was Sampson Gideon Kemble, Mrs. Nugent's cousin, and the position was that of Surveyor in the Customs at Kingston. This was not ordinarily in the Governor's gift, but he had the power of appointing *pro tempore* to posts which fell vacant.

[2] This expedition is referred to in a note from Mrs. Nugent to Admiral Duckworth, which is printed in Appendix B.

had been waiting some time, and Sir J. Duckworth was so impatient, that it was announced to us before we were ourselves half dressed. Poor dear N. was worse off than myself, as he had to shave, and had only just begun. Got ready as soon as possible, and beg the party to sit down, and that General N. would soon join them. He came in about the middle of the dinner, in as high a fever as myself. Two tables were laid, for an immensely crowded party. Only two ladies besides myself, Mrs. Peacocke and Mrs. Griffiths; so there was no dancing, and we got to bed as soon as we could.

7*th*. General N., thank God, quite prosperous this morning, and he set off at 5 to review the 6th battalion, 60th regiment, at Up Park Camp. A large party of naval men to attend the Admiral and me, to a breakfast given by Mr. Griffiths. General N. met us there. A room as full as possible; and, what with the heat of the sun and the crowd, the atmosphere was almost insupportable. The breakfast table was loaded with ragouts, fricassées, &c. and beefsteaks!! As General N. had business in Kingston, we got away as soon as we could. – Return to the Admiral's about 4, dress and dine almost immediately. A large party – Mrs. Hibbert, Mrs. Symes, Mrs. and Miss Cochrane, were the ladies to-day.

8*th*. General N. off soon after 4, to review the 2nd battalion, 60th regiment. – A large party, of Navy officers in particular, to breakfast with the Admiral; I making the agreeable to them as well as I can. – Mrs. Griffiths called soon after, and we all drove to Kingston, to shop and visit. The heat dreadful. Got back at 3; my dear N. was just returned. Both of us half-fatigued and hurried to death; the first with the heat, and the second with the Admiral's impatience to sit down to dinner, for fear it should be spoiled. The party was a complete crowd. – Before 6 drove to Greenwich, where the Admiral's barge was in waiting for us, and we rowed to Port Henderson; there we took to our carriages, and got safe to the Penn soon after nine.

9*th*. Up very early, but can't get to church; there being such a crowd of people, and my dear N. so full of business. – Captains Ross and Hatley of the Navy, Colonel Gordon and some officers of General N.'s regiment (the 85th), Colonel Roberts, Captains Maitland, and D'Arcy, and (I beg his pardon) Major Mackenzie. Then to dinner came Colonel Gillespie, 20th dragoons, Colonel Brisbane, 69th regiment, Major and Mrs. Pye: in all twenty-six people.

10*th*. Up early, and again an immense party; twenty to breakfast. Soon after General N. went off to his Court of Chancery, and was not at home again till near 6. He was much fatigued, and worn out with long causes. Major Mackenzie, 85th, Mr. Whyte, Mr. Hely, 69th regiment, and altogether twenty-five people at dinner.

11*th*. The Speaker, Mr. Edwards, &c. at breakfast. General N. at the King's House soon after. – Captain Elrington, 2nd W.I. regiment, from Fort Augusta, in the morning.

12*th*. Drive to Port Henderson soon after 5. Received Mr. Scott at breakfast. – General N. at the King's House all the morning. – Dr. Lind says that no one can be going on better than I am, and I trust in God he is right. – King Mitchell, the Speaker, Mr. Edwards, Mr. Hinchliffe, Rev. Mr. Scott, and a large party, at dinner.

13*th*. Mr. Campbell, and Mr. Jones, at breakfast. General N. as usual, at the King's House, as Chancellor, all the morning. – For a wonder, all our staff dine out.

14*th*. Mr. Peacocke, with the staff, at breakfast. At 5, General N. with delightful letters, and several nice presents, from dear Lady Buckingham and dear Lady Temple. Twenty-six people at dinner, among them were the new Attorney-General, Mr. Ross, Mr. Redwood, Messrs. Jackson, Affleck, and Lewis, Privy Counsellors, Captain Mends, R.N., Captain Broome, 20th dragoons, Major and Mrs. Pye, &c.

16*th*. Honourable Major Macdonald, and several of the staff at breakfast. At dinner, Mr. and Mrs. Woodham, Mr. Edwards, Captain Dixon, and Mr. Kelly (just from England) and Mr. Parkinson, 20th dragoons, &c. &c.

17*th*. At dinner, Major and Mrs. Pye, Captain Bartlett, and Lieutenant Le Breton of the Engineers, from England, and another lieutenant of the same corps, whose name I could not learn. Mr. Bankes and Mr. Foster, of the Navy, with the staff.

18*th*. Colonel Ramsay and Major Cookson at breakfast, with Mr. Halkett, and Mr. Grant, just arrived, who remained all day. – Talk a great deal about England to-day, but, alas! our new comers don't know any of our friends.

19*th*. Colonel Gordon, Captain Dobbin, Mr. March, and Mr. O'Farrell, at breakfast. Have a long conversation with Colonel G. afterwards. Send carriages for the Admiral, Captain Boyles, &c.

20*th*. Sir J. T. Duckworth off at 5, for Port Royal. Colonel Gordon went long before. – Captain Elrington at breakfast.

21*st*. A very large party of lawyers at dinner. Three ladies, Mrs. Hughes, Mrs. Tonge, and Mrs. Cunningham, and Mr. Redwood, a clergyman from Montserrat, to whom General N. has given a living at the request of the Speaker, were also of the party.

23rd. General N. so much engaged that we can't go to church. Send the staff and the servants, and we stayed at home together. – Mr. Corbet on St. Domingo affairs; and Mr. and Mrs. Woodham, and Mr. Drummond, of the 60th, at dinner. Am so unwell that I am obliged to leave the table.

24th. After a restless night, up before 4, and off for Fort Augusta. Arrive there just as the sun was rising, and General N. immediately reviewed the 55th regiment, which had just landed. A grand breakfast. – Then the 2nd West India regiment was reviewed. Walk down the line with General N. and speak to many of the new soldiers; though they did not understand, they tried to look pleased. – Cake, wine, &c. set out at Mrs. Cruchley's, who, with Mrs. Elrington, did the honours of their apartments to me. Return to the Penn a good deal fatigued, but my dear N. was obliged to start for Spanish Town immediately, to hold a Bishop's Court. He returned to dinner at 6.

25th. Drive to Port Henderson at 5, where General N. inspected some invalids of the 55th regiment. He bought a fine American horse. He did not go to the King's House, but stayed at home, and wrote letters all the morning. – At dinner, Colonels Lethbridge and Roberts, and Dr. Veitch.

26th. Kemble came to-day to thank General N., and seems very happy in his situation.

27th. The blackies perfect in their prayers. Read to them myself this evening, and intend doing so in future.

28th. Colonel de Charmilly and Mr. Lewis at breakfast. – Give a farewell dinner to the officers of the 2nd West India regiment and their wives. All depart at ten, excepting Mrs. Elrington, who sleeps here. – We had a few drops of rain to-day for a wonder, and how tantalizing that there were not a few showers.

29th. Rise at 5, and write letters for General N. till breakfast time, and begin again immediately after, and write till 1, when he despatched forty circulars to the different Members of the Assembly, upon the subject of the ensuing meeting. – At dinner, only Mrs. Elrington and our staff. – Heard the servants their catechism, and to bed at nine.

30th. The Admiral, &c. send to beg for the carriages. This prevents us from going to church. These Sunday parties are sad things; but in the present instance it can't be avoided. Read prayers at home. – Sir J. T. Duckworth, Admiral Campbell, and Captains Dunn, Gardner, Eyles,

Grindall, and Mends; in all about twenty-four. All left us for Port Royal at 8, and we were in bed at nine.

31st. Drive to Port Henderson at 5. Took leave of Mrs. Elrington, and sent her under the escort of Captain Duckworth to Fort Augusta. – All the morning preparing despatches to go by the *Juno* frigate to England.

June 1st. Send off my letters by Hallam, who goes in the *Juno* to England. Only Mr. Corbet added to our dinner party.

2nd. Try to drink the Spa water, but it won't do.[1] – At dinner only Mr. Coleman, of the 60th, and our own party. – Drive to see poor little Dr. Lind, who is ill in bed, but not I trust seriously so. He thinks well of my case, and I am happy.

3rd. Drive to Spanish Town at 5 o'clock. Give orders for the grand dinner to-morrow. Only Captain Macintosh, of the 85th, added to our party to-day. General N. has given him a fort, and he seems delighted.

4th. General N. &c. started early for Spanish Town. The troops out. Salutes, &c.; and then a levee held. – Mrs. Pye and Mrs. Elrington came to dine with me, and General N. had all the civil and military at the King's House, to celebrate the King's birthday. *A great let off.* Returned to the Penn at 10, and all in bed soon after. God bless our dear good old King!

5th. Major Mosheim, Captain and Mrs. Elrington, and Mr. and Mrs. Davies, 2nd W.I. regiment, at dinner. – Almost all our servants ill with the fatigues of yesterday.

6th. Whitsunday. – Up early, and to church at 10. The service well performed, and the Communion well attended. – Only Mr. and Mrs. Woodham, Monsieur and Madame Grandjean, and Madlle. Robert, at dinner.

7th. General Churchill and his Aide-de-camp, &c. at breakfast. Not well all the morning. General C. &c. amused themselves as well as they could, for General N. was obliged to attend to business. Major and Mrs. Pye, Captain and Mrs. Elrington, and Major Stapleton, added to our party at dinner.

---

[1] I do not know which Spa is meant. The chalybeate spring near Silver Hill Gap in the Blue Mountains was known as the Jamaica Spa, but although the Government had in 1776 purchased the site, they had done nothing about it. In 1806 when a committee of the Assembly went to inspect it, with a view to "rendering the institution more useful to the country", they found buildings erected by a neighbouring proprietor who claimed to have been in peaceful possession of the site for the past twenty years. Mrs. Nugent's draught may have come from Bath in St. Thomas, or even from Port Henderson, or it may have been imported; in the *Royal Gazette* of 1794, a list of provisions advertised by a Kingston merchant as "just imported" includes "Hot-well water, in hampers of 2½ dozen each."

8th. Major and Mrs. Pye came to enquire, and remained to breakfast. The whole morning strong symptoms of all going on right and well with me, and though very poorly, I rejoice and keep up my spirits.

9th. Captain and Mrs. Elrington went back to Fort Augusta. – General N. and I most comfortably alone all the morning. He wrote a letter to the Speaker, and I worked by his side. – I am now teaching some of the ladies to make shoes, in the style of Vanderville, and am very busy at the pattern pair.[1] Only our own staff at dinner, and prayers, as usual now, in the evening.

10th. My dear husband's birthday, and may God bless and preserve him in all things! Offer up this morning a more than usually fervent prayer for his welfare. He is, however, sadly harassed with business, and has scarcely ever the pen out of his hand. Colonel Gillespie and Mr. Edwards to breakfast. A great deal of conversation after, with the latter. When they were gone, my dear N. finished his speech, message, &c. and is now ready for the opening of the session. Colonel Roberts, Major and Mrs. Pye, &c. at dinner. To bed at 10, but poor General N. had to write to the Admiral, and so much to arrange in the way of business, that he was much later.

11th. General N. off, at 4, to review the 20th dragoons. Not well enough to go with him. – An immense party at dinner, at 5, and a dance in the evening. Colonel Gillespie and I opened the ball, and, in spite of my illness, this morning, I got through all extremely well, and did not get to bed till half-past twelve.

12th. General N. and part of his staff went to visit Admiral Campbell. Colonel Roberts, Mr. Leicester, and Mr. Sutherland of the 85th, who slept here, breakfasted with me. About 1, General N. returned much heated, and more fatigued than usual. Persuaded him to lie down, and, in consequence, he was much refreshed by 5. – At 6, a large party, General Rose, &c.

13th. Send the chariot for Miss Murphy and Major and Mrs. Pye.

14th. General N. &c. early in Spanish Town, to meet the Council, &c. The Attorney-General and Mr. Campbell, 2nd West India regiment.

15th. Rise very early, anxious for the result of the business to be brought before the Assembly, and particularly on account of all the vexations that may arise to my dear husband. Mrs. Pye, Mrs. Griffiths, and Mrs.

---

[1] A list of London shopkeepers in *Holden's Triennial Directory* for 1805–7 includes both Levinus Vandervelde, boot and shoe maker, 7 Wardour Street, and Vandervell, ladies' shoe maker, 16 Old Cavendish Street.

Elrington, and Lord Aylmer, &c. at breakfast. – General N. went to town at 2, and returned before 6. – Much business expected to-morrow. – Lord Aylmer and I had a great deal of talk about old times.

16th. The Speaker, Mr. Scott, Mr. Murphy, &c. &c. and some military. Two young Messrs. Murphy, Mr. Grant, and Colonel Skerrett, were among our guests. – Most of them returned to dinner at 6, so we did not get to bed till half-past ten o'clock.

17th. At breakfast, Mr. Simon Taylor. – General N. went to Spanish Town, and sent his first message to the House of Assembly, on the subject of his communications from Lord Hobart. – Dine at 6. The Speaker, General Rose, Captain Carr, &c. added to our party. Anxiety has made me so unwell, that I can scarcely sit out the dinner, and was glad to get away, and go to bed, without seeing any more of the gentlemen.

18th. Only our own party at breakfast, and dine between 2 and 3 o'clock; after which General N. went into Spanish Town, for the meeting of the Assembly. – At 6, Mrs. Elrington and Miss Murphy accompanied me, and we all dressed for the ball at the King's House. An immense crowd of gentlemen, but few ladies, as, at this season of the year, they are all in the country. I declined dancing, and no one seemed surprised; but I promised old Sir John Duckworth[1] to open the first ball with him after October next. God grant it, and how happy I shall be then! Even at this distance of time, the happiness is almost too great to think of. I played cassino, and did all I could to keep the *big wigs*, &c. in good humour. – We supped between 12 and 1, and got home at 4 o'clock, my knee aching with making curtsies, and my temper tried with amusing and making fine speeches; but, thank God, my dearest N. is not at all the worse for the anxieties and his writing fatigues, &c. which have been severe of late. – I must mention, that I wore a pink and silver dress this evening, given me by Madame Le Clerc, and which was the admiration of the whole room.

19th. Don't get up till 8, and breakfast at 9. Sir J. Duckworth, Admiral Campbell, and several Navy men, at breakfast. They stayed all the morning, and we dined at 4: having an addition to our party of some officers of the 85th. My dear N. sat down, but, after taking a little soup, was obliged to be off to Spanish Town, where indispensable business awaited him. He returned at 8, and the party was kindly broken up. Only Captain Elrington and young Drury stayed to sleep. To bed soon after 9, fatigued

[1] He was fifty-four.

PLATE 9

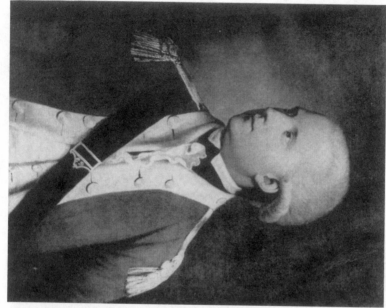

(a) ALEXANDER LINDSAY, 6th EARL BALCARRES
From a photograph of an oil painting by an artist unknown

(b) ADMIRAL SIR JOHN THOMAS DUCKWORTH
From a mezzotint by George Clint after a painting by
Sir William Beechey

both in body and mind, and very anxious for my dear N., who has many embarrassing affairs on his hands at present, and every thing going wrong in the House of Assembly.

20th. Our thoughts are so engaged with business that we have no comfort of our prayers to-day. – My dear N. is much harassed. – At dinner, Mr. and Mrs. Woodham, the Pyes, the Murphys, and the Elringtons – the latter left us in the evening, to go on board the *Druid* frigate.[1] Heard of the arrival of a packet, just as we were going to bed.

21st. At breakfast, the Speaker, Mr. Edwards, and the Reverend Mr. Scott. All went with General N. to Spanish Town after, and Miss Murphy also left the Penn. Glad to be alone, and read my English letters sent me by express from the King's House. All pleasant, but the fuss and agitation of reading them increased the heat so much, that I was quite ill when General N. returned home to dinner at 6. – Feel more annoyance than I own, when I think of the vexatious proceedings of the House of Assembly, and also my dear N.'s fatigues and anxieties.

22nd. The Pyes, Mr. Herring, Mr. Griffiths, and some military, at breakfast. – General N. went to town at 11, and then all the rest departed, and I was happy to be left alone. – The Speaker and a few Members dined with us.

23rd. The Reverend Mr. Donaldson only, in addition to our staff, at breakfast to-day. General N. went to the King's House, to prorogue the Assembly, and came back to dine at 5.

24th. Drive to Port Henderson, and return before 7. – Messrs. Grant, Minott, Corbet, and Whitfield, with Lord Aylmer, at breakfast, and Mr. Murphy and Major Maitland added to the party for dinner.

25th. Drive to the Salt-Ponds early. – Only our own party at breakfast. – The morning quiet. Captains Carthew and Mends of the Navy, Mr. Coleman, the Pyes, Messrs. Griffiths and Kemble, at dinner. The latter is now Surveyor of Kingston, and my brother Downes Collector of Savanna-la-Mar.

26th. Captains Bartlett and Carr at breakfast. – Send for the Admirals,

[1] The 2nd West India Regiment, under Captain Elrington's command, had been embarked for some days, but Nugent was holding them as a bargaining counter, as he explained to Duckworth (June 14th): " . . . altho' I mean they should sail for Barbadoes . . ., yet by remaining *in terrorem* merely a few Days here, it might facilitate my Operations essentially." The operations consisted in persuading the Assembly to vote the military supplies requested in Lord Hobart's despatch from the War Department (Introduction p. xxiv). When they refused, the sailing of the West India Regiment was cancelled.

&c. at 2, to dinner. They, together with Lord Aylmer, Colonel Roberts, and Mr. Nixon of the 85th regiment, the Reverend Mr. Scott, Captain Walker, R.N. &c. formed our party. The Admirals slept here, and we played cards.

27*th*. A cloudy morning. – The Admirals went away early. – A few showers in the course of the day. – After we returned from church General N. was full of business, and sat up late writing, after our dinner party broke up.

28*th*. At 4, General N. off, to see the troops embark at Port Henderson. Mr. Scott returned with him. General N. engaged all day with English despatches. I also write my letters. Only our own party (now fourteen) at dinner.

29*th*. Writing all day. Only Lord Aylmer at dinner.

July 1*st*. Drive to the King's House before 5. – Send carriages for Navy men. – A very large party at dinner, and all left us before 10, excepting Lord Aylmer and Mrs. Pye, who remain at night.

2*nd*. Up very early, and finish my letters before breakfast. – Lord Aylmer came to gossip in my own room, while General N. finished his, and this was not till our dinner time. Feel low and unwell all dinner, thinking of England, &c. Lord A. left us at 6, to embark for England.

3*rd*. Drove to Spanish Town early, but am particularly heavy, and feel the heat exceedingly all day.

4*th*. To church at 10, and bring back with us Monsieur Grandjean and Madlle. Robert. – Not well, and retire to my own room, and leave them to amuse themselves. Have a consultation with Dr. Veitch, and dress for dinner in much better spirits. Several officers of the 85th, and altogether a very large dinner party.

5*th*. Copy despatches for General N. from 5 till near 9, and am delighted to be useful. Colonel Ramsay and a party at breakfast; and feel so much better to-day, that, as soon as they were gone, wrote again, not only my own letters, but helped to copy my dear N.'s. – Mr. Cuthbert and Mr. Lindo upon business. The latter about lending money to the French in St. Domingo. – Send off our despatches by the *Crescent* frigate, Captain Carthew.

6*th*. General N. reviewed the 2nd battalion of the 85th regiment, on the race course, near Spanish Town, before 6, and returned before the sun was over-powerful. At 4, my dear N. off for Spanish Town again, to dine with the 85th. – Mrs. Pye, Kemble, and Duckworth, to dine with me.

7*th*. General N. up at half-past two. I also got up, and wrote Mems. for him, while he dressed. At half-past three, he was off for Kingston, Stony Hill, &c. about barracks, and other military arrangements. I laid down till 5, but could not sleep, I was so uneasy about my dear N., who has so much fatigue of body and mind, and in such broiling weather. After breakfast Mrs. Pye was sent for express, Mrs. Rossington being taken very ill in Spanish Town; and she was dead at 11 o'clock, only having complained a few hours before. Very much shocked, and feel quite unwell in consequence.

8th. Have had a tolerable night's rest, and cheer myself with looking forward to the return of my dear husband. God protect him! All the party went into Spanish Town, after breakfast, and I remained at home till dinner time.

9th. Colonel Gordon, and some of the 85th, at breakfast. About 2 o'clock, the Admiral, his Secretary, Captains Mends and Ross, of the Navy, with some civilians, made a large party. Had spasms in my side all dinner time, and went to bed as soon as our guests left us, before ten.

11th. Feel so well that I return thanks fervently to God, and now look forward with more certainty and joy than ever to the arrival of my expected darling baby. Mr. Gore, of the *Cerberus*, at breakfast. – Read prayers at home, Mr. Woodham being so ill he could not leave his house. – Mrs. Pye took leave in the evening, and we were in bed at ten.

12th. Up at 4, and set off for the Decoy,[1] Mr. Murphy's estate, in St. Mary's Parish. – Arrive at Berkshire Hall at half-past nine. Find a breakfast prepared, and Mr. and Miss Murphy waiting for us. – Proceed on our journey at 11. A dreadful hill to mount, and the heat beyond description. A tremendous thunderstorm met us, just as we were in a narrow road, with a great precipice on one side, and a hanging rock on the other. The flashes of lightning, and the rain, beating in our faces, almost blinded the poor horses as well as ourselves. We were wet through, for General N. was obliged to throw away the umbrella to save our lives, as we were very near being down the precipice. The kittareen, that was driven by Captain Johnson, close behind us, was thrown down the precipice, and dashed to pieces, but he was active and saved himself.

[1] The Decoy was a property formerly owned by Sir Charles Price, Speaker of the Assembly 1756–63, whose hospitality made it a well-known resort. Sir Charles' son, who succeeded him as Speaker, dedicated to him a poem on the Decoy, which began:

> To dust and suffocating heats,
>   Well pleased, we bade adue;
> To taste your garden's rural sweets,
>   And pay respects to you.

Arrived at the Decoy about 2, but so stiff and heavy with the weight of water about me, my shoes even being full, that I was obliged to be lifted out of the carriage. My clothes were immediately taken off by the ladies of the house, who thought I was all over bruises; but soon found that the green and yellow stripes on my skin proceeded only from the dye of the umbrella having run in streams down my back. I was washed all over with rum, and then took some warm soup, and in two hours I was as well as ever and as gay. My dearest N. would not take care of himself, and only thought of me, so I fear he will suffer. God grant he may escape, and all the party; for, like myself, every creature is wet through. – Only Mr. Hinchliffe, who came with us, in addition to the family party. – Very snug and comfortable, and all uncommonly cheerful and well, this evening.

13*th*. All well, except being a little stiff this morning. My dear N. really enjoying himself very much; walking about, shooting, and fishing on the lake, till dinner time. Dine at 4. – A nice walk in the garden in the evening. Fine broad gravel walks, cabbage and cocoa-nut trees, and many ornamental shrubs. Have a syllabub on the lawn. The gentlemen play at bowls, and the young people swing. The comparative coolness of the climate is quite refreshing, and all things are so comfortable about us, that I felt almost as if I were in England; and, besides, I have so many secret sources of comfort and delight at present, that my mind is in a heavenly state, and I am as perfectly happy as any mortal can be. – Two Messrs. Grant joined our party, but we all separated, and went to bed at nine.

14*th*. Up at 5, and walk in the garden with my maid. At 7, we all assembled at breakfast. – Visit the dairy, &c. and feel quite well, but my dear Nugent's hands are very much inflamed and swelled, and his face is redder than ever, from being so much exposed to the sun all day yesterday. Captain Cox from the East Indies, and Kemble and Duckworth came. – At 8, I went to bed from prudential motives. The rest of the party went at ten.

15*th*. An early walk again. – A working party of ladies in the morning. – More gentlemen joined us at dinner to-day, and we had a large party. – In the evening in the garden, bowls and syllabub, &c. and then cards till ten.

16*th*. Walk more than an hour in the garden with Miss Murphy, and my maid attending us. – A large breakfast party at 7. General N. rather heated and not quite well. Oblige him to rest and be quiet, till dinner time.

Some people, however, upon business. Captain Vanderbruck, &c. of the 60th. I was in hopes we should not have had anything of the sort, for a few days at least. In the evening General N. quite well, and I am happy.

17*th*. An early walk as usual. After breakfast, General N., with a party of gentlemen, explored the country on horseback, and came back much pleased with the views, &c. Dine at 4 o'clock. Afterwards; first, the usual lawn amusements, and then chess and cards till 9. I played at the former, beat and was beaten.

19*th*. Before I returned from my morning walk, the Chief Justice, Mr. Kirby, and Mr. Cuthbert, arrived. – Some of our party returned to Spanish Town, and Majors Irvine and Drummond replaced them; so they will all in turn enjoy a little cooler atmosphere.

20*th*. Mr. K. and Mr. C. off early. – At 4, our packet letters; all delightful. Go to dinner in high spirits, at 5. A little thunder and rain, for about a quarter of an hour, and then beautiful and fresh all the evening; quite delightful.

21*st*. A grand holiday given to the blackies, on our account. A most amusing dance on the lawn, and all very merry.

22*nd*. Rise soon after 4, and breakfast at 6. – Begin our journey homewards. A sad fright soon after we started. The horses took it into their heads to back partly down the hill. Thank God, no accident, and I behaved quite heroically! The reflection on the dear one I have in charge, gave me presence of mind, and a degree of fortitude I did not think that I possessed; thank God! Carried in a chair to Berkshire Hall, where we took leave of our kind host and his daughters, and paid my black ponies for my journey. Arrive at the Penn, without accident or fright, at 4.

23*rd*. Colonel Roberts and Mr. Mackenzie, of the 85th, and Mr. Gore, R.N., at breakfast.

24*th*. Our new butler, Short, arrived. – Drive to Dr. Lind's in the evening.

25*th*. Colonels Gordon and Roberts, of the 85th, and Captain Bartlett, of the Engineers, at breakfast. Mr. Woodham still ill, and no church in consequence, but I read prayers to the family at 11. Dine at 3. – Only Captain Bartlett and Lieutenant Le Breton, R.E. in addition to our party of the staff. To-day I have written to some, and lectured others, of the young men of our staff. All very silly people, but I keep their folly from General N. as well as I can.

26*th*. General Churchill, Mr. March, &c. at breakfast, and also some officers of the 2nd battalion of the 85th. – Send off our despatches by the

Sans Pareil, and dine at 4. – Then a drive to Dr. Lind's. He pronounces me very flourishing. Alas! poor man, he appears sadly declining, I am grieved to say.

27*th.* Major Mackenzie, and Messrs. Nixon and Rogers, of the 85th, at dinner. – Drive out in the evening on the race-course.

28*th.* Colonel Gordon and the Pyes at breakfast. Major Pye just returned from St. Domingo, whither General N. had sent him on a mission to General Le Clerc. He brought me a second cargo of Parisian fashions, from Madame Le Clerc (subsequently La Princesse Borghese),[1] sister to the great Buonaparte. – In the evening, drive to Port Henderson, where Colonel Gordon embarked for England on board the *Nimrod* frigate, commanded by Captain Mends.

31*st.* King Mitchell, the Attorney-General, and a large dinner party.

August 1*st.* The Admiral, &c. attended our family prayers. – Capt. Honyman, R.N. came to ask our commands for England.

2*nd.* Sir J. Duckworth, &c. left us. – Officers of the 2nd battalion of the 85th at breakfast. Dine at 3. – Visit Dr. Lind in the evening.

3*rd.* Young Creyke and Grace, of the *Ganges,* at breakfast. – General N. went to the King's House soon after, to hold a Board of Works. Expected all the officers of the 85th, second battalion, at dinner. A delightful tropical rain kept most of them from coming. Those that did come got away soon after 8, and we went to bed, much refreshed by the air being cooled.

4*th.* Sent Grace and Creyke to Port Henderson at 4. – Only Major Mackenzie at dinner.

5*th.* Out, before gun-fire, in the carriage, by myself. Only the maids. General N. rode. – Captain Bartlett, &c. at breakfast.

7*th.* Mr. and Mrs. Woodham, and their little girl, Captain Bartlett, and Mr. Le Breton, &c. at breakfast. They all took their leave at 10.

8*th.* Mr. Woodham too weak to perform the service, so we read prayers at home. – Despatch our English letters before dinner. – The Grandjeans, Mademoiselle Robert, Mr. Edwards, 5th West India Regiment, Mr. Coleman, 60th, Mr. Thompson, 85th, &c. were our guests.

9*th.* A dreadful and sudden tornado for half an hour this morning. The whole house in consternation, for fear of a hurricane. General N. in alarm for me, and thinking of a place of safety. However, all passed over, and we were truly thankful. – Only Major Gould and Mr. Browne

---

[1] She married Prince Camillo Borghese in August 1803. These words seem to be the only example of afterthought in the Journal.

at dinner. Set off immediately after for the Admiral's Penn. – Mr. Waterhouse, Mr. Ludlow, and some Navy men.

10*th*. General N. off before 5, for Up Park Camp, on barrack business. – Some Kingston ladies after breakfast. Go into town with them to *shop*, &c. Return at 3, and try to rest a little.

11*th*. All our party go to breakfast, at Mr. Griffiths', at 8. All the gentlemen attend my dear N. to his daily labours of inspection of barracks, seeing about *money matters*, &c. at Kingston. Soon after 2, he returned for me, and we went back to the Admiral's Penn. – A large party of Navy men, Army, &c. at 4. The ladies were Mrs. Griffiths, Miss Moss her sister, Mrs. Symes, and Miss Cockburn her sister, soon to be married, they say, to Captain Ross, R.N.

12*th*. Return home before breakfast. – My dear N. full of business, and writing despatches for England, to go by the *Topaze* frigate, Capt. Honyman. – A magnificent present of peaches to-day from Sir J. Duckworth; a very great treat to me.

13*th*. Drive to Spanish Town, and look at a house soon to be occupied by Mr. and Mrs. Murphy. See Dr. Lind. He says I do a great deal too much. Determined to rest; to bed at eight.

14*th*. Take my walk till sunrise in the piazza. – Captain Bartlett at breakfast. Mr. Ramsay came to pay General N. an escheat. – Dine at half-past three, and drive out. Lose our way in a wood, and don't get home till past 8, much fatigued. – Make Captain Johnson read prayers, and hear the servants their catechism, and go to bed myself.

15*th*. At dinner, Mr. and Mrs. Woodham, Major Maitland, 60th, Captain Jeffries, 60th, Mr. Thompson, 85th, and three officers whose names I did not hear.

16*th*. My dear N. and I talk over many interesting arrangements, in the piazza, before breakfast. – Only Mr. Edwards, 6th West India regiment, with our staff at dinner. – Drive to Port Henderson.

17*th*. General N. out with his gun till 7. – Receive dear English letters. Every thing delightful. All our friends well, and General N.'s public despatches of the most flattering nature. His conduct in all respects highly approved of, thank God! His applications, too, all attended to, and all successful. – Drive to Dr. Lind's, and have the happiness of telling him of General N.'s success in his favour. Call also for General N. to make communications to Mr. Cuthbert and Mr. Mitchell. – Have prayers, and go happier to bed than usual, and feel uncommonly well. Ease of mind is the best medicine for all my little ills, I am sure.

18th. I often think what a curious sight it would be in England, to see General N. and me, in only our *robes de chambre*, strolling about at daylight, eating fruit, &c. This morning was fresher than usual, and we really enjoyed ourselves. Captain Bartlett and Colonel Roberts at breakfast; they staid all day. – Write letters to go by the *Syren* frigate. – Call upon Mr. March, &c. after dinner.

19th. Send the carriage early to Fort Augusta, for Captain and Mrs. Elrington, and their little girl, only five weeks old. All day nursing the little baby. Feel deeply at the sight of an infant. A sort of happy agitation kept me awake all night. Oh, my God, hear my prayers, and grant me the blessing of a healthy child, endowed with such good and amiable qualities and disposition as may make it a blessing to its dear father and myself, and grant it may ever be worthy of thy care and protection, by doing good in its generation, and serving thee faithfully all its days, through our Lord and Saviour Jesus Christ.

20th. Up at half-past five. Send for the baby, and walk with it in the piazza. – Finish our letters, to go by the *Syren.* – At dinner, Captain Carr, Mr. D'Arcy Whittington (a complete quiz), &c. were of our party.

21st. Send to Port Henderson for the Admiral, &c. Mrs. E. confined to her bed, and the poor baby not at all well. – Dined with the gentlemen at 4. Feel very uneasy, from hearing the poor baby crying continually. Obliged to play my part, and have cards, &c. to amuse my gentlemen. – The baby better.

22nd. Walk with General N. in the piazza till sun-rise. – Our house overflowing with guests. – Go to church at 10. – Mrs. E. well enough to return to Fort Augusta at 2. – A large party at dinner. Mr. Supple, the new clergyman, was of the number.

23rd. Sir J. Duckworth, and Captains Dunn and Ross, amuse themselves exceedingly well, and give me no trouble, while General N. goes on with his business uninterruptedly. – Twenty-six people at dinner, the principal guests being of the Council and Assembly, with General Churchill, his Aide-de-camp, &c. All go to the King's House in the evening, where we had a ball and supper. Did not get to bed till 1. This is not keeping strictly to poor little Dr. Lind's quiet directions; but, though I was as merry as any of the party, I did not even think of dancing.

24th. Dine at half-past two. Then all set off, at 4, for New Hall, King Mitchell's.[1] Get there before 8, and feel so fatigued that, as I was the

[1] Of this visit Nugent had written to Duckworth on Aug. 18: "I trust you will be at Leisure to pay a Visit to Mr. Mitchell at New Hall, St. Thomas in the Vale, for a Day

only lady, I long to go to my own room and to bed immediately, but the heat and the musquitoes would scarcely let me sleep the whole night.

25th. After breakfast the gentlemen attend General N. to explore the country. I kept quiet, but took too long a walk in the evening, and was glad to get away from the party, very early.

26th. Up very early. The heat, the musquitoes, the roars of laughter from the gentlemen till a late hour, and the dancing and jollity of the servants all night, all combined together to spoil our repose, so that we got very little sleep, and I feel this now very much. My dear N. is, thank God, quite well, and that is a consolation.

27th. Start at daylight for home. – The Admiral and Captain Dunn near having their necks broken, by the horse Captain Dunn was driving becoming unruly, and the carriage was indeed in a sad shattered state, in consequence. All get home safe, however, thank God! and soon after breakfast, all retire to sleep, and rest ourselves. I undressed completely, and had a most sound and refreshing nap; and, when we all met at dinner, were very merry, and there was no complaint. – Captain Dunn drove the Admiral to Port Henderson, but we gave them a quieter horse, and all was well. Only Mr. Hanson, in addition to our dinner party to-day.

28th. General N. off before daylight, to look for a lady donkey for me, as I am desired to drink the milk every morning, to keep up my strength in this cruel hot weather. But it is my mind more than my body that is affected, by hearing of the constant deaths that occur at this very unhealthy season, which always throws a gloom over this time of the year; and, just now, the island is particularly sickly. Keep up my spirits as well as I can, and try to think of every thing cheerful.

29th. Go to church at 10. The rest of the day quiet, and only Mr. and Mrs. Woodham in addition to our staff, at dinner.

30th. Up at 5. – The appearance of the morning most extraordinary. All over the mountains to the east, were thick clouds, apparently tinged with fire. From these issued rumbling thunder, and vivid flashes of lightning. This lasted for a quarter of an hour, and was most awful. Then, the sun broke through all with his brightest rays, and nothing could be more sublime. The black clouds became first a sheet of fire, and then dispersed entirely. After looking with wonder and admiration,

or two next Week, as it will tend to reconcile us. Mrs. Nugent has promised to be of the Party, as Advances from the Great here are not to be rejected we find with Impunity."

and some little anxiety, at this scene, my dear N. and I had a most delight-ful conversation, on the subject of our happy prospect in becoming a father and mother. Our hearts are full of gratitude and joy, and we said our prayers with more than usual fervour this morning. – After breakfast, he went to hold a Court of Chancery, at the King's House, and I remained quietly alone till 3, when he returned with the staff, and after our family dinner drove me to Dr. Lind's, whom we found better.

31*st*. General N. again in the Court of Chancery all day. – Poor Henry Rogers taken ill. Send for Dr. Adolphus. – A shower of rain, of ten minutes only, was so heavy, that it prevented us from driving out this evening. – Henry Rogers much better.

September 1*st*. General N. in the Court of Chancery, and I pass my morning alone; for, as there are only young Aides-de-camp here, I leave them to themselves. – Dr. Adolphus came to tell me that Henry Rogers was much better. – My dear N. much fatigued when he returned from Spanish Town.

2*nd*. General N. out with his gun early. I walked in the piazza. – The Pyes and Captain Bartlett to breakfast. – Thank fortune the odious Chancery Court is over to-day. My dear N. home at three. Take a delight-ful drive in the evening, and to bed early.

4*th*. General N. rode out with Rogers, Duckworth, and Drury; but I preferred being quiet till breakfast. – General N. read prayers for me, for I was too much fatigued.

5*th*. General N. rode with the young Aides-de-camp, and I kept quiet, for the heat is most oppressive.

6*th*. Only Captain Bartlett at breakfast. – General N. now rides, and I keep quiet in the piazza before breakfast. Captain Bartlett, as usual, at-tended General N. to Spanish Town, to hold a Board of Works. I employed my morning most delightfully, in making arrangements for my nursery, and for the accommodation of our gentlemen in town, who must now soon leave the Penn. – My dear N. read to me for an hour, on his return home.

7*th*. My little lady donkey arrived, and I took my dose. – General N. out with his gun, for an hour before breakfast. – The morning quiet. – Mr. and Mrs. Hughes, Mr. and Miss Affleck, Captain Saunders, Captain Bartlett, and his officers, at dinner. The heat intolerable, and all the party panting and perspiring to excess.

9*th*. Find the ass's milk agree extremely well with me, but it can't revive my spirits quite, or make me forget the many who are suffering

PLATE 10

SEGAR SMOKING SOCIETY IN JAMAICA!

SEGAR SMOKING SOCIETY IN JAMAICA!
From a print by William Holland after a drawing by A. James

from illness at this cruel season of the year. – Send carriages for the Admiral, &c. – A large party; Messrs. Hylton and Goreham were the only civilians. – Doctor Adolphus taken ill at dinner, and obliged to go home. The heat more than usual, and all complaining. The present season, they say, is more than usually sick. Numbers, both civil and military, are ill, and most of the medical staff too, which is particularly distressing.

10*th*. General N., the Admiral, &c. all rode out early. – After breakfast, the usual routine; writing, reading, and creolizing.[1] – An immense party at dinner. – Mr. Mitchell, Mr. Cuthbert, Mr. Shand, Mr. and Mrs. Rodon, Mrs. and the Misses Rennalls, Dr. Brodbelt, &c. were of the number. Send to Port Royal, for young Brooke and Pakenham. We all gasped in the piazza, after dinner, but really could not play at cards. – The night a perfect calm, and the moon so bright, that I got my small Bible, and read some verses in it, as easy as I could by daylight.

11*th*. All up at half-past four. – Drive with the Admiral to Port Henderson. He went on board the *Leviathan*, and General N. went to Fort Augusta, to inspect the invalids there, and to see what can be done for the comfort of the poor sick soldiers. I returned home a little melancholy: but, thank God, this dreadful season of the year is so far advanced. I now long for two months to be over. – General N. did not get home till 1. – Am wretched on account of the heat, but he has not suffered from it. Only a morning party. – Drove to Major Cookson's Penn in the evening.

12*th*. The heat so great, that I can't go to church. Prayers at home. – The Woodhams, two Messrs. Hylton, &c. at dinner. The heat overpowering, and I am now in a constant state of fatigue from it.

13*th*. Major Otway, of the 85th, dined with us. Drive to Dr. Lind's.

14*th*. All our gentlemen, excepting Major Drummond, Rogers, and Drury, gone to dine on board the *Leviathan*. Feel ourselves very comfortable, in having such a snug party. – Send off carriages for Dr. and Mrs. Ludford to-day, and expect them to-morrow by dinner time.

15*th*. My domestics are so zealous in giving me the ass's milk, that I am obliged to beg they will not get up in the middle of the night; for now they bring it to me at three instead of an hour and a half later, which is rather hard upon me, as well as themselves. – Just as we had breakfasted

---

[1] "Creolizing is an easy and elegant mode of lounging in a warm climate; so called, because much in fashion among the ladies of the West Indies: that is, reclining back in one arm-chair, with their feet upon another, and sometimes upon the table." (John McLeod, *Narrative of a voyage in his Majesty's late ship Alceste, to the Yellow Sea,* 1817).

to-day, an Aide-de-camp of General Le Clerc's (Capitaine le Brun) arrived
with despatches. He gives a sad account of the state of the French troops
in St. Domingo. In the course of the last few months they have buried
14,000 men of the yellow fever. Fifteen general officers have also died,
with a proportion of other officers. Captain Le Brun says, that they have
had 25,000 men well, and now not 5000 effective men remain; and that
their guards have been obliged to be made up latterly of black troops;
rather a dangerous experiment under their present circumstances. The
island is full of brigands, who come in strong parties from the mountains,
and harass the troops continually; murdering, also, not only every white
man they meet, but any black man they suppose to be attached to the
French cause. In short, nothing can be more dreadful than the account
this poor young man gives, who appears really sinking into his grave
from hardship and fatigue. He and Colonel Bourke are the only two
remaining Aides-de-camp out of ten that General Le Clerc brought with
him from France! He laid down almost all the morning. We had a present,
of English cut-glass and trinkets, made up for Madame Le Clerc, and
have purchased a hobby-horse, with silver appointments, for her son,
Astyanax Le Clerc.[1]

Mr. Forbes, from St. Domingo, joined our dinner party, with Monsieur Grandjean and Mr. Thompson, of the 85th; and Dr. and Mrs. Ludford came just before we sat down. Had a little conversation with him,
in the evening. He thinks me very large, I am sure, from what he said, but
thinks me wonderfully well. Our minds are now at rest, for, having the
doctor in the house, we need not fear a surprise. I only think about it
with joy and thankfulness.

16th. The ass's milk at 4 this morning. Beg for another half hour to-
morrow; for it is not daylight now, till much after that time. – General
N. drove the doctor into Spanish Town. On their way they met a Mrs.
Hamilton, the wife of one of the Irish soldiers of the 85th. It seems that
she has come to offer herself as my nurse. I like her appearance very much.
She is pretty and good humoured, which makes Doctor L. anxious I
should take her, and he has persuaded General N. it will be such a good
thing to have her in the house, in case I can't take charge of the dear baby

---

[1] A Nugent family joke, perhaps. The name of Pauline Leclerc's four-year-old son
was not Astyanax but Dermide Louis-Napoléon. Astyanax, in the legendary siege of
Troy, was the infant son of Hector and Andromache; at the capture of Troy he was
thrown from the city walls by Ulysses. Dermide Leclerc safely returned to France with
his mother in December 1802, but died of fever in Italy a few years later.

myself. I have consented, if her character answers, to receive her, and to give up the delightful idea of nursing, if it should be found best for the darling child. – Drive out in the evening, but my mind so agitated all day, that I am quite unwell, and good for nothing. Mr. Holmes, of the 85th, and Captain Bartlett, our only additional guests to-day.

17*th*. Don't sleep all night for thinking of nurse Hamilton and the future. After breakfast, Dr. and Mrs. Ludford go to Spanish Town. My dear N. and I all alone during the morning, and he consoles me very much; for he says it would be impossible for me to do justice to my dear baby in this horrid climate, and with the many anxieties of a public situation, and that Mrs. Hamilton's fair and fat little boy shews what a good nurse she really does make. Try to be satisfied. – Am much shocked to hear of Captain Bartlett's being seized with the yellow fever. He only left us at 8 o'clock last night, in perfect health, and now they say that his life is almost despaired of. As soon as we had dined, General N. drove into Spanish Town, and we called upon Doctor Rennalls, desiring that he would also take charge of Captain Bartlett, and at General N.'s expense, that nothing may be omitted to save the poor man. Major Maitland rather better, and hopes are entertained of his recovery. Call upon the Attorney-General.

18*th*. The Attorney-General, his bride, and her mother, Mrs. Tinker, at dinner.

19*th*. Visit poor Captain Bartlett. Hear that his symptoms are more favourable. – Mr. Griffiths, Mrs. Rennalls, Mrs. Israell, the Honourable Mr. and Mrs. Leslie, General Le Clerc's Aide-de-camp, the Commissary-General, &c. &c. in all twenty-eight people, at dinner. Much fatigued, though much amused. The Leslies perfect strangers, and boring poor General N. sadly about their affairs. – I was cruelly fatigued too, and the thunder and lightning were so frightful, the greatest part of the night, none of us could sleep. The rain fell in torrents, but for this we are most grateful.

20*th*. Feel good for nothing, but my dear N. is much cooler, thank God; for he is so full of business, I don't know how he will ever get through it all. What with St. Domingo, the black corps question, and the Court of Chancery, (which begins again to-day), it is enough really to distract him. Both of us shocked, too, by hearing that poor Captain Bartlett was given over. – Mr. Leslie and a large party at breakfast. General N. went into Spanish Town soon after, attended by all his plagues. Did not return till 4. The heat dreadful; but it threatens rain again to-night. God grant we may have it. – Some cases of claret sent by the French to General N., which he immediately ordered to be returned.

21st. Dr. and Mrs. Ludford off, at daylight, for Kingston. – General N. and I comfortable and alone, till breakfast, when the Admiral and a large party came, for whom we had sent carriages early. General N. and all the family went into Spanish Town, and the latter attended poor Captain Bartlett's funeral. General N. in the Court of Chancery all the morning, and I had to amuse the Admiral, &c. Perhaps it was better for me, as I should otherwise only have thought of poor Captain B. who had so often been our guest, and to whom we had taken a great liking. – A remonstrance from the French officers, about the claret, sent as a present, *they said*, from General Le Clerc; still coolly refused, and for particular reasons, but too long to state to-day – however, I hope to amuse myself shortly, with detailing this transaction, so worthy of the modern French character.[1] In the evening, drive with the Admiral and his party to Port Henderson.

23rd. Up at gun-fire. The heat dreadful. – General N. in Spanish Town, the whole morning. Drive to Dr. Lind's after dinner, but hurry home on account of a threatened thunderstorm. The air was quite on fire. I just got in before the rain began, which poured down like a torrent. Then came the most tremendous thunder, with flashes of lightning almost blinding. We sat round the table, and were taking some wine and water with Dr. Ludford and Henry Rogers, who had both come in wet through, when, all at once, there was peal upon peal, and so rapid, that I asked General N. to see by his watch if there was the interval of a second between them, in order to judge of the distance; but, just as I spoke, the house seemed to be on fire, and two dreadful claps of thunder came as it were at once. All I recollect was, finding myself under the table, on my knees, and quite *crumpled* up. The Doctor ordered the table to be removed, and no one to touch me, but to let me straighten myself gradually. Soon after, I was able to move, and, after a hearty fit of crying, and seeing that no one was hurt, and the thunder becoming every minute more distant, I recovered myself entirely. All the servants had run out of the house, in spite of the rain; and they say that a ball of fire passed close to the offices, but for-

---

[1] The transaction is not mentioned again. It was probably connected with Nugent's displeasure on discovering that Capt. Lebrun had succeeded in raising a loan of £60,000 (Jamaica currency) from the Jewish merchant Alexandre Lindo, and had had goods and specie of this value shipped aboard his frigate without customs clearance or Nugent's knowledge.

tunately no one was hurt. Yet the whole thing was, for a moment, more tremendous and frightful that I can possibly describe. All was comparatively quiet by 10, when we went to bed, only the rain pouring, and the thunder distant.

24*th*. No one the worse for the fright of last night, and I slept well, notwithstanding, to the Doctor's great astonishment, who did not know what might have been the consequence. – General N., the Doctor and his lady, in Spanish Town all the morning. – Alone with my own agreeable thoughts till dinner time. – Heavy rain in the evening.

25*th*. Up before daylight. – General N. finished his Chancery business to-day, to my great joy. – A large party at dinner, at 5. The Admiral, Mr. Mitchell, the Attorney-General, and Mrs. Ross, Mr. Tinker, Mrs. and Miss Rennalls, Mr. and Mrs. Hughes, Mr. and Miss Affleck, &c. &c., twenty-six in number. The whole party dispersed at 9, excepting the Admiral. About 10, a shock of an earthquake, that alarmed me a good deal, and another at half-past one, shook our bed very much. Keep myself as composed as I can, but cannot help feeling the greatest alarm.

26*th*. The Admiral off at 6, for Port Royal. I think he was as much frightened at the earthquake as I was, for he looked *blue* when he talked of it this morning. All the family went to church, except myself. The Doctor thought I had better rest. – Only the Woodhams at dinner. Thank God we have had neither thunder nor earthquake to-day.

27*th*. Major Ottley just from England, came to breakfast, and Captain Drummond, 2nd W.I. regiment, they both stay all day. – Poor Captain Johnson ill. – After dinner, took leave of our party, and drove to enquire about him, and see Dr. Lind.

28*th*. Mr. Le Breton on business as engineer, now that poor Captain Bartlett is no more. – Feel the heat sadly, and am very faint and poorly till dinner time, and indeed after. Then better, and go to bed comfortable, having had a most refreshing drive.

29*th*. Colonel Roberts and Captain Munro of the 85th, and Captain Elrington, at breakfast. They stayed all day: and the 85th men to sleep.

30*th*. We were awoke, in the night, by another shock of earthquake; it was not severe, yet most awful. – My dear N. and I comfortably alone till one, when General Churchill and Captain Coatquelvin came to spend the day. Left them, with Colonel Roberts, Captain Munro, &c. to creolize. General N. found General C. so sound asleep on the sofa, in the drawing room, that we were tempted to play him a trick, by making an old black woman steal a pair of gloves, which awoke him in horror. He bore it, however, with great good humour, and it served for a laugh the rest of the day. – Captain Munro went back to Stony Hill; Colonel Roberts remained.

October 1*st*. Nurse Hamilton came; feel half angry at her superseding me in one of the most precious parts of my expected duty, but play with her fair little boy, till I was quite in good humour with the mother. – Colonel Roberts returned to the regiment. Still full of jealousy and worry about nurse Hamilton, for why should I not be a mother indeed.

2nd. Colonel Ramsay and Major Cookson, R.A. at breakfast, and Mr. Douglas of the 85th. The latter taken ill, and obliged to lie down all the morning. Soon as it was cool enough, order the carriage, and send him to his quarters, at Fort Augusta, and we took our drive to the race course.

3rd. General N. read prayers to me at home, and our morning would have been quite satisfactory, if it had not been for the English despatches, to be closed to go by the *Tisiphone*. At 5, a large dinner party. The Honourable Mr. and Mrs. Leslie, sad bores to General N. Mrs. Woodham, too, exhibited herself in an odd way, talking all sorts of nonsense, though this rather amused many of the company. My dear N. really worn out with letters and applications, &c.

4th. General N. off, before 4, for Kingston, to settle a variety of affairs. – The heat most oppressive, and the musquitoes in swarms. I am so tormented by them, that I can get no rest. – Have the staff with Dr. and Mrs. Ludford to dine with me at 5.

5th. Dr. and Mrs. Ludford went into Spanish Town for the morning. – Admiral Duckworth returned with General N. to dinner, having joined him at the King's House. – Drive to Fort Augusta with him after dinner. – Before we retired to our nests we were almost devoured with musquitoes, and when there were dying with the heat; but there is an appearance of more rain, and so I trust the atmosphere will soon be cooled.

6th. The morning cooler, but the musquitoes, if possible, more intolerable than ever. Their buzzing really makes me nervous. – Only Major and Mrs. Pye. – Advised by Dr. Ludford not to drive out any more, till after my confinement.

7th. Poor Mr. Radford, of the Engineers, died this morning, and Mr. Le Breton is dangerously ill. Try not to dwell upon these horrors, but alas! how can I help it. Some nice showers to-day. Nothing new in society here, but all talking of the yellow fever, &c.

8th. Feel very low. Poor Mr. Le Breton is also dead of the fever. Nothing can be more melancholy than the accounts from all parts of the country. Endeavour to support myself as well as possible, but my mind is sadly harassed with a thousand fears for my dearest N. and many friends. – Poor young Browne much affected by the death of his brother officers, and kindly reprimanded, and put in arrest, by General N. for a supposed fault, to prevent his attending the funeral this evening.

9*th*. Rise early, as usual, and try to shake off my depression of spirits, by playing with nurse Hamilton's baby, and thinking of my own. – General N. went into town, and was full of business all the morning. Dr. L. also absent till dinner time. – Get Mrs. Ludford to help me to make camphor bags, for all our friends, to preserve them from infection.

* * * * * *

Here has been a great chasm in my Journal, and, oh my God! with what gratitude and joy do I once more renew my usual occupations! But I will try to detail the past as accurately as I can. About 3 o'clock on Sunday morning, the 10th of October, I began to feel very unwell, but I did not see the doctor till 5, when I was sitting on the sofa, and all things were prepared for the approaching event. At 8, the staff, and Mr. Perry, a Member of the Assembly, came to breakfast. I sat down with them, and endeavoured to appear at ease; but I suffered sadly, and was forced to go to my own room before they took their leave. From that time till half-past five o'clock on Tuesday evening, my misery was great indeed; but the moment my darling boy was born compensated for all past suffering, and never can I forget the delightful sensation of first beholding my precious child, and feeling that I was a mother. Oh my Heavenly Father, how shall I ever express my gratitude to thee, or the joy that now fills my heart, for the great blessing thou hast bestowed upon me! My future life, prolonged as it may be, will be too short, to shew the sense I have of thy bounties and mercies. Yes, even if it should be lengthened to the utmost extent of the age of man, at every moment that I breathe I will endeavour, as much as in me lies, to promote thy honour and glory; not only with my lips but in my life, by giving up myself to thy service, and doing all the good I can to my fellow-creatures. That child, too, thou hast given me, that precious child, shall be taught, as far as I am capable, to glorify thee by word and deed. Endow him, oh my God! with such good and holy dispositions, as may render him always acceptable in thy sight. Grant that he may be a faithful servant to thee; a comfort to his dear, dear father, and myself, and an useful as well as amiable member of society, kind and compassionate to the poor, and that he may, in every action of his life, prove himself a faithful follower of our Lord and Saviour Jesus Christ. – Here I must again leave off writing; for my heart is still too full, and my frame too weak, not to feel the exertion and excitement of writing. I cannot yet be at all composed or coherent. A few days will, I trust, give me more strength of both body and mind.

Before I attempt to begin my journal regularly, as usual, I will try to describe some of the *agrémens* of a Creole confinement. First, the heat is so dreadful, that it is impossible to go to bed. Then, to mitigate it a little, the blinds are kept closed. Then, the dark shade of the room brings swarms of musquitoes. With these teasing, tormenting insects I am half buzzed out of my senses, and nearly stung to death. Then, the old black nurse brought a cargo of herbs, and wished to try various charms, to expedite the birth of the child, and told me so many stories of pinching and tying women to the bed-post, to hasten matters, that sometimes, in spite of my agony, I could not help laughing, and, at others, I was really in a fright, for fear she would try some of her experiments upon me. But the maids took all her herbs from her, and made her remove all the smoking apparatus she had prepared for my benefit.

The very night my dear baby was born, it was nearly devoured by the musquitoes, in spite of all my care, in exposing my own arms and neck to their attacks; and, for a day or two, his dear little eyes were almost closed up. – Poor nurse Hamilton suffered sadly from the heat, in keeping him under my curtain, and behaved so kindly that I am quite *reconciled* to her. – My English maids too, were so attentive, and took such care, that old nurse Flora should not pinch, or suffocate me to death with her charms, that I shall not forget it. As for Margaret Clifford, I am sure if I had been her own child, she could not have appeared to feel more.

The morning after my darling boy was born, I was allowed the luxury of a warm bath, of all sorts of sweet herbs and scented leaves; such as orange blossoms, &c. It was so contrived, that I could enjoy it without much fatigue for a few minutes, and those few minutes were an indescribable refreshment. This I continued every day, while I kept my room. The third day I sat, or rather lay upon my sofa, with my *cherub* on a pillow by my side; and who can describe or imagine my delightful sensation, in looking at this dear baby! My heart is always in prayer, and never can I be sufficiently thankful.

Passed the first three weeks quietly. – Did not admit all our family, but had two or three only to visit me, and now and then to dine. – On the 30th of October, however, they all came once more, as usual, and our former way of life was renewed. – My dear N. was engaged every morning, with the House of Assembly, but the great happiness he feels, when he returns from the labours of the day, in seeing our little darling, makes him forget all, and join with me in my joy and delight. I am indeed thankful, and only wish all the world felt the gratitude and happiness I do, or had cause to feel it equally with myself. In speaking of the kindness of domestics, I ought not to forget Cupid, who was the picture of woe I am told, and would neither eat, drink, nor sleep, while I was ill; and then danced and sung, and seemed half mad with joy, when my dear baby was born. And I have rewarded him, by letting him be the first of all the blackies about the house to see the baby, and he is also to be his valet-de-chambre by-and-bye.

*   *   *   *   *   *

November 1*st*. I will now resume my journal, and go on regularly, as usual; and what an additional subject I have – the progress and improvement of our dear little boy! – I rise now at gun-fire, and take my walk in the piazza, for it will be three weeks to-morrow since my confinement; but I find the comparatively cool air strengthens me, though I don't go out, because I don't wish yet to leave my dear baby, and go into the world, which I must do if I am seen beyond the lodge gate. We have our staff now, as usual, at breakfast and at dinner, with Dr. and Mrs. Ludford; but, as we are not upon ceremony with them, all goes on well, and as we like.

2*nd*. The early morning happy in the society of my dear N. and baby. He makes an excellent nurse already, and I delight in seeing him so happy. At 10, he went to Spanish Town, as the House of Assembly meet again to-day; but he has had a holiday since Friday, and this is the case every week, that the Members may attend to their private affairs. – A most comfortable evening, and to bed at 8.

3*rd*. A day of distress. Soon after General N. went into Spanish Town, this morning, and Mrs. Ludford also had gone to visit and shop, poor nurse alarmed me with looking very unwell, and seeming really to have a fever. I prevented her nursing the dear child, till I could get the doctor's opinion. Doctor Adolphus luckily arrived, and prescribed for her, and desired that we would feed the little darling till she was better. Kept all my anxiety from my dear N., who is obliged to remain at the King's House, as it is Wednesday, and his dinner day to the Assembly. Forty or fifty dine with him on this day every week. – Passed a miserable day, and was quite overcome when General N. came home at 10.

7th. The Admiral, &c. only, in the day, and all arrangements were made for the christening of the dear little man. – At 4, the company assembled. They consisted of some few ladies, Mrs. and the Misses Murphy, Mrs. Woodham, Mrs. Pye, Mrs. Ludford, and Mrs. Elrington, who were staying at the Penn. There were about twenty or thirty gentlemen; Sir J. T. Duckworth, General Churchill, King Mitchell, Simon Taylor, Mr. Scott, Mr. Warren, &c. &c.

After dinner, the black servants, about forty men and women, with their children and sweethearts, &c. had a dance in the back piazza; the white ladies and gentlemen having had theirs before we sat down to dinner. At half past 8, the whole family were assembled in the piazza, and the guests in the dining room. The dear baby was christened by the names of George Edmund. – The Rev. Mr. Woodham performed the service. Admiral Duckworth and King Mitchell stood proxies for the Marquess of Buckingham and Admiral Nugent, and Mrs. Murphy and Mrs. Ludford for Lady Gage and dear Lady Buckingham.

After the ceremony, cake and wine were handed round, and all the gentlemen stood up to drink the new Christian's health, with three times three. The white and black servants, too, had cake and wine, and vociferated heartily also. After which, the blackies sang and danced and made merry. My dear baby looked beautiful in his christening dress, and was wrapped, by way of mantle, in a beautiful muslin handkerchief, embroidered in gold, sent me by Madame Le Clerc. I am much flattered by the pleasure all the Members of the Assembly, &c. expressed, on the birth of our little boy. He is, it seems, the first child that has been born in this situation; for none of the former Governors have had children, excepting Sir J. Dalling, and they were not born in Jamaica[1]. Old Mr. Simon Taylor and Mr. Mitchell could never say enough upon the subject, and they seemed to think that he should now be so attached to the island, and should become quite one of themselves. I own, although I am grateful for their kindness, I could not carry my gratitude so far. As to Mr. Simon Taylor, he really talked to me like an affectionate father, though in a sort of gruff way.

8th. General N. took his little boy his usual walk at gunfire; for he has done this every morning, since the dear child was a fortnight old. He makes, indeed, an excellent nurse, and spends every leisure moment in playing with his darling little son. Should this book be ever read by

[1] Not true. George, son of Sir William Henry Lyttelton, was born in Jamaica in 1764.

our dearest George, he will then know that, should there be any fault hereafter in our care of him, or any mistakes in his education, &c. the errors have been those of our judgment only, or an over-anxious tenderness; for never did parents feel a more lively affection for a child, than we do for him, nor look forward to its future happiness and respectability with more anxiety than we do to his. His welfare, is indeed, far beyond our own. We would, either of us, willingly sacrifice our lives even, to promote his interest. Our prayers to God are more fervently offered for him than they ever have been for ourselves.

Although still agitated with the interesting event of yesterday, this has been a day of peace, joy, and comfort inexpressible.

9*th*. Yesterday my cards of thanks were distributed, and I expect all the world to drink caudle. General N. took the baby his walk, but has promised me never again to lay his little charge down on a sofa, and run with his gun to shoot a hawk, which I found he had done to-day. General N. in Spanish Town early, and at 12 the ladies began to come. Cake, caudle, chocolate, &c. were devoured. The baby was shewn in his little cot, and much admired; the gauze curtains and bows of ribbons being particularly becoming. I sat in state till near 4 o'clock, and then, finding no more guests arrive, went to rest. – Had a sad alarm, for poor Clifford, I found, had been taken ill with a sad pain and inflammation in her leg. Send a carriage immediately for Dr. Adolphus, who, thank God, does not think seriously of her case. Heard, before dinner, that Captain Munro, of the 85th, was dying, and many others ill. I do my best, but how can one help such melancholy circumstances preying on the mind! General N., too, has received a card, to attend the funeral of poor Miss Affleck. She was a fine young woman, and, when she dined here last, was anticipating the pleasures of my intended balls, for which she had just received her cards.

10*th*. Poor dear Clifford better, and nurse and baby merry, and as well as possible. Find a large party in the breakfast room. – General N. away all the morning, to meet the Assembly, and to give his weekly dinner, and did not get home till 10. The two ladies and the staff absent all the morning. I nursed the baby, and amused myself, and was as happy as I could be under present circumstances.

11*th*. Send carriages for the Admiral, &c. and had a large breakfast party. – Clifford better. – Crowds of ladies, from 12 till 3 o'clock. All chattering, gossiping, eating cake, and drinking caudle, &c. I can't say I enjoyed the party much, for I was kept in a fidget about my dear baby.

Some one took him out of his cot, contrary to my wishes, or rather orders; I did not see it done however. – They pulled him about and passed him from one to the other, till I thought they would break his neck. At 3 I was heartily fatigued, and glad to see them all depart. There were two Mrs. Baillies, Mesdames Clement, McGlashan, Tonge, Cookson, Yeates, Maxwell, Crackley, Ecuyer, Fermor, Ramsay, Millward, two Mrs. Bullocks, Rodon, Sherriff, two Misses Armstead, two Rennalls, Misses Hanson, Fermor, Cargill, Kelsall, Mrs. Ross, Mrs. Tinker, Dolmage, Kelsall, Simon, &c. &c.; but I don't recollect the names of half that came to-day. Only Mr. Corbet at dinner. – Opened a little book to-day, to keep an account of my dear baby's health, and know, from hour to hour, how he goes on, that I may be ready in case of any illness.

12*th*. George took his walk in the piazza, with his papa, and they both enjoyed it very much. Soon after, General N. went into Spanish Town. The Admiral, Captain Dunn, Mr. Edwards, &c. came, but only stayed till 2, for second breakfast. Feel the time lost, as I could not be with little George. A white satin hat for him to-day, and sent him dressed very smart, to meet his dear papa, at half-past five.

13*th*. Little George and his father took their walk early, as usual. – Find Mr. Murphy and Mr. Sherriff in the breakfast room. They are deputed, by the House of Assembly, to congratulate me on my recovery, and the birth of my dear little boy, and to say that that House wished to give me an entertainment on the occasion, and requested I would name the day. – In consequence, Tuesday the 30th, is fixed upon for that purpose; and though I feel very grateful for this attention, yet I dread the fatigue of balls, &c. the present session, and, more particularly, because they will oblige me to be so much absent from my little darling. But it can't be helped, and I must only try to make up my mind to little crosses, and think of my great blessings.

At 12, the ladies began to come again. They were chiefly from Kingston to-day, mixed with the military and Members' wives, from Spanish Town again. The crowd and heat were very great, but I got through all much better than the last time, as my wish not to have the baby taken out of his cot was complied with, and so my mind was at ease.

14*th*. The early morning as usual. To church at 10. After the service, a certain number of ladies and gentlemen stayed, and I returned thanks, and then the Communion was administered to us. Called at the King's House afterwards, and found a present of six ring-tailed pigeons, from my friend Mr. Simon Taylor. – At dinner, the Woodhams, Pyes, Major Mait-

land, Captain and Mrs. Lomax, Dr. Adolphus, &c. Prayers, and to bed at
nine.

15*th*. This day five years I was married, and I can say sincerely from
my heart, that I have never one moment repented it, nor have I ever
experienced the smallest degree of slight or unkindness from my dear
husband; and this year finds me a happier woman than ever I was in my
life. I am so truly blest, that if I could but see my dearest N. a little less
fatigued with business, and a little less anxious, I should pronounce
myself that *rara avis*, a perfectly happy human being. I have all my heart
can wish; an excellent husband, a beautiful, fine and healthy boy. We
have not only an independence for ourselves, but ample means to serve
our fellow-creatures. In short, we have all that any reasonable beings can
possibly want or wish for; and oh, my God, give us grateful hearts, that
we may be worthy of the continuance of thy great and manifold favours
and mercies.

The Rev. Messrs. Warren and Scott came to breakfast. It was the first
time I had seen the latter since he was struck with lightning; and, poor
man, he is a sad object; he is deaf, his ideas are confused, his speech is
imperfect, half his teeth are gone, and his whole frame is shaking and
shattered. From his former liveliness and intelligence what a change!
But may these misfortunes here be beneficial by turning his thoughts
more to hereafter! The sight of him, however, made me very low, and,
unfortunately, he remained all the day.[1] In the course of the morning,
the officers of the 60th came in a body, to congratulate me upon dear
George's birth. Was glad when the visit was over, as all these demands
upon my time are cruel interruptions to my morning engagements.

16*th*. A new carpet for dear baby. A beautiful tiger skin, on which he
lies in the veranda, and enjoys the fresh air, early in the morning.

17*th*. Doctors Brodbelt and Adolphus, soon after, to see Mrs. Ludford,
who, they say, has a strong tendency to consumption, but that she is in

---

[1] The Rev. Alexander John Scott, 1768–1840, a naval chaplain, and a linguist, had
been employed by Admirals Hyde Parker and Nelson as secretary and interpreter at
Copenhagen. Parker had also procured him the living of St. John's parish in Jamaica,
tenable simultaneously with his chaplaincy. In 1802 Admiral Duckworth appointed
him chaplain of the flagship, *Leviathan*, and in July sent him in HMS *Topaze* on a
mission to Gen. Leclerc at Cap François. On the return voyage the ship was struck by
lightning, which "extended itself to two of the powder horns in the Captain's cabin",
and also to the Rev. Scott, who was in his hammock there. In December 1804 Scott
left Jamaica, having been presented with a living in England, but soon afterwards
went to sea again with Nelson, and as chaplain of the *Victory* attended the dying
Admiral at Trafalgar.

no immediate danger. – My dear boy is prospering, but, alas, we must soon think of giving him the small-pox.

19*th.* This is to be a day of bustle and fatigue, and to-night I give my first ball this session. – Send for the Admiral, &c. early. At breakfast, in addition to the Navy, Colonel Roberts and Mr. Hogg, of the 85th. At second breakfast, Captains Walker and Dundas, of the Navy. Joined the party, but all went to dine at King Mitchell's. I dined alone here, with only Mrs. Ludford, and at 8 went to the King's House, to meet my company. Dear little George was with me while I dressed for the ball, and really seemed pleased with my gay appearance; for I put on one of Madame Le Clerc's spangled dresses, on purpose, and the glitter I am sure attracted his notice. Opened the ball with the Admiral, according to promise. At supper my little darling's health was given with three times three. General N. thanked them, and drank success to the Island of Jamaica. I only curtsied, but my heart was full. My fatigue was so great all day, that General N. kindly got the chariot as soon as supper was over, and we brought off Drury and Rogers with us, to sleep here, leaving Mrs. Ludford, &c. to follow at leisure. Found the dear boy sleeping nicely in his cot at half-past two o'clock, and went to bed satisfied and thankful; but the noise I had heard of cheering, &c. at supper, the speeches, and the fatigue, altogether, were almost too much for me.

20*th.* Was told this morning two melancholy circumstances. My poor little Cupid's mother (Venus) died at the King's House, on Thursday. They had kept her illness from me out of kindness, but every thing had been done for her comfort, &c. I am assured. The other is the death of poor Mr. Blakeney, of the 85th. The chief cause of his death was the distress of his mind (poor fellow) for the loss of his brother officers. Poor Captain Munro's death, in particular, affected him. It is remarkable that poor Mr. Blakeney had scarcely any fever, and his death was almost sudden.

21*st.* General N. crowded with unexpected business, and trying to get through all in time for church; and particularly as we have asked for the Sacrament to be administered to us to-day. Order our breakfast in our own room, and I help to copy as well as I can, but, in spite af all, found it impossible to be ready by 10. I therefore wrote to Mr. Woodham, begging that the service might proceed without us, and that we would be at church in time for the Communion, &c. Accordingly, we went at 12, but the sermon had begun, so we retired to the King's House, that we might not distract the congregation; but returned exactly in time for the

Sacrament, at which Mr. Kirby, just from England, assisted Mr. Woodham. Returned to our business, at the Penn, with satisfied minds. My
dear N. finished all his despatches before dinner; but really the fatigue
was overpowering. He copied Simon Taylor's calculations,[1] made
out all the St. Domingo Reports, &c. &c. in all of which I could be of
no use, to my great regret. – At dinner, the Woodhams, Messrs. Herring,
Donaldson, &c.

22*nd*. The Assembly have sent out their cards for the grand ball and
entertainment, to be given to me.

23*rd*. Received an express from Stony Hill, giving an account of the
death of poor nurse's husband. Poor creature, I don't know how to tell
her, and am much distressed on her account. Get Mrs. Ludford, towards
evening, to break it to her, and do all I can to comfort her. She has promised to feel as little as possible, on account of the dear baby; and I will
do all I can for hers.

24*th*. Out early in the sociable, with nurse and dear baby. – Poor nurse
trying to look cheerful, not to distress me. Make her some presents, and
talk of her boy, &c. and we returned home tolerably at ease. – Mrs.
Murphy and her daughters at breakfast. – Quite grateful to poor nurse,
for keeping up her spirits as she does. – Heard of a packet, and immediately after, my dear N. received his English despatches. Nothing can be
more flattering than the expressions of all his official correspondents.
Our private letters also delightful, and most cheering to the spirits. – At
dinner Colonel Malcolm, Member for Hanover, and Dr. Maxwell.
General N. shocked Colonel M. when he introduced dear George, by
saying, how much obliged our little man had been, for his hospitality
in the spring.

25*th*. General N. drove with me and the nursery party to Port Henderson, in the sociable, and we enjoyed ourselves very much. – Dr. Ludford
went to Kingston, to see the child from whom our dear boy is to be

---

[1] On August 20 Nugent had written to the Colonial Office: "Mr. Simon Taylor a
very rich Proprietor in Jamaica, who by a Misrepresentation to the Members of the
House of Assembly, was the principal Cause of their refusing to grant any further
Supplies to his Majesty for the Maintenance of the Military Establishment (having
stated to them that it was in contemplation in England to lay an additional Tax of 20s.
on Sugars, & which he attempted to prove by producing a Letter on the Subject from
his Correspondent in Liverpool) is very busy at this moment preparing some diffuse
Calculations to prove that the Planters cannot support any additional Burthens."
(Their real author was supposed to be the West India merchant George Hibbert).
    Several sheets of the diffuse calculations, copied by Nugent, are among his papers
at the Institute of Jamaica.

inoculated, and brought such quantities of baby's things, sent by the packet, and just landed from England. Much admired, and a great amusement to us all day.

26*th*. Dr. L. returned from Kingston, and at 12 o'clock my beloved child was inoculated. Much agitated, in consequence, the rest of the day, but obliged to dress, and go to the King's House, soon after 4. Find most of the company assembled. Sit down at 5, with about thirty or forty people at dinner. The dancing people began to come before the cloth was removed. Only open the ball with Sir J. Duckworth, and then walk about, and say civil things, till about 11 o'clock, when we returned to the Penn. General N. and I sat up afterwards to discuss the politics of the day. Much of an uncomfortable nature has been debated in the House of Assembly, and the Members are more than ever divided, and more than ever inclined to cavil at every measure of the British Government. I regret all deeply, on account of my dear N; but he will do his duty, and trust to the rest.

27*th*. Mr. Corbet at breakfast. One of the Aides-de-camp made me his confidant, about his pecuniary distresses: do what I can to relieve his mind; but these sort of things make me exceedingly uncomfortable, and particularly on account of the friends of these very inconsiderate young men.

28*th*. Mr. Stewart, of Trelawny, at breakfast. I don't like him at all, he seems such a republican. Am very low, and unwell all the morning. My dear boy again inoculated, as the first attempt does not appear to have answered. This keeps me in great anxiety. – Mr. Stewart returned to dinner, with Dr. Adolphus.

29*th*. Drove to Port Henderson, at daylight. – Thank God, our dear child appears to have taken the infection, but I hope what was done yesterday will not increase the eruption. – Rain at 4, and so heavy, that none of our expected company came to dinner. – Young Grace only.

30*th*. Dress at 7, for the ball given to me to-night, by the Assembly. Dear little George at my toilet. For the benefit of posterity I will describe my dress on this grand occasion. A crape dress, embroidered in silver spangles, also sent me by Madame Le Clerc, but much richer than that which I wore at the last ball. Scarcely any sleeves to my dress, but a broad silver spangled border to the shoulder straps. The body made very like a child's frock, tying behind, and the skirt round, with not much train. A turban of spangled crape, like the dress, looped with pearls, and a paradise feather; altogether looking like a *Sultana*. Diamond bandeau, cross, &c.; and a pearl necklace and bracelets, with diamond clasps. This dress, the admiration of all the world over, will perhaps, fifty years hence, be laughed at and considered as ridiculous as our grandmother's hoops and tissures appear to us now. – But, to return to our proceedings; all well here at 8, and we started in high spirits for the ball. We were met at the door by the four stewards, and marched up the room to the tune of "God save the King." I then stood by the state sofa, receiving the compliments of all the company, and making curtsies for near an hour. After which, I opened the ball with the Admiral, danced with a Member of Council and one of the Assembly, and then thought it *dignified* to play a rubber of cassino. This over, General N. and I walked about the room, toadying and being toadied till supper time. A splendid supper soon after 12. Transparencies and appropriate devices, &c. Soon after we had sat down, the company all stood up round the table, with filled glasses, and drank my health, with a fine complimentary speech, and three times three. Then General N.'s health followed, with the same sort of speech, and applause: and last of all, our dear child's health, with blessings and good wishes, most grateful to our hearts. General N. thanked them, and I curtsied and looked my thanks, but I could not speak, and really felt so much overcome with the whole thing, that I was glad when the uproar ceased, and the attention of the company was drawn to some other toasts, proposed on the part of General N. about the concerns of the Island, Kingston,[1] &c. Got back to the Penn at three.

December 1st. Up at 8. What an hour for us! General N. in town all the morning. At 5, some gentlemen, and Mrs. Griffiths, Miss Moss and Miss Williams, at dinner.

2nd. Dear babe and his arm as well as possible. Crowds of visitors all the morning, coming and going till 4 o'clock. Then drive with General N. to Spanish Town. We gave a dinner to a large party of the Assembly, at the King's House, and Mrs. Ludford and I dined quietly with the Murphy family.

3rd. Dressed and went into town. A great crowd. Sit between Mr. Mitchell and Simon Taylor; both very kind, and telling me to please myself, and leave the company to take care of themselves; but hear at 8, that all is going on well at the Penn, and I begin the ball, which was at last adjourned to the Egyptian Hall, for the company became so numerous that the gallery, where we usually met on Fridays, could not contain

[1] Probably refers to the impending incorporation of Kingston as a city, which took place 12 January 1803.

half of them. One of the longest and most disagreeable evenings I ever spent, but get away at eleven.

4th. My dear N. full of business, all the morning, with Mr. Corbet and Sir R. Basset; the latter endeavouring to vindicate his conduct, when he was Superintendent of Honduras. Mr. Corbet was bringing forward his proof to the contrary; being employed some little time since by General N. to enquire into the charges, brought against Sir Richard Basset by the settlers of Honduras. – It appears altogether to have been a scene of the saddest fraud and peculation possible. Yet the wretched man looks so miserable, that I can't help pitying him, as he is dismissed the service; and it is thought several others will share his fate. – Heard, in the evening, of poor Downes' illness, and go to bed low on his account; though they say it is not the fever, and that when the last account came he was better.

5th. To church with the staff at 10. My dear N. full of despatches, to go by the *Cerberus* frigate to England. Our sermon to-day was very long. The clergyman that preached was a Mr. Davies, just arrived, and he treated of botany and astronomy, as well as divinity. It appeared altogether an essay, more fit for the drawing room than the pulpit. He dined with us, as well as Mr. and Mrs. Woodham, and Mr. Ramsey, of the 60th regiment.

6th. Up at daylight, and help dear N. with his despatches, by copying letters. – Major and Mrs. Pye, &c. at breakfast. – The despatches sent off at 12. A quiet dinner, and a drive in the curricle.

9th. Till after 2 this morning, the little darling was feverish and very uneasy; but, thank God, he appears better to-day. Drive with him to Port Henderson. Only nurse and Johnson with me. General N. holding the dear child, on a leather pillow, the greatest part of the way. – Mr. Scott, of the Council, to breakfast. – A great deal of business for dear N. in Spanish Town, and he can't return till 5. I pity him, for his heart is here, and I am sure he suffers much from anxiety.

10th. Poor N. obliged to be in town all day, to dress there for King Mitchell's grand dinner. I dined with only Mrs. Ludford, at 3, and dressed and went into Spanish Town at 8. Found a crowd assembling, for this is what they call the King's Ball; and every one that can afford a dress is allowed to come to it. General N. &c. came at 10, and we all marched into the ball-room, to the tune of "God save the King." I danced three dances, and then played cassino till 12, at which hour we went to supper. – Began dancing again, but heard from Mr. Sherriff that the greatest danger was when the small-pox was turning, and that then some nourishment should be given. Got the carriage as soon as possible, and returned to the Penn, to change poor nurse's diet. Found that she had had a bason of fresh milk, and that both were quietly asleep.

12*th*. General N. too full of business to stir from the Penn, and we gave up church to-day, but had prayers by ourselves. – A large party at dinner. Sent the sociable and four for Miss Williams and a party of ladies. All stayed for family prayers: Mr. and Mrs. Woodham, &c.

14*th*. Just as we were stepping into the carriage, at daylight, an express arrived from Fort Augusta, with a despatch for General N., to say that a packet was in the offing, and that General Carmichael, the Captain of the packet, and Mr. Mackinnon, had landed in an open boat, in the middle of the night. Drove immediately to Port Henderson, to meet the gentlemen, and full of conjectures as to the nature of the news we were to receive – the King's death, a war, a change of ministry, or some grand affair, could be the only probable causes of such an express, and such haste. – Met the gentlemen, and brought them home to breakfast. It turned out to be only the usual communication from the British Government, and the gentlemen's haste was to get ashore. They spent the morning refreshing at the Penn. We dined at 4, and then we took them to the King's House. They were Brigadier-General Carmichael, who is appointed to the staff here, Captain Fellowes, who commands the packet, and Mr. Daniel Mackinnon, on his private affairs. Found a large party assembled, for the Colts' Ball. This is a kind of subscription fête, given by the new Members of Assembly, who are always considered colts, and the Governor too, till he has gone through the ceremony of this entertainment. General N., therefore, was a party concerned; and it was very gay, with transparencies, &c. in the supper room, and a very fine set-out altogether. I danced, and did all that *was agreeable*; and so did General N. – Sir J. Duckworth was in a rage with Captain Fellowes, and it was with great difficulty I effected a reconciliation, and prevented his reporting him to the Admiralty. After supper, poor Mrs. Ludford was taken ill.

15*th*. A party at breakfast; Colonel Lethbridge, General Carmichael, Mr. Mackinnon, Captain Fellowes, &c. – Am anxious all day about poor Mrs. Ludford. Do not ask our company to stay dinner. Only four sat down. All out of spirits, poor Mrs. L. seems so ill, and can be heard in any part of this thin house.

16*th*. We all went into Spanish Town, to breakfast with Mr. and Mrs. Murphy. I say all, but General N., nurse, baby, and myself, were the party. A large breakfast. The crowd and heat great; but dear Georgy had a cool part of the veranda for his tiger skin, and enjoyed himself very much. Excused myself to Mrs. Rodon, for not attending her ball this evening, as it is impossible for me to go out to-night, and to entertain the whole town, as I must to-morrow.

Drs. Ludford and Adolphus backward and forward, in attendance upon poor Mrs. L., who seems to be growing worse rather than better. – The melancholy scenes that we are daily witnessing, the extraordinary characters that we meet with, and the manœuvres of party which we witness, will, I hope, be useful lessons to us for the rest of our lives, by shewing us the vanity of all things, and reminding us more and more of the shortness and uncertainty of this life.

17*th*. A dreadful night for us all, listening to poor Mrs. Ludford's groans. Put off our dinner and dance for this evening, and give all our attention to her. Our great consolation at this moment is, the health and prosperity of our dear child. – No further news of poor Downes, so we hope he is doing well. – The day melancholy indeed to me, as my dear N. was obliged to go to the King's House, upon business, and did not return till 6. – In the evening no hopes given of our friend.

18*th*. Quite wretched to-day. Poor Mrs. Ludford raving incessantly all night, and it was impossible not to hear her. About 5 o'clock she became quiet, and we flattered ourselves that a favourable change had taken place; but, alas! no, the mortification had begun, and she expired at 11 o'clock to-day! We went immediately to the King's House, leaving my maid in charge of the Penn, and have passed a melancholy day indeed.

19*th*. Go in my night-cap and dressing-gown, with dear baby, to Mrs. Murphy's, at daylight, and remain till late in the day. Poor Mrs. Ludford was buried at 9 o'clock. The procession set out from the King's House. General N. attended, and shewed every possible respect to her memory. Dr. Ludford set off for St. Elizabeth's (his parish) after the funeral, and we returned to the King's House, as there was no service in the church to-day. – At 5 o'clock, send the carriage for the Murphy family, which, with our own, made twenty-two at dinner. It was all gloomy enough, and both General N. and I were so worn out, we were glad to get to bed when 10 o'clock struck.

20*th*. Feel quite ill, and can't go out. My spirits sadly low all day, and my dear N. so full of business, that I scarcely see him.

21*st*. Low and miserable all day. – Try to rally my spirits, for my dear N.'s sake whose greatest comfort is to find me cheerful when he returns to our own apartments, after the business of the day. The evening quiet again, and this will do us more good than anything.

22nd. A wretched day indeed! It seems that poor Downes has been dead some time. How sad and wretched for his miserable wife and child! Give way entirely, and pass a sad evening, my imagination constantly presents such a dark cloud before me, that I am quite overcome. But God's will be done! He knows what is best for his erring creatures.

23rd. Sad dreams all night. Rise very early, and drive out. Am determined to occupy my mind, and not to dwell upon painful subjects. It makes poor N. so miserable, and wears out my own health and spirits. – Write to poor Downes' widow, and try all I can to console her.

24th. Only Mr. Cathcart at dinner; but my dear N. is very unwell, and overwhelmed with business, and, at this moment, much teased with French intrigue, about getting money at Kingston. Try to support myself for his sake, and not add to his cares.

25th. Christmas Day. But very warm, and so unlike Christmas Day in our own dear country. – A shock of an earthquake, just as I was preparing for church. My dear N. not well, and advised to stay at home. I trust it is only over-occupation that occasions his illness. However, in this climate, the most trifling attack is a source of alarm. He promised to come to the Communion, and when I missed him, I did indeed feel cruelly anxious and nervous, and this was not diminished by finding him so unwell as to be lying down, and very feverish, when I returned from church. God preserve him! – At 3, the Aide-de-camp returned from visiting the French officers, on board their frigate at Port Royal, and carriages were sent to bring them here to dinner. – The Doctor says, that General N. must not leave his room, and, politically, the General does not wish to receive them, except merely making his bow, and then I am to do the honours of the dinner table. They came at half-past four o'clock, when the Vicomte de Noailles declared himself also too unwell to sit up; and actually followed General N. to his room, and remained there conversing with him all the time we were at dinner. – With the assistance of the staff I got through the dinner business pretty well, but in the midst of it lost my voice entirely, and yet I have no cold. Dr. Adolphus says it is nervous, and I dare say it is, for inwardly I am very low and wretched.

The Vicomte de Noailles' conversation was chiefly on the subject of St. Domingo, but he talked also of the golden key, namely, the access he hoped to obtain to the South American treasures. He told General N. that the French plan was, to put to death every negro who had borne arms, and to hamstring the others! – General N. then asked him, what would the colony be worth in that case; but to this he was not prepared for an answer. In short, it appears, that, though the French may have had a great deal of the monkey in their composition and character formerly, they have now more than a double proportion of the tiger. For never were there such a set of cruel heartless wretches, and I rejoiced to see them depart at eight.

26th. I was sadly ill all night. My dear N., though, much better, thank God! – He has taken, within the last twenty-four hours, no less than forty grains of calomel, and scarcely seems to have felt it at all. – The Woodhams and Pyes to dinner. I am still *speechless*, but not otherwise ill, and continue to get through the day tolerably well.

27th. Noise of rude music, &c. &c. all night. – My dear N. better, but particularly unwell myself all the morning. The streets crowded with singing men and women. Nothing but noise and bustle all day. At dinner, Major Maitland, Dr. Gallagher, and our own party. General N. quite himself again, and my voice is returning.

28th. As soon as it was light, set off for the Admiral's Penn, baby, nurse, and all. General N. &c. rode. Arrive at the Admiral's about 8, and find the Vicomte de Noailles and four other Frenchmen there before us. A long discussion, upon money matters, between General N. and the Vicomte; not at all satisfactory to the latter, I fancy, who took his leave about 12, and we rested ourselves till 4, when we joined a large dinner party.[1] Mrs. Hibbert and Mrs. Bogle were the only ladies besides myself.

29th. Drive to Up Park, at daybreak. Sir J. Duckworth in the sociable with me and baby. General N. &c. on horseback. – The 6th battalion, 60th regiment, reviewed. – General N. then inspected the works, new barracks, hospital, &c. and we returned to the Admiral's at 8, for breakfast. Colonel Mosheim, and a few officers, with us. Mrs. Griffiths came to ask if I wished to go into Kingston. Went with her to a few shops, and returned to rest a little before dinner. A larger party than usual of ladies; Mrs. Laws, Mrs. Griffiths, Misses Stewart, Miss Cockburn, &c. &c.

30th. The Admiral, &c. accompanied General N. to Stony Hill, at 5. I drove out with the child and maids, and then breakfasted with the Navy men here; Captain Dunn, and Mr. Muddle, Aide-de-camp to Sir J.

---

[1] Noailles had been trying to negotiate another loan from Alexandre Lindo.

Duckworth, and Mr. Headlam, his secretary. Mr. and Mrs. Peacocke soon joined us. She, poor thing, was so unwell, that she was obliged to remain in my room all the morning. She told me her history, and I really feel for her very much. She is lady-like, and well informed, and appears to be perfectly thrown away upon an unfeeling, speculating, foolish man, to say the least of him. – A large dinner party at 4. Mrs. Hibbert, Mrs. Symes, and Miss Cockburn at dinner. – A number of ladies came in the evening, and we had quite a ball. My dearest Georgy made his appearance among the dancers, and was greatly admired. I thought he looked like a little angel. General N. was particularly merry, and danced a great deal. Thank God, he bears all his fatigues so well.

31st. Too tired to drive out. Colonel Roberts and Captain Ross, in addition to the Admiral's usual party. – A packet arrived in the night, and we got papers as late as the 23rd of November. Peace or war doubtful. – General N.'s despatches were very comfortable to his own private feelings. – After breakfast, drive into Kingston, and make a few visits. See poor Mr. Edwards, who is still very ill. At 4, go to Mrs. Griffiths', and after a short toilette, meet a large party at dinner. The heat dreadful, and am obliged to leave the table. I don't know what is the matter with me, but I certainly don't stand the climate as well as I did last year. – Return to the Admiral's Penn, at 9.

CHAPTER III

JANUARY 1, 1803 – DECEMBER 31, 1803

January 1st, 1803. – As soon as we had breakfasted, took leave of the Admiral, and arrived at the King's House at 12. General N. had some business with the Secretary, &c. as usual; and baby danced and enjoyed himself in the gallery till near 3, when we got safe to the Penn, and found all so clean and nice there, that we felt the delight of being once more at home. – Only two of the staff, and ourselves, except Mr. D. Mackinnon, who has been of all our parties.

2nd. Dine at half-past three. The Woodhams, the Pyes, Mrs. Hodges, and two Mr. Lewises, General Carmichael, Majors Ottley and Darley, and Dr. Gallagher, in addition to our own party.

3rd. Drive to Port Henderson at gun-fire. – My dearest baby bathed in the sea for the first time. General N. took charge of him, but my heart was in my mouth the whole time, and I could not look at the proceeding. He was bathed out of a boat, and the waves splashing so high that it was really very frightful. My spirits too, are now so easily alarmed, that the least danger for my dear, dear child makes me wretched. Lie on the bed the greatest part of the morning, and find it difficult to recover my spirits. The Admiral came at 3. – Only a small dinner party. Captain Dunn went back to his ship at 8.

4th. The Admiral and General N. rode out at gun-fire, and I took my drive with the maids and dear Georgy. Never was there a dearer baby. He is scarcely ever heard to cry, and is always well and merry. I am, however, poorly, and begin to think that something unusual is the matter with me. If I should have a dear little girl, how delightful! Receive a packet of books from England, for the instruction of poor children, Sunday Schools, &c. but alas, they can be of little use to us here!

After breakfast, General N. drove the Admiral to Spanish Town. They visited Mr. Edwards, and several invalids. – A large party at dinner to-day; Major Maitland, Captain Jeffries of the 4th battalion, 60th, Mrs. Rennalls and family, Mr. and Mrs. Rodon, Mr. and Mrs. Herring,

Mr. Mitchell and Mr. Lane; in all, about twenty-four. – Captain Johnson just returned from his voyage to New Providence.

5th. Rise before day, and set off for Port Henderson, where Clifford bathed my little darling in the sea before the sun was up. General N., the Admiral, &c. went on to Fort Augusta. I was not so much alarmed to-day, because Clifford stood only in the water, close to the shore, and not in a boat, which made it much less dangerous and frightful to look at. – On my return to the Penn, find Mrs. Hodges, and two Messrs. Jarvis, to breakfast with me. At dinner, the Admiral, Captains Dunn and Dundas, Mr. Headlam, Mrs. Kelsall and family, Mr. and Mrs. Dolmage, Mr. and Mrs. Ramsay, Mr. and Mrs. Woodham; in all twenty-six.

The Admiral was so unwell that he left the party before we removed from table. I then had a treat, for General N. and myself, in seeing the dear baby prepared for the night in the drawing-room. Just as his fresh dress was put on, a large centipede came creeping out from the very spot where we were playing with him; and judge of our alarm! The sofa pillow was thrown to the other side of the room, and General N. soon put the reptile to death; but we hunted over every part of the room, and his room too, before we could put the dear boy into his cot for the night.

6th. Am much shocked to hear of the sudden death of poor Mr. Wolfrys. We dined with him, at the Admiral's Penn, last week, and he was very anxious for us to visit him in the mountains this week. At first we partly promised, but afterwards, on account of the journey being too long for little George, we excused ourselves; and most fortunate it was, for we should just have been present at the melancholy scene of his death. Events like these fill the mind with horror and awe, and make us think indeed. – Go with General N., at gun-fire, to review the 4th battalion, 60th regiment. The Admiral not well enough to be of the party. General N. much pleased with the corps, and commended, in particular, the rifle companies. I returned home with my little G. to breakfast. General N. remained for the breakfast given by the corps. – Drs. Ogilvie and Blair in attendance upon the Admiral, who kept his bed; but Dr. Blair, on whose opinion I rely, thinks it merely a bilious attack, and that shortly he will be as well as ever. – We had a very large dinner party, and, to our surprise, the Admiral made his appearance. Mr. Parker, of the *Leviathan*, came with Dr. Blair. There were also Mr. Halkett, from New Providence, Mr. Mitchell, General Carmichael, Major Darley, Major Maitland, and officers of 4th battalion, 60th, Mr. Whitehorne, Mr. Bullock, Mr. Clement; in short, an immense party. The Admiral soon got tired, and was obliged to go to bed; so the party broke up very early, and the house was quiet by ten.

7*th*. The Admiral still unwell, and can't go with us to the dinner, given to-day by Mr. Rodon, the Custos of the parish. Order dinner for him and his secretary here, and go with our own party to dine in Spanish Town. Hear of much illness, and so many deaths, that my usual uncomfortable feelings were greatly added to, and I could scarcely sit out the dinner. So very faint and sick indeed was I, that at 9 the carriage was ordered, and General N. and I returned home, just as the gaieties of the evening were beginning, as there was a dance.

8*th*. General N. and I drove with little George to Port Henderson, so early that the moon was shining brightly the whole way. General N., after seeing dear baby bathe, went on with the staff to Port Royal, in the Admiral's barge, to review the artillery stationed there. – After breakfast, the Admiral, &c. took their leave. He was nearly as well as ever, but his attack has been rather a severe one, and he looks very ill. – General N. &c. all back before three.

9*th*. After the service drive about Spanish Town, and find all the invalids better, and Major Drummond and Mr. Edwards recovering fast. – Only the Woodhams at dinner.

10*th*. Very unwell this morning, but drive, before sunrise, into Spanish Town; General N. on horseback. At breakfast, Colonel Barrow, from England, to take the command, as Superintendent of Honduras. General N. engaged all the morning, in giving him instructions. He stayed to dinner, with Messrs. Hanbury and Cathcart, Major and Mrs. Pye.

11*th*. Am so alarmed to-day at seeing George bathed, that I am determined not to be present again on the occasion. Indeed General N. seems himself inclined to give it up; thank God! for I am sure it does not do him any good, and it is very dangerous.

12*th*. The dear child bathed again, but I could not look at it. I hope this may be the last time. – Our own family early at breakfast. – Poor Drummond so ill, that he has been removed to the King's House, to be better taken care of. General N. himself rode into Spanish Town, to give the necessary orders respecting him, and to procure the best advice, so I trust he will do well. – A packet from England; delightful news. – Go to dinner at 4, in a *happy fuss*. Dear Miss Acheson tells me of her intended marriage with Lord William Bentinck. God bless and make them happy! Go to bed most comfortable to-night, and hear that poor Drummond is much better.

13*th*. Mr. Griffiths came to take leave in the evening, as he is to be off in the packet. Drummond better.

15*th*. Dress by candle-light, and drive to Port Henderson, where General N. reviewed the black corps (2nd W.I. regiment). A great breakfast afterwards at the inn, and did not get home again till 11 o'clock.

16*th*. General Carmichael, Major Darley, Colonel Roberts, the Pyes, &c. at dinner.

17*th*. Again make my toilet by candle-light, and arrive at the race-course before sun-rise. General N. reviewed the St. Catherine's militia. We returned to breakfast at the Penn. General Carmichael, &c. left us soon afterwards. Had a present from Colonel Ramsay, who came from Port Royal, of two beautiful tiny tortoises, in a glass case. – At dinner, Mr. Unitt, from Curaçoa, who has just arrived with the Governor, Colonel Hughes, from that island, to whom he is secretary.[1]

18*th*. Mr. Unitt left us very early, with General N.'s instructions for Colonel Hughes. Mr. Scott, of the Council, and Miss Williams, &c. at breakfast. Various people in the course of the morning, on business of accounts, &c.

19*th*. Send carriages for Colonel Hughes, &c. and my baby took his walk; for, thank God, bathing is given up. Colonel Hughes, Captain Miller, Mr. Unitt, and Mr. Du Vernet to breakfast.

20*th*. The Admiral, &c. at breakfast, and to spend the day. – Dine at 4. – General Carmichael and his Brigade-Major, Mr. Ross, Mr. Scott, &c. in addition to Colonel Hughes, and his party.

21*st*. Start at half-past four, with our whole party, for Bushy Park (Mr. Mitchell's); breakfasted there, and then proceeded on to Spring Gardens, where General N. reviewed the St. John's and St. Dorothy's militia. Returned and dined at Mr. M.'s, and then home again to sleep.

22*nd*. After breakfast, Admiral D., Colonel Hughes, &c. all went to Port Royal. – Sir J. Duckworth returned to dinner, with Commodore Bayntun.

23*rd*. The Admiral and Commodore went to Port Royal. Saw poor Drummond after church, and he is getting well slowly. – The Chief Justice still ill. At dinner Mr. and Mrs. Woodham, Mr. Underwood, Mr. Irving, Major Maitland, &c.

24*th*. General N. off before day, with General Carmichael, Colonel Hughes, &c. to review the militia of St. Thomas in the Vale. I drove out

---

[1] The British occupied Curaçao from September 1800 until the Treaty of Amiens in 1802, and Col. Hughes was joint Governor during that time.

with dear little George, &c. Not at all well the whole morning, and glad to be alone. Only Mr. Unitt, and one Aide-de-camp at dinner with me. General N. &c. returned before we left the table, and all our guests took their departure soon after 8. – Poor Downes's widow and her little girl came, just as we were concluding prayers.

25th. Go to Mrs. Skinner's room at daylight. Find her and the little girl quite well, but no one disposed for an early drive. At breakfast, an unusually large party; sixteen persons. – My morning, after a long conversation, was spent, as usual, in writing, reading, and nursing my dear little boy. – Dine at half-past four; Mr. Mitchell, Mr. Edwards, and some officers of the 87th regiment. Mrs. S.'s spirits better than I expected. Rather sickish myself, and glad, at 9, to go to bed.

26th. Drive with Mrs. S. and our two children, to Port Henderson. Again bathe my little darling. – At breakfast, only Major and Mrs. Pye added to our party.

27th. Some officers of the 87th regiment, at breakfast. – Another horrid Court of Chancery, and I did not see my dear N. till half-past four. Eighteen persons at dinner.

29th. Only Colonel Hughes, and Mr. Unitt, at breakfast. – General N. in Spanish Town, on Chancery duty. – Messrs. Irving, Cunningham, McNeil, and Mr. Browne, 87th, at dinner. Colonel Hughes and Mr. Unitt took leave before 8, and went on board the packet, to sail for England on Monday.

February 1st. Too sick myself to drive out. Baby better than usual, and took his airing with Mrs. S. and her little girl. – Mr. McAnuff at dinner.

2nd. Dine later, on account of the *grand* cause between Lindo and Lake not being decided. – General N. determined to settle the business to-morrow, without hearing further pleadings.

3rd. Am persuaded to drive in the curricle early, with General N., the baby, &c. in the sociable. Colonel Ramsay, Major Cookson, and Mr. Du Vernet, at breakfast. – To-day my dear N. settled the cause between Lindo and Lake, to the entire satisfaction of every one; and even the parties concerned themselves acknowledge the thorough justice of the decision.[1] This is delightful to me, as it makes his mind so easy and comfortable. – Major and Mrs. Pye, Dr. McNeil, and Captain D'Arcy, of the 85th, at dinner. – Settled arrangements with Dr. McNeil, about poor nurse's eldest little boy, to be sent to Stony Hill, and better taken care of.

---

[1] Richard Lake and Alexandre Lindo had formerly been in partnership as Guinea factors, i.e. slave dealers.

5th. Rise before 3. Feel very, very sick this morning. Set off, however, as soon as dressed, with Mrs. S. in the sociable, for Kingston. General N. on horseback, with his staff. Arrived on the race course just as the sun was about to rise, and the scene was really sublime. The hills, and all, tinted with the most brilliant colours. The Kingston militia were then reviewed. The crowd was immense. After the review, met a large party, at the Admiral's Penn, at breakfast. After which, Mrs. Griffiths came, and we drove into Kingston, for shopping, &c. and did not get back again to the Penn till after 2. – A party of thirty at the Admiral's dinner. Sick all the time, and wish myself home again. Set off for our own Penn as soon as we had taken our coffee.

7th. Mr. Blair (Lady Mary Blair's son) arrived from England, with letters from Lords Westmoreland, Hobart, &c. and dear Lady Buckingham. Invite him and his wife here, and do all that is civil and kind by them.

9th. A delightful shower of rain. – The people from Stony Hill, with contracts for the barrack, &c. Only the Pyes at dinner; and to bed at an early hour.

10th. At daylight set off, with our whole party, for the Ferry House,[1] from six to eight miles on the Kingston road. – After breakfast, proceeded to review the St. Andrew's militia. Among the spectators was one of the fattest brown ladies and her child that ever were seen, and General Carmichael brought them up, to be introduced to me. Got back to the Penn before 4. Notwithstanding a delightful shower of rain, we all suffered very much from the sun to-day, and poor little Grace's face was almost one blister. – Prayers, and to bed at 8. – Observed forty people of our family at prayers, this evening.

11th. Have more distressing letters, &c. than usual the last few days, and get up early, to reply to them all as well as I can. I know it is not in my dear Nugent's power to listen to many of them, but I will do my best, though my task is often painful. – Send the sociable for the Admiral, &c. to Port Henderson, and the chariot to Spanish Town, for Mr. and Mrs. Blair. The Admiral brought Mr. and Mrs. Ledwich and Captain Dunn with him. Exert myself to make the agreeable, as my dear N. had so many letters to write, but the day passed off extremely well. Mrs. Blair is

---

[1] Before the building of the railway in 1845–6, it was the regular halfway house between Spanish Town and Kingston. The present Ferry Inn incorporates some of the old structure.

very pretty, but I thought her ten times more so, for the admiration she expressed of my dear little G.

12*th*. My little darling is four months old to-day, and has already a tooth. The nurse got a guinea and a smart ribbon on the occasion, and is merrier, *if possible*, than ever. – Only Mr. Minott, one of the Members for Portland, at breakfast. The rest of the day quiet, and enjoying the society of the dear little ones. Mrs. Skinner's little *Bonella* is a sweet child, but so spoiled that I am afraid she will be a little tyrant. Mrs. S., like all Creole ladies, has a number of servants with her, and all are obliged to attend to any caprice of the little girl, as well as her mamma; and I grieve to see it. – It will, however, be a good lesson for me, and I am determined to make my dear little boy so amiable, that he shall be loved by all, and not feared. But, in this country, it will be difficult to prevent him from thinking himself a little king at least, and then will come arrogance, I fear, and all the petty vices of little tyrants. – I have taken little Bonella in hand, and she really seems already to be much better in temper, and is, indeed, a most attractive dear little thing.

13*th*. General N. off early for Kingston, not to return to-night, as he is to review the Port Royal militia, at Castile Fort, to-morrow.[1] Feel low and depressed about him, as I cannot help fancying the ill effects of so much fatigue and exposure to the sun; but he says he feels it less than so much letter-writing, &c. after anxious business. God protect him! Read and remain quiet all day. – Poor dear Clifford to sleep in my room, as I am a sad coward when General N. is away from me.

14*th*. My dear N. came at 4, not at all the worse for the sun; but he and Mr. Duckworth (Aide-de-camp) nearly lost their lives, by the overturn of the kittareen, and being dragged a considerable way. Thank God, they came off with only a few bruises and scratches; but the account of their disaster made me sadly nervous.

15*th*. My mind much harassed by many painful circumstances and unpleasant subjects; but this must always be the case in public situations. Keep as much as I can to myself, and took up my dear healthy child, and make myself happy. I am so thankful, too, to see my dear N. so well.

16*th*. Drive to Port Henderson, and take dear little G. – General Carmichael, Captain Maclean, and Mr. Doughty, at breakfast. After they were gone, a nice long morning with my dear N., talking over many affairs, upon some of which he has made my mind quite easy, and I shall

---

[1] In 1805 it was renamed Fort Nugent.

try not to be anxious about any one or any thing, as long as I see my dear husband and baby as well and prosperous as they are at present, thank God!

17th. General N. out with his gun at daylight. I walked in the piazza with my dear little boy, and then amused myself with reading and writing, till breakfast.

20th. Go to church at 10. – Rain came on towards dinner-time; so we had only a snug party, instead of the many we expected. Hear a great deal of myself from Mrs. S. People find fault with me, for having no intimates; but Mrs. Pye has cured me of that, and the only way to keep clear of nonsense and party business is, I am sure, to keep all my confidential talk for my dear N.

21st. Drive, at daylight, both to Dr. Lind's and Dr. McNeil's, and General N. gave them many charges, respecting the sick of our family. All are, however, better to-day, and will, I trust, do well. – Several ladies came to a second breakfast, and Mrs. William Bullock brought two of her children. How injudiciously treated the poor little things are in this country! They are allowed to eat every thing improper, to the injury of their health, and are made truly unamiable, by being most absurdly indulged. I look at all this as a good lesson for our care of dearest little George.

23rd. Only Mr. Sherriff, Drs. McNeil and Adolphus, at breakfast. All our invalids are mending. – Mrs. S. in Spanish Town, visiting all day. I took charge of little Bonella, who was as good and amiable as possible all day.

24th. Take little Grace to Port Henderson, to go on board the *Ganges*, after passing a fortnight here. General Carmichael and Major Darley at breakfast. – Mr. March, Dr. Gallagher, &c. joined the dinner party.

25th. General N. out with his gun at daylight. I was not quite well, and did not drive out as usual. After breakfast, General N. went to Spanish Town, upon business, and I remained quiet. – Only our family at dinner, and about 7 we all drove to Spanish Town, to see Mr. Cussans's exhibition. It was a performance something in the style of Dibdin. We could not help laughing at the nonsense; but, at the same time, it made me melancholy to think, that the folly and extravagance of a person who had been brought up as a gentleman, and who is really of a respectable family, should compel him to expose himself in that way to the public.[1]

---

[1] Charles Dibdin, 1745–1814, was an actor who wrote "Tom Bowling" and other songs, and gave one-man performances in which he sang and accompanied himself

The audience were of all colours and descriptions; blacks, browns, Jews, and whites.

26th. Dress by candle-light, and drive to Port Henderson, the Admiral's barge taking us to Port Royal. A delightful row. The water like glass, and the scene altogether, as the sun rose, sublime. General N. reviewed the 87th, just landed from the *De Ruyter* troop-ship, after which we had a fine breakfast, on board the *Leviathan*. Mrs. Blair and Mrs. S. were the only ladies, besides myself. – The ship was in high order, and we went all over it with Sir J. T. Duckworth, who did the honours himself *beautifully*; but, I believe, we were great bores to the officers and ship's company. The Admiral, General Carmichael, &c. came home with us, and we had a large dinner party. Among the number were Mr. Douglas, just from England, Mr. Quarrell and Mr. Meyler with him, and Mr. and Mrs. Rodon: in all twenty-six.

27th. Admiral Duckworth went at 10 to church with us. After church, made a round of visits with him. – The Chief Justice, and his brother, the Rev. Mr. Kirby, Mr. Millward, Mr. Mitchell, &c. at dinner.

28th. General N. off at 4, for Stony Hill. I had my little George in bed with me till 6, and then got up, to drive with the Admiral to Port Henderson. The Pyes, &c. came to breakfast, and I brought back little Brooke. – Mr. Affleck, a sensible sort of man, came from Manchioneal, to invite General N. to his uncle's house, in that place. Had a long conversation with him, upon education, and get some useful hints about the university part of it, that I shall reflect upon for the sake of my dear Georgy. Mr. A. is a good classic, and, I am told, a very well educated man. He appears so to me at least. – At 5, my dear N. returned to dinner. Halkett, the Attorney-General, and Mrs. Ross, and Major and Mrs. Pye, at dinner. All go away at 9. My dear N. sadly heated, and a little fatigued; but quite well in health, thank God!

March 2nd. Drove out, as usual. – General Carmichael, and Mr. and Miss Ludlow, from America, at breakfast. All went soon after. – The day quiet, and to bed at 8. – Gave little Brooke a severe lecture. He is a naughty boy, and I am in constant terror of some accident happening to him, yet I can't help laughing at his tricks.

"on an instrument which was a concert in itself" *(Dictionary of National Biography).* John Cussans was a nephew of Thomas Cussans (d. 1796) of Amity Hall, in St. Thomas, Jamaica. He was well known in the London theatre world as a clowning character, and the reputed composer of a comic song, Oh, poor Robinson Crusoe!, which he sang "at the Royal Circus and Sadler's Wells with great applause."

3rd. Delightful letters by the packet from all our friends, and General N.'s public despatches most satisfactory.

4th. Still writing English despatches, and General N. too busy to drive out, as the letters are to be sent off by a merchant ship immediately, and not by the regular packet. – Twenty-four people at dinner.

5th. A melancholy day for me; my dear N. so full of business, and so surrounded with visitors, and people coming for orders, that I can scarcely speak to him, and this lasted till the moment of his departure, at 2 o'clock. Had a dull and sad day after, but tried to cheer myself with my little darling. After prayers, I spoke to all the servants, on the subject of their conduct during my dear N.'s absence, and they promised the utmost order and regularity, poor creatures! and I rely upon them.

6th. Went with the whole family into Spanish Town. – Made a visit to Dr. Lind after church. – At dinner, Mr. –, of the *Leviathan*, Dr. Clare, and the Pyes, &c. A delightful letter from my dear N. in the evening. – All my guests stayed for prayers at eight.

7th. In spite of myself, my spirits will sink, and I feel a thousand apprehensions about my dear N., and forebodings that I can't describe. God preserve him, and grant us once more a happy meeting.

8th. This is, thank God, the third day of my dear N.'s absence, and I shall count the hours till we meet again. – The Admiral has, very kindly, given Mrs. S. a little vessel, to take her to Black River, close to her own home. I feel greatly obliged to him for this considerate accommodation, as it will make her and the dear little girl truly comfortable.

9th. All the morning assisting Mrs. S. in the preparations for her little voyage. Dine at 3, and at 5 drive to Port Henderson in the sociable, Mrs. Pye of the party. See Mrs. S. and her little girl safely embarked. Sir J. D.'s boat, and every sort of attention shewn her. – On our return to the Penn, the Pyes, &c. took leave, and we had prayers, and to bed at nine.

10th. Mrs. Pye came to breakfast, and, as she said, out of compassion, to pass the day with me. – Have a lecture to give the young men; Kemble and Browne both very silly, but I keep all their foolish démêlés to myself, and they have promised to think no more of the nonsensical disagreement. Played cassino, &c. with the party till nine. Then prayers, and to bed. – A message in the evening by Major Darley, from General Carmichael, who will be here early to-morrow.

11th. General Carmichael, &c. for the day. – Mr. Morelle, at 11 o'clock, to draw my dear baby, and I hope to surprise General N. with a nice likeness of him, which I mean to send to meet him, across the country. –

Many sketches made, but none of them satisfactory, and I fear, after all, it will be a sad performance. However, not to throw poor Mr. Morelle into despair, sit to him myself, with dear G. on my lap. Am heartily tired of the business, as he kept me till 5 o'clock. General Carmichael, &c. all talking and commenting on the subject. Little G. stared and wondered, but was so good, he was the admiration of every one. Rain came on, just as we were going to dinner, so all the party agreed to sleep here, excepting General C., who returned to Fort Augusta. – A delightful letter from my dear N. before I went to bed. – Next Monday, I shall take my departure for the country, and then we shall meet for a few days at least; and while I remain here I can have no rest, as, out of kindness, people are coming continually, and I shall not be able to avoid a large party every day.

12*th.* It is a week to-day since my dear N. left me, and this day my darling George is five months old. – The morning as usual. – Write a long letter, and tell my dear N. all my plans for our meeting, but don't speak of the portraits, as I hope to surprise him agreeably, for dear Georgie is better represented than I expected. I am an old sharp-nosed fright. – The day as usual; sitting for my picture, and talking, &c. with the young Aides-de-camp.

13*th.* Could not go to church, as the carriage was sent early for Sir John Duckworth, and all were preparing for the journey to-morrow. – Read prayers to the maids in my own room. – The Admiral brought young Baker with him, and he is to be of our party to-morrow. – General Carmichael, Major Darley, Mr. Mitchell, Mr. Edwards, the Pyes, Woodhams, &c. at dinner. Very gay and lively. – The pictures not approved of, and they say that Mr. Morelle has been only a cook. The Admiral, Mr. Baker, and Mr. Kemble slept here.

14*th.* Up at three, and proceed first to the King's House, to give my last directions, and to take the papers lying there for General N. Sir J. Duckworth, nurse, Johnson, and baby, with me in the sociable. Mr. Baker and the Admiral's valet-de-chambre, in a curricle; white George (a German groom), with Mrs. Clifford, in a kittareen; Prince and Peggy in another; then, a white groom, and two black men on horseback before us early, to get all the wains laden with sugar casks out of the way, as they are dangerous to pass on the road, being drawn by oxen; and, lastly, two sumpter mules; forming in all a great cavalcade.

Nothing could be more prosperous than the first part of our journey, till we arrived at Rio Magno. Baby well and merry, and all of us in gay spirits. Just before we came to the river, we met the Speaker, and Mr. Redwood, and Mr. Blackburn, Members of the Assembly.[1] They advised us to lose no time in fording the river, as the water was increasing very much, and, indeed, pouring down from the mountains, quite like a torrent. They kindly turned back with us, as not a moment should be lost, and they directed one of the black men to go before on horseback, as soon as possible, through the most shallow part of the river. They next ordered our sociable to follow, and the rest to proceed in the same line, as quietly as possible. The servant's horse could not well stem the torrent, and it stopped. Ours began to plunge, and the traces were loosened on one side of the wheel horses. The roaring of the water, and the cry of the people, "Go on, go on," made it a most terrific moment. The carriage began to move up and down; the maids wrung their hands; and poor Sir J. Duckworth really turned black. I took the baby to myself, and sat upon the back of the carriage, with my feet upon the seat. All I could do was to call out for some one to take my precious child. Good Mr. Blackburn (I shall never forget him) threw himself into the water, and, by the help of the several carriage wheels, got to the side of the sociable, and held the dear baby above the water with one hand, and making his way with the other, got his precious charge safe to the land. I watched him with my eyes till all was safe, and then I felt as if all the danger was over, though I saw poor Clifford dragged out of the stream half drowned. – Just as I turned to Sir John Duckworth, to say that now we had all our senses about us, and we could save ourselves, good Mr. Blackburn plunged in again, and asked if I would trust myself with him. In an instant we were struggling with the stream, and I must have been a sad weight; but he kept my head above water, and we were soon safe with the dear baby. Sir John Duckworth mounted one of the carriage horses, behind my maid, and Kemble, I believe, behind the nurse; but the confusion was so great they themselves could hardly tell how they got out. It seems that poor Clifford threw herself into the water, and was saved by one of Mr. Blackburn's servants. The groom, &c. &c. were dragged out safe, about a hundred yards down the stream.[2]

The sun was pouring on our heads, and there was no shelter near, except an overseer's half-finished house. A piece of cloth was hung up,

[1] Philip Redwood was himself Speaker at this time, having been elected in place of Kean Osborn in October 1802. There is possibly some confusion in the text.
[2] In 1816 Samuel Whitehorne, Member for St. Ann, was drowned at this fording on his way to Spanish Town to attend the Assembly.

as a screen for the maids and myself. Little George was not at all wet, but so full of fun, that he seemed to enjoy the scene altogether. We laid him on a mat, to kick about, while we washed ourselves with rum, to prevent cold, and the gentlemen did the same, in a sort of half-finished veranda. Our spirituous bath put us all in a glow, and we were advised, each of us, to take half a glass of the same nectar; and after waiting for nearly two hours, it was said the water was rather low, and we all again attempted to pass the Rio Magno. I was mounted on a horse, with four negroes as guides and supports, and got safe through. Darling George was close to me, on a negro's head, and supported by several others. It was a most cruelly anxious sight altogether, and, when it was all safe over, my spirits forsook me, and I fainted. However, a shower of tears soon restored me, and we proceeded on to Berkshire Hall, where we found good Mr. and Mrs. Murphy had sent a chair, and several negroes, to Mr. Vidal's, to carry me and the child to the Hall, which is seven long miles, and chiefly on the edge of a precipice. Poor little fellow, he was so heated and fatigued, that he cried sadly, which delayed and distressed us all very much. He was so thirsty, that he wanted his nurse continually; so I put her into the chair with him, and mounted my horse, and then, thank God! before 7 o'clock, we were all safe and well at the Decoy. – In the evening, our treasure was so well and lively, that I lost all apprehension about him, and sent off an express to General N. to let him know how prosperous we all were, for fear of evil reports reaching him. – Thank God all well; to bed at ten.

15*th*. Could not sleep all night, for the roaring of waters in my ears; but no one was ill, thank God; and as for myself, my strength and spirits are the astonishment of every one. – Pass a most comfortable and quiet day, with only the party in the house.

16*th*. Rain all day. Very comfortable in the house.

17*th*. The Admiral off early in the morning. Send off my despatch to General N. – The day sociable and comfortable.

19*th*. This day fortnight my dear N. left me. It appears a month, and how I long to see him again. – Receive delightful letters from him, and write him a full account of the progress and improvement of our dear baby. – Quiet, and to bed soon after nine.

20*th*. As there is no church near, send little George to walk, and pass the time myself till breakfast in reading. – Prayers at 11 o'clock in the dining-room. – Have a nice letter from my dear N. On Thursday I shall see him at the Ramble, and have the delight of shewing him how much our darling is improved. – Dine at 3. Walk in the garden, and have a syllabub, as usual.

22nd. Up early, and started, soon after breakfast, for the Ramble. Baby with me in a chair; the rest on horseback. Stopped at Pembroke Hall a short time, and then complete our journey, about ten miles, before 3 o'clock. Found two long letters from my dear husband, and both so affectionate, and so full of anxiety about the effects of our water disaster, that I cried like a ninny, and made my eyes so red, I was half ashamed to shew myself at dinner. Only Messrs. Henry and Whitehorne, in addition to our party. My baby well, and looking beautiful, with his fair skin and bright *purple* eyes.

23rd. At 2 o'clock my dear N. arrived, and quite well, thank God! but has gone through much fatigue, and run several risks, from bad roads, &c. – He was delighted with little G.'s improvement; though, at first, the little darling cried, and would not go to him; but he soon seemed to recollect his voice, and laughed and patted his face, as if to make up for his unkind reception; and to shew that he did then remember him.

25th. Spend the morning with my dear N. who has much writing, and we remained almost entirely in our own room till dinner. Then walk afterwards, see the sugar making, and amuse ourselves till eight.

28th. General N. off early, to review the St. Mary's militia. The day quiet. The gentlemen did not return till 7. Mr. Grant and Captain Macintosh, of the 85th, had joined the party, and dined here.

29th. Ride to the cottage, about a mile off. Have the baby taken there, and General N. and I walked with him back, by a shorter road. – Dine at 4: Captain Marlton of the 60th, two Messrs. Minott, and Mr. Fitzgerald, in addition to our party. – Messrs. Henry and Whitehorne off for St. Ann's, to prepare for General N.'s reception there; for, alas! he must renew his tour to-morrow.

30th. At 12 my dear N. left us. A dreary day indeed to me. – A servant came back in the evening, with a little despatch, to say he was safe over the worst part of the road to St. Ann's Bay.

31st. A wet morning. Had a long conversation with Mr. Murphy, upon public matters. Most of it will, I am sure, be useful to my dear N.; so I shall keep it in store for our meeting, as I don't like to write upon such subjects. – After 10 o'clock to-day, the weather was fine, and much cooler for the rain in the morning. Rejoice on General N.'s account, as he reviews the St. Ann's militia to-day.

April 4th. Set off to return to the Decoy at 9. – Take a second breakfast at Mr. Mason's, and get to the Decoy to dine.

6th. Walk early; breakfast at 7; dine at 3. – Take syllabub, and swing in the garden.

7th. After dinner explore the negro houses. Most of them neat, and very comfortable, with poultry, &c. &c. about them.

8th. *Good Friday*. – Prayers at 11. – This day (as many lately past) has been one of much reflection and seriousness to me, for which, I trust, I shall be all the better in future.

9th. Walk in the garden with little G., and then breakfast at half-past six. – Prince returned from Spanish Town, and brought the portraits. Alas! the day as usual.

10th. A pioneer, with letters from my dear N. early this morning.[1]

12th. This day my baby is six months old, and there cannot be a finer creature; so fat and fair, and so full of health and spirits. God bless him. It is also Miss Murphy's birthday, and we shall make it a day of rejoicing. – Very merry, and to bed at eight.

13th. Young Baker left us, to join the Admiral.

14th. Doctor Hanson joined the party.

15th. A great deal of talk with Mr. Murphy, about black corps, &c. Treasure it all up for my dear N., that he may know general opinions on the subject.

17th. Mr. and Mrs. Whitehorne, with their two children, and Miss Henry, Captain Johnson, and Mr. Browne, arrived just as we were taking our second breakfast in the piazza. – Dine at 5. – The ladies in white and silver at dinner, and the children all over beads; the party exceedingly smart. – Made many observations on Creole education, and pity the poor things, for being so stuffed with all sorts of unwholesome food.

18th. Did not sit down to breakfast till 9, the ladies being so long making their toilette. They seem to bestow much pains and attention to their dress, and examine me most minutely. – A dance in the evening, in which I joined *politically*, and do all that I can to be *agreeable* till 10, and then am really so much fatigued, that I am obliged to go to bed.[2] – Heard this evening of the death of poor nurse's child; poor soul! I am

[1] Pioneers were a slave labour corps, hired out by Government to the army. A few were regularly employed as postal carriers between Spanish Town and Port Henderson, etc.

[2] Thomas Murphy, Mrs. Nugent's host at the Decoy, and Charles Grant, the other Member for St. Mary's, had been "considered as the Heads of a democratic Party in the Assembly, & Leaders of the Opposition to Lord Balcarres . . . I courted the two latter

indeed distressed for her, and don't know how I shall be able to break the sad news to her.

19th. Intended to return to Spanish Town to-day, but the rain prevented me, and I am not sorry; for thinking of poor nurse's affairs kept me awake and I am far from well to-day. Towards the middle of the day make up my mind to let her know the sad tidings.

20th. Nurse came to my room early to-day, with a much more cheerful countenance than I had dared to expect, and I am really grateful to her for the effort she evidently makes, to conquer her own feelings, on account of my precious boy. – Captain Palmer joined our party to-day, and gives so favourable an account of the roads, that I hope to return home to-morrow. I danced one *political* dance to-night, and got to bed soon after.

21st. A sad tropical rain, this morning, prevented my thinking of moving to-day; for the precipice roads must be so very dangerous. – Another dance in the evening.

22nd. The weather fine, and the report of the roads so favourable, that I set off for Spanish Town, soon after 8. The Misses Murphy, &c. with me. All rode down to Berkshire Hall; little George in the chair part of the time, and behaving delightfully. Got home soon after 6, all well. Had a most comfortable dinner, and a letter from my dear husband; and all went to rest, with minds at ease, excepting, I fear, poor nurse, in whose eyes I saw tears as we passed on to the Penn from Spanish Town, near to where her little boy died. I could not help remarking to-day, the number of servants attending the Misses Murphy and myself. There were no less than twenty, independently of my white maids.

23rd. Rise at 6, but don't drive out. A letter from the Admiral, asking for carriages for himself, the Blairs, &c. to-morrow; and spend the day as well as sleep. – Only Major Maitland and Dr. McNeil, in addition to our party to-day.

24th. Could not go to church, on account of sending the carriages for the Admiral, &c. The Admiral, Mr. and Mrs. Blair, General Carmichael, Major Darley, Major Maitland, and Dr. Clare; in all a large party. All in high spirits. – Prayers in the evening; the Admiral, the Blairs, &c. remaining. The rest went away at 9. – Heard of the arrival of the packet, and my spirits were rather lowered, by the reports of the renewal of the war, &c.

Gentlemen in order to break up their Party, which has succeeded to my Wish" (Nugent to Hobart, 28 June 1802).

25th. Admiral D. &c. left us. The Blairs remained till after dinner. Then, sent them on to Spanish Town in the chariot.

26th. A note from my dear N. to say that he will certainly be at home by 7 or 8 this evening. Order the servants a fête in consequence, and, with the assistance of the Misses Murphy, make all my preparations in the best manner. Dined with the gentlemen of the family, before 3, and immediately after take our stations in the piazza, to see the blackies enjoy themselves.

A long table was spread on the green, with all their most favourite dishes, of barbecued hog, jerked hog, pepper-pot, yams, plantains, &c. There were tubs of punch, and each of them had three glasses of Madeira, to drink three toasts – "Massa Gubernor, and Missis, and little Massa"– all of which were drank with three times three, by the men, women and children, and their sweethearts. The little children were all allowed a little sip, out of the grown up people's glasses.

As soon as that ceremony was over, I began the ball with an old negro man. The gentlemen each selected a partner, according to rank, by age or service, and we all danced. However, I was not aware how much I shocked the Misses Murphy by doing this; for I did exactly the same as I would have done at a servants' hall birthday in England. They told me, afterwards, that they were nearly fainting, and could hardly forbear shedding a flood of tears, at such an unusual and extraordinary sight; for in this country, and among slaves, it was necessary to keep up so much more distant respect! They may be right. I meant nothing wrong, and all the poor creatures seemed so delighted, and so much pleased, that I could scarcely repent it. I was, nevertheless, very sorry to have hurt their feelings, and particularly too as they seemed to think the example dangerous; as making the blacks of too much consequence, or putting them at all on a footing with the whites, they said, might make a serious change in their conduct, and even produce a rebellion in the island.

But to proceed with my fête. – I had people on the look-out for the arrival of my dear N., and about 8 o'clock his approach was announced. I then marched at the head of the whole party, with little George in my arms, to meet him; the music playing, "God save the King." As he got out of his carriage to join us, we saluted him, with three cheers. Dear Georgy was at first a little frightened with the noise and bustle, but he soon began to laugh, and appeared to enjoy all that was going forwards, as if he understood the whole thing. We had a little supper in the piazza. The blackies resumed their dancing, and kept up their gaiety the greatest part of the night.

27th. Rise early, and all well and happy, to be once more settled at home. – General Carmichael, Major Darley, and the staff, at dinner.

28th. At dinner, Colonel Roberts, Mr. Hanbury, Major Cookson, and Major and Mrs. Ottley, with Drs. Gallagher and McNeil, Major F. and M. Grandjean, made a large party.

29th. Little Grace came to breakfast, and to take leave for England. Mr. Ince arrived from St. Domingo. He belongs to the 55th, and has just escaped from the brigands. He gives a most dreadful account of the state of that island.[1]

30th. General N. full of business in Spanish Town, almost the whole day. – Only Mr. Steel, of the 87th, at dinner.

May 1st. To church at 10, with the Misses Murphy, &c. Young Grace went early on board the *Ganges*, to sail for England. Gave him a letter to dear Lady Temple. Wish we could all have gone with him to England.

2nd. Sent the maids to Kingston, and drove out, with nurse and my little treasure, to Port Henderson. Began again to bathe him in the sea. They tell me it is good for him, but it is a sad ordeal. – General Carmichael, Major Darley, and Major and Mrs. Ottley, at dinner. – Young Stewart arrived, with letters from his father. A most unpromising young man in appearance, but, for Colonel Stewart's sake, General N. will do all he can to serve him.

3rd. The Admiral and Mr. Conolly were sent for early. – Dinner at 4. – General N. full of business, and I amusing our guests as well as I can.

4th. At this season of the year we are really tormented with ants. My dressing table covered. My bason, jugs and goblets, full of them, and nothing can be more disgusting or distressing. – Only Mr. Parsons at breakfast and dinner.

5th. Set off, with the Misses Murphy, at daylight, for the Admiral's Penn. A large party assembled there, to breakfast. The heat and dust intolerable to-day. All the morning talking with Mrs. Blair and the ladies, but thinking of my dear little Georgy at home. – An immense dinner party. – Had a bath from a large glass of water spilt over me. My ball dress all dripping. Return to the company in my dressing-gown, not to lose

---

[1] Lt. Ince, whose ship had been driven ashore near Tiburon, had been kept a prisoner by the indigenous forces and claimed to have gathered valuable information by feigning ignorance of French.

time to dress after dinner. Danced three couples only. Did not get to bed till 12. – Long to get home again.

6th. Set off for the Penn at daylight, by a new, short, and most beautiful road. – My sweet babe quite well, and seeming almost as glad to see me as I was to see him once more. General N. loaded with business of all sorts, but particularly about St. Domingo. – The day quiet, and happy as it can be while we see him so harassed. This is a sad drawback to my comfort, but, thank God, his health does not appear to suffer.

7th. A day of trouble. – The Spanish Town election took place. Mr. Mitchell, Mr. Redwood, and Mr. Falconer, chosen; Mr. Cuthbert thrown out.[1] – General N. less occupied, and more with me, the latter part of the day; so we enjoyed talking over affairs, and playing with dear little G. together. In the evening, the young people played Pope Joan, and *we* walked most sociably in the piazza.

8th. To church at 10. – To the King's House afterwards, where General N. settled some business. Dine at 4. – A visit from the Duchess of Port Royal. Make her a present, as usual; and these presents are, I find, rather a heavy tax; for all my prettiest things go that way.

9th. Send the Misses Murphy into Spanish Town, to make visits, and pass the morning with their friends.

10th. At breakfast, Mr. F. Smith, Mr. Lawson, and Mr. Stevenson. Only Mr. Lawson remained for dinner. – At 8, went with our young ladies to a ball, given in Spanish Town by Mrs. Ramsay. – Danced one dance. Was much amused by a great deal of nonsense, and ashamed of laughing so much.

11th. A despatch at daylight, to tell General N. of the arrival of some French officers, with some communications from St. Domingo. Send off carriages for them immediately, but the wind coming on to blow almost a hurricane, prevented their landing, and at 5 the carriages returned empty.

12th. Send young Stewart to Port Henderson, to go on board the *Dési-rée* frigate. – The Admiral came to breakfast, but left us soon after, to return to Port Royal. Then came General Carmichael, &c. for orders. – All in a fuss about the news from St. Domingo. The French officers were sent for again, and four of them made their appearance at 3 o'clock. After a little discussion with General N., dinner was ordered, and the conversa-

---

[1] There was a general election, since the Assembly, elected in 1796, had completed its term of seven years. The result of the poll (for St. Catherine's Parish) in Spanish Town was: Redwood, 101; Mitchell, 93; Falconer, 65; Cuthbert, 55.

tion was unusually lively and gay, though how they could keep it up with such spirit I cannot imagine, after all the horrors they have been witness to in St. Domingo. But they are light-hearted Frenchmen. The gaiety on our part was assumed, and in a certain degree political, to prevent the introduction of serious subjects, as they have come (poor souls!) to ask for assistance that cannot be granted to them; and, in short, my poor dear N. is in a sadly embarrassing situation with them and their affairs. When little G. was brought in to them, *to be admired*, after dinner, he amused us all very much, by the profound attention he paid when the Frenchmen spoke, and then saying, *Mo, Mo,* which appeared as if he asked to hear more; and this, in fact, was the case, as nurse has taught him this word, and he makes use of it, as a signal to repeat any thing he likes. – After dinner, we had coffee in the piazza, and then got rid of our French friends, as soon as we could.

13*th*. A refreshing breeze, at 5 this morning, which they say portends the continuance of the May rains, which have never fairly set in, and the last two days we have had nice showers, regularly at the same hour. General N. full of business all day.

14*th*. An officer from Antigua, with despatches, and brought an account of the *De Ruyter* troop-ship having put in there in distress. Left the *Trent* at sea, in even a worse condition, and much fear is consequently entertained for her safety; as she was, according to the sailor's phrase, less seaworthy, when she left Port Royal, than the *De Ruyter*, though not so old a ship.

16*th*. Have a conversation with Dr. McNeil, on the subject of Dr. Clare, and decide upon having the attendance of the latter. – Drive to Port Henderson.

18*th*. Rise at daylight. Bathe my boy at Port Henderson. – Mr. and Mrs. Woodham brought their little girl, four years old, to breakfast. Measured George with her, and, except in height, he is much the largest; but she is the most puny thing I ever saw, and all from bad nursing and improper food, I am sure. – A large party of gentlemen at breakfast, and all upon business. As soon as General N. could get away, he mounted his horse, in spite of the broiling sun, and rode to Spanish Town, having apppointed to meet many gentlemen of the country there, on particular business. – Captain Loring, and another Captain of the Navy, Mr. and Mrs. Ross, Mr. Stevenson, &c. at dinner. Before we parted for the night, I gave Captain Johnson a good deal of advice, about precipitate marriages, but I don't think it will do any good.

19*th*. Drive early to Mrs. Tonge's Penn, and see her little baby, but don't get home till 7, when the heat was so overcoming, that we were all subdued, and I am determined not to be out so late again. Mr. Smith, recommended by Lord Fingal, dined with us.

25*th*. My dear N. still harassed with business, and in the Court of Chancery; and I shall be on the *qui vive* till it is all over. At 5, a large dinner party. – Mr. and Miss Millward, Attorney-General, and Mrs. Ross, Doctors Clare, Brodbelt, and Adolphus, Major Maitland, General Carmichael, and Major Darley, &c.

26*th*. Mrs. Rodon and two Misses Rennalls at breakfast. Sent for the Admiral, Captain Dunn, &c. – General N. in Spanish Town all the morning, but joined our party at 4. Mr. Campbell and Captain and Mrs. Lomax, at dinner also.

27*th*. The Admiral and Captain Dunn set off, at 5 for Port Royal. General N. went out with his gun. – Most of our family dined at the Ferry House, on the Kingston road, and our dinner party was very small.

29*th*. The Misses Murphy did not go out. Mr. Woodham ill, and no church service. Assemble the family, and read prayers at 10. Duckworth and Rogers in great disgrace, and have a severe lecture from General N. They dined yesterday at Fort Augusta, and returned home in such a state that they are absolutely objects to-day; they having their faces cut and scratched, by making their way through the fences, it is supposed, not being able to find the direct road. In fact, it is quite a mercy they were not both killed.

About 2 o'clock, there was an alarm of fire, the sun having caught the penguin fence, that separates the guinea-grass field from the lawn. All the neighbouring Penns sent assistance, the instant that one of our blacks blew the shell,[1] and it was soon got under; though the grass and everything were so dry, that they seemed to burn like touchwood. The poor rabbits[2] ran out of the fence by dozens, and many of them were half roasted; and, in short, it was a scene of great confusion. While the servants were engaged in the field, we were very near being burnt in the house; for Monsieur Baptiste left his kitchen, and ran out with the rest to assist, and during his absence, a log of wood fell out of the fire, and burned several

---

[1] "The [conch] is not only the instrument of calling the negroes to their labour, but being sounded in a particular tone is the signal of alarm, either for fire or rebellion" (Anon., *A short journey to the West Indies*, 1790).
[2] Richard Hill, quoted in P. Gosse, *A naturalist's sojourn in Jamaica*, 1851, says that this is the earliest reference he could find to wild rabbits in the neighbourhood of Spanish Town.

articles, and the house would certainly have been the sacrifice, if one of the maids had not fortunately smelt the fire, and had the courage to run in, and pull out all the burning linen, &c.; which, with the aid of a few buckets of water, soon set all right again. At dinner, only General Carmichael and Major D. with our own party. The disgraced gentlemen did not make their appearance till quite late in the evening.

30th. The day as usual. – The gentlemen of the family, excepting Duckworth and Rogers, all dined on board the *Leviathan; they* stayed at home with us quietly, to hide their *scratches.* The young ladies helped to console them, and the evening was very sociable.

31st. Rain, with thunder and lightning, the greatest part of the night. Thank God for it! It has cooled the air very much, and I feel particularly happy and comfortable, in consequence. – General N., for a wonder, made use of the chariot, to go into Spanish Town to-day, it rained so very heavily; but his business pressed; Chancery, &c. ,&c.

June 1st. A Mr. Black, from Ireland, with letters. – Mr. Waterhouse, too, upon business.

2nd. Poor Varty died this morning. – The Misses Murphy were afraid of the damp air. Mr. Clement, from America, Mrs. Dolmage, and Mrs. Ramsay, dined with us. A great deal of Creole conversation, and many prejudices that amused me, but I cannot enter into them.

3rd. A delightful though very hot morning. – My dear N. closed the Court of Chancery for this quarter, at 4 o'clock. Only Major Otway, of the 85th, at dinner.

4th. Rejoice that my dear N. has no Chancery business to-day. He has, however, to hold a levée at the King's House, at 1, and to give a grand dinner, in honour of his Majesty's birthday. – General C., Major D., &c. at breakfast, and to attend General N. into Spanish Town. Salutes were fired, and all manner of respect shewn on the occasion, but I remained quietly with the Misses M. at the Penn.

5th. No service again to-day. – Read prayers to the family, as usual. Colonel Roberts, Captain and Mrs. Emmerson, and a Miss Kempsey, came from Stony Hill to dine. – General N. closed and sent off his despatches for England.

6th. Send the young ladies and gentlemen into Spanish Town, in the sociable, &c.; they brought back a large party of the Murphy family to dinner; Mr. and Mrs. M., with their daughter Eliza, having arrived there yesterday.

7th. Mr. and Mrs. Murphy join our breakfast party, and the ladies remained with me all the morning. The rest accompanied General N. to town, as this is his first audience day.

8*th*. Major and Mrs. Ottley, and Dr. McNeil, at dinner.

9*th*. Mr. C. Grant and the Murphy family at dinner. – In the evening, had to settle a dispute between the young gentlemen. Made them mutually apologize, and shake hands; but Miss Murphy is playing a foolish and girlish part, which adds much to these misunderstandings. Give her some good advice.

10*th*. General N. out with his gun at daylight. I had to rest, as I have some fatigue to encounter to-day; but the musquitoes were more intolerable than ever. They are indeed in such swarms, that it took more than an hour last night to get them out of my darling George's net, who could not sleep for their tormenting him. When, just as we thought all was safe, close to his cot crept out a large centipede, and renewed all my distress and anxiety about him. – The Admiral, and a large party, at breakfast; and at 4, an immense dinner party. The Murphy family, Mr. Minott, Mr. Henry, Mr. Headlam, Captain Cottrell, R.N., &c. – At 7, a crowd came from Spanish Town, and we had a dance till 11, when a supper was laid in the back piazza, and it was near 1 before they all dispersed. – The officers of the 85th, and the whole of the Murphy family, remaining here; but all sadly crowded, I am afraid.

11*th*. Colonels Lethbridge and Turner, of Vere, with the family, made our party to-day. – The musquitoes intolerable.

12*th*. Drive to Port Henderson, and bathe dear Georgy; but the sea was turbulent, and I was rather unhappy. Breakfast before 8. – Mr. and Mrs. Murphy, with their family, and some of ours, dine at Mr. Rodon's. We had a snug party of ten. – Only Captain Cottrell and Dr. McNeil, with ourselves, and the disengaged part of the staff, at dinner.

13*th*. Send carriages, soon after 5, into Spanish Town, for the Murphy family, who slept there. Soon after breakfast, General N. set off with Mr. M. in the curricle, to visit the estates between this and Kingston, called the Camoens.[1] – After second breakfast, Mrs. and the Misses Murphy with me in the sociable. The rest of the party in kittareens, phaetons, and on horseback, all proceeded to the Ferry Inn, to meet the Admiral and a large party at dinner. We had sent on to order the dinner, a few days before, and all that Jamaica produces was ready to be served up. The poor Admiral, however, was so overcome, with fatigue and the heat of the day,

---

[1] Caymanas.

that he was quite ill, and obliged to leave the table. In consequence, we all separated early. Mr. and Mrs. M. went with the Admiral, and are to be his guests till Wednesday. I took my seat in the curricle with General N., and all our young people went in the sociable; and really, if it had not been for Sir J. T. Duckworth's illness, it would have been a merry party. As it was, I was much entertained; for the Inn is situated on the road, between Kingston and Spanish Town, and it was very diverting to see the odd figures, and extraordinary equipages, constantly passing – kittareens, sulkies, mules, and donkeys. – Then a host of gentlemen, who were taking their *sangaree* in the piazza; and their vulgar buckism amused me very much. Some of them got half tipsy, and then began petitioning me for my interest with *his Honour* – to redress the grievance of one, to give a place to another, and so forth; in short, it was a picture for Hogarth. – When we got home, a packet had arrived, announcing the certainty of a war. – I had a merry hour with the young ladies and gentlemen, who are all good friends now, and in high spirits.

14*th*. Receive private letters, and all delightful. – General N.'s audience day. – Mine spent with dear baby. – Captain Lawson, Mr. Vidal, and Major Codd, at dinner.

15*th*. My dear N. so harassed with business, that he is very unwell, and I tremble for his health; this keeps me in a state of the greatest anxiety, for fear it should be seriously affected. – Only General C. in addition to our party.

16*th*. General N. too unwell to join the breakfast party. I drove out with the Murphy family, and then had eighteen people to breakfast with me. Amongst them was a Mr. D'Arcy, from Cork, recommended by Baron Hussey, &c. &c. General N. joined the dinner party, but felt so unwell he left the table, and I rejoined him, when they all went, and I could be with him. Dr. McNeil says, however, he has no fever, and only requires quiet. Thank God!

17*th*. General N. had a much better night, but is still far from well; and, contrary to Dr. McNeil's advice, would go into Spanish Town, as this is his audience day. – It is said that much mischief is brewing in the country, and that it is connected with the St. Domingo French, &c.; but all this is secret information, and must be enquired into privately. – An old acquaintance of General N.'s arrived to-day – a Mr. Brent. He, with Mr. Codd, and the Doctors, and our staff, made up the dinner party to-day. – In the evening, I drove, with the Murphy family and dear Georgy, into Spanish Town. Mr. and Mrs. Murphy, with their daughter Mary, remained there,

on their way to the Decoy. The other two ladies returned with me. –
Prayers, and to bed at 9. – Heard from my dear N. that there was much
further information respecting the plots, but still all is very obscure. He
is, however, thank God! much better, and I try to keep my mind at ease.

18*th*. Think all night of the late discoveries, and fear this wretched
country is devoted to the same destruction that has overtaken St. Domingo. Should anything decidedly take place, we have agreed that my best
plan would be to go on board ship, and remain there till after my confinement; but I will not think about it, in my present helpless state, but
hope and trust all will yet be well. – General N. still complaining, and so
full of business of all sorts, that we scarcely meet a minute in the day, except at meals.

19*th*. No service in the church to-day, Mr. Woodham being absent at
Port Royal, on account of health. Read prayers to the family in the back
piazza.

20*th*. Drove to Major Cookson's Penn, and returned before 6. After
breakfast, heard Bessy and Becky their prayers and catechism, &c.

21*st*. This is General N.'s audience day, and he is very busy all the mor-
ning. Messrs. Sherriff and Perry, and Mr. and Mrs. Rennalls, from Up-
Park, the Admiral, and Captain Loring, at dinner. – Many people ill in
Spanish Town, about whom I am very anxious. – Mr. Campbell, Dr.
McNeil, &c. Hear better accounts of them this evening; and go to bed
more comfortable.

22*nd*. About 12, an express from Port Royal. The *Hunter* brig arrived
with the news of war with France and Holland. This obliged the Admiral
to leave us, and put us all in a fuss; for the certainty of war with France,
just now, adds much to our embarrassments here. God protect us!

23*rd*. The day as usual with me, all but my being with poor N. – Only
Mr. Younghusband, of the Artillery, recommended by Mr. Addington, in
addition to our party.

24*th*. General N.'s audience day. – At 5 o'clock a large dinner party;
among which were officers of the 85th and 2nd West India regiments, &c.
Messrs. Sherriff and Robertson, &c. Asked Mr. S. for his vote for Mr.
Lyon, as Agent for the Island, and hope to get it.[1] – Some of the 85th
stayed for prayers.

25*th*. General N. set off early in the curricle, for Kingston. At 1, I fol-

---

[1] Edmund Pusey Lyon, a nephew of William Mitchell, succeeded Robert Sewell as
Agent for Jamaica in London in 1803. The Agent was elected by a joint conference
of the Assembly and Council.

lowed in the sociable, with the Misses Murphy, to meet him at the Admiral's Penn, to celebrate Mr. Duckworth's birthday. – A large party; very merry, dancing, &c. The heat, however, was dreadful, and I got to bed as soon as I could.

26th. The Admiral had given notice to the clergyman at Kingston, that we should attend the service; otherwise I would not have gone, for we were obliged to pass close by the pole, on which was stuck the head of the black man who was executed a few days ago.[1] We came so late, that we found all the congregation had been waiting a long time for us. The church is pretty, and well fitted up, but the service was miserably performed, by a *Scotch* reader, and a *Welsh* preacher. The latter is the vicar. The other, a respectable looking old man, who is curate, bears an excellent character, and General N. says he will give him a living, as soon as possible. I own I made interest for him. After the service, we had to run the gauntlet quite, for a lane was formed from our pew to the carriage door, and all were standing still till we passed; not a very comfortable exhibition to me at present, with my round-about figure, in a high wind. After church, General N. went to inspect the messing of the regiment, in the King's barrack. The Admiral and the ladies returned with me to the Penn. At 5, a dinner party. – Little George made his appearance both before and after dinner, and was the admiration of every one.

27th. General N. off with the whole staff to Stony Hill, to inspect the 85th, who give him a grand dinner to-day. – The Admiral and my party all dined at Mrs. Griffiths'. The heat wonderful, and nearly intolerable, and we managed to get away at 9. – General N. almost at the same moment, at the Penn. – The Admiral went to-day on board the Spanish ships of war, to invite the officers to dine with him to-morrow, and we also have asked them for Wednesday.

28th. Returned to the Penn. – General N. remained in Spanish Town, this being his audience day. I should explain, that these audience days are to prevent so many people coming constantly to the Penn upon business, and it answers perfectly well.

---

[1] The *St. Jago de la Vega Gazette* of June 18–25 reported: "Monday last a Slave Court was held in the Court House in Kingston, when two negro men named *Fidelle* alias *Dundo* and *Goodluck* (the former belonging to Mr. Solomon Flash and the latter to Mr. Joseph Cantelow), were tried for forming a rebellious Conspiracy; of which being found guilty after a long trial, and on the clearest evidence, they were sentenced to be hanged by the neck on the Parade of Kingston, their heads severed from their bodies and placed on poles – one on the Slipe Pen Road, the other on that adjoining the City, leading to Windward: which sentence was accordingly put in execution on Tuesday."

29th. The morning as usual till 9, when the Admiral and his party came, and soon after the Spanish Commodore and his suite; for we had sent carriages for them all to Port Henderson. There were six Spaniards, and we had a very pleasant and lively dinner party. Two or three of them spoke French, and translated for the others. – General N. made them happy by speaking Spanish, which they insisted upon, and spoke rather with disgust of the frivolity of the French. Then we discussed matrimony; which seemed most particularly to interest the Commodore, who, like all old bachelors, is fond of talking of a wife; though they never mean to have one. They all smoked their cigars, and, after coffee, set off again, so happy that we heard them begin to sing, as soon as the carriage drove off. Captain Cottrell, &c. then took their leave, and we all retired to rest. Only the Admiral slept here.

30th. The Admiral off at daylight. Only Mr. Woodham and Mr. Craskell to-day, in addition to our usual party

July 1st. Messrs. Edwards and Baillie, and Major and Mrs. Ottley, at breakfast. The two latter remained, but Messrs. E. and B. accompanied General N. to his audience. – Young Stewart drawing bills, and proving himself worthless, to our great annoyance. – Mr. Lawrance, of the Navy, is also in disgrace. Write to the Admiral respecting him, who will shew him all the favour his case will admit of.

2nd. General N. very busy all day with English despatches, &c. Have the Rev. Mr. and Mrs. Ledwich, and Messrs. Brent and Kemble, from Kingston.

3rd. General N. received an express, from Mr. Henry of St. Mary's Parish, with an account of several negroes having suddenly disappeared, from the different estates in that neighbourhood, and that from his own place fifteen had gone off at once. This is indeed alarming, and especially when coupled with the late intelligence of a conspiracy, &c. God preserve us from the horrors of an insurrection! To church at 10. Not well the whole time, and my mind harassed by the sad reports of the morning. – At 5, a large dinner party. – The Woodhams, Captain Craskell, Mr. Brent, Mr. William Murphy, &c. – Feel sadly low, but was rather comforted after dinner, by General Carmichael's account of the state of the country, and the observations he had made on his little tour, from which he returned this morning only, and has spent all the day at the Penn. To bed in rather better spirits, about the state of opinions on the subject.

4th. The Misses Murphy set off at 6 to-day for the Decoy, escorted by their brother and some of our young men.

5th. General N.'s audience day. He is much occupied with the situation of this Government, both externally and internally. We drove early to Major Cookson's Penn.

6th. Get up at half-past four, after an almost sleepless night, thinking of the state of this wretched country. The heat, too, most overpowering. Drive with General N. and dear Georgy as far as Port Henderson, where we were met by General Carmichael, Major Darley, and the staff, and they all proceeded to Fort Augusta, while I returned to the Penn. – Ordered my solitary breakfast in the boudoir, which I have lately made in the piazza. Mr. Parsons came, but I ordered his breakfast in the dining room, and did not admit Colonel Irvine, who also came to breakfast, but sent him to join Mr. Parsons. General N., &c. returned in a most dreadful heat, their faces quite scarlet, and their hair black with perspiration.

7th. From the reports to-day, the country appears in a sad state, and there is every reason to think, that the French have their emissaries among us. God protect us! I try to support myself, but my spirits are at times deeply affected. Yet I must bear up, for the sake of my dearest N., whose cares would be greatly increased by my alarms.

8th. A night of terror and anxiety, but I must not give way, for the sake of my dear N. and all around me. – We had a nice drive round the race-course early; and after breakfast, General N. full of business, as usual, in Spanish Town. – General Carmichael, Mr. Wm. Murphy, Kemble, &c. at dinner.

9th. A most awful night. For several hours the sky was quite a sheet of fire, and the thunder came, peal on peal, with scarcely a second between them. The house shook so that the servants declared it was an earthquake. We intended to breakfast with the Admiral, but sent off an express, to prevent him from waiting for us, and mean to go to dinner. – Dearest little G. slept though the whole storm and is perfectly well this morning. – Soon after 10, set off for the Admiral's Penn. At dinner, the Spanish Commodore, two French naval commanders, General Morgan, and his two Aides-de-camp, with the Admiral's and our families made the party. – In the evening, played cards, and had a great deal of conversation with the French General,[1] upon his sufferings, and the present state of St. Domingo. – To bed at 10, and certainly not in high spirits with all I have heard to-day.

---

[1] General Morgan, who had been intercepted at sea on his way from Cap François to take command in the south of Saint-Domingue.

10*th*. Returned home. – Only private prayers to-day. – Only the Woodhams and the staff at dinner. A storm threatening, they all dispersed very early. Had prayers directly, and were in bed when the gun fired for 8 o'clock.

11*th*. The heat dreadful. – General N. read prayers to me very early, and we then walked with little G. in the piazza, till breakfast time. – At one, sent a carriage to Port Henderson, for Sir J. Duckworth, Captain Bayntun, &c.; and at 3, the sociable for the French gentlemen. At 5, our party were all assembled; Messrs. Scott, Mitchell and Edwards, the civilians; General Carmichael, and Colonel Lethbridge, the military; then the Spanish Commodore, and his officers. I was the only lady, as usual, but the dinner was exceedingly cheerful. In the evening an express, with an account of the taking of St. Lucia and Tobago, by our troops, and decided hostilities with the French. For the first few minutes General Morgan, &c. seemed to feel a little, but, like true Frenchmen, soon recovered their spirits; and I am sure are glad to be prisoners, and to have nothing to do with all these disasters. – At 10, we sent them all to Spanish Town, where we had provided beds for them at Charlotte Beckford's, and the Admiral with Captain Bayntun remained here.

12*th*. Send carriages into Spanish Town for the gentlemen, who all arrive to breakfast by 8. An immense crowd and three tables laid; fruit, wines, &c. and the gentlemen all took their bottle of claret, in addition to coffee, and the usual breakfast. Much discussion between General N., the Admiral, and General Morgan, on the subject of the French officers being on their parole in Spanish Town, instead of Kingston. General N. does not quite approve of the arrangement, but so I believe it is to be. I don't like General Morgan, he appears so inimical and designing, notwithstanding all that has been done to make him comfortable; and indeed seems to be a real enemy to every thing English, though he affects to profess the reverse. – Tuesday being General N.'s audience day, he made an early move, and the whole party accompanied him to Spanish Town.

15*th*. Both of us had a restless night. – Drive to Port Henderson at daylight. – General N. reviewed the 2nd West India regiment.

16*th*. Wrote letters, in favour of Mr. Lyon, and sent a present to Mrs. Sherriff, which will, I hope, secure Mr. S.'s vote. – Mrs. Skinner, with her little girl, and Miss Williams, came at 1, with a cavalcade of blackies. Her brother, Mr. W., soon after.

17*th*. Go to church at 10. At dinner, the Woodhams, and Major and

Mrs. Lomax, in addition to our party. – Mr. W. read the prayers this evening, and General N. has given Mrs. Woodham's brother, Mr. Craskell, the fort at the Apostles' battery; so all were well pleased.

18*th*. Drive out early with Georgy and the ladies. – Sad accounts from St. Domingo. – General N. full of business all day. General N., Major D., and the Grandjeans, at dinner.

19*th*. A sad night. Those poor wretches in St. Domingo prey upon my spirits. – The morning as usual. – Colonel Roberts, a Mr. Nugent from the north of Ireland, Mr. Hanbury, and Mr. W. of the Artillery, &c. at dinner.

20*th*. Had Major Lomax and the Grandjeans to spend the day. Mrs. Cookson and her little girl came to see me, and the nurse brought her own little black child to shew me. It was only seven months old yesterday, and could stand by a chair, and crawl about anywhere; and really seemed, in every respect, like a child of a year old.

21*st*. General N. and I walked, in our dressing gowns, for an hour in the piazza, before the sun rose, with little Georgy as our companion. All the rest of the day preparing despatches, to go by the *Leviathan*. – At 5, a large dinner party; Dr. and Miss Grant – like them much.

22*nd*. General N. so full of business and letters, that he could not drive out with me. Miss Williams went into Spanish Town in the chariot, and brought out Mr. and Mrs. Campbell, of the 60th regiment, to dinner. Poor people, they are full of gratitude to General N., who has appointed Mr. C. Barrack-master of Spanish Town. Sent them back happy in the evening, and went to bed satisfied.

23*rd*. An anxious day. Much teasing business, and much misconduct on the part of many in whom we placed confidence; but I must try not to think of these things, for the sake of my health. General N. much engaged all day, with arrangements for the emigrants and French prisoners, that arrived in Spanish Town to-day.

24*th*. To church at 10. Several of the French officers (prisoners on parole) there, so I suppose they are Protestants; but some say they only came out of curiosity, or to pass away time. Drove to the King's House afterwards, and had a talk with Dr. Clare, as now it is probable I shall be confined there, instead of the Penn, and we made arrangements for the family being accommodated elsewhere. At dinner, only the Woodhams and Kemble from Kingston, in addition to our own party.

25*th*. The heat dreadful, although we got in from our drive before the sun was up half an hour. Persuaded General N. to sit to Morelle for his portrait, though more out of charity than any thing else. – About 12 o'clock, a frightful tornado, but it lasted only a short time.

26th. Take out little G. and Bonella, with only nurse and Johnson. Find B. very docile when she is without her mother. Send for the Admiral, &c. in the morning. – Dine at 5. – The two Mrs. Rennalls, Miss Rennalls, Mr. Mitchell, &c. at dinner. Mr. M. brought me two plums of the Orleans kind (black); the first that were ever produced in Jamaica.

27th. The Admiral, &c. left us at 5, and General N. walked out with his gun. Mr. Whitfield came to breakfast, and to receive orders, respecting the French emigrants. A long discussion on the subject, with General N., who will do all in his power to make them comfortable, consistently with the security of the island; but they must be watched a little, under present circumstances.

28th. This day two years we landed at Port Royal, and I was strongly reminded of it, by the salute that was fired for Sir J. Duckworth, who went out of harbour on a cruise. I feel truly thankful to God Almighty, who has been pleased to spare our lives thus far, for the health we have enjoyed, and for the addition to our happiness in the birth of our dearest George; and now, for the near prospect of having another darling. May we ever be grateful, and shew that we are really so, by our obedience to the commands of the Almighty, in all things, and by doing all the good we can to our fellow-creatures! The day quiet and more comfortable than usual; yet my plans for being confined here, or at the King's House, are not quite settled, and so I can make no decided preparations.

30th. General N. off before daylight, to go on board the *Vanguard*, which brought into harbour, yesterday, a French 74-gun ship, *Le Duquesne*. He did not get back till 12, when the heat was dreadful.

31st. The heat so great, that I was advised not to go to church. The rest of the family went. – Only the Woodhams and the Grandjeans, with Mr. Airy, at dinner.

August 1st. Send off the sociable very early, to Port Henderson, to bring the French deputies, from St. Domingo, to breakfast here. Messieurs Fitzgerald and Guien, with Monsieur Hillier of the Navy, came. We breakfasted at 7, and they remained the rest of the day. Their mission seems to be of the greatest importance; for the wish of the planters and remaining inhabitants is, to give the colony up to the English – they have been so ill treated by the French troops, and suffered so much from their rapacity and injustice, that they say it is impossible to look to them for any security. They speak indeed of their profligacy and misconduct, altogether, with the greatest disgust. It is, upon the whole, a most embarrassing situation for my dear N., and what he is to do, I can't imagine.

2nd. General N. in Spanish Town all day. – At dinner, Major Codd, Captain Aldred, and Mr. Chandler.

3rd. An express, in the night, from Captain Walker of the *Vanguard,* which General N. was obliged to answer immediately, and to desire Captain Walker to breakfast here, which he did, and there was much discussion all day, on the subject of St. Domingo, &c. which, indeed, was carried on till a late hour, after the family had retired to bed.

4th. General C. and Captain Mackintosh, of the 85th, came to spend the day. The Rev. Mr. Simcocks, from Port Royal, got a severe lecture from General N. about his marrying a young naval officer with some good-for-nothing woman there. The rest of the day occupied by St. Domingo discussion, &c.

5th. Sent a carriage to Port Henderson for Captain Perkins, who had much business with General N. He returned to his ship soon after breakfast, and General N. was in Spanish Town the rest of the day. – Am much shocked to hear, in the evening, that young Stewart had forged a bill, and must be got out of the country as soon as possible. How unkind of Colonel Stewart to send out such a young man to us!

6th. General N. out on horseback early. I amused myself with little G. in the Piazza. Send carriages to Port Henderson for Captains Walker and Perkins, and Dr. Blair, R.N. The latter gives a fearful account of the jail fever, brought from St. Domingo by the last prizes. At 4, send carriages for the French Commodore, &c. – A very large party at dinner, at 5. Have a great deal of conversation with the Commodore, who is the ugliest creature my eyes ever beheld, but who asserted, that at twenty he was "*beau comme l'amour,*" that all the ladies were in love with him, &c. – very modest indeed, with a nose like Bardolph's, eyes that look *transversely,* and teeth of all sizes, and shapes, and colours, green and black predominating! But it was all very amusing, and made us very merry after he was gone.

9th. A crowd of Frenchmen at breakfast, for whom the carriage was sent early. I did not make my appearance, as we have agreed it will be good policy for me to be declared unequal to society, till after my confinement; and so all will be settled, and I shall know by that time what ladies to receive. – The French Commodore, with his friends, and Grandjean, went on board the *Vanguard,* to dine with Captain Walker; while General N. went with General Fressinet into Spanish Town; he to his business, and they to their lodgings.

10*th*. The day quiet, but the heat dreadful. It is now so long since we have had a shower, that every thing is burnt up, and even the well is, I fear, getting dry. – Remonstrate with some of our young men upon the improper lives they lead, and the miseries that must result from the horrid connections they have formed. Get very fair promises, but fear that is all I am to expect, from my exertions to save them from ruin. This is, indeed, a sad immoral country, but it is of no use worrying myself.

12*th*. General N. went into Spanish Town as usual. Captain Dundas, R.N., General C., &c. came to visit me. Drive out, in the evening; meet a large party of French people – Madame Fressinet, &c. Affect to lie back in the carriage, like an invalid, to keep up the character I have politically adopted. – In the evening despatches from St. Domingo, and much harassing business for my dear husband.

13*th*. The heat excessive. Drive out, in the evening, and avoid Spanish Town, for fear of encountering the French again.

14*th*. General N. rode out early, and went with the staff, &c. to church, at 10. I read my prayers at home. – The Grandjeans at dinner, with Monsieur Bellause, from St. Domingo. Mr. B. came to express the wishes of the inhabitants of St. Domingo, to place themselves under British protection. A difficult card for my dear N.

15*th*. A cloudy day, and some tremendous thunder and lightning, with heavy rain. We rejoice, for the moisture of the air is refreshing to the poor animals, as well as ourselves, and they seem to enjoy it as much as we do. This is the first whole day of clouds that I have ever seen in this country. The sun has not been visible, and what a treat the comparative coolness is!

16*th*. Send off carriages for the Admiral, who came to discuss St. Domingo business, &c. with General N.; and, as soon as their talk was over, the Admiral hastened back to Port Royal, and General N. into Spanish Town. For reasons too long to explain, the French Commodore, &c. dined here, with General Carmichael, Major D., &c.

17*th*. General N. off, before day, for the Admiral's Penn. While I was at breakfast, came Monsieur Bellause, with Monsieur Grandjean, upon St. Domingo business. Finding General N. gone, nothing would satisfy them, but laying all their papers before me, and it was with great difficulty I got rid of them, by 12 o'clock. – General N. at 4. All more satisfactory. Evening as usual.

18*th*. Send a carriage early, for Monsieur Bellause, &c. and General N. arranged a great deal about St. Domingo. After they left the Penn, Gen-

PLATE II

DR. GALLAGHER'S BILL FOR ATTENDING THE NEGROES AT KING'S HOUSE AND GOVERN-
MENT PEN

eral N. wrote to the black chiefs, and sent also his secret instructions to Captain Walker and Mr. Cathcart, &c. who are to proceed immediately to St. Domingo.

19*th*. A present of cake and a pin-cushion, from the Duchess of Port Royal. – Was much shocked in the evening, to hear of the sudden death of poor Mrs. Ottley, who expected to be confined in a few months.

20*th*. The day as usual, but my spirits a good deal affected by the many deaths announced within the last few days, and particularly among the young, and those newly arrived in the country. Keep quiet, and have the comfort of my dear N.'s society, almost the whole day.

21*st*. The Woodhams, Dr. and Mrs. Brodbelt, Mr. Husband, &c. at dinner. – Sad accounts to-day of the many deaths at Up-Park camp. – God preserve my dear husband and child!

22*nd*. The carriage sent early to Port Henderson for Captain Dufour, Aide-de-camp to one of the Brigand generals. He is a much more gentleman-like sort of man than I expected; and, although a mulatto, is not very dark, and has a pleasing countenance. The account he gave of the conduct of the French general officers, as well as those under them, was dreadful indeed, and their cruelties were not to be contemplated without horror. I was surprised at the good language he spoke. At 10, he left us, and at 4, we sent the sociable for Generals Fressinet and Merck, Commodore Quérangal, Captains Courvoisier, &c. who, with General C., Major D., &c. dined with General N. I kept close to my apartment, till they took their leave, and then we had a snug little supper, and went to bed at ten.

26*th*. A long conversation with my dear N., about the misconduct of some of our young men, in forming improper connections, and thus involving themselves in future. – Poor foolish Captain Johnson is in great distress, about an ugly mulatto favourite, who has been accused of theft. General N. will give all the good advice he can; but *cui bono?*

27*th*. Duckworth, &c. went early to Kingston, to bear testimony to the amiable character of the mulatto lady; but the stolen shoes were found in her pocket! However, they all say it was a conspiracy, and Captain Johnson's constancy is unshaken.[1]

28*th*. All go to church but me. – Only the Woodhams at dinner. Am not a little disgusted with him, as they say he got tipsy, and beat his wife

---

[1] A year later, Captain Johnson (Nugent's ADC and military secretary) "expressed a very earnest desire to enter holy orders" and Nugent recommended him to the Bishop of London for ordination and promised him a living.

the other day. I can't believe it, and yet he is not at all like any idea I have formed of a clergyman.

29th. General N. in Spanish Town all day. Much to do with the prisoners and emigrants.

30th. Drive out, and bathe dear little Georgy. He and nurse dance and sing all day, in spite of the heat, and neither of them appear to suffer from it; but I fainted to-day, and felt very poorly in consequence. However, my dear N. stands it well, and so shall I, I trust, after a few months more.

September 1st. General N. &c. not at home till after 10 at night. He and all the staff went, at 2 o'clock, to the Ferry House, to meet a large military party, at dinner. – My day quiet. Drive out with Mrs. Skinner, Bonella, and little G. in the evening. Prayers, and to bed at nine.

3rd. Dr. Adolphus at dinner, and consult him about poor dear Clifford, who seems much debilitated by the climate, and he promises to do all he can for her.

4th. Little G. slept last night, for the first time, in his new bed, and my mind is much easier about him. – All the family went to church. – Only the Woodhams at dinner.

5th. High wind, and a prospect of rain, thank God! A slight shower, but scarcely enough to wet the surface of the ground, which is now as hard as marble.

6th. General N. in Spanish Town all the morning, and I wrote all my notes and letters, as I shall soon not be able to write. – Obliged to send Mr. Heslop a negative, about Rock Fort; but don't feel much for him, he has so little delicacy in his applications, and so indeed have very many people, as well as him.

7th. Henry Rogers taken ill at breakfast. Send for Dr. Adolphus, and have the comfort of finding it only a bilious attack. General N. as usual, very busy, and in a state of great anxiety about St. Domingo.

*   *   *   *   *   *

12th. Here has been a great chasm in my journal. But to-day I must write a few lines. – My dear N. is gone to Kingston, and I am sitting on my sofa, a truly happy creature, and most grateful to God Almighty for the great and undeserved blessing He has bestowed upon me. I will try, in spite of the little nervous weakness which I feel at present, to give a detail of the last four days. About ten minutes before 4 o'clock, on Thursday the 8th, I was awoke with slight pains. The house was immediately in a bustle, and an express was sent for Dr. Clare, who arrived about 5, and found me in bed safe, with my dearest little fat girl by my side. My illness was literally nothing, for I was actually speaking, and walking towards the sofa, the instant before it was all over. No words can speak my delight and gratitude, or the joy of my dear N., who, as well as myself, I am sure, expected great and protracted suffering for me. I was immediately so well, and in such spirits, that, in the course of the day, I saw, not only the doctor, but all the gentlemen of the family, who came to enquire after me and the dear baby. – Had some anxiety, on account of the misunderstanding of my deaf maid Johnson, but am too happy to let any thing dwell upon my mind that is at all unpleasant. My dear little George delighted with his sister, and this is his monthly birthday. He is now eleven months old, and never was there a more lovely child. – I am happy to be allowed to nurse my little girl; but, alas! I fear, from my anxiety, and the heat of the climate, I may not be able to do her justice, and this lowers my spirits a little. My dear N. was delighted, when he returned from Kingston this evening, to find the baby with me, and all going on well. He brought each of the maids a present, and I had quite a scene with poor Johnson, after she received hers, for she thought she had not deserved it. However, she is penitent, and I am sure I forgive her with all my heart.

15*th*. Quite a different creature, from having had a better night. Dr. Clare at 10. Surprised to find me up, and walking about my room. Drank some porter at dinner, for the sake of my little Louisa.

16*th*. Saw Dr. Robertson and Colonel Irvine, for a short time this morning. – Make an excellent *day nurse*, and feel quite happy.

17*th*. Major Pye, Captain Johnson, and Mr. Browne, were admitted for half an hour to-day.

18*th*. General N. read prayers to me, and we passed a most comfortable morning. A shower of rain, and hope for more, as the heat is intolerable, and the *prickly heat* almost insupportable. Had two of the family to dine with us, for the first time. – Feel it rather a fatigue.

19*th*. General N. in Spanish Town, engaged in the horrid Court of Chancery. – My darling little girl quite the admiration of the whole house; just as healthy, quiet, and good, as dear Georgy.

20*th*. Dear baby seems to have a cold, and is a little feverish. Am afraid the taking two milks may disagree with her. Consult with Dr. Clare, and am fearful poor dear Georgy must be weaned, and resign his room to his sweet little sister. – Rather better towards evening, and go to bed more comfortable.

22nd. All well and happy. – A packet, and private letters most comfortable; but I fear poor Ireland is in a sad state. My baby quite well, and dear little Georgy prosperous. Admiral Duckworth at breakfast. Mr. Murphy at dinner.

23rd. The prickly heat most distressing. – Major Pye and Mr. Browne at breakfast. – Dr Clare came, and ordered me saline draughts for the prickly heat; but I don't think they do me much good.

24th. General Carmichael and Captain Johnson at breakfast.

25th. Colonel Irvine and Dr. Robertson with Duckworth and Kemble, to breakfast, and all go to church with General N. I read my prayers at home. Am rather low, as dear little George must be weaned, and I must give up all charge of my sweet little baby.

26th. Mrs. S. and Bonella accompanied General N. and little George, and spent the morning at the King's House. This is our first *real* attempt to wean the dear child. My heart is heavy, but I am thankful, and will not repine. He returned in good spirits, dear boy, and we gave him to nurse again for the night, Mrs. Moore resuming her charge of baby.

29th. I long for the Court of Chancery to be over, for it is a sad drawback to our comfort.

30th. Assembled all the servants, and made them presents, for my dear little girl; or rather, she did, for everything was put into her little hand, to give them. Read the family prayers, and a thanksgiving for myself, and now all will go on as usual.

October 1st. General N. drove me out; Mrs. S., nurse, and the children went in the sociable. All the family at breakfast. Doctor Clare, to announce that he had vaccinated two healthy children, from the virus sent from England, and if the infection takes, my darling little girl is to be vaccinated, the latter end of next week. This day, at 4, the Court of Chancery for this quarter was finished, and now my dear N. will be less absent from home.

2nd. No service in the church to-day, Mr. and Mrs. Woodham being absent, on account of health. General N. read prayers at 11. – Hear of poor Captain Henry, of the Navy, being given over. These are melancholy times, and indeed these annual visitations are most trying to the spirits.

3rd. Drove to Port Henderson, but returned quite melancholy, on hearing minute guns firing, for Captain Henry's death. General N. and I feel deeply for him. – Alone all the morning, my dear N. holding an Ecclesiastical Court, in Spanish Town.

4th. General N. off, at 3, for Stony Hill. Returned at 4 in the afternoon, having gone forty miles to-day, besides walking a great deal, inspecting barracks, &c.; but he does not seem at all the worse, for either the great heat or the fatigue – but many of the staff could not come to dine; only Colonel Irvine and Dr. Robertson, and they did not go to Stony Hill. Drury is, I find, so much of an invalid, that, by the advice of the Doctor, he is to be sent to England, as soon as possible.

5th. General N, off again, very early, for Fort Augusta, to review the troops, and to inspect the barracks, &c. there. I drove with Mrs. S. and the babies to Port Henderson. At 5, General N. brought a party to dinner. – General C., Major D., Captains Cassan and Dobbin, and Mr. Cowen; but he had previously been at the King's House, transacting business for the prisoners, and emigrants from St. Domingo.

7th. Drive to Port Henderson. Both little G. and Bonella bathed in the cold salt water bath there, and behaved extremely well. General N. obliged by business to be in Spanish Town all day.

8th. From daylight till dinner time my dear N. was shut up with papers, and did not even appear at breakfast. – My time as usual, till 12, when Dr. Clare came, with a nice little mulatto child, from whose arm my dear baby was vaccinated in both legs. Feel much agitated, and wish this could be deferred, till after she is made a Christian; but Mr. Woodham's absence may delay that too long, and it is best not to run the risk of small-pox. God grant that this may succeed! Colonel Roberts, in addition to our dinner party; he came to take leave for England. An express, to say that Mr. Woodham had returned, and there will be service to-morrow.

9th. Little G. not well, and complaining with his teeth, but try to compose myself for church; yet was so nervous, that, when the congregation crowded round me, I was near fainting. A few remained after the service, and I returned thanks, and took the Sacrament. After which, we drove to the King's House, where Colonel Roberts took our English despatches, and set off for the *Lord Charles Spencer* packet, in which he sails to-morrow. – Only Messrs. Woodham and Airy, in addition to our party. – Talk of fixing the day for the christening, but don't decide, for reasons too long to detail to-day. – Dear baby's legs both look rather red, so I hope the vaccine matter has taken. Her name is to be Louisa, and I think it very pretty.

10*th*. The early morning as usual, and then sit up for company; but rain coming on, Captain Johnson and Captain Duckworth, the Aides-de-camp for the day, to hand up the ladies, actually sat down and nearly devoured all the cake and caudle themselves, to the great amusement of us all.

11*th*. General N. at the King's House, and full of business all the morning. – At 12, the ladies began to come, and I had a crowd around me, till 4 o'clock. – In the evening, drove into Spanish Town to inquire how little Eve, who has got a little daughter, is to-day.

12*th*. This day, my dearest, dear George is one year old complete. God bless and preserve him, and grant him many, many happy, very happy years! Drove out, with my precious children, to Port Henderson. All prosperous. Little G. quite well; baby the same; and this is to be a day of joy. – At 5, the company began to assemble. – The Admiral and his party. – The Messrs. Mitchell, S. Taylor, Edwards, Cuthbert, General Carmichael, Major Darley, Mr. Cowen, the Doctors, &c. &c. After dinner, little G's. health was given with three times three, and he was led about the table, to receive the compliments of the company. Before we took our coffee, we went to see the blackies enjoying themselves, who had also a grand entertainment. After which they drank young *Massa*, with a sort of shout, that was more like an Indian war-whoop than any thing else. Then young *Missis*, with the same vociferation. *Old Massa* and *Old Missis* came next; and, in short, they were very merry. A ball afterwards, and all dispersed before 12. The 8th of November is fixed for my dear baby's christening. I wish it was sooner; but, for *reasons of state*, thus it must be.[1] It is not, however, quite comfortable to my dear N. or me.

13*th*. In the morning the Admiral, &c. to make enquiries. Colonel Lethbridge and Mr. Nolan, at dinner.

14*th*. Drive early to the King's House. Little Eve's child like a wrinkled old monkey. But she thinks it beautiful, no doubt. – At 12, a crowd of ladies. Every one, indeed, on my list, but one family, that is out of town.

15*th*. Dr. Clare early. His opinion, alas! is, that my sweet baby has not taken the cow-pox. So that disagreeable and distressing operation

---

[1] Conceivably the christening was postponed until the Assembly was in session, for the convenience of Simon Taylor and Mr. Edwards who were to stand proxy as god-fathers, and other members of the Assembly.

must be gone over again, or perhaps, after all, we must give her the small-pox.[1] Drive to Port Henderson, with little G. – At breakfast, Major Nugent Smith, of the 55th regiment, Mr. and Mrs. Cunningham, of Montego Bay, Mr. Taylor, and Mrs. and Miss Correvont, from Kingston. All leave us soon after. – Poor little Drury, from Stony Hill, and appearing very ill indeed.

17th. Set off for the Admiral's Penn, to pass a few days, for change of air. Leave my little cherub with her nurse, under the care of my dear N.; but take little G. as my companion. Mrs. S. and Bonella went to Kingston, on a visit to a cousin of hers. Get to the Admiral's to breakfast. Only Navy men at dinner; a large mixed party, but only two ladies, Mrs. Moore and Mrs. Griffiths. Cassino in the evening, and to bed at ten.

18th. Dream all the night (when I did sleep) of my dear N. and sweet Louisa. – The musquitoes so tormented little G., that more than half the night was spent in watching him. – Drive early to Greenwich, to the Admiral's bath. Just close to me, when I jumped in, was a large turtle. Dear little G. had only been dipped an instant before. It looked frightful, though they say there is no danger; but I was so unwell, after I returned to the Penn, that Dr. Blair advised me not to attempt to bathe any more. – At dinner, Mrs. Ross, Mrs. Symes, and a large party of men.

19th. Go into Kingston in the morning, and am much diverted with the easy manners and familiarity of the ladies and the shopkeepers, who all seem intimate acquaintances. At dinner, only the Misses Stewart, with Mrs. Ross, the rest all gentlemen.

20th. Mrs. Yates and Mr. and Mrs. Cole at breakfast. – At dinner, Mrs. and Miss Grant, Mrs. Ross, and Miss Williams.

21st. Drove into Kingston, and visited till dinner time. On my return to the Penn, receive the dreadful account of an affray in the 85th regiment, and the death of poor Captain Cassan.[2] Am such shocked, and am sure my dear N. must feel it very much. – Mrs. and the Misses Johnstone were the ladies at dinner to-day. – A number of gentlemen as usual, and Captain Scobell, who gave a most horrible description of the evacuation of Aux Cayes and Port au Prince; barbarous and strange beyond conception indeed!

[1] The older method, of smallpox inoculation, had been used in the case of Mrs. Nugent's firstborn the previous year. Dr. Dancer in the 1809 edition of his *Medical Assistant* says that at that date cowpox vaccination (introduced by Jenner in 1798) had not yet been generally adopted in Jamaica owing to some early failures.
[2] Capt. Cassan was "unfortunately run through the body" by a brother officer, who was acquitted of murder by a court which accepted his plea of "extreme provocation."

23*rd.* All well, only the Woodhams, and Captain and Mrs. Craskell, in addition to our family party.

24*th.* Drive to the Penn, before breakfast, with the dear little ones. All the morning, a bustle, and crowds of gentlemen visitors. Mr. Dobbs, from Ireland, amongst them. An immense dinner party of gentlemen, who sat very late. I dined quietly in my own apartment, with Mrs. S. and her sister, Miss Mary Williams.

28*th.* A very large party at second breakfast. Then, at 5, a party of French people. Received them in the ball-room, and dined in the Egyptian hall. Generals Fressinet, Brunet, d'Henin, le Fevre, Commodore Quéran-gal, Captain Fogue, &c. &c. with Madame Fressinet, Monsieur and Madame Grandjean, Mademoiselle Robert, Captain Murray, &c. &c. I really was much amused. I sat between Generals Fressinet and d'Henin. The first a gentleman-like sort of man, but, like a true Frenchman, did nothing but compliment me, and almost make love to me. They say he was a barber, before the Revolution, and I can easily believe it. He did nothing but talk of himself and his wife. He said she was a most charming person, and so clever, that she could talk upon any subject; physics, metaphysics, &c. &c., in short, all subjects of conversation were equal to her. In the evening, eight or ten more French gentlemen came, who belonged to the staff of the several Generals, and we had a dance. I got up a French country dance for Madame Fressinet, but the exhibition was so extraordinary, that I almost repented my civility; for her clothes were very thin and she kicked about, and looked as if she had no covering at all. She is very pretty, though the least creature I ever saw; and I cannot help pitying her, for the disastrous scenes she has gone through; though she talks of all the St. Domingo horrors with astonishing *sang froid.* At 12, all dispersed.

31*st.* At second breakfast, Commodore Quérangal, Monsieur Cour-voisier, Mr. Fogue, &c. My dear N. far from well, heated, and much harassed with business. The Commodore &c. took leave for England.

November 1*st.* Many members of the Council and Assembly called, and were very civil indeed.

2*nd.* The Admiral, &c. at 5. A larger dinner party than usual to-day. The ladies were Mrs. Brodbelt, Mrs. Millward, and Mrs. and the Misses Perry. All the rest gentlemen. – Much *politics* going on, and many deep schemes laid, by some of the old Members. I hope all may end well, but I fear there is a great deal of vexation likely arise to my dear N. therefrom.

3*rd.* At second breakfast, Madame la Marquise de Piquières and her

PLATE 12

FIRST PAGE OF A LETTER TO GEN. NUGENT FROM LEFEBVRE DESVEAUX, A FRENCH
PRISONER OF WAR

The writer complains that his Negro servant, whom he sent to be registered in compliance with the Admiral's order, has not been returned to him.

daughter. The latter was brought up in America, and speaks sad English!

4th. A large party of gentlemen at dinner. – In the evening a crowd, amongst whom were General and Madame Fressinet, La Marquise and Mademoiselle Piquières, &c. &c.

6th. Several at second breakfast; Mrs. and Miss Grant, the Rennalls, &c.

7th. I don't know how it is of late – I have no time for keeping a journal. – It is a task to me. I see a great deal of company. I have a large and *anxious* household to attend to. I have constant applications and notes to answer; and then, my dear little ones occupy too delightfully my leisure moments, to allow of my giving any sort of description of persons or things, or what is going on here. Besides, I regret to say, that my dear N. has many and great vexations, which, added to the heat of the climate, fill my mind, more than anything, to make me constantly tremble for his health. – Drove out this morning, as usual, but at second breakfast a chill came over me. Drs. Drumgold and Adolphus were here, and they both advised me to go to bed. I really was in a fever till near 12 o'clock at night, when my head was relieved, and I got a nice sleep.

8th. Take bark and saline draughts, and do all I can to be well to-day, to receive my company, and have my dear baby made a Christian. – At 1, we all assembled in the chapel; Mr. Simon Taylor, and Mr. Edwards standing proxies for Governor Nugent and Major Osborne; Mrs. Rennalls and Mrs. Skinner for dear Lady Temple and Lady William Bentinck. Mr Mitchell (King Mitchell) gives us a grand dinner to-day, and I am to have a ball upon this happy occasion. – But I should mention, that my dear little girl's names are Louisa Elizabeth.– After the ceremony, cake, wine, &c.; all the servants had the same; and, in short, health and happiness was drank to the dear little Christian, with every demonstration of affection and joy. Find myself, after all this, not quite equal to the dinner party; so send my excuse to King Mitchell, and take a quiet little repast at home. – At 8, dress for the ball. A numerous company. Don't dance, but play cards till 11, and then take leave of our guests, and go to bed. – The gaieties were kept up till one.

9th. Much better this morning. – A packet from England, with most comfortable letters, and a parcel containing more of the vaccine virus. Send for Dr. Clare, who immediately inoculated my little Louisa with it. God grant it may succeed! – Poor little Drury does not gain ground at all, and General N. has sent him to make a cruise in the *Hercule*, in hopes of his recovering, and not being obliged to return to England.

10th. Only Mr. Dobbs and Miss Grant at dinner, with our own family.

11*th*. General and Madame Fressinet to take leave. To-morrow they go to Kingston, to prepare for their voyage.

16*th*. Thirty-three people at dinner. Doing the honours and making the agreeable, was a severe task to me to-day, for my heart was in the nursery. – At dinner to-day, Mr. Redwood (the Speaker), Mr. Rodon (the Custos), and his lady, Mr. and Mrs. Sherriff, Mrs. and Miss Tanner, King Mitchell, Mr. Simon Taylor, Mrs. Affleck, Mr. Minott, Mr. Christie, Mr. Lewis, Mr. Johnstone, Mr. and Mrs. Herring, Mr. and Mrs. Marshall, Mr. Stewart, Mr. Shand, and Mr. Edwards. In short, we go the round of society, I think, over and over again.

17*th*. Hear from Mrs. Skinner and her sister very amusing accounts, of remarks made upon General N. and myself, and find that every word, look, and action, and article of dress, is canvassed; but what does it signify?

A large party at second breakfast, and all the conversation about a sad affair that has just taken place. A Mr. Irvine, in a fit of jealousy, having murdered one of his servants. It seems the favourite was a brown lady; and to, mend the matter, Mr. Irvine is a married man, and his unfortunate wife has been long nearly broken-hearted, as his attachment to this *lady* had occasioned his treating her often with the greatest cruelty even. His own brother endeavoured to secure him after the murder, but he has made his escape. It is to be hoped that he may lead a life of penitence, if for the present he eludes justice. – We had a quiet dinner party to-day, and we rejoiced at it, for we heard, just before we sat down, of the death of poor Mr. Hillary, after a very short illness. It is indeed shocking to hear of the many deaths that occur every day, and my mind is constantly anxious for those I love. Thank God! our family have been unusually healthy hitherto, and I pray that we may continue to be equally fortunate. – Dr. Clare, as usual, three times a day. He thinks dear little G. decidedly better; but we are still cruelly anxious about him.

18*th*. Dear Georgy rather better. Doctor Dancer, as well as Doctor Clare, to-day. They both give a comfortable opinion of the dear child. – A large party in the evening, but I could not dance, and was glad when 11 o'clock came.

20*th*. A great lecture, in the papers of yesterday, to the gigglers at church, and a fine *puff* for General N. and me, for our conduct there, &c.[1]

---

[1] The *St. Jago de la Vega Gazette* referred editorially to a letter from a correspondent signing himself Clericus, who complained that "his attention to the sermon was entirely interrupted by the chattering, giggling, and otherwise indecorous behaviour

21st. Packed up the necklaces, to go by the *Cumberland*, to dear Lady Temple and Lady Mary Grenville.[1]

22nd. General N. made old Grandjean a present of the house and garden that he has hitherto rented of Dr. Robertson. I was much affected by the manner in which the poor old gentleman expressed his gratitude. – This is, however, only paying *one little part of our debt*. If ever this meets the eye of my dear Nugent, he will quite understand it, and know all I mean.

23rd. All the morning obliged to listen to long histories, of the events of the evening before; and to accommodate all differences, as well as I can. The brown ladies, as usual, concerned. Don't let General N. know of these disagreeable affairs, as it would only make him uncomfortable, and he has already enough to do, with public business.

24th. The Admiral, Mr. Waterhouse, &c. at breakfast.

25th. Colonel Lethbridge, Captain Campbell, and several gentlemen from Kingston, at dinner.

26th. A large dinner, and go, in number between thirty and forty, to see Mr. Rannie perform. We were all much amused with his ventriloquism.[2]

(we are sorry to say) of the fair sex, and of that part of them, too, from whose situation in life we should have expected better things . . . Our correspondent further observes, that many French people were present, and he is hurt to think what an unfavourable impression they must have received of our religious principles . . ." Happily, however, "the pious demeanour of his Honour the Lieutenant-Governor, and his amiable consort, was truly exemplary."

[1] Among the gifts which the Nugents sent to Lord and Lady Buckingham were Jamaican plants and seeds, South American birds, and "an Honduras canoe, with its appurtenances."

[2] Advertised in the *St. Jago Gazette* of 12–19 November 1803:

"FOR TWO NIGHTS ONLY.

The Ladies and Gentlemen of Spanish Town are respectfully informed, that Mr. RANNIE intends displaying his

VENTRILOQUIAL POWERS,

On Thursday evening, Nov. 24th, and Saturday, the 26th, at the Masons' Lodge.

Mr. RANNIE possesses by nature the power of causing a voice to give responses to whatever questions he pleases to ask, from closets, drawers, under tables, chairs, or from the ceiling of the room; this curiosity is so singular, that we have no account of any Ventriloquists but three since the woman of Endor, who is described in the Hebrew language, as having a familiar spirit. Mr. R. will also cause the voice of a child to appear to speak from the pocket of any lady or gentleman present . . . The whole to conclude with the imitation of an OLD SCOTCH LANDLORD, disturbed

29th. King Mitchell brought his brother, Mr. Robt. Mitchell, who had just arrived in the packet, to introduce him to us. Mr. Edwards, also, at breakfast. General N. then held a Court of Appeal, in the Council Chamber, which took up his whole morning, and I received visitors for him. Amongst them was Mr. Holland, just arrived as Judge of the Admiralty. He has brought his wife with him. She was a Miss Eden, and will, I hope, be an acquisition to our society. I asked him to dinner. At 4, General N.'s Court was over, but he was so full of business, with the House of Assembly, that Captain Johnson, his Military Secretary, was sent with repeated messages to the House, till 6 o'clock, the Private Secretary being confined to his room with a fever, though nothing dangerous. Much fuss about the troops and their pay, &c., and my poor N. had not a moment to join the company at dinner, till near 7. – We both like Mr. Holland's manner much.

30th. A Court of Errors, or Appeal, again this morning, and I am sorry to say it is to continue a fortnight. I pity poor dear N. very much, for he really has not now one leisure moment; and I pity myself too, for I scarcely ever see him, but in a crowd.

December 3rd. A large dinner party to-day for the Admiral, &c., but the only ladies were the Misses Murphy, except those in the house. Mr. Holland drank so many bumpers of claret, that he got into high spirits, and gave up, in the Court of Admiralty, every point of which he had been so tenacious in the morning. – Though this is the very beginning of December, we all agree it is like the dog-days; and, even while sitting still, the perspiration bubbles out, and drops from the forehead, nose, and chin, so that many of the company really looked like so many living drip-stones.

5th. Hear that poor Captain Murray has the fever. Of late I have omitted to mention illness; for it only makes one melancholy, and miserable; but there are, in fact, only three subjects of conversation here, – debt, disease, and death. It is, indeed, truly shocking.

6th. General N. all the morning in the Court of Appeal. – A small dinner party; and, at 8, the company began to assemble for the King's

at night by a traveller.

Mr. R. deems it necessary to inform the ladies and gentlemen of this town, that he is the person named in the Encyclopedia, who caused the great alarm that took place at Edinburgh a few years since, by causing a fish that was exposed for sale, apparently to speak to its owner.

Admittance 13s. 4d. Doors to be opened at half past six, and the performance to commence at seven o'clock."

PLATE 13

King's House 22 Dec. 1803

Rec. Pt. Recev'd 20 lbs of Tea

M. Clifford

Rec. 6/8 his

Witness R Rountree   Jos. + Morris
                            Mark

My dear Sir,

Will you be as good as to pay to the order
of Dr. Alexr. Robertson the Sum of two hundred
& fifty pounds Currency on my Account for a
small House & Land which I have made a Present
of to old Monsieur Grandjean D'Aubancourt in
Spanish Town —

Yours sincerely

G. Nugent

King's House, Novr. 22d. 1803 —

30th Novr Received Alexr Robertson
1803.

(Entd)

A. Atkinson Esqr.

KING'S HOUSE TRANSACTIONS: MRS. NUGENT'S MAID TAKES DELIVERY OF GROCERIES,
AND GEN. NUGENT BUYS A HOUSE FOR MONS. GRANDJEAN

Ball.[1] The Admiral, with a large party, Mr. and Mrs. Holland, &c. came from Kingston; and every one seemed merry and well pleased. Supper at 12. To bed at two.

7*th*. Only Captain Adams, of the 55th, and Mr. Nixon, of the 85th, at dinner.

8*th*. A large party of the Members, with their wives and daughters, at dinner. Mrs. Broughton is quite a character. She had been married before, and we asked her if she had had any children by Mr. Roper, her former husband, of the firm of Roper, Cocker and Co. She replied "No, nothing at all like it, no chance whatever of it; no such thing, I can assure you." Just before the company assembled at dinner, Dr Clare came and inoculated my little darling Louisa. God preserve her to us! After much discussion, we agreed to have the puncture made in her dear little leg; for if the present fashion of excessive short sleeves lasts till she grows up, it will not be becoming to expose a scar on the arm, which I now see disfiguring many pretty young ladies. – A ball given to me to-night, by the Attorney-General. With our party of nearly forty persons, we proceeded thither about 9, and were received with much ceremony and kindness. Mrs. Skinner and Miss Williams were much pleased with the attention shewn them. A gay dance, and supper at twelve.

9*th*. Poor Captain Murray was buried yesterday, but, as I had much to do, they did not tell me, till to-day, that he was no more. He was a fine man; and how I pity his poor mother, Lady George Murray, when she hears of his sad fate! – Only two new gentlemen, from England, at dinner; the Rev. Mr. Humphries and Mr. Skelton. The usual Friday dance. Mrs. Skinner very unwell, and poor Duckworth taken very ill

---

[1] The Ball was advertised as follows in the *Royal Gazette:* –

"KING'S HOUSE, *Oct.* 27, 1803

KING'S BALL

There will be a BALL given by His Honour the LIEUTENANT-GOVERNOR on Tuesday evening, the 6th day of December next, in honour of

HIS MAJESTY'S BIRTHDAY.

To prevent confusion, Ladies and Gentlemen are requested to order their carriages to come by the Old Court House, and go off by the Long Room.

N.B. – No Gentlemen can possibly be admitted in boots, or otherwise improperly dressed."

in the course of the evening. If not better to-morrow, the Admiral must be sent for.

10*th*. My morning spent in nursing, and anxiety, for my dear N., too, is very complaining. The Admiral came at about 3, and is in a sad state about his son, and almost despairing. General N. not able to leave his room for dinner. Mrs. S. still in bed, and all the family in distress. Doctors Blair, Clare, and Adolphus, in constant attendance. Sit down to dinner with the gentlemen, and do all I can to comfort the Admiral, and support my own spirits. In the evening, the Doctors were astonished at the quantity of calomel General N. had taken in the course of the day; and I was indeed alarmed; but he says it is his only chance of cure. Before we went to bed, all were evidently better, and Doctor Blair speaks most favourably of poor Duckworth; so his father went to bed, much more at ease.

11*th*. Mr. Duckworth better. Mrs. S. out of bed, and, about 10 o'clock this morning, the Doctor pronounced my dear N. without fever; but says, he must never take such a quantity of calomel again; nearly, if not quite forty-two grains! and he must indeed have a wonderful constitution to bear it. The Admiral left us before dinner, but Dr. Blair remained in attendance upon Duckworth. Part of my dear N.'s illness, I am sure, is owing to worry, and the battles he is obliged to fight with the House of Assembly, to carry into effect the measures of Government. In private society we are all good friends, but, as Governor, they speak most harshly of his conduct, and try to bully him into giving up his intentions, &c. I wish the session was well over, and they were all once more peaceably settled at their homes, and we at the Penn again. – Did not go to church, but had the Woodhams, General Carmichael, &c. at dinner. Leave us at 8. – General N. is very much better, thank God!

12*th*. On our return to breakfast, find Henry Rogers taken ill. Don't wait a moment, but give him a good dose of calomel, and, in two hours after, some castor oil. Duckworth better, and General N. quite himself again. Write to the Admiral, and give him an account of his son, which will, I am sure, be a great comfort to him. Keep H. Rogers upon water-gruel all day, and in the evening he was quite well. I adopted this plan from an old lady, who told me, there was nothing so safe, in this country, as scouring out the patient immediately. – At dinner, only Drs. Blair and Robertson, and Captain McDonald, in addition to the usual party and staff.

13*th*. I spent half an hour in the chapel alone, and comfortably. Christmas Day, Easter, and Whitsuntide, are the only days in the year for the Communion, and I am anxious to be well prepared to take it the next time, if I live, please God! – In the evening, many unpleasant and alarming reports, respecting the French prisoners on parole and the negroes in this town. One of the black men, a Dutch negro, had absented himself from prayers, and it was observed, by one of the staff, that he was seen making signs to one of the sentries, from a window. This, together with the rumours all day, of an understanding between the French prisoners and the free blacks, and their tampering with the negro slaves, was indeed most frightful. Before we went to bed, General N. sent to the officer of the guard, and made enquiry respecting the two sentries, placed at the front door of the King's House, during prayers; and found that they are Irish convicts, of notoriously bad character, and the rest of the guard chiefly recruits, from the French prisoners.[1] I cannot describe the anxiety I suffered, nor the thousand horrid ideas that pressed upon my mind; and, especially, as there has appeared of late a general apprehension throughout the country, and various reports have been made, within the last few weeks, of the alarming state of the negro population, &c. Before we went to bed, General N. secured his own arms. All the staff, too, were on the alert, and, as the nursery door did not lock well, I begged to have it nailed up for the night.

14*th*. The alarm continued, though secretly, all day. French prisoners coming in constantly, and it is suggested that the best plan will be to disarm them. Many Members of Assembly closeted with General N., but he tells me that, with the precautions taken, nothing is to be feared. – The Murphy family at dinner.

15*th*. General N. much engaged with the state of the country. Several messages passed between him and the House of Assembly, on the subject of French prisoners, &c. &c. A petition also from the corporation of Kingston – they seem all sadly alarmed; but he says, with the arrangements he is making for stationing the troops, &c. that he can answer for the security of the island. God grant that all may go well.

16*th*. At breakfast, the Admiral, &c. General Carmichael, Major Cookson, and Major Darley. An unusually large dinner party, and a crowd in the evening. All danced and were very gay. Many flirtations going on, but the season is now drawing so near to a close, that many looked anxious, and I fear there will be several disappointments. – To-day, the

[1] More than 500 Germans, Poles and Swiss were recruited from the prisoners, formerly in French service.

Assembly have expressed much anxiety for the arrival of the troops, and I hope, indeed, they will be here to-morrow, at the latest.

17*th*. Drive out early with General N., and meet the troops marching in; and what a relief to the minds of the Assembly, as well as mine! A few days will end the session. – A large party of Members and their ladies, at dinner. In the evening, several took their final leave, and the civilest things were said on all sides. Much as I wish for quiet, I have received so much kindness, from many of them, that I was quite sorry to say, adieu!

18*th*. Fred. Berkeley, R.N. (a son of Earl Berkeley's) came on a visit.

19*th*. Warwick Lake, R.N. (Lord Lake's youngest son) came to us.

24*th*. Write letters to go by the *Revolutionnaire*. The *Leicester* packet arrived.

25*th. Christmas Day!* Rise very early, and prepare for church. The Communion well attended. – A large dinner party; but before we joined the company, General N. had written *private* letters, to the Duke of York and Lord Hobart, which I copied for him, as he did not wish even his secretary to see their contents. Some part of them related to a secret business with Spain.[1]

26*th*. The general negro masquerade began at daylight, and nothing could exceed the noise and bustle of the day. Little G. was delighted with *Johnny Canoe*, and with throwing money for the blackies to scramble for. – Our usual dinner party late, in the back drawing-room; for the hall was public property, the whole day. Scolded General N. for being as silly as his little boy, in throwing money for the blackies to scramble for, and really some of them had all their finery torn to pieces in the struggle, and very narrowly escaped in whole skins. – In the evening, a report from Stony Hill, that the regimental chest had been broken open, and nearly £2000 taken out.

27*th*. An express very early. One of the men has turned King's evidence, and has impeached the others. – The town and house still in an uproar; but it is really diverting, and very astonishing too, to see the mixture of

---

[1] Nugent asked the Duke of York to lay before the King his request for a "red ribband", the decoration of a Knight of the Bath. After referring to his thirty years' service, he pointed out that his colleague Duckworth already had a K.B., and that it would increase his prestige with foreigners.

War with Spain was expected to begin again at any time (though it did not break out for another year), and the letter to Lord Hobart referred to the project of a British thrust in Spanish Central America, involving an advance perhaps up the Belize river to Guatemala or an expedition up the St. Juan river in Nicaragua. Nugent was collecting information from recent travellers in that area (25 December 1803).

PLATE 14

THE ROYAL GAZETTE.

JAMAICA: PUBLISHED BY *ALEXANDER AIKMAN & SON,*

PRINTERS TO THE KING'S MOST EXCELLENT MAJESTY.

☞ ADVERTISEMENTS *from the Country must be sent to a Correspondent in Kingston, otherwise they will not be inserted.*

☞ *No* ADVERTISEMENTS *can be received for insertion after One o'Clock on Friday, those from Government excepted.*

VOL. XXV. FROM SATURDAY, DECEMBER 17, TO SATURDAY, DECEMBER 24, 1803. No. 52.

☞ PRICE, Three Pounds Five Shillings *per annum, when called for, and* Four Pounds *when sent by Post.*
☞ ADVERTISEMENTS *not exceeding* Sixteen Lines, *are inserted at* Four Dollars *per Month, and longer ones in proportion.*

Kingston, November 25, 1803.
For Freight or Charter,

To LIVERPOOL, GLASGOW, or BRISTOL,

THE SHIP

BROOKE,

JOSEPH TUCKER, Master, 352 Tons per Register.

And for **LIVERPOOL,**
To Sail with the First Convoy,
THE SHIP

CRESCENT,

M. HAYES, Master,
235 Tons per Register. Both staunch copper-bottomed Ships. Apply to
BOGLE, JOPP, & CO.

Kingston, Nov 25, 1803.

OR SALE, for Cash, Bills of Exchange, or Produce,

343 *Prime Young and Healthy*

NEGROES

Imported in the ship Rox, from Angola.
BOGLE, JOPP, & CO.

Kingston, Dec. 10, 1803.

TO BE SOLD, for Cash or Bills of Exchange,

225 *Choice Young Congo*

SLAVES.

Imported in the ship BEDFORD, Capt. Lane.
SHAW, INGLIS, & MILLS.

Kingston, March 11, 1803.

OR SALE, for Cash, Produce, or approved Bills of Exchange,

315 *Young Healthy*

SLAVES,

Imported in the ship Polly, James Blake, Master, from Congo.
FAIRCLOUGH, BARNES, & WILSON.

September 8, 1803.

FOR SALE,

Six Young Healthy and well-disposed

NEGROES,

Coopers by trade.
For particulars apply to
JOHN STONE.

October 5, 1803.

OR SALE, by Personal Agreement, in the parish of St. James,

00 Prime **NEGROES,**

accustomed to Plantation Work; among whom are several valuable Tradesmen. For terms apply to
Messrs. Atkinson, Hanbury, & Co.

GENERAL MILITIA ORDERS.

King's House, December 14, 1803.

AS the QUARTERMASTERS of the TROOPS of MILITIA LIGHT HORSE and DRAGOONS, lately reduced by order of the Commander in Chief, have held commissions in the service, they are hereby directed to be placed *on second* in the REGIMENTS of FOOT, in the parishes in which they respectively reside, in order to be recommended, according to their seniority, by the several Commanding Officers, for the first Exigencies which may become vacant.

By order of the Commander in Chief,

J. TYRRELL, *Sec.*

His Majesty's Printing-Office,
October 8, 1803.

For Sale, a few Copies of a scarce Edition of the Third Volume of the

LAWS OF JAMAICA,

WITH ITS ABRIDGMENT,

Comprising those from 33d to 39th GEORGE III. inclusive;

The Abridgment being an Alphabetical Digest of the Laws contained in the 3d Volume.—Price, £.10 Cash.

His Majesty's Printing-Office,
Dec. 17, 1803.

ALL Accounts with ALEXANDER AIKMAN, SENIOR, to the 31st December, 1800, not settled previously to the ensuing GRAND and PETTY COURTS, will then be put in Suit without distinction.
ALEX. AIKMAN, JUNIOR,
Attorney to Alex. Aikman, Senior.

October 8, 1803.

MUNDS & M'INTOSH,

Booksellers and Stationers,

Have always on Sale, at his Majesty's Printing-Office, BOOKS in various Branches of Literature, STATIONARY of a superior quality, &c.

** *Books Re-bound to any Pattern, on the shortest Notice.*

June 11, 1803.

FOR SALE, *at his Majesty's Printing-Office,*

MONTHLY RETURNS

Of the Transactions on Sugar Estates, Coffee Plantations, &c.

December 16, 1803.

TO BE SOLD, at Old Shaft en Pen, in Westmorland, on the 1st day of February next,

About 130 **HORNED CATTLE,**

A few MARES and their FOLLOWERS:

Bills of Exchange, Cash, or good Orders on Kingston, will be received in payment.

JOHN WHITE,
PATRICK WHITE,
Exors. of ROBERT DELLAP, Esq. dec.

FRENCH REVOLUTION.

THE following very comprehensive and sensible account of the general primary causes, and great leading events, which induced the revolution in France, is taken from the Preface of a work entitled, "Historical Epochs of the French Revolution."

"Various causes contributed to effect, generally speaking, a revolution in the minds of Frenchmen, and led the way to a revolution in the State. The arbitrary nature of the government had long been submitted to, and perhaps would have continued so much longer, if France had not taken part in the American war.

"The perfidious policy of Vergennes, who, with a view of humbling the pride of England, assisted the subject in arms against his Sovereign, soon imparted into his own nation the seeds of liberty, which it had helped to cultivate in a country of rebellion; and the clown of France, as I once heard it emphatically observed, was lost in the plains of America.

"The soldier returned to Europe with new doctrines instead of new discipline, and the army in general soon grew dissatisfied with the monarch, on account of unusual, and, as they thought, ignominious rigours, which were introduced into it from the military school of Germany. The king also, from a necessity of retrenchment, had induced his ministers to adopt some mistaken measures of economy respecting the troops, and thus increased the odium which pride had fostered, and by diminishing the splendour of the crown, stripped it of its security and protection.

"To this was added the wanton profusion of the Court in other expences, and the external parade and brilliancy, which, if they impoverish, often dazzle and *gratify* the people; were exchanged for *familiar* entertainments, which gave rise to frequent jealousies among the nobles, and tended to lower that sense of *awe* and respect for royalty among the people, which, in monarchies, it is of the utmost importance to preserve.

"At this time, also, philosophical discussion had reached its pinnacle of boldness. Infidelity had woven the web of discord in the human mind, which was now ripe for experiment, and Rousseau and Voltaire were the favourite authors.

"Previous to the year 1789, from the extreme disorder of the finances, it became necessary to raise money by extraordinary taxes, which the common powers of the parliament were deemed insufficient to authorize; and, afraid, in the present temper of the

savage and civilized amusements. – The heat great, and a large military party at dinner, in a room too small for such a number, added to it greatly.

28*th*. More intelligence from Stony Hill. Many people implicated in the robbery; but as yet no chance of recovering the money. The sum is now said to be £2400.[1] – Have not driven out these three days, but General N. has rode and drove, and the little ones have had their exercise and air regularly, and are, thank God! quite well. – A military party at dinner again. Obliged to give Drury a lecture, for his very improper conduct.

29*th*. Write early my thanks to Dr. Clare, and send him a present of two hundred pounds from General N., for his attention to me, &c. – Dine at 2 o'clock, and then set off for the Apostles' battery, with General N., General Carmichael, Major Darley, Colonel Irvine, and Captain Johnson. A beautiful situation, but the house quite a hovel. However, it is all to be made quite comfortable, and we have decided to go there the 8th of next month, for the benefit of sea air, and bathing the dear little ones. Home again by 8 o'clock.

30*th*. Mrs. S. and her sister, with little Bonella, off early for Kingston, on a visit to a relation of theirs. Little G. will miss his companion very much, as he is very fond of little Bon. – General N. busy, writing a paragraph for the newspapers, in answer to a false statement, respecting some measures of his government. He sent it off before dinner.[2] – Young Drury in great disgrace, and to be sent to his regiment immediately. He is a foolish and tiresome boy, and it is the more provoking, as he has some talent, and many good points. Write him a long letter of advice, but I fear it won't do much good. To-day, also, I had a long conversation with Major Fraser, on the subject of his officers; and then on some of the émigrés. Send them what relief I can. This was a day of *contretemps*, for, in the evening, the Inspector of Hospitals was so urgent with General N. about returning to England, and giving up his charge here, that he got a

---

[1] Among those implicated were the C.O.'s orderly and a woman of the regiment named Mrs. Bushnell, who, Nugent told Duckworth, "was pursued and taken up returning from your Penn to Kingston on Thursday Afternoon last and immediately searched but nothing found upon her. It seems that she was conversing a very considerable Time with John Wallis a Marine at the Signal House there, supposed [*sic*] for the Purpose of hearing what Opportunities there might be of getting a Passage and of escaping from the Island." The accounts of the Kingston gaol show that Lucy Bushnell and six men charged with robbery spent 89 days in the gaol awaiting trial by the Assize Court, which acquitted them on April 29.

[2] The result seems to have been an article signed Atlanticus, dealing with the familiar question of the black corps, which appeared in the *Supplement to the Royal Gazette* of 7–14 January 1804.

most severe lecture, in the presence of all the staff. Poor man, he is lately married to a young wife! He is alarmed at the climate, too, I believe (although he had been previously ten years at a time in the island); and, in short, ever since his arrival, has never been a day without annoying General N. with his complaints, though in perfect health the whole time. The whole party were aghast, and I was more distressed than I can describe. He had come out on promotion, so that, in giving him leave, ultimately General N. told him that he went at his peril, as he should report his conduct to the Duke of York.

31st. As soon as I could, I sent Colonel Irvine to Dr. Robertson, with a message, which will, I hope, set his mind at ease, and make all comfortable again. – General N. feels hurt, that he spoke so warmly to him; but his anxiety for the service, and more especially the medical department, obliged him to do so, and he says that were he to give way to all such applications, the fears of every one would soon take them back to England, and we should have none left to do the duty here.

CHAPTER IV

JANUARY 1, 1804 – SEPTEMBER 2, 1805

January 1st. After the service poor Dr. Robertson came by appointment. Had a long conversation, and arranged matters for him with General N. It was quite shocking to see the state he was in, crying and sobbing like a child; and with such a robust figure as his, made the scene altogether most deplorable. – Woodhams, Grandjeans, and the usual Sunday party.

2nd. All out before day, to review the Spanish Town garrison. A grand breakfast after. The rest of the day with Johnny Canoe, &c. for the last time this year, or at least till Christmas.

3rd. General N. ordered a Court of Enquiry, upon a Monsieur la Violette, for his cruelties to British officers, when prisoners of war, at Guadeloupe. If they are true, he must be a wretch indeed.[1]

4th. La Violette found guilty of the dreadful crimes laid to his charge. At least the evidence against him is as strong as possible; but to-morrow he is to make his defence, so we must not prejudge him.

5th. La Violette has most completely condemned himself, by contradictions and prevarications. He has been sent on board the prison-ship, in the most ignominious manner; even his own countrymen and brother officers detest and despise him, and say that his cruelties and murders are beyond belief. In short, that he is a monster and a complete *mauvais sujet*. What a horrid world! and to this man I had shewn kindness and the greatest civility!

6th. More company than usual, both at breakfast and dinner. At the latter, a large party, and all military, excepting the Rev. Mr. Donaldson. No ladies; but before we left the table, they began to come, and we had a very gay dance, till 11 o'clock. Then, as this is to be my last party this season, another hour was asked for, and the evening ended most merrily. How glad I am!

---

[1] La Violette was a prisoner of war on parole. Attention was drawn to his identity when the *Kingston Daily Advertiser* happened to reprint a letter which had appeared in the London *Evening Post*, describing his conduct at Guadeloupe.

7*th*. During our drive this morning, General N. talked to me a great deal, about my taking the children to England in the spring, and not waiting for his being relieved; but we could neither of us make up our minds quite to part, and so will not think any more of it at present. The dear little ones have their health now, and the quiet life I hope to lead, with the good air of the Apostles' battery, will, I trust, soon restore my strength. – Receive a favourable answer from the Admiral, to a letter I wrote to him yesterday, about one of the French prisoners; Lieut. Babor and his son. Send off Major Fraser instantly, with the glad tidings, to the poor man.

8*th*. To church, and hear a very good sermon from Mr. Campbell, jun., just arrived from England, to whom General N. has given the living of Portland.

9*th*. A visit from poor Mr. Babor and his son, Thomas Jermyn, to return thanks, and they are to be off for France as soon as possible. – Dine at 2, and set off with the darlings, to the Apostles' battery; all well, and delighted with the beautiful view.

10*th*. The maids and little ones bathed in the salt-water bath, at the bottom of the rock, and all seemed to enjoy it. The cook went over to Port Royal, to market for us, and we passed the day most agreeably. Only Major Ottley and Captain Iseltevin called, but we did not ask them to stay dinner. This situation is beautiful. The house, if it may be so called, stands on a high rock, overlooking the sea; Port Royal, Port Henderson, Fort Augusta, Kingston, and the Liguanea mountains, are all in sight. – In short, it is enchanting, and really very tolerably cool in the evening.

12*th*. Soon after breakfast, Mr. Dolmage came to announce the sudden death of poor Mr. Holland, which shocked us both very much.[1] Doctor Blair and Captain Dundas, with Major Cookson, came at three, and stayed dinner. We took a little walk in the evening, on the rock, and examined the twelve guns, which give the name to the fort. – The company all left us soon, and we went to bed at eight.

16*th*. Major Codd and Major Fraser, to breakfast. We hoisted our flag for the first time, and the Admiral came over from Port Royal, to visit us; but they all left us before dinner, excepting General Carmichael, Majors Darley, Fraser and Codd. General C. not well, and glad to get away early. His nephew very ill, at Fort Augusta.

17*th*. Doctor McNeil came early to tell us that General C. was in

---

[1] Nugent learned that Mr. Holland had "just fired a Gun at some Cattle which had broken into his Garden when a blood Vessel burst & he died."

PLATE 15

VIEW OF KINGSTON HARBOUR FROM THE APOSTLES BATTERY

From a drawing by James Lomax

great distress, and very ill, too, himself. His nephew, Mr. Cowen, died in the night, of convulsions, after the fever had left him, and he was supposed likely to recover. These awful circumstances, do indeed affect the spirits, but we must try not to think of them. Our boat (the *Maria*), came for the first time this evening, and we rowed to Green Bay, where we were received by an old man, of 72, a Mr. Robertson, formerly the purser of a man of war, who was expecting us, as an Aide-de-camp had gone the day before, to let him know we should probably make him a visit. It seems that he has settled the place entirely himself, and lived in it forty-two years. The purser of the *Blanche* was on a visit to him, for his health; and he has a white housekeeper (Mrs. Washbourn), who begged that my ladyship would allow her young ladies, Clifford, Johnson, and nurse Hamilton, to pay her a tea visit, they would be such *pretty company*. As soon as the sun got behind the mountain, we explored the place, which is very wild, romantic, and pretty. A great deal of cotton growing,[1] and altogether very curious. But the most wonderful thing we saw, was the tomb of a man, who was swallowed up in the great earthquake of 1692; but I have sketched the tomb and inscription exactly, and that will give the history, without my repeating it. We returned home delighted with our little voyage.

Here lyes the Body of
Lewis Galdy, Esq.
who departed this Life at Port Royal,
The 22d December, 1739, aged 80.

———

He was born at Montpelier in France,
but left that Country for his Religion,
and came to settle in this Island, where he
was swallowed up in the great Earthquake,
in the Year 1692,
And, by the Providence of God, was by
Another Shock
thrown into the Sea, and miraculously
saved, by swimming untill a Boat took
him up. He lived many years after in
great Reputation, beloved by all who
knew him, and much lamented at his
Death.

———

Dieu sur Tout.[2]

[1] In the late eighteenth century, much of the additional supply of raw cotton needed for the new textile machines in Britain was grown in the West Indies.

[2] In 1955, since the cemetery at Green Bay had become difficult of access, the Jamaica Historical Society arranged for the transfer of the tomb to Port Royal, where Galdy's remains were formally re-interred in St. Peter's churchyard.

18*th*. Captain Dundas's barge ready for us, at gun-fire, and with little ones and all, went on board the *Elephant* immediately. The Admiral, Commissioner Stirling, and a large party, to meet us, spend a very pleasant morning, walk over the ship, and little George much amused and astonished at all he saw; all the sailors admiring him very much, as well as dear little Louisa. On our return home, at 12, salutes were fired from Fort Augusta, Fort Charles, and all the ships of war at Port Royal. Captain Craskell was at the Apostles' battery, and fired a salute also.[1] Little L. did not mind the noise, but little George started and jumped every time that I did so, and at last was so much frightened, that he cried sadly. Kemble, Duckworth, and Rogers, came over in a canoe, from Kingston, to dinner, and returned at night; it was rather a hazardous voyage, which we begged them not to repeat.

20*th*. Mr. Hinchliffe at breakfast, full of gratitude for his appointment, as Judge of the Admiralty Court, and to take the oaths, &c. Dr. Robertson also came to breakfast, and seems perfectly satisfied with the justice of General N.'s conduct towards him.

22*nd*. General Carmichael, Major Darley, Mr. K., &c. at breakfast. The question respecting the Inspector of Prize Tonnage decided satisfactorily in the evening, before the party broke up. I rejoice, for, although I don't like to have anything to say to public matters, I can't help hearing all about them, and they are very often a great worry and anxiety to me.[2]

23*rd*. Just as we were going to dinner, Duckworth, Browne and Rogers, with Majors Codd and Fraser, came and stayed till eight.

24*th*. Received a present of two macaws, and a Spanish hammock, by a Mid from the *Hunter* brig, just arrived from Honduras. – Some of the staff at dinner.

25*th*. Captain Perkins of the *Tartar*, at 7 o'clock. He arrived last night, from St. Domingo, and brought back Mr. Corbet; who was sent by General N. with proposals for a treaty of commerce, &c. to His *Excel-*

---

[1] Long calculates that 28,600 lbs. of powder, costing £2145, were consumed annually in the firing of the morning and evening guns and ceremonial salutes in Kingston harbour. In firing a salute on the King's birthday in 1804, two of the guns at Fort Balcarres in Falmouth exploded and "two men of His Majesty's 55th Regiment were unfortunately destroyed" (*Royal Gazette*).

[2] Nugent and the conscientious Edward Corbet, shortly to be appointed Collector of Customs, were much exercised about irregularities in the disposal of prize cargoes, the trouble being that "the present Prize Agent, Mr. Waterhouse, who is a Man of too acute Talents for that Situation as it stands at present, may ship from, or land anything at, his Wharf without Fear of Detection"; and, as Corbet pointed out, the temptation for him to sell the goods in Saint-Domingue at twice the Jamaica price was very great.

lency General Dessalines, the black Emperor. Then came the Admiral, the Commissioner, and several Navy men, Mr. Corbet, and Doctors Robertson and Edgar. In short, our little front drawing-room was so full, that many sat in the veranda. Mr. C. has not succeeded in his negotiation. General Dessalines wishes to make some terms on his own part, that certainly will not be acceded to by General N. Moreover, General N.'s intention is, I believe, to send Mr. Corbet over once more, and then I shall state all matters in this book; at present, therefore, I shall be silent.[1] The Admiral, &c. took their leave before dinner, but the rest remained to dine; and, immediately after, we began our voyage in the *Maria*, to Fort Clarence; old Mr. Robertson, from Green Bay, having come in the morning, and offered to pilot us thither. We were much pleased with our excursion, and got home at 8. All the young men returned to Spanish Town. – Only Henry Rogers slept here.

26th. The horrid Court of Chancery begins to-day, and will interfere sadly with our comfort. General Carmichael came, most provokingly, to spend the day, and stayed till General N. returned, at 4, to dinner.

27th. General Carmichael and Major Darley, with fifty men of the 2nd West India regiment, came to mend our roads, and they are so good natured, and so anxious for our accommodation, that I feel quite angry with myself, for not enjoying General C.'s society yesterday, and preferring my dear nursery party. As soon as General N. returned, Mr. Corbet and Mr. Whitfield came, on St. Domingo business, and we were not left to ourselves till near 8. Then, we enjoyed the sea air a little while, before we shut up for the night.

31st. Made Duckworth read me one of Blair's Sermons,[2] and he really seemed as much interested in it as I was.

February 2nd. Mr. Duckworth off, at daylight, to fish. – Brought home a shoal of fish of all sorts.

3rd. I am afraid the climate has at last disagreed with me, for I was near fainting twice from actual weakness, while I was dressing for my

[1] The author forgets to keep her promise. Dessalines, who was later crowned Emperor of Haiti, complained in February of Nugent's refusal to recognise him as Governor-General. He objected to a proposed restriction on trade in neutral (North American) ships, and demanded arms and ammunition on a scale which Nugent was not prepared to meet. Nugent blamed the failure of the negotiations partly on the Royal Navy, which during the blockade had angered Dessalines by depriving him of the capture of French stocks of arms.

[2] *Sermons*, 5 vols., 1777–1801, by the Rev. Hugh Blair, was a widely read work of which Dr. Johnson said: "I love Blair's *Sermons;* though the dog is a Scotchman, and a Presbyterian, and everything he should not be, I was the first to praise them."

platform walk, with the little ones. – Mr. D. off again to fish. I hope he will not be in the sun as late as he was yesterday, for it is a sad risk for him; but he is so fond of the sport! General Carmichael and Captain Ross came at 7, to spend the day. I would have excused them for omitting the kindness they intended me.

5*th*. The Admiral and Captain Garth surprised us, just before we went to dinner, and six of the staff. So our little Fort room was quite crowded; but we had a pleasant dinner, and all were off at 8, and we walked down the rock with them.

6*th*. A white man from the Admiral, with a letter to me recommending him as a butler, but declined to take him. Then came a madman, who talked of General Brunet, and plots among the blacks, &c. but it all ended in asking charity. General N. gave him a guinea, and he was seen safely down the rock; though I own his stories made me go to bed most uncomfortably, and revived all the alarms of plots, &c. &c.

8*th*. General N. and H. Rogers (who returned to sleep in the Fort) off at daylight, to fish and shoot. Returned at 4, having been all day coasting, and a great risk I am sure they have run, by having been so long out. They brought home immense sport, having shot two pelicans, and a variety of other birds. The pelican is indeed a curious bird; the bill is very long, and the sides of it as sharp as a razor. The chest is of an elastic texture, and stretches to an enormous size. General N. talks of getting some of his day's sport stuffed and preserved, to take home with us.

10*th*. Captain Whitby, of the *Désirée*, came just as we were going to dinner.

11*th*. General N. out again with his gun, till breakfast time; and then again till 1, to see the Look-out[1] with General Carmichael, and some of the staff, who came to breakfast.

12*th*. Walk on the platform till 7. Prayers after breakfast, and then prepare to return to the Penn. – About 12, I laid down again, with little G. by my side, and soon after was seized with a most dreadful spasm in my head, and so suddenly, that, although I knew all that was going forward around me, I could not utter a word, the pain was so violent. Most fortunately, I had the presence of mind not to let go of my dear G., who was in my arms at the time; otherwise he might have been killed. Doctor C. was sent for; but, before he arrived, dear good Clifford, at the risk of her life, had gone off to Spanish Town, and procured every necessary

---

[1] On the hills behind Port Henderson are the ruins of two look-outs or watch towers, and a house, said to have been used by Admiral Rodney in the 1770's.

medicine for me, and when the Doctor arrived, he found nothing wanting. Several of the staff, &c. were coming to dine with us. Poor Clifford had a side saddle put on the first horse that arrived, and, at the hazard of her existence, rode off to the Penn. Never shall I forget her kindness. She came into my room, streaming with perspiration, and loaded with bottles of medicine. I saw, but could not speak to thank her, or express my fears for the risk she had run. – Till 4 in the morning my agony was great. Doctor C. remained on the sofa, and poor dear Clifford on the floor, by my bed-side, on a mattrass. Doctor Clare says, that my complaint is a *Coup-de-Soleil*, owing to the sun pouring upon the low roof of the battery room, and I suppose it is, for there is no ceiling, and the roof is as hot as a furnace. He advises my return to the Penn without delay.

13*th*. Rejoiced to be once more at the Penn, which has been put into the nicest order, for our reception.

17*th*. An express from General Carmichael to General N. He has discovered a spring of fresh water close to Fort Augusta, which will be a great acquisition indeed.[1]

20*th*. General N. held a Board of Forts, &c. which kept him all day in Spanish Town. Have several notes, about *white ladies'* disputes and little gossip. Keep clear of it all as well as I can.

22*nd*. General N. off before day, with the doctors and several of the staff, to see and decide upon the newly discovered well, at Fort Augusta.

23*rd*. Mr. Humphries at breakfast. – General N. made him happy, by giving him the living of Vere, vacant by the death of poor Mr. Underwood. No events; only they say the wild cats have destroyed a great deal of our poultry.

25*th*. A packet arrives; all prosperous, both public and private, except that from Trinidad there is an account of poor Edward Rogers' death, which we have the melancholy task of breaking to his brother Henry. He was much affected, poor fellow, and I made him my companion the rest of the day.

26*th*. In the evening unfavourable accounts from Curaçoa.

29*th*. Took the Admiral to Port Henderson at daylight. He is in a sad fright about Curaçoa and not at all in spirits, as he undertook the whole affair, without saying a word to General N., and so feels that

---

[1] In 1800, £4003 12s. 6d. (Jamaica currency) was paid to two contractors for supplying Fort Charles (at Port Royal), Fort Augusta and Apostles Battery with water and boats for one year. Long puts the cost of supplying Fort Augusta with water from the Rio Cobre at £400.

all the responsibility will rest upon himself. But General N. has met his very late communication, of the state of affairs there, in the kindest manner; and in this, as in every other case, has set aside his own private feelings, and only considered the public service. The poor Admiral seemed rather humbled, and very grateful; and I sincerely hope their joint arrangements will not prove to be too late.[1]

March 3rd. Dearest little Louisa stood to-day, for the first time, all alone by a chair, and she will not be six months old till the 8th. It was a *beautiful* sight; she is so very short, so fat, and so very pretty. At least we think she is. She is indeed like a little fat wax doll. But I have desired that she shall only be allowed to stand now and then, as a show; but not long at a time, for fear of making her dear little legs crooked.

4th. The heat excessive. Mr. and Mrs. Affleck, and Mrs. and Miss Rennalls, &c. at dinner. Go to bed with a thousand apprehensions, and in low spirits. People here are so very imprudent in their conversation. The splendour of the black chiefs of St. Domingo, their superior strength, their firmness of character, and their living so much longer in these climates, and enjoying so much better health, are the common topics at dinner; and the blackies in attendance seem so much interested, that they hardly change a plate, or do anything but listen. How very imprudent, and what *must* it all lead to!

7th. No guests to-day, excepting Mr. White, recommended to General N. by Lord Fingal. He is very importunate to get some place or appointment.

8th. Settle Madame Jolie's affairs, by writing to Captain Saville, &c. More information received from General Merck.[2]

10th. Drive to the King's House early. Call at several places, and surprise some of the staff, whose secret ménage was unknown to us before; but this is a sad, sad country! See the fattest black baby I ever beheld, quite a little monster, and all owing to stuffing it with food. How unwholesome it must be! Mine, I am determined, shall at least be fed

---

[1] The Admiral had ordered Capt. John Bligh with two ships of the line, two frigates and an armed schooner to proceed to Curaçao and demand its surrender. Bligh landed 800 men but encountered unexpected resistance from the French and Dutch defenders, and had to call off the attack.

[2] Captain Saville, RN, was Commissioner for French prisoners of war. General Merck, a German by birth, one of the officers on parole, was the madman at Apostles Battery referred to above. He afterwards claimed to have revealed to Nugent a plot by Gen. Brunet and other French prisoners to seize the barracks and arsenal, rouse the slaves, and get control of Jamaica with the help of French forces from Cuba.

moderately, and I take care that none of the blackies shall ever give them a morsel.

11*th*. Hear from Major Fraser a great many distresses of the St. Domingo emigrants, and give him all my gold pocket-pieces, for distribution, though they won't do any great good, I fear. – Begin to take jelly to-day, and think it promises to agree with me.

12*th*. Colonel and Mrs. Horsford arrived from England yesterday. He breakfasted here, but she only comes to dinner. – We invited them to be with us till they can get a house, and accordingly they come to-morrow.

13*th*. Colonel Ramsay, and Major Cookson, at breakfast. – The latter to take leave for England.

15*th*. Mr. Edwards, of Vere, joined our party.

17*th*. Spoke to Mrs. Horsford, as a friend, on the subject of her *vivacity*, occasionally, in speaking to her husband. Now that I have a daughter of my own, I feel interested in the conduct of every woman. She took it in good part, and has promised to command her temper.

18*th*. Finish my letters to go by the *Duquesne*, in which poor wretched, but now happy, Doctor Robertson sails for England.

20*th*. Dr. Robertson at dinner, for the last time. He was full of gratitude and happiness. – Mr. Cathcart, and Mr. Fitzgerald; the latter just arrived from Cuba. He gives a dreadful account of the suffering of the poor people in St. Domingo, and of the treachery of the French generals, before they left the island.

24*th*. An immense yellow snake was shot close to the house.[1]

26*th*. Dress by candle-light, and drive with the whole party to Port Henderson. Find General Carmichael's boat waiting for us. Land at Fort Augusta soon after sunrise. See the West India regiment out, and all the new recruits. They made a most savage appearance, having only just arrived from Africa; all their names were written on cards, tied round their necks! Saw the regimental school, after which General Carmichael gave us a grand breakfast, and we left Fort Augusta at 11. – The heat was excessive, but when we came near the newly discovered spring, I could not resist getting out of the carriage to explore it; though the sand burnt my feet, and the sun scorched my temples and nose sadly. Mrs. Horsford was certainly more prudent, in not leaving the carriage.

---

[1] Gosse, *op. cit.*, describes the snake, *epicrates subflavus*, as not infrequently found in houses, and as commonly attaining a length of eight or ten feet. Non-poisonous like all Jamaican snakes, it is now rare.

31*st*. Dress by candle-light, and our whole party proceeded to Port Royal, where the Admiral gave us a grand breakfast on board the *Hercule*. All the Captains of the fleet, the Murphy family, &c. &c. Lord Wm. Fitzroy was the only new Captain, and is a very nice-looking young man. The *lion* for the morning, for the gentlemen, was a large cannon taken from the French, but I own it did not interest me much. Saw poor Captain Walker, just before he left the *Hercule*. Never was there a truer picture of woe, and most sincerely do I feel for him.[1]

April 1*st. Easter Day*. – Go to church at 10. – Mrs. Horsford was not well, from the fatigue of yesterday, and could not go. The church was strewed with pimento and orange blossoms, and the pews were ornamented with branches of both. The scent was most refreshing. The Communion was tolerably well attended, and Mr. Rose (who now has preached) assisted Mr. Woodham. Saw Colonel Dessources at the King's House afterwards, and asked him to dinner. We had an unusually large party, and the servants, too, had a feast, and were made very happy; General N. having ordered an ox to be killed for them last night.

3*rd*. General N. out early with his gun, but I did not drive out, as the servants were dancing all night, and I am sure must want a little more rest than usual this morning.

4*th*. Drive very early to Port Henderson. – General Carmichael, Major Darley, and the Rev. Mr. Rose, at breakfast, and stayed all day. Mr. Nugent was added to our dinner party. – Hear a salute fired, while we were at dinner, and at 8, receive notes from Admiral Dacres, announcing to General N. his arrival, to assume the naval command on the station, and to me the arrival, under his care, of two boxes; one full of straw bonnets from dear kind Lady Buckingham, and the other, lace veils, &c. from dear, dear Lady Temple. Go to bed in high spirits, at having heard from our beloved friends; for Admiral Dacres sent me a large packet of letters from them all.

5*th*. Mr. O'Keeffe, recommended by the Duke of Clarence, came to pay his compliments, on his arrival in this country. – We had a large dinner party; several officers of the 60th, Messrs. Fishback, Petrie, Campbell, &c. and Mr. (Chancellor) White.

---

[1] Ten days before, Capt. Walker had sailed for England in command of the captured ship *Duquesne*, but now faced a court martial for having grounded the ship on the west end of Morant Keys on the morning of the 25th March. The court let him off with a reprimand.

PLATE 16

HMS *Hercule* IN PORT ROYAL HARBOUR, 1806
From a watercolour sketch by T. Stuart
Port Royal on the left, Apostles Battery on the extreme right

6th. Colonel Mellifont, just arrived to join the 85th, with Major Otway and Mr. Spears, at dinner.

9th. Hear of the arrival of the *Queen Charlotte* packet. Meet our letters on our morning's drive. All delightful, and the dear old King much better than we had dared to hope from our last accounts. The Murphy family, and Mr. Minott in addition to our staff party, at dinner.

10th. Mr. Sharpe just arrived, and Captain Hance of Rock Fort.

11th. General N., with the staff, off at gun-fire, for Port Henderson. My morning as usual. – Poor Browne taken ill at the King's House. One of my little black boys in a dangerous way, and poor little Hortense *in labour.* In short, I was anxious all day, and saw only the doctors, who all stayed dinner. – General N. returned about 4 o'clock, having done all he wished of business and civility to-day; and he likes Admiral Dacres even better on this second visit, than on the first. – All the invalids better in the evening, and wretched *little* Hortense, has a great German boy.

15th. Mr. Croft, with letters of introduction from England, and Major Campbell of the 60th, in addition to our usual Sunday party.

17th. General N. off before day, to review the 60th on the race-course. Mr. Hall, and Mr. C. Grant, Member for St. Mary's, at dinner.

18th. Up at half-past two, and arrive at the Admiral's Penn soon after daylight. Admiral Dacres there, with Sir J. T. Duckworth, to receive us, with a large party of Navy men and a few civilians. Like Admiral Dacres very much; he seems such a good natured, *domestic* man, always talking of his family.[1] The morning spent in gossiping and talking nonsense, but we were all merry and much amused; and I should have been very comfortable, if the dear little ones had been here. – At dinner, the party was added to, by Captains Bligh, Croft, Vansittart, Evans and Dunn, General Carmichael, Mr. and Mrs. Symes, and Mrs. Ross.

19th. General N. &c. off at daylight, to review the 6th battalion of the 60th regiment, at Up-Park camp. Large dinner party at 5 o'clock. – The ladies were Mrs. and Miss Grant, Mrs. Ross, and Mrs. Affleck.

After dinner, I begged them to excuse me, and I would lie down a short time before the ball, which I was sorry for afterwards, as I found

---

[1] Mrs. Nugent was not the first one to be charmed by this. Mrs. Fremantle, aboard her husband's ship off Toulon in 1797, had written in her diary:

"Captain Dakers of the *Barfleur* paid us a long visit this morning, he is a great favourite of mine for he seems to be so fond of his wife and children, he always talks of his family" (Anne Fremantle, *Wynne diaries*).

on my return to the drawing-room, the ladies looking very odd, and certainly cool to each other; for poor Mrs. Horsford had injudiciously talked nonsense about the *natives*, and offended them all very much, as I learnt from the gentlemen, in the course of the evening. Began the ball with Sir J. T. Duckworth, and then danced with several other Navy men, as well as military and civilians; and, in short, in spite of the remains of my headache, did all I could to be *agreeable*. Never since we have been in this island have we been shewn more kindness, nor have we ever been received with more respect and distinction; and this proves to me, that, though they may not like many measures that my dear N. is obliged to enforce, yet that they cannot help liking him, as a man, and appreciating his character.

20*th*. At breakfast, Commodore Barré, and Monsieur and Madame Vatière, in addition to our party. Am very much amused with the French people. When they quitted us, we drove into Kingston, and were imprudently out till 3 o'clock, in a broiling sun. However, we were none of us the worse for it.

At 5, a very numerous dinner party indeed. The ladies, Mrs. Marshall, Mrs. Griffiths, and two Misses Stewart. – In the middle of dinner, a sad scene occurred. A scorpion crept from under the flap of the table, up one of the Misses Stewart's sleeve, and stung her severely. It was really frightful to see the reptile under the thin muslin sleeve, striking with all its force, and the poor girl in an agony; and it was some time before it could be got hold of. Mr. Hinchliffe produced a little bag of indigo, which he wetted with water, and applied to the wound, and it seemed immediately to allay the pain, and by its cooling quality certainly prevented the part from inflaming, for the young lady did not feel any bad effects from it afterwards. I sat opposite to her, between the two Admirals, and could not help crying from real fright. – To-morrow we did intend to go home, but alas! it will now be Sunday, before I see my dear little ones again; for Mr. S. Taylor expressed great anxiety to give us a dinner to-morrow, and, from *political motives*, it was thought we should not refuse. Indeed, in the present situation of my dear N. with the House of Assembly, we ought to do everything possible, to conciliate the Members, and must not consider our private feelings. – Cards, and to bed at ten.

21*st*. Hear that poor Miss Stewart has not suffered from the odious scorpion. – Visitors and gossip till 4; then proceed to Mr. Simon Taylor's Penn, where there was a grand entertainment. Mr. S. T. was more than ever kind to me, and he spoke in the highest terms of my dear N., and ended by saying: "Ah, he is an honest man, though I don't like some of his measures." – Saw a number of black and brown ladies in the evening, to please the old housekeeper; but I don't know whether the white ladies, whom I left in the drawing-room when I gave audience, quite approved of my conduct. Back to the Admiral's Penn soon after 10, and to bed immediately.

22nd. Start at daylight for home, and find my dear little ones quite well, and rejoiced to see us return. Particularly delighted with the toys I bought for them in Kingston.

24th. The Navy were full of the Kingston business, and say, that the ladies have got a Directory, in which they have discovered, that Mrs. Horsford's father, Mr. Brocksopp, is a slop-seller at Wapping.[1] I do lament her being so silly, and bringing all this upon herself; though probably she will never hear of the offence she has given. I shall give her a friendly hint, to be more discreet in her conversation in future.

25th. Brought young Berkeley home with us, as he has leave of absence, from the *Blanche,* for a few days.

26th. Mr. Smith at breakfast, who expressed much gratitude to General N. for appointing him Island Engineer, though only *pro tempore.*

May 5th. At 7, send the chariot for Mrs. Wright, from Carolina, and Mr. La Motte. The lady was introduced to me by an old friend, Mrs. Middleton.

9th. Hear of the death of Mr. O'Keeffe and poor Miss Bigsby, whose fate is indeed a lamentable one.

12th. Mr. La Motte and Captain Dobbin at breakfast. A deputation, composed of Messrs. Kelly and Markland, from the merchants of Kingston, to General N., to detain the packet for one week. After much discussion, this was acceded to.

14th. Mr. Harris (of the *Nonsuch*) at dinner.[2] – General N. played Colonel Irvine rather a naughty trick, by ordering an extraordinary fricassée for dinner, of which the Colonel ate twice, and highly commended it. It passed for chicken, but was really a guana. When he hears, to-morrow, what it was, I expect to see wry faces, and a good laugh too.

15th. At breakfast, the story of the guana made the party very merry;

---

[1] Slop-seller: a seller of cheap clothing for seamen. Brocksopp and Bilbie, stationers and rag merchants, Upper Thames Street, are listed in *Kent's London Directory* for 1800.
[2] Mrs. Nugent misheard the name of the ship. William Harris was a midshipman in the *Hunter* brig.

and, as it had perfectly agreed with those that ate it, they joined in the joke; indeed, it is considered not only a wholesome dish, but a great delicacy, by many Creoles; but the sight of it, while living, is disgusting, as it is covered with scales, and looks frightful altogether. We had two at the King's House, but one of them fell into a covered tank there, and was lost; the other pined, and its death was decreed, to prevent it from sharing the fate of its companion. – It is, in fact, to give some idea of it, nothing in appearance but a small crocodile.[1] Wrote to Mr. S. Taylor to-day, about Mrs. Wright's affairs, and did a great deal of business for several people, all of which, I hope, will spare my dear N. some little trouble.

16*th*. Colonel Gordon, Major Drummond, Mr. Edwards, &c. at dinner.

22*nd*. Send the sociable at 2, for the Admiral and Captain King, who, with Mr. Hinchliffe, &c. made our dinner party. – Sir. J. T. Duckworth and Captain Loring stayed all night. The latter to take leave on going to England. – Admiral Dacres is on a cruise for the present. – I shall no longer speak of my own health; it is a stupid and monotonous subject.

25*th*. Only Mons. de Mansigny at dinner, in addition to our party. – He is a sensible, gentleman-like old Frenchman, and I like him much.

26*th*. General Carmichael, Major Darley, Major Ottley, Captain Kingscote, &c. at dinner, and Colonel Lethbridge to take leave for England.

27*th*. Kemble came from Kingston, to announce to us his intended marriage. – Foolish man! but I wish him well with all my heart.

29*th*. The early part of the day as usual. – Colonel Mosheim, Major Campbell, and Mr. Bowes (a solicitor in the Court of Chancery), at dinner.

30*th*. Captains Dundas and Lake, R.N. in addition to our dinner party.

June 4*th*. Our dear old King's birthday. – I pray that he may receive the reward of his virtues in a better world. – The Doctors advise for me an immediate change of air, and Colonel Mellifont came in the morning, to settle about my going to Stony Hill.

5*th*. Hear of the serious illness of poor Captain Cathcart. He is a fine young man, and I trust may be spared. – General N. in Spanish Town

---

[1] Sir Hans Sloane, in *A voyage to the islands of Madera, Barbados . . . and Jamaica*, 1707–25, says that in his time guanas ("very fat and good meat") were commonly eaten in Jamaica and "were of great use when the English first took the island." The Jamaican guana continued to be of use until recent years, when it became extinct. At about the same time as Gen. Nugent fooled Col. Irvine, some officers of the 3rd Regiment (the Buffs) at the Mosquito Shore gave a dinner party at which the menu included guana fricasseed, manati soused, monkey barbacued, armadillo curry, and parrot pie (Capt. G. Henderson, *An account of the British settlement at Honduras*, 1811).

all the morning, holding a Bishop's Court. – Mr. Alexander, of the 85th, was the only addition to our party at dinner.

6th. We all went melancholy to bed, having heard not only of the death of Captain Cathcart, but also of five of his officers!

7th. General N. rode with Mr. Smith at daylight to Fort Clarence. – General Carmichael and Mr. Hinchliffe at breakfast; after which, General N. rode again to inspect the Apostles' battery, to see with his own eyes all that may be necessary to be done there.

9th. Set off from the Penn at 4 o'clock; both the dear children quite well. Arrive at Stony Hill before 8. My dearest N. my escort and comforter. – At dinner, Colonel Mellifont, Major Otway, Captain Austin, with C. Meredith. The band playing for me till 8. – Nothing can exceed the kindness of Colonel M., and indeed every officer of the regiment. – Colonel M. has given up his apartments in the barrack to me, and the other officers are so anxious to do every thing for my accommodation, that I am only distressed for fear of putting them to great inconvenience, by their desire to study my comfort.[1]

10th. And my dearest N.'s birthday. Most fervently do I offer up my prayers for his health and happiness. – Before dinner, saw all the gentlemen of the regiment; the Lieut.-Colonel and Major taking their breakfast with us. At 3, my dear N. left me for the Admiral's Penn, and I dined alone; but Colonel M., Major O., and Captain M., spent part of the evening with me. – The band played, and all the women and children, too, were paraded. I went out and spoke to most of them, but felt so exhausted at last, that Dr. Doughty (the surgeon of the regiment) advised me to go to bed, and take a composing draught.

11th. Major Fraser and Mrs. Wright came to breakfast. – Colonel Mellifont and the Doctor also joined the party. My dear N., after reviewing the St. Catherine's regiment, returned to Stony Hill, about 3 o'clock. – At dinner, Captains D'Arcy and Macintosh, with the Colonel and Major; the band playing as usual in the evening. – Sergeant Murphy, a fine tall handsome man, was appointed my orderly, and to be constantly in attendance.

12th. Feel rather better this morning, and try to be well, that I may

---

[1] "Mrs. Nugent I am happy to say has benefitted by the Change of Air and Scene, and by roughing it at Stony Hill, as it has directed her Attention from her own Situation to other Matters. She is Queen here and of course commands her Subjects to give her whatever Comforts the Barracks afford, which are however much circumscribed for a Family" (Nugent to Duckworth, 13 June 1804).

Some of the old barrack buildings form part of the present Industrial School.

fulfil my promise of dining with the regiment to-day, at the mess. – Mrs. Piercy and Mrs. Nolan, with a large party of officers, to call upon me in the morning. – At 4, went to the mess, and walked afterwards for a short time on the parade. Have some of the party to take tea with me, but at 8 retire to my room. – General N. has promised that my dear little ones shall come up to me, as soon as possible; to-morrow or the next day, I hope.

13th. After breakfast, Colonels Mosheim and Unwin, Major Drummond, &c. to call upon me. General N. set off for the Penn at 3; and, at 4, Colonel Mellifont, Major Otway, Captain Wilkins, and Messrs. Longfield, Grant, and Campbell, dined with me.

14th. The Rev. Mr. Campbell, the Lieut-Colonel, the Major, Captain Etherington, Lieutenants Cully and Cruice, dined with me, with Ensign Sutherland. Feel better, and in better spirits, for I shall see all my darlings, (please God!) to-morrow.

15th. Up at, 4, and prepare for my dear babies, who are to come at 8. All well and happy. Spend my day with them, and my dear N., most delightfully.

16th. General N. rode early to Bellevue[1], in hopes of engaging that place for us, but was disappointed.

17th. Mrs. Burrowes and Mrs. Chapman, of the regiment, dined at the mess, and a large party came home with me to tea. Get rid of the ladies as soon as possible, and left General N. to manage the gentlemen, who stayed talking till near ten.

18th. General N. went at daylight, to review the St. Andrew's regiment. – A quiet dinner in our own apartment. – In the evening we went to the parade. I preceded General N., the children being anxious to go out, and was received by the regiment like a general officer, according to Colonel Mellifont's order.

19th. Mr. Plunkett came early this morning, to offer us Mount Salus. – General N. rode over to see the place, and has engaged it. – Colonel and Mrs. Horsford came to spend the day, and we had the Lieutenant-Colonel, Major, Captain Austin, and Mr. Plunkett to dinner.

21st. General N. off before daylight, to review the Kingston regiment.

22nd. Walk out before parade, for a short time; Cupid carrying my chair, and the orderly sergeant Murphy following.

---

[1] This Bellevue, near Stony Hill, and now occupied by St. Michael's Roman Catholic Seminary, is to be distinguished from Mr. March's Bellevue near Spanish Town.

25th. At breakfast, Mr. Watson, and several of the staff. I have now had every officer of the regiment at dinner, and must begin the list again.

26th. The two Admirals at breakfast. They remained the whole day.

July 5th. A stormy night, General N. up from 1 till 2, writing letters, to postpone the execution of the poor deserter, which was to take place at 5, this morning. Poor soul, it is only a short respite! – General N. and I writing, or arranging his tour round the island, and my moving to Mount Salus on Saturday.

We are invited to see Mr. Cully, Adjutant of the 85th, married to Mrs. Chapman, a Kingston widow. Went there, with the Colonel, Major, &c. &c. at 4 o'clock. A sad scene, the bride was shut up, and in tears, not having been able to get any white satin ribbon from Kingston, nor any onions or sage, to stuff the ducks, that were to appear at the wedding feast. Sage and onions, it was not in our power to bestow; but, fortunately, I had a whole piece of white satin ribbon, for which I sent to my room immediately; and, while she was decorating herself, General N. stood godfather for Mrs. Burrowes's little boy; who was christened *Doctor* George William David, to the great astonishment of the clergyman and us all; but his father very sagaciously accounted for it, by saying, he intended him for his own profession, and it might save a diploma.

As soon as that ceremony was over, the bride made her appearance, all over bows of white satin, having cut up the whole piece of ribbon to ornament herself; which was rather an annoyance to me, as I could not replace it, without sending to England. General N. stood papa, and gave the lady away, and we then sat down to a sumptuous dinner, with no less than two couple of ducks smoking on the table, but, alas! without sage and onions. There was a large party of the regiment at dinner, and the whole business was very entertaining. – Before 8, General N., the Colonel, and I, returned to our barrack, and then our thoughts took a different turn, as my dear N. is to get up at 3 o'clock to-morrow, on a most painful service, that of shooting a wretched deserter, who has been already pardoned sixteen times.

6th. We neither of us slept much, and General N. was up at 2 o'clock. At 3, he was off for Halfway Tree, where the poor man was shot. He was attended home by a large party to breakfast; among whom were a lady and gentleman, that he called Donellan or Donaldson; but we found when they were gone, that the name was Campbell. However, the hospitality was the same, and they seemed much pleased. – Dine at the mess; order the regiment grog, and the same entertainment, as a take leave, that they had on our arrival. After the parade, saw the women of the regiment all assembled, and then called upon the bride and the ladies of the garrison, and took a *tender* leave of them all.

7*th*. A little after 4, we mounted our horses, and had a most beautiful romantic and tremendous ride, over the mountains, and on the edges of precipices, to Mount Salus.[1] Find the house and every thing very comfortable, and feel myself much better, and less fatigued than I could have expected. Mount Salus appears really almost out of the world, and, although I have a guard, I dread my dear N.'s leaving me, though his tour this time will be short. – The late rains have made the insects and reptiles appear in swarms innumerable, and their hum is quite extraordinary. – Our gentlemen all took leave, and I hope got over the precipice road before dark.

8*th*. The air was so cool and pleasant, that we quite enjoyed the early morning. Read prayers at 11, and at 1 my dear N. left to me to dine at Mr. Taylor's, and to commence his tour round the island. – The afternoon was extremely rainy, with tremendous thunder and lightning. Awful as it was to me, now alone with only the poor *blackies* and my guard, I occupied myself with watching it over the plains of Liguanea, from the piazza. At times, all was clear above, while the storm raged below; the thunder roaring, and the lightning flashing on the dark curtain, which hid all the plain from my sight. It was indeed most impressive, and added much to my sad and melancholy contemplations, in being absent from my dear husband and children.

9*th*. Two Messrs. Pinnock, and Mr. G. Cuthbert, with four officers of the 85th, to breakfast. The latter stayed and dined at 3 o'clock, and then returned to Stony Hill.

10*th*. When I was writing in the veranda this morning at half-past six, Colonel Mellifont and Mr. Austin came to breakfast with me; and, soon after, Captain Meredith escorted Mrs. Wright up the mountain, having gone to Kingston for that purpose. Hear a great deal of the sickliness of the season, and of many deaths in Kingston, &c.; but this is always more particularly the case at this time of the year. – Three officers of the 85th at dinner.

12*th*. Nurse and my darling little girl came.

---

[1] In the Red Hills, southwest of Stony Hill. It may have been the hill residence occasionally used by the Admiral, to which signals from the flagship in the harbour could be relayed by semaphore from the Admiral's Pen.

16th. Hear of the deaths of Major Otway and Mrs. Burrowes, at Stony Hill. – Go very melancholy to bed.

21st. At dinner, Mr. Harwood, Mr. Longfield, Mr. Dugard, Mr. Grant, and Mr. Nixon, and all go away at six.

22nd. Rise very, very early, and at sunrise had the happiness of seeing my dear N. and little Georgy, all well, thank God!

23rd. Walked in the evening to Mr. Pinnock's mountain; almost too much in my present situation, and contrary to Dr. Clare's injunctions.

24th. Rev. Mr. Humphries at dinner. Much disgusted with his cant of vulgarity, and am ashamed to say, that I was barely civil to him at last, and heartily glad to get rid of him at eight.

25th. Mrs. Cummins (my new nurse), and her child came. Don't very much like her manner, but she seems a good creature, and I must not be fastidious.

27th. Major Drummond, Colonel Irvine, Captain Duckworth, Mr. Browne and Dr. Adolphus, at breakfast, and to stay the whole day. Rain came on, and we were obliged to lodge them all as well as we could at night.

29th. Mr. Nugent came, and bored us all day.

30th. Only our own party at breakfast, with Mrs. Wright, and young Browne, who is here for his health. Soon after, General Carmichael and the Rev. Mr. Campbell came to spend the day. From Stony Hill came Mr. Grant, Mr. Campbell, Mr. Nixon, and Captain Hance. All left us at 6. Little G. and L. amused the party very much, and are, indeed, remarkably intelligent, lively, little things, and oh! how I long to shew them to our English friends!

31st. General N. off early for Kingston, and did not return till 3. – General N. found much consternation at Up-Park barracks, to-day, on account of several soldiers having died, in consequence of the bite of a spider. It is described as a small, round, black spider, with a red spot at the tail, containing a subtle poison.[1] In fifteen minutes or less, after the person is bitten or stung, he goes into convulsions, and very often it proves fatal. General N. saw a man in the hospital, a few hours after he was bitten, and says that his agonies were dreadful, and the doctors thought he could not possibly live. Before we went to bed, I had all the rooms thoroughly examined, and my darling children's cots in particular. God protect them!

---

[1] The black widow spider, *latrodectus mactans*, found on the American continent and West Indian islands.

August 1*st*. Only young Hylton at dinner, who came to thank General N. for his King's commission, which was in the 85th regiment. Write several letters to the young men of our staff, and endeavour to guide them to what is for their future welfare. I have daily fair promises from many, but alas! this is a sad country for the morals.

2*nd*. Captain Meredith's servant, this morning, brought in, from a little plantation close to the house, a curious nest, of one of the little black venomous spiders, that have been so fatal at Up-Park camp; at least it answers the description given of it. It is a little round black thing, with a very red spot close to the tail, or rather almost under the stomach. We have it preserved in rum, and I look at it with horror, thinking how fatal such a reptile may be to those I love. Our watchfulness and care will now be doubled, and I have desired that the children may never he allowed to touch any thing, not even a fly, for fear of that dreadful venomous creature.

3*rd*. Amuse my dear children, by shewing them a little humming-bird's nest, the progress of which I have been watching for several days past. The little mother is scarcely larger than a bee, and her nest is like a very tiny tea cup. It is placed under the leaf of a tree, which shelters it like a roof, and keeps even the dew from her young. The nest has a small branch running through it, as a security, and contained two little eggs, which are now hatched. The young birds are really not larger than what we call in England horse-flies, and are indeed the most ridiculous things. We were much amused, in seeing the little mother taking such care of them; and it was with difficulty I could get George and Louisa to allow themselves to be carried into the house again, they were so delighted with the sight. –Not a little melancholy, as, alas! to-morrow, my dearest N. begins his second tour.

4*th*. A melancholy day indeed! Dear N. off at 6. – The little ones were asking for papa all day. – Meredith went to Stony Hill, and brought back Drury, to spend a few days here. Gave them both a great deal of advice. Hear in the evening, from my dear N.

5*th*. Another letter from my dear husband. He is well in health, thank God! but greatly harassed with a variety of business. – Speculations upon his resigning the Government; politics; shabby and ungrateful conduct of many whom he has served, &c. &c. In short, he is very much disgusted with many, and so am I.

6*th*. Our young men all off to see a race, between the silly boys of the 85th, who will, no doubt, suffer severely for their folly.

11th. An express from General N., to say, that *the King of the Musquito Indians, and his uncle,* wished to come to Mount Salus, and that I must receive them in his absence.[1]

13th. The King, &c. did not arrive till 9, on account of the heavy rain, which has made the mountain road very difficult. I must now describe his little savage Majesty. – He is about six or eight years old, a plain puny looking child, but seems to have a very high and determined spirit. His features are rather better than those of negroes, and his hair is so much straighter, that he is evidently of a mixed breed; but his uncle has the woolly hair of the negro, with flat features, and a very wide mouth. – It is said that, many years ago, a large slave ship, from Africa, was wrecked on the Musquito shore, and no doubt this may account for the hair and features of the uncle, and for the mixture of the breed.

The young King was dressed in a scarlet uniform, and wore a crown upon his head, of which he seemed very proud. The crown was of silver gilt, ornamented with mock stones, and was sent from England, some years ago, for his father. Both the little King and his uncle seemed to hold it in high estimation. When it was placed on the table, and little G. and L. wished to handle it, the uncle got up, and placed it in a little box, brought with him for that purpose, shaking his head and saying, *na, na,* all the time. – Mr. Doughty, Mr. Cully, and Mr. Grant, arrived from Stony Hill, and then General Carmichael, Major Darley, Captain Etherington, and Mr. Nixon, composed our party.

At dinner, the uncle (Count Stamford, or the Duke of York, for he announced himself to have both these titles) ate of every dish, or rather devoured every thing that came within his reach. The little King had a small table for himself, and was helped by his uncle, who seemed to attend him quite as a servant. The uncle did not drink much wine, but what he did take soon got into his head; and as for the little King, he became quite savage in a short time. He cried, roared, and yelled horribly, and began to pull off all his clothes, in the most violent manner, and was nearly naked before we could have him carried out of the room. He was then put under the care of some of the negro women, for the night, but he shrieked and roared several hours, before he went to sleep.

---

[1] The King, whom Nugent had sent for to go to school in Spanish Town, was the eldest surviving son of the murdered George the Second (p. 37n. above). His elder brother had previously been sent to school in Kingston by Lord Balcarres, but died of smallpox. Mrs. Nugent's guest is possibly the George Frederick who in 1816 was crowned King of the Mosquito Shore in the Anglican church at Belize. The Mosquito territory continued to be a British "protectorate" until 1860.

The uncle soon lost all his diffidence, and began to talk to us so freely, of the good and hospitable customs of his country, that I spoke to General Carmichael, to get him also put to bed. Poor General Carmichael had, I am sure, drank too much wine too, by his manner, and therefore the 85th gentlemen were my greatest comfort. They got the General to bed, and also the Duke of York, placing a black man to guard the door of the latter, and then Captain Etherington, and Mr. Grant, got each a blanket, and laid themselves down at Mrs. Wright's door, and mine, and were our guards for the rest of the night.

14th. At daylight, to my great joy, all the party set off for Stony Hill, and I hope never to see the like again. Dear little G. and L. were quite sorry that the little King and his crown were gone, but thought him very naughty to say so much last night. I promised myself a quiet day, but, to my great annoyance, came Mr. Campbell, and Mr. Harwood, of the 85th, to dinner, but they went away in the evening.

18th. Receive several letters, from different members of the staff, and all full of fair promises, but I have lost my faith very much in them.

22nd. A most kind note from Mr. Simon Taylor, with a present of grapes and other fruit.[1] Took the opportunity, in reply, of being equally kind and flattering; and so I do hope, if he is not an active friend, he will not be an implacable enemy to my dear N. the next session.

23rd. Herman (our German butler) found an immense hairy spider, close to the piazza, but crushed it so much in his fright, that we could hardly ascertain its real shape; but, from every appearance that was left, I should imagine it was the tarantula. Have every place searched, but find nothing of the kind near, and so make up our minds to hope, that this one coming so near the house was a rare occurrence.[2] A quiet day; teaching the children how to tell papa he is welcome home.

26th. Read, &c. early, as usual on this day. – At breakfast the eternal and tiresome Mr. Nugent. – Prayers at 10. – The rest of the day quiet and comfortable.

29th. Preparing letters for England all the morning. General N. wrote a long epistle to dear Lord Buckingham, about a residence in Bucks, and Oving in particular. Duckworth, Browne, Kemble, and Rogers, came to spend the day, but all left us in the evening.

September 5th. At 7, the Admiral and Mr. Hinchliffe, to spend the day. –

[1] Long says that white and red grape vines, introduced from Europe, seemed to thrive on low-lying sites in Jamaica.
[2] The true tarantula is unknown in Jamaica.

The fact is, that this situation tempts many to come to breathe a little
fresh air. – Talk till 3, when we dined, and they left us soon after 6. –
Both General N. and I dreadfully fatigued, with our long talking day.

6th. Hear from the Admiral, of Mr. and Lady Margaret Cameron and
their family. Mr. Cameron is on his way to the Bahama Islands, of which
he is Governor. – Despatches upon despatches, and all the early part of the
day devoted to papers, by my dear Nugent. – Dine at 3; and, soon after
5, mounted my horse, and General N. walked by my side, to see a house
from a neighbouring mountain, from which we had a most magnificent
view. Returned, just as the day was closing in, much refreshed. – Settled
that we would go down to Spanish Town, to receive the Camerons at
the King's House. Both of us full of regret, but it can't be helped, and
we must make up our minds to it.

9th. Rise at 4, and all set off, to go down the mountain before the sun
rose. All the party on horseback, excepting myself, who performed the
journey in a chair, carried by four pioneers, and the little ones in men's
arms. Find the carriages waiting for us, at Swallowfield estate. Proceeded
to Spanish Town, where we arrived about ten.

11th. At 8, Mr. Cameron, Lady Margaret, and four children, arrived
in the carriages we sent to the Admiral's Penn for them, last night. He
was received with the ceremonies due to his rank as Governor, and we had
a grand dinner, and a ball in the evening. I like Lady Margaret very much,
and he appears an excellent, good, and most pleasing man. The children
are plain, but good-humoured and intelligent, and exactly what children
at their age ought to be. They are delighted with my little loves, and
particularly Louisa, who has been with them almost the whole day.

13th. Have, at 11, a second breakfast, of fruit, wine, cake, &c., and, at
12, all set off for the Admiral's Penn; Lady M., her young people, and
myself, in the sociable, with our two black postillions, in scarlet liveries,
but with black ankles peeping out of their particulars, and altogether
rather a novel sort of appearance, to Europeans just arrived. General N.
and Mr. Cameron in the curricle. Aides-de-camp, servants, &c. in kittareens, and on horseback; and all arrived in grand procession, at the
Admiral's, at about 3. Refreshments were ready, and then we all creolized
till 5 o'clock. A large party, of the Navy chiefly, at dinner.

14th. Immediately after breakfast we all went to see Kingston, and
make purchases. – Left Lady M. C. a short time at a milliner's, and called
upon Mr. and Mrs. Kemble to make her acquaintance, for the first time.
Return to the Admiral's about 2. A second breakfast was ready, of

mutton chops, &c. Then creolized till 3, when we went to dinner in our morning dresses; and, notwithstanding the late second breakfast, the whole party did ample justice to the Admiral's dinner. At 5, the carriages came to the door, and we all separated with real regret. – The Cameron children sent toys to little G. and L., and I gave them all keepsakes, at the jeweller's, in their names. – Governor Cameron and his family went to Greenwich to embark for the Bahamas, and we returned with our party to Spanish Town. Get home at 8, and found both our children quite well, and go to bed as soon as we could. – Lady M. Cameron and I amused ourselves to-day, on the subject of precedency. I was obliged, as Governor's lady, to take rank of her, but have promised her, her *revenge* in England, and shall be delighted to give it.

15*th*. Breakfast in my dressing-room this morning. Soon after, General Carmichael, and the young Indian King, with his uncle, came to spend the day. Amuse his little Majesty in my apartment, with sugar-plums and the children's toys. – General C., Major D., &c. returned to Fort Augusta in the evening. The King and his uncle remained with us. The latter was taken ill, but it is thought to be merely from eating too much dinner.

17*th*. Drive to the Penn at daylight. At 10, General N. began his quarterly Court of Chancery. – Obliged to send the little Musquito King *forcibly* to school; but not before, in his rage and reluctance, he had broken the poor orderly sergeant's watch to pieces, and scratched his face sadly. The uncle was still ill, and so we had all to manage for him ourselves. George says, "naughty, naughty boy." – A staff dinner only, and to bed at nine.

23*rd*. The Duke of York so well, that we sent him off, before dinner, to Fort Augusta, to embark for the Musquito Shore. He took a great many presents with him, which he considered very handsome.

25*th*. Try to learn to play at *brelan*.[1] – To bed soon after nine.

26*th*. The early morning, as usual. – Went to the gallery, and heard Mr. White make his first speech in the Court of Chancery. – Mr. Campbell, Mr. Storer, Colonel Unwin, Major Drummond, &c. at dinner.

28*th*. In my drive this morning, met several of the unfortunate half-black progeny of some of our staff; all in fine muslin, lace, &c. with wreaths of flowers in their hats. What ruin for these worse than thoughtless young men! But advice is of no use, and they must stand the consequences; yet I cannot help pitying their families, and it makes me truly melancholy to think of their future distress.

[1] A French gambling game, something like poker.

October 4th. Mr. Gaven, recommended by the Irish Chancellor, at dinner, with our staff.

11*th*. Alas! poor Dr. Clare is no more. He breathed his last before the day dawned, and we have indeed lost a most excellent friend and agreeable companion, as well as an able physician.

12*th*. My darling little George is two years old to-day, and it was to have been a day of joy and thankfulness, but the loss of poor Doctor Clare has thrown a sad cloud upon my spirits. The house full, all day. – Little G. was dressed in boy's clothes, for the first time, and little L. had a pair of shoes for the first time also. Two grand events, that occupied the whole family, as well as their dear little selves. – A grand dinner at 5, and a large party, or rather a ball. The band played all dinner time, to George's great delight, and Louisa danced round the shades on the dinner table, to the amusement and astonishment of every one. At 11, the party separated, and all the noise ceased, to my great joy; for what with the drinking of healths, the huzzaing, the music, and the contrast of my own feelings, I really was worn out. But may God bless my dear boy, and may every future birthday be as happy to him as this has been, for he and Louisa have been almost wild with spirits, the whole day.

15*th*. Hear all the new blackies their prayers, &c. previously to their being made Christians. – The *Chesterfield* packet sailed to-day, with General N.'s despatches.

16*th*. Messrs. Sedgwick, Donaldson, and Taylor, and General Carmichael, &c. at dinner.

17*th*. Captain Trollope and Mr. Markland at dinner.

18*th*. A large garrison dinner party to-day. – A Mrs. Campbell was the only lady, who entertained me with histories of land crabs, &c. and all the disasters of a poor military man's wife.

21*st*. Mr. Woodham, &c. at dinner. At 7 o'clock, all repaired to the chapel, where all the new servants, and infants lately born, were baptized; and I trust in God, they may turn out good Christians, and peaceable members of society at least; for I have tried to make them understand their duty.

22*nd*. All day the house was in a bustle, crowded with visitors. Eighty-five people at dinner. The band playing, the huzzaing, &c. were almost stunning, and I did not go to bed till after 11 o'clock. Poor General N. was obliged to sit up much longer.

23*rd*. The gentlemen did not separate till after 1 this morning, and yet we were all up at 6, as usual. – Several people at breakfast, and at 11, General N. held a Council. At 3, the House of Assembly came over in a body, when he delivered his speech. – At 6, an immense crowd; the House of Assembly, the public officers, and the military, all at dinner, and exactly the same bustle and noise as we had yesterday. I pity poor dear N., who must go through it all, and with so much business on his hands, at the same time. – I got to bed at 10, but the party in the great hall did not break up till three.

24*th*. A quiet day, thank God! at least I hope so, as I have not heard of any company being invited. – Ten o'clock. – My dear N. writing in my room, the greatest part of the morning, and amusing himself with the children, till dinner time; and then only the Rev. Mr. Donaldson was added to our party.

25*th*. Our new medical Inspector-General (Mr. Rocket) arrived from England.

28*th*. Major Watson, just from England, the only addition.

29*th*. Mrs. Wright, the young widow staying here, and who was introduced to us by Mr. and Mrs. Middleton, now Minister at the Court of Russia, has, I am afraid, taken a fancy to Mr. Rocket, and all the gentlemen of the staff are already making a joke of her *attentions* to him. I am sorry she makes herself so foolish, but it can't be helped.

30*th*. A large dinner party of Navy, Military, and Members of Assembly. Just before we sat down, an express from Port Royal. A ship had arrived from England, with private despatches for General N. and Sir J. Duckworth. Strong rumours of a Spanish war, so we must be additionally alert now.

November 2nd. Frederick Berkeley came early, and is to spend a few days with us. He is an excellent creature, and a great acquisition. – A comfortable day altogether. Some visitors, and military men in the morning, and at second breakfast. – At dinner, Messrs. Malcolm and Perry of the Assembly, with Colonels Unwin and Gordon, and in the evening a very large and very merry party. Young Berkeley enjoyed his dance beyond anything, and as he sleeps in the house, and does not run the risk of a chill afterwards, the exercise is good for him.

3*rd*. Mr. and Mrs. Kemble came on a visit.

4*th*. To church at ten. I am sorry to say, we have had two large parties today. One at second breakfast, and the other at dinner; but, during the sitting of the Assembly, it can't be avoided. Prayers, and to bed at nine.

5th. Heard of the old President of the Council being ill. – Only our own party, and Mr. and Mrs. Cully at dinner; but the table is now crowded every day. – Just before we went to bed, heard of the poor old President's death. Several hours previous to it, his *disconsolate* widow had sent to know how he should be buried, what the ceremony ought to be, &c. &c.!![1]

6th. Drive out early. – This is to be a day of bustle, as our very grand ball takes place to-night. – Dined at 3, and at 4, my dear N. went to attend the President's funeral, which was conducted with much pomp and state; and I hope his widow will have all the consolation possible.

15th. Our wedding anniversary, and may every future one find us as happy in each other, as we really are this day! – All the morning as quiet as possible. At 6, the Admirals, with Captains Dunn, Gardner, Hawker, Temple, &c., Messrs. Mitchell, Edwards, Hinchliffe and Scott. Got through it all very well, and very merry we were. The children came in after dinner, and behaved delightfully.

22nd. I am wicked enough to wish a month of my life over, for I am most heartily sick of dissipation and politics, and long for a little rest of body and mind.

23rd. The late rainy season has produced millions of horrid reptiles, and I found a large scorpion on my dressing-gown this morning. – Mr. Gaven, and Mrs. and Miss Fermor, in addition to our staff dinner.

24th. Drive out early with the dear children. After breakfast, a scene with poor Mrs. Wright, who took her leave for Charlestown. – Mr. Rocket was particularly cold yesterday, and she shed many tears in remarking upon his conduct; but I dare say she will soon forget all about it, as she seems rather *volage* in her feelings.

25th. To church at 10. – Returned home much fatigued with the length of the service, as our old chaplain preached, and he is so worn out, that he can hardly utter a distinct word; and his pauses, hesitation, and mistakes, kept me in a constant fidget.

30th. Sent the sociable at 6, for Colonel and Mrs. Smith and family, who have lately arrived from England. She seems a pleasing woman, and her sister, Miss Wauchope, a good humoured, "bonnie lassie."

December 1st. Dr. Clare (our poor friend's brother, but alas! how

---

[1] Thomas Wallen, the President of the Council, had remarried four months before his death, at the age of eighty-four. He was on the Council for twenty-eight years, and for the last six received a "humane bounty" of £700 per annum on account of his reduced circumstances.

inferior) came to see me, and he and Mr. McAnuff were the only additions to the dinner party to-day.

2*nd*. Captain D'Arcy, Mr. Piercy, and Mr. Doughty, of the 85th, at dinner.

10*th*. The Colts' Ball. Young Berkeley and Lake, with the Kembles, delighted with all the fuss and noise of the day. Soon after 8, all were assembled, and we proceeded in great state, up the ball room, to the tune of "God save the King." Supper at 12; very magnificent, with transparencies, and finery of all sorts. My chair was decorated with wreaths of flowers, and, in short, it was a gay affair altogether. Toasts, &c. were given, and all were as merry as possible; many lamenting that this was likely to be the last of our gaieties this session, and probably our last in Jamaica.

12*th*. Several people called to take leave to-day, and our chaplain, Mr. Warren, was quite pathetic in bidding adieu to the *Prince of Wales*, as he calls little George.

15*th*. A quiet day. – Discuss with Mrs. Horsford the advantages of a public situation. She says, that people don't take the trouble to find out her good qualities, while all mine are exaggerated; and that I hear nothing, from morning till night, but my own praises. I said, not *my* praises, but those of the *Governor's lady*. Her reply had some truth in it, for she said, "Aye, that may be in some respects, and yet all your good qualities are found out, by the trouble people take in enquiring into them, while I am passed over and unknown, merely because no one thinks of examining into my character."

18*th*. The morning full of company, and my dear N. so much engaged in business, that I scarcely saw him. At half-past five, he prorogued the House of Assembly; but not without having first gained his point, for the £500 due to the 4th battalion of the 60th regiment. At 6, a large dinner party of Members, &c. Mrs. Levingstone the only lady, except those belonging to the family at present. Every body in great good humour, and we did not break up till 11 o'clock.

22*nd*. Take my drive, and Mr. and Mrs. Kemble set off for Kingston, at the same time. It is a foolish marriage, but I hope they may prosper. – After breakfast, little G. distributed money to the black servants for Christmas.

24*th*. All the blackies half mad with their preparations for to-morrow.

25*th*. *Christmas Day*. – We both went to church, at 10. A long service, and, in my present weak state, very fatiguing.

26th. Nothing but bonjoes, drums, and tom-toms, going all night, and dancing and singing and madness, all the morning. – The Horsfords, the Grandjeans, &c. at second breakfast, and to see the sports at the King's House. Some of our blackies were most superbly dressed, and so were several of their friends, who came to join in the masquerade; gold and silver fringe, spangles, beads, &c. &c. and really a most wonderful expense altogether. General N. gave the children money, and threw some himself among them from the gallery, and in the scramble all the finery was nearly torn to pieces, to my great vexation. However, they seemed not to mind it, but began dancing with the same spirit as if nothing had happened, putting their smart clothes into the best order they could. We gave them a bullock, a sheep and a lamb, with a dollar to every person in the house, from the oldest individual to the youngest infant; besides a complete new dress, with two changes of linen. – This is the case every Christmas, and at all festivals they have a present of clothing. Perhaps, however, it is more than is usually done; but, for the short time we are with them, we will make them as happy as we can.

27th. Noise all night; and, if possible, to-day worse than ever. – At dinner we had only Captain Quayle of the Artillery, in addition to our little party. – At 9, all was profoundly quiet throughout the town; for almost every woman as well as every man was so exceedingly tipsy, they could do nothing but sleep; and I may say, too, so thoroughly fatigued with their dancing and masquerading, poor things! though people say, they are all really so drunk they are unable to move.

28th. Order again restored, and all going on as usual. – Poor General N. much harassed and vexed, by the dispute between Colonels Horsford and Gordon. They are both married men, and have families, which adds much to his anxiety to reconcile them.

29th. After breakfast General N. had the two Colonels with him in the Council Chamber, and insisted upon the quarrel being made up in an amicable manner. After a length of time, all was settled, satisfactorily, and poor Mrs. Horsford was made quite happy.

January 1st. Go to church at 10. Much noise of tom-toms, &c. all the morning. After the service, the whole garrison came to pay me the compliments of the season. A grand collation of wines, fruit, &c. was laid out in the ball-room, where I received them, and we made ourselves mutually agreeable for an hour, when I was glad to get to my own room. Only our own party at dinner.

2nd. My only visitor, Dr. Rennalls.[1] Carmichael blistered, &c. and hopes are entertained of his recovery. – The same dinner party, and evening, as usual.

7th. General N. received despatches from England, early this morning, by the *Princess Augusta* packet. I got delightful letters from all my family and friends, and dear Lord Buckingham has sent me a most beautiful lace cloak, with a nice and most valuable letter from himself.

9th. To-day we had unexpectedly a large dinner party, chiefly of French; Monsieur Mansigny was of the number. – To bed at 9. – I can't spell the Frenchmen's names, for I did not hear them distinctly pronounced.

10th. Monsieur Mansigny, &c. again. – All day poor General N. had to discuss their affairs with them. They dined here, but, to my great joy, set off for Kingston, in the evening.

11th. General Carmichael so well, that we sent him in the chariot to the Rev. Mr. Campbell's, near Kingston, for a change of air. – Surprised by the two Admirals coming to breakfast, and to spend the day. – Sir J. T. Duckworth to announce his approaching departure for England, and Admiral Dacres to succeed him in the command of this station. They stayed till quite late in the evening, and then slept in Spanish Town, to be off for Port Royal, at daylight to-morrow.

22nd. In returning home from our drive this morning, we met a gang of Eboe negroes, just landed, and marching up the country. – I ordered the postillions to stop, that I might examine their countenances as they passed, and see if they looked unhappy; but they appeared perfectly the reverse. I bowed, kissed my hand, and laughed; they did the same. The women, in particular, seemed pleased, and all admired the carriage, &c. One man attempted to shew more pleasure than the rest, by opening his mouth as wide as possible to laugh, which was rather a horrible grin. He shewed such truly cannibal teeth, all filed as they have them, that I could not help shuddering. He was of Herculean size, and really a tremendous looking creature. They were all dressed in new clothes, and the women had tied their coloured petticoats round their waists as aprons, and the rest had very little covering.

February 1st. At dinner, Mr. and Mrs. Tucker (a new lawyer and his wife) in addition to our own family.

---

[1] Mrs. Nugent was expecting another child. On January 9 Nugent wrote to Duckworth: "She is very uncertain as to the period of her confinement, but it may happen this week." On January 22 the doctor told her she had miscalculated, and on February 5 she was "still *in statu quo*"; nothing more is heard of the matter.

5th. Only Mr. Griffiths, of the Artillery, in addition to our party to-day. He brought letters from Sir W. W. Wynn.

7th. At dinner, Captains Whinyates and Younghusband, to take leave for England.

8th. All the morning, visitors. – Mrs. J. Mitchell, &c. from England. Mrs. Rennalls, to introduce them .– At dinner, Mr. Sill, Captain Campbell, Mr. Hylton and Drs. Reid and Doughty, of the 85th, and our own party.

12th. Send carriages early for the officers of the Artillery, just arrived from England. Colonel Smith came, and introduced Captains Dixon and Campbell, and Lieutenants Lindsay, Scott, Chambers and Foley, who stayed the whole day.

14th. Mr. Storer officiating as Aide-de-camp for the first time, and seems much pleased with his appointment.

16th. Drive out to meet my dear Nugent, on his return from Kingston. Mr. Edwards and Mr. W. J. Hall were with him, who dined with us. Saw Mr. Edwards in my own room, who shewed me the intended addresses for the Admiral, on his leaving this station. He made a joke of most of them, the phrases were so high flown and so bombastical; and indeed I think it would be much better, if they were in a plainer and more sensible form.[1]

18th. Conversation with Sir J. T. Duckworth, before dinner. At 9, he took leave, and actually shed tears. I envy him his return to dear old England, and wish we could at least be of the party.

20th. The carriages were sent, before daylight, for Commissioner Dilkes and his lady, Colonel and Mrs. Smith, and Miss Wauchope, Captain and Mrs. Dixon, Mr. Browne, &c. who all arrived at eight.

25th. The *Pickle* sloop of war, with despatches, arrived; and, just before we went to bed, we learnt that a Spanish war was declared.

28th. At dinner, Captain Humphries, of the 60th, and Mr. Doyle, of the 55th, in addition to our party.

March 2nd. Only Mr. De Boss, of the 60th, in addition to our family party.

---

[1] The Assembly voted him thanks for his effectual preservation of the commerce and coasts of the island, and a thousand guineas for a ceremonial sword.

On arrival in England, Duckworth was charged before a court martial with having "in the most shameful and scandalous manner loaded, received on board, and suffered to be received on board HM Ship *Acasta* [in which he had sailed from Jamaica] an immense quantity of goods and merchandize, other than for the use of the ship." The court accepted the Admiral's explanation that the goods were intended for presents and not for sale, and acquitted him.

4th. See Martin's (the Duchess of Port Royal as she is called) daughter, soon after breakfast. It is a sad thing to see even this good kind of woman in other respects, so easy on the subject of what a decent kind of woman in England would be ashamed of and shocked at. She told me of all her children by different fathers, with the greatest *sang-froid*. The mother is quite looked up to at Port Royal, and yet her life has been most profligate, as we should think, at least in England.

5th. An unhappy day! A consultation with the doctors, and they all agree, that neither George nor I should encounter another summer here. Will do my best to make up my mind, to leave my dear husband, but if he could go with me, what joy!

8th. After a great deal of discussion, before we went to sleep last night, decide upon going at daylight to Old Harbour, to see the *Augustus Cæsar*, as we had promised the owner, Captain Bell, that we would, if possible, this morning. Every thing looked so nice and comfortable, that General N. settled with him about our accommodation, &c. and so the die is really cast! – After our return to the King's House, what with the dust, the fatigue, and the agitation of my own mind, I was quite ill, and could not leave my room .– General N. had a party at dinner; all gentlemen, however; but it was hard upon him, as he was almost as far from well as I was. Then, in the evening, just as he came to my room, intending to have half-an-hour's quiet, before we went to bed, an express arrived from General Myers, to say, that several French ships of war, with troops, had appeared to windward. They had attacked Dominica, but their success there, and future destination, were not known; but this island was their object, probably. – Of course, my dear N., ill as he was, was obliged to set about immediate arrangements for our defence, as well as to prepare all the dependencies of Jamaica for theirs.[1] This kept him up, with his Military Secretary, in my dressing-room, the greatest part of the night. We had, in consequence, scarcely a doze.

9th. The doctor says that an immediate change of air is necessary for dear little G., and to-morrow we remove to Port Henderson; but alas! General N.'s business will not admit of his being of the party.

10th. After church, General N. full of business, and crowds of people continually coming; all much alarmed at the idea of a French force coming to this part of the world. – As soon as we had taken a 3 o'clock dinner, General N. set off with us to Port Henderson. An express from

---

[1] Probably means (British) Honduras and Mosquito Shore, and Cayman Islands.

the Admiral overtook us, giving an account of the capture of Roseau, &c.[1] After staying a couple of hours, to see us settled in our new house, he was obliged to return to Spanish Town, and all his anxious business.

14*th.* An early walk on the sea shore with the dear children, who picked up some shells, and were delighted. Did not see a creature the whole day; heard from and wrote to General N. At 4, ordered a boat and rowed with the maids and little ones to Fort Augusta. General Carmichael much better. Go back soon after 6, and was in bed before eight.

15*th.* Row again with the children, &c. to Green Bay, and get back before seven.

17*th.* No church to go to. – Put the children to sleep as soon as we could after breakfast, that they might look well, and be in spirits to receive dear papa, who came soon after 2, and found us all improved in looks. He seems sadly worn, and sun-burnt, though he says he is quite well; but he has undergone immense fatigue, walking seven miles up the bed of a river, under a broiling sun, and over rocks, &c. where no horse could be of use. Captain Meredith, who came to Port Henderson with him, tells me, that all the party were knocked up. Thank God! however, he has not suffered in health in the least. Took a nice walk in the evening, and the little ones delighted to shew papa the shells, &c. &c.

18*th.* General N. sent off the despatch to windward, to Admiral Dacres; and extracts from General Myers's letter, &c. to the printer. – A few of the staff to dinner. Get rid of them at 6, and take our nice little walk again.

21*st.* General N. off again to inspect the black corps at Fort Augusta, and returned at 11 o'clock. All the staff then proceeded to Spanish Town, and we dined *tête-à-tête* at 3. At 5, however, he was obliged to leave us. Our little ones went part of the way with us, and when we were obliged to take leave of dear papa it was a sad scene, and they could scarcely be prevailed upon to return with me and the maids. I could not help re-marking the difference between the feelings of a boy and of a girl. George did not shed tears, but kept calling for the black horse, on which his papa rode, while Louisa covered her dear little face, and sobbed, Papa, Papa, for a length of time, before we could pacify her. During the evening, before she went to sleep, she called for papa, and seemed to

[1] Roseau, the capital of Dominica, surrendered to a force landed by Admiral Missi-essy, but the French contented themselves with levying a ransom of £7500 and sailed away to repeat the process at St. Kitts, Nevis and Montserrat.

think of nothing else; while George took his little whip to bed with him, and would make me tell him stories, about the black horse, &c.

22nd. Take an early walk with the children. Find the Commissioner on my return, waiting to ask if I will go to Port Royal to-morrow, to see the *Theseus* man of war laid down. Appoint 12 to-morrow, when he is to come for me. – Have little G. to dine with me, at 12 to-day, and order a guinea-fowl, with bread-sauce, with which he was delighted. – My new boat and boat's crew came for orders. Fix 5 o'clock, and take a nice row. Home again soon after 6. – A comfortable letter from dear N.; all well, thank God! but he is sadly harassed with business, I fear.

23rd. Rise early, not to disappoint the children of their row. On our return find the old Commissioner, with the Admiral's barge, waiting to take me to Port Royal, as the ship was to be laid down at 8 or 9 o'clock, instead of 12, as he said yesterday. Feel quite vexed to be so hurried, but set off without delay, and get to Port Royal about 8. A great many Navy officers to meet me. Mrs. Smith and Miss Wauchope, the only ladies. Stayed till near 11, under an awning, put up for that purpose, before the ship was fairly on her side; and then, indeed, it was a very fine and a very wonderful sight. The dexterity of the sailors accomplished the whole affair in a most astonishing manner. As the water flowed in, it was extraordinary to see the number of reptiles that tried to escape up her sides; scorpions, centipedes, cockroaches innumerable. We then returned to the Commissioner's, where numbers of the Navy captains, &c. came to pay their compliments to me, but only the Admiral and Captain Balderston, with a few military, were of the dinner party at 4. At 6, my dear N. surprised us by his appearance, just as I was stepping into the Admiral's barge, to return to Port Henderson. Poor fellow! though I was rejoiced to see him, I was sorry he had come, for he had had a most fatiguing day. A ride of twenty-four miles in the sun, and no dinner, or any refreshment. – Get home at half-past seven, when he had a comfortable dinner, and seemed quite well.

25th. Two whales made their appearance in the harbour yesterday, and to-night were seen close in front of the house. Explained all about them to little G., who wishes to see them again.

27th. My morning was spent in writing about Mrs. Wright's affairs. Settle them all, as well as they will admit of.

28th. Despatches from the north side of the island. All the arrangements perfectly made, and all well.

30th. Row to Port Royal early. At breakfast, the Admiral and Major

Gould. Did not stay to dinner. Just as we sat down *tête-à-tête*, came Mr. Browne of the Artillery, with the intelligence of a French fleet being seen off St. Domingo, steering this way. The account was brought by a vessel, that left Port Royal this morning, and had seen some of them. General N. desired him to return to his duty immediately, then drank a glass of wine, and ordered his horse. I will not say what were my feelings, when he took the dear children in his arms and kissed them, for perhaps the last time. He wrote a few lines in his pocket–book, which he left with me, and which I found, after he was gone, were instructions for the safety of myself and children. I ordered the maids to put everything ready to move at a moment's notice, and then sat down almost stunned, and could not think clearly of anything. – An express from the Admiral in the course of an hour, to tell me, that it was thought the enemy was not so near us as had been reported in the morning. In consequence, I decided upon remaining here, for fear my dear children should suffer, from being exposed to the night air, and a journey at such an unusual hour. Wrote to General Carmichael, and sent my boat's crew to Fort Augusta, to join their regiment there. Write also to Captain Dobbin, at the Apostles' battery, and arranged an express, in case of alarm, or any information coming during the night. Saw all the doors fastened, and said all I could to quiet the alarms of the maids, &c. At 10, prepared for bed. – I soon after received an express from my dear N., advising me to remain at this place, till further intelligence of the enemy's movements could be obtained. I replied immediately, giving him every comfort in my power, respecting myself and the children. – In the course of the night, Henry Rogers came, but only stayed a few minutes, just to see how we were. – The rest of the time was quiet, and I rejoiced to see the day dawn, without further alarm.

31st. Major Fraser early, with a letter from General N. All at the King's House were up almost the whole night, writing circular letters, and copying General N.'s orders, &c. for different parts of the country; and he himself was off before day for Kingston, where he will probably remain till all is over. God bless and preserve him from all dangers, and grant that all may soon end happily for us!

Eight o'clock in the evening. This day has indeed passed most miserably. Not a creature have I seen since the morning, but have walked in the piazza the whole day, with a glass in my hand, looking continually towards the sea for the enemy. Nothing has been heard but the scaling the guns[1] in the different forts and ships in the harbour, and the practice

[1] Cleaning the bore of the gun by firing a charge of powder.

of the artillery. The ships of war have manœuvred, and are now arranged as a sort of battery across Port Royal harbour, and when the Admiral's ship had her sails hoisted, and moved to her station, I could not help smiling at George and Louisa, calling it *"Grandmamma"*; for, being talked to of their grandmothers being two great people, they thought such a large and splendid object must be a grandmamma at least.

As soon as the sun would allow us to go out this evening, I went with them to Port Henderson, where we had an extensive view of the sea. It was a dead calm, and, as far as the eye could reach, like a sheet of glass. Not a speck was to be seen on the horizon, and God grant an enemy may not cloud it! I have just received a letter from my dear N. He is in Kingston, and undergoing wonderful fatigue, in assembling a force for the protection of that place, and in making the best arrangements possible, for the defence of the island, by placing in the most vulnerable situations all the troops he can collect; but, with our present force of regular troops, it is impossible to do this effectually. For, alas! all parts are vulnerable, and our force, from sickness and various other causes, is very small and inadequate. Martial law is to be declared, and to-morrow he means to hold a Council of War, for that purpose. – I try to be as composed and as calm as possible, but I can't fix my attention to any one object for comfort, nor think distinctly on any subject. – I see the dear little ones put to bed, after saying a little prayer for dear papa; and may their dear little innocent voices be heard!

April 1st. We have passed a sad night of alarms. Several shots were fired from a house near, and our black servants said it was to frighten thieves, as many were seen about in the evening. General Carmichael sent back my boatmen to me this morning; and, as they appear to be trusty people, I have desired they may sleep in the stable every night, till General N. (please God!) returns. – Dear Clifford returned here yesterday, and she is so courageous that she is a great comfort to me; but she tells me that, before she left Spanish Town, the negroes appeared to be inclined to riot, and to make a noise in the streets, when the troops marched out, but they were soon dispersed by the militia. The black servants here seem to rejoice at the bustle, but, as they profess to hate the French, their pleasure is only that of change; for, like children, they are fond of fuss and noise, and have no reflection.

2nd. After another anxious and sleepless night, I rowed with the children round the ships in Port Royal harbour. Saw and spoke to several naval friends, who were all most friendly and comfortable. About 10 o'clock, a letter from General N. He writes in tolerable spirits, and is quite well, thank God! The Council of War was held in Kingston, and martial law declared yesterday. The day passed in my usual anxiety and watchfulness, and I have now fixed the glass in the Venetian blinds, so that I can look out constantly, without the fatigue of holding it. Every now and then I feel quite blind, but getting into a dark corner, and shutting my eyes for a few minutes, enables me to see clearly again.

The sea was rather rough this evening, and I took a walk with the little ones, instead of a row. We met a horrid looking black man, who passed us several times, without making any bow, although I recollected him as one of the boatmen of the canoe we used to go out in, before we had the *Maria*. He was then very humble, but to-night he only grinned, and gave us a sort of fierce look, that struck me with a terror I could not shake off. – This evening, nurse sung again to the children, who had their usual dance, and went to bed happy, dear little innocent souls! Clifford tells me that all the black people know there is some alarm, but are ignorant of the cause of it, and most of them, it is to be feared, are ready for every sort of mischief. However, I feel confident in our own servants, who all seem as anxious to secure the house, and to be as much afraid of depredators, as I am.

3rd. How little do we know what calamities may befall us in this world! Yesterday I thought my cup of anxiety was full, but to-day I have been near losing my dear George. He was romping with his nurse and little sister, and fell from off the bed, with his head against the corner of an open drawer. He gave a shriek, and then appeared quite stunned with the violence of the blow. The wound was directly on the back of the head, and it bled frightfully. We immediately sent off for Dr. McNeil; but, in the mean time, I took courage, and had him laid upon my lap, and held him there, while I cut away all the hair near the wound, and then applied some court plaister, upon which I kept my hand, till Dr. McNeil arrived, when he found the dear child in a nice sleep, and the blood quite staunched. He said I had done all he could have done, with only this difference, that he would have sewed up the part, to which I had applied the court plaister, and this did quite as well. After a few hours, thank God! the little darling was as well, and as playful as ever; but it will be many days before I can cease to think of the past without trembling.

Mr. and Mrs. Edward Bullock, and their family, arrived at Port Henderson to-day, but I was too much agitated to see any one. I sent, however, to offer them all civilities, and the use of the boat, &c. &c.

for taking the morning air.[1] In the evening, I myself took to Fort Augusta my answer to my dear N.'s darling letter, and the children were of the party, that General Carmichael may be able to tell General N. how we all are, and to give a good account of them; but don't mention the accident little George met with. – The evening cooler than usual, but the weather is now dreadfully hot, and my anxiety is great, for fear my dear N. should suffer seriously from the heat of Kingston, which is, I believe, the most broiling place in the universe.

4*th*. A letter from General N. All in the same anxious state, but we are now prepared, as far as possible, for the worst. – Mrs. E. Bullock, and Mrs. Whitehorne, with their little ones, came, and spent a few hours, to the great delight of my children. – Dined with little G. at 12, and at 3, drank tea, and then ordered the boat, and took a long row, which delighted my little party. – Home, and to bed at 8. – Little G. quite well, and seems not to have suffered in the least from the fall.

5*th*. At gun-fire take Mr. and Mrs. E. Bullock and their little ones a nice row round the fleet. Soon after breakfast, a Navy officer, with a despatch from the Admiral, to tell me, that, after the French fleet had reinforced the city of Santo Domingo,[2] they had shaped their course towards the Mona Passage, and that consequently we had much less to apprehend from their attacks; at all events no immediate descent on this island can be in contemplation. Write to my dear N., and am all joy, to think the danger is at a distance at least. – Have Mr. and Mrs. E. B., Mrs. Whitehorne, Mr. Andrews, and the little people, all at dinner at 3 o'clock. A table laid in the piazza, for the children, and enjoyed the scene very much myself; dear little G. and L. doing the honours *beautifully*. – Soon after 4, rowed with the whole party to Port Royal, and, on our return, they all took leave. – A nice letter from my dear N.; he writes in great spirits, and will be in Spanish Town to-morrow. Thank God! thank God!

7*th*. About 4, an express from Port Royal, with despatches from Barbadoes and England. A letter from Sir W. Myers, announcing the near approach of an English squadron to windward, and the prospect of our naval force being sufficient to pursue and chase the enemy out of these

---

[1] One of the ruined buildings at Port Henderson is known as Bullock's Lodge, perhaps after William Bullock, who was Secretary to the Governor, 1811–32, and presumably related to Edward Bullock.
[2] The capital of the former Spanish colony, where a French garrison held out until 1809.

seas. The Minister's letter from home, giving much the same intelligence, and expressing great anxiety for these colonies in general, &c.

13*th*. Pack up, and all return in the sociable. Quite happy to be together again, and all in much better health than when we left Spanish Town.

14*th*. To church at 10. A full congregation, and all the church strewed and ornamented with pimento.

15*th*. Much hurry all the morning, and General N. was obliged to dictate his speech, for me to write, as he went in and out of the room, to receive different Members of the Assembly, who were continually coming. Before 2 o'clock it was ready, and he delivered it in the Council Chamber, the House having come over in state, with the Speaker at their head, as usual. At 5, an immense dinner party. Every one much pleased, and all went off extremely well. I was complimented very much, upon the improved looks of myself and children, and I only wish I could feel as much improved as they say I appear to be. At 10 o'clock all was quiet, and martial law had this one good effect, that it obliged us all to be much more sober, and to keep earlier hours, than we should otherwise have been, or felt inclined to do. Yet the great flag, flying in the middle of the square, and the number of red coats moving about in different directions continually, gave a warlike appearance, and all looked too hostile to give one very comfortable or pleasing contemplations, in considering the future.

16*th*. The Assembly all in great good humour with General N., approve of all his measures, and seem really grateful for his activity and arrangements for the protection of the island.

18*th*. All sorts of arrangements making for future defence. All in good humour, and every one anxious to do his duty. General N. satisfied, and more comfortable in spirits than I have seen him for a long time. The 18th regiment is very unhealthy, and I am sorry to say, are to be sent to Stony Hill, and then the poor fellows there must encounter this hot, unhealthy town. – A review this morning, at daylight, on the race-course. Took little G. in the carriage, dressed in an Aide-de-camp's uniform; scarlet, with blue facings and gold embroidery, a staff hat and feather, and he really looked lovely; in my eyes at least.

19*th*. The 85th marched into Spanish Town, early this morning, and alas! many of them, I fear, will suffer from the dreadful heat of this town. – A party at second breakfast, and another at dinner. – All glad to meet once more, but many are *gone* since I was at Stony Hill, and my thoughts in consequence are most melancholy.

20th. Admiral Cochrane and his Flag-Captain at breakfast.¹ Make the agreeable to them till 12. My dear N. very busy as usual, but to-day he had a most flattering address, and an answer to his statement respecting American intercourse, and all of the most gratifying nature.² He will now make his prorogation speech, with much more comfortable feelings. – Visitors innumerable coming in, and interrupting his business all day. – A large dinner party – King Mitchell, Colonel Edwards, Mr. Hinchliffe, Aide-de-camp (for he is now one of General N.'s militia Aides-de-camp, which gives him the rank of Colonel), Major of Brigade Pallmer, Aides-de-camp Ross and Bullock, General Scott, and Major Grant, of the Artillery, with the Admiral and his Captain, made our dinner party. Have a great deal of talk with the Admiral, who knows all my family, and it is wonderful, at this distance, how great an intimacy is formed immediately with those that know them we love.

22nd. Lament the change in the poor 85th. Within one month three officers have died of the yellow fever, and several once healthy looking young men are now quite ghastly. If the climate has affected them so much in the mountains, what may they not suffer in the lowlands! Poor General Carmichael, too, who slept here last night, is so ill, that General N. has given him leave of absence, and advised his going to St. Thomas in the East, for change of air, which the doctors say is his only chance of living; that he never can recover his health here. Poor little man! It is a great pity he can't make up his mind to go to Europe; but, unfortunately, his finances are in such a state, that his emoluments are of the utmost consequence to his family; and, most probably, his life will be the sacrifice. – Mr. Vernon brought young Gordon, of the *Northumberland*, to-day, and we are glad to shew him any kindness, on account of his family, and he really is a fine boy.

23rd. Arrived at the Admiral's Penn at 3. At 4, an immense party, chiefly of the Navy, and almost all of them the new arrivals. Most of them seemed sadly alarmed about the climate, and afraid to eat or drink any thing, and are making constant enquiries about the yellow fever.

24th. Start for the King's House, the carriage loaded with toys. The children were delighted to see us. Dine at 5. The heat overpowering, and feel the fatigue of the day sadly.

¹ Rear-Admiral Alexander Cochrane had left the fleet blockading Ferrol to pursue Missiessy's squadron with six ships, four of which were detained by Dacres for the protection of Jamaica.
² They were gratifying about the defence measures taken, but protested strongly against the proposed restriction on trade with the United States (Introduction p. xxiii).

25th. Beg Colonel Mellifont not to turn out the guard to me and the children, when we take our morning's drive. It is fatiguing the men, and makes us appear quite ridiculous, I am sure.

26th. My dear N. has had the painful task of deciding upon the fate of the 4th battalion of the 60th regiment; they are now to be drafted, a necessity that could not be avoided, owing to their continual broils, their insubordination, and constant cabals, and party business, against their commanding officer, Colonel Unwin. He is quite delighted with the idea of getting home, and leaving this horrid climate, and I only hope and pray, that the Duke of York may approve of the step General N. has found it so necessary to take.

27th. The dinner party rather melancholy to me. Captain Bell, of the *Augustus Cæsar*, dined here, and the whole evening there was nothing but discussions about our voyage, sea stock, &c.; and now there is no hope of my dear N. being relieved in time to go with us. – The thunder and lightning so very dreadful this evening, that none of us went to bed till 11 o'clock.

29th. Take the children, at daylight, to the review of the Kingston regiment. A good breakfast, at Mr. S. Taylor's, afterwards. – At 5, a very large dinner party, or rather parties, for there were two rooms full. Mrs. Holgate, Mrs. and Miss Farmer, and the two Misses Stewart, were the only ladies. – Don't get to bed till after 11, and very much fatigued; but particularly anxious about dear little G. and L., who, if I had not taken the greatest care, would have been stuffed with all sorts of trash, and so perhaps made quite ill, from the derangement of their dear little stomachs. I am determined never to take them out again, while they are so young.

30th. The children had a nice night, and were quite well this morning, thank God! After breakfast, leave Mr. Taylor's hospitable mansion, and return to the King's House, all well; and here ends another month, and our whole party alive and prosperous, thank God!

May 1st. – Write and read till breakfast time. Poor Mrs. (Lieut.) Campbell came in the morning. I kept her all day. Made her all the useful presents I could, and in short said and did all in my power towards her comfort. Lieutenant Campbell came to dinner.

2nd. Rise very early, and settle various affairs, public and private; and at 10 set off, with General N. and the children, to Port Henderson. At 3, General Carmichael came to dine with us, and to take leave, on going into the country for his health. He looks sadly, and, in all probability, it is the last time we shall see him in this world; though he talks boldly of his recovery. Poor Doctor Reid, who has attended him so faithfully, during his long illness, is actually dead of the fatigue, &c. and was buried yesterday. I could not help remarking the nervous effects of this climate, in a circumstance that occurred in our walk this evening. Just as we were returning home, we heard a horse coming full speed towards Port Henderson. We both stopped, with a sort of shuddering, and, when we explained our thoughts to each other, it appeared they were the same, and that General N., as well as I, imagined that it was an express to announce the death of poor General Carmichael, who had just left us. So suddenly and so frequently do these melancholy circumstances take place, that the mind is constantly prepared, and constantly anticipating them too.

3rd. General N. and the children, with the two Misses Rennalls, were of our rowing party this morning. At 7, we breakfasted, when Mr. Longfield, of the 85th, made his appearance, and, after a most extraordinary conversation about conspiracies, &c. &c. we discovered that he was really mad. The children were playing about, and I really dreaded that he would do them some mischief; he seized upon their toys, and eyed them in so odd a manner. General N. and I kept him engaged as well as we could, till Major Fraser arrived from Spanish Town, and we persuaded him to accompany him back; but it was with much difficulty we got rid of him. The poor man looks the shadow of what he was when he first arrived from England, about a year ago. Then he was a fine-looking, healthy young man, and now he is a poor, emaciated, wrinkled old man.

4th. Our usual row early. Return soon after sunrise. Captain Smith of the Engineers, Meredith, and Rogers, at breakfast. Colonel Espinasse, and Mr. Baker, of the 85th, and Mr. Browne of the Artillery, at dinner. A short walk in the evening, and to bed at 8. – Poor Longfield is in a strait waistcoat.

7th. Colonel Mellifont at breakfast, and had a full account of poor Longfield's situation. He is really insane, but the doctors think change of climate may restore him, and he is to sail in the next packet. The Honourable Captain Gardner came from Port Royal, and sat with me some hours. I was in a fright all the time, as the newspapers were on the table, with a full detail of his elder brother's affairs, his wife's trial, &c.[1] General N. came at 5, and asked him to dine; and, in the evening, we all accompanied

---

[1] Capt. Francis Gardner, RN, was second son of Admiral Lord Gardner. His elder brother, Capt. Alan Gardner, had obtained £1000 damages from his wife's lover in an action for criminal conversation, and in 1805 a private Act of Parliament was passed dissolving the marriage.

him to Port Royal, and drank tea with the Commissioner. To our great surprise, Captain G. offered to come back with us, and, after a little supper, opened the whole history himself, and discussed all his brother's affairs fully; so my delicacy in the morning was not at all necessary. The night was beautiful, and Captain Gardner returned to Port Royal at eleven.

8th. Did not row out, we were so late this morning. While we were at breakfast, Captain Reeves, of the 18th, came to ask leave to return to England. Poor man! he seemed ready to resign his commission, rather than remain here; he is so much alarmed about the climate. General N. was obliged to leave him with me, and go into Spanish Town. As soon as he was gone, poor Captain Reeves frightened me very much, by being seized with a cold shivering fit. He told me he had felt quite ill all the morning, but did not like to complain to General N., for fear he should think it was only owing to alarm about the yellow fever. I begged him to take some Madeira, that was on the side table, and advised his going back to his quarters, as soon as possible. After taking two large bumpers of old Madeira, he returned to his boat, and I hope to hear to-morrow that his illness is of no material consequence. – Dr. Rennalls in the morning. – General N. brought home with him, to dinner, Colonel Irvine, Mr. Smith, and Dr. McNeil. The doctor says, I could not have prescribed any thing better than the Madeira wine for Captain Reeves, so probably his complaint is chiefly on the spirits; a disorder so frequent, and often so fatal in this country. A dreadful thunderstorm in the evening, and the gentlemen obliged to sleep at the inn.

9th. A row round the ships at Port Royal again, this morning. – Mr. Scott of the Artillery, and Mr. Dundas, at breakfast. Poor Mr. Scott is just out of the fever, and looks like a ghost. When these gentlemen left us, and just as we were congratulating ourselves upon the present quiet state of the island, and our prospect of being safe in England by this time next year, Captain Bouverie arrived, in the *Mercury*, with despatches from Sir John Orde. The Toulon squadron passed Cadiz, on the 9th of April, and is supposed to have steered westward; so we are all again in bustle and confusion; and most likely no convoy will be able to leave Jamaica, till the hurricane season begins, and then it would be madness to think of going. – Colonel Drummond came to spend the day, which was certainly not very agreeable to either General N. or me, as our minds were so occupied, with the despatches, &c. that we had much to think of, and could not give our attention to any other subject. – Mr. Scott and Colonel

Drummond at dinner. – Hear of poor Captain Reeves, who is desperately
ill. – A thunderstorm again obliged the gentlemen to remain at Port
Henderson. – Little G. slept in his new bed in my room, for the first time.

10th. We attempted to row out in the evening, but I was so nervous,
and so much alarmed at every thing, that we returned almost immediately.
A quiet little talk calmed and comforted me a good deal, before we went
to bed.

11th. Captains Bouverie and Hardyman at breakfast, and to take leave.
The former takes the mail to England, and, in consequence of this, the
regular packet will not sail till Monday se'en-night. Mr. Smith, the Island
Engineer, on business, the greatest part of the morning.

15th. General N. early in town, as he holds a Council to-day, on the
subject of American intercourse, and various other matters.

17th. One of the lieutenants of the Apostles' battery came as we were
going to breakfast, to announce the death of poor wretched Captain
Dobbin. He died without seeing his children, and it is said has left all he
is worth to his black mistress and her child. This is, I am afraid, but too
common a case in Jamaica.

19th. To-day, three events here – Little Becky, a black child, bitten by
a conger eel, a large centipede found in the nursery, and a snake close to
the window. Have all the house well searched, before we went to bed, as
the late storms have brought reptiles without number out of their holes.

22nd. The heat dreadful, but the sea as smooth as glass, and the scene
altogether beautiful. We were so early in our boat, that the sun did not
quite get from behind the mountains till we were returning from our
row, when the whole atmosphere was of a silver colour. General N. received an express from Admiral Dacres, to tell him, that, after all, it is not
thought that the Toulon fleet is coming westward.

23rd. General N. off at 3, to review the Saint Catherine's regiment,
before he begins his Court of Chancery. I remained quietly by myself,
writing, &c. till 12, when Mr. Browne came from Port Royal, with despatches, by the packet, and alas! some from the windward, announcing
the arrival of the French combined force there. – To describe the state of
my mind is quite impossible, and now I tremble so much, I can hardly
hold my pen, and my mind is really half distracted, with various distressing thoughts that assail me; I have sent off an express to my dear N., and
begged to join him and the little ones, in Spanish Town, immediately,
and am now waiting with the greatest impatience for the result. – About
4, he came in the chariot, and after taking a hasty dinner, we set off for the

King's House, where the affectionate caresses of my dear children enabled me to shed a plentiful shower of tears, which relieved my head and heart wonderfully; and I shall now, I trust, resume all my courage and cheerfulness, and be a comfort, rather than a burthen, to my dear husband, whose mind is at present sadly harassed.

24th. At 10, General N. held a Council of War. Martial law was declared, and the great flag unfurled in the square, immediately after. – Got all our private letters, and (thank Heaven!) all our friends well and happy in England. General N.'s private despatch, from Lord Camden, is particularly comfortable, and I now look forward with the hope of his being able to go home with me, if I am detained here much longer by the circumstances in which we are now placed; or of his joining me soon in England, if we are obliged to separate. – The morning full of bustle. All the colonels of militia in their uniforms, coming continually. Orders issuing in every direction, and expresses going off, to every part of the country. Every now and then my strength fails me, and I run to my own room to lament, and stretch myself out for a short time on the bed, and then I can return with fresh vigour to the business of the day.

25th. Send the maids and children out in the sociable. Remain with my dear N., who has passed a day of continual business, writing and giving audience, etc. Don't dine till near six.

26th. To church at 10; an immense congregation, and all in scarlet. The heat extreme. The poor Jews looked uncomfortable the whole service, but they would have lost their pay, of five shillings a day, if they had not attended.[1] A large party at second breakfast, and the Attorney-General was of the number; he is wishing for leave to go home, if possible, on account of ill-health, and indeed, he does look sadly. – All the day full of bustle; militia generals and colonels coming continually. George and Louisa were much amused, with seeing all the red coats parading the square, and I could not help smiling, to see a militia soldier, with a black boy carrying his firelock behind him, and the serjeants, with each an attendant carrying his halbert, &c. Major Gould arrived, before dinner, with various reports, respecting the enemy, as well as *domestic* affairs. – The clergy as usual at dinner. – Much anxious discussion, before we go to bed at ten.

27th. Go out early with the children. – Poor General N. shut up from daylight, and not a moment to breathe scarcely, he has so much writing

---

[1] During martial law, non-commissioned officers and privates in the militia were paid five shillings a day "while on actual duty."

and business of all sorts. Breakfast at 7 o'clock. Till 3, incessant business and visiting. Then an express, with a confirmation of the enemy being in these seas. If they really do come, we have the comfort at least to know, that we are as well prepared as we possibly can be from the nature of our situation, resources, &c. &c.; and that we have nothing to accuse ourselves of, in point of negligence, or being off our guard. In fact, the security of this island depends mainly upon our superiority at sea, and the vigilance of our squadrons.

Poor General N. has been particularly harassed to-day, with business, and teased and vexed at the same time, by the new militia general officers. – They are all so tenacious of attention, command, &c.! King (now General) Mitchell, is quite *sulky*, and out of humour, because he is not given enough to do, and that General N. has given more orders to General Farmer than to him, the last day or two. – We had a large dinner party, and many people also in the evening, and all paying me the greatest attention, King Mitchell in particular; and this has always been the case, whenever he is displeased with General N. for any of his measures. Then, I am sure of being overpowered with flattery and fine speeches.[1]

28*th.* General N. again too much engaged to go out with us before breakfast; and, as soon as that was over, was at his desk again before 8. –

[1] The print reproduced in Plate 17 is a caricature of the militia by a regular army officer (Ensign A. James, 67th Regt.) The captions are:

1. Martial Law declared by beat of Drum, and the Standard hoisted in St. Jago de la Vega.
2. The Generals preparing for the defence of their respective Districts.
3. Subordinate degrees qualifying themselves for both the offensive and defensive Arts of war.
4. The flower of the Isle performing the eighteen Manoeuvres under the experienced eye of a creolized Adjutant.
5. Captn. Cheeks kicks the shop to hell, and speedily unmuftifies!
6. Major Replevin goes thro saluting motions in the presence of his astounded Rib!
7. Lieut. Coffee assuming l'air militaire under the aiding fist of Miss Carolina Yam.
8. Ensign Caveat awaiting the warning Drum for Field Day, with slumbering vigilance.
9. Volunteer Spruce in the act of marching to Parade.
10. Corporal Benjamin turning out with mosiacal fierté for morning exercise.
11. A Sample of native infantry practising his manoeuvres.
12. Manumitted Quashire ready to lay down his life pro aris et Focis.
13. The Forlorn Hope – or a party going to reconnoitre the summits of the Blue Mountains.
14. Creolean mode of firing grape Shot.
15. The vigilant defenders of the Country on the qui vive!
16. A Horse in the execution of the great duties of his Corps!
17. Beau Jenkins practising the Militia Band in the new German Waltz.

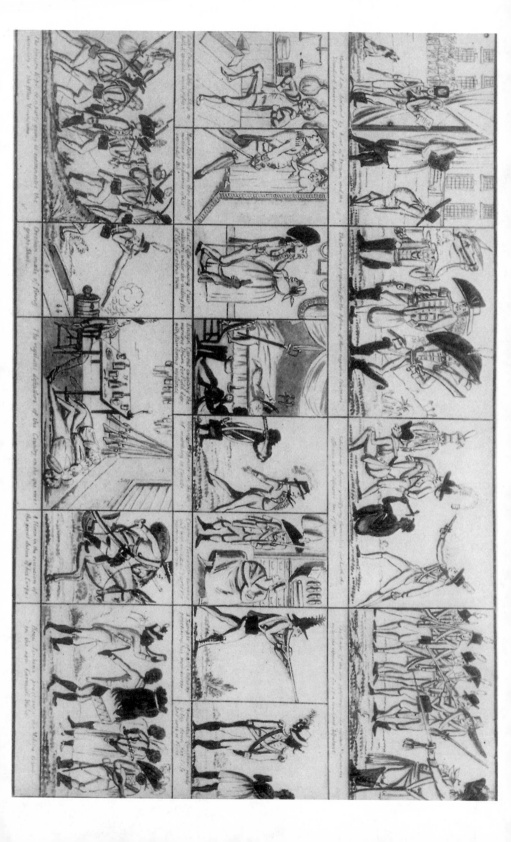

General Carmichael surprised us with his appearance to take the command of the troops, and General N. has appointed him a Lieutenant-General, – good, little, zealous, but *broken down* man! Colonels Mellifont, Horsford, Irvine, Rainy, &c. are all Major-Generals.[1] – A crowd of military at dinner, and in the evening; myself the only woman.

29th. General N. off, before day, to Kingston, and I drove out with the children. Breakfast at 7, with the gentlemen of the family that remained. Mr. Knox, lately from England, came, and I asked him to dine, as he is introduced by Mr. Staples and my brother Cortland. – General N. returned at 5, and the reports of the enemy are less favourable. My spirits are not a little depressed, as he hinted the necessity of perhaps sending me and the dear children into the interior of the island, where Mr. Mitchell has kindly offered us an asylum; but I am sure that the blacks are to be as much dreaded as the French. – Messrs. O'Hara and Knox at dinner, and a large party in the evening; Mrs. Rennalls was of the number, to hear the news.

31st. A stormy night, and the thunder dreadful. – Business, visitors, and anxiety all day. When will our suspense be over? I really rejoice at every hour that passes, in hopes that the next may bring some tidings to put an end to it. – An unfortunate man of colour was brought into Spanish Town, to-day, to be tried for mutiny. He is a serjeant in the militia, and his abuse of his colonel, and white people in general, has had, they say, already a most serious effect; among the men of his company in particular. – At dinner, only the staff, but so many gentlemen in the evening, and about a dozen ladies, that I thought it was best to set them all dancing, and this kept up their spirits till 11 o'clock. To-morrow several of them go into the country, where most of the women and children are gone already; as the interior of the island is now considered the safest place. So it certainly is, from the French, but how will they guard against the insurrection of the negroes? – Poor Captain Campbell, of the Artillery, is dead, after a very few hours' illness; I am afraid that fatigue and exposure to the sun, for some days past, have been the cause.

June 1st. The day as usual, full of business and anxiety, from reports of all sorts, and of a contradictory nature. General N. half angry with some

---

[1] "A scale of regular and colonial rank is very properly established in the West Indies, in order to prevent disputes, and with a view of transferring commands, in times of danger, to the proper hands. According to this scale, a regular Lt.-Col. takes the rank of Major-General, and, in actual service, the command of the troops (both regulars and militia) in the district . . ." (J. Stewart, *Account of Jamaica*).

of the staff, for telling me all the rumours. – In the evening, a crowd of people, as usual, for nearly three hours.

2nd. Whitsunday. Dreadful thunder and lightning all night. The rain and the storm altogether continued, and it was so very damp, there was no service in the church. – The maids, &c. all in a bustle, preparing for the marriage of Mrs. Cummins (a nursery maid) with Ensign Brockmüller, which is to take place before dinner. The rain, &c. they say is a bad omen, and occasions, I observe, many anxious looks and mysterious remarks. The storm kept the party from assembling, till it was so late, that we went to dinner. At 7, Ensign Brockmüller made his appearance, and soon after was united to nurse Cummins, who is now an officer's lady, and has, in consequence, thrown off her cap, and been dressed in her own hair. Yet the Ensign offered to let her remain, and do her *work* here, as long as I remained in the country; but I declined so great an honour, and she returned with him, in the evening, to his quarters.

3rd. The wretched serjeant of militia's Court Martial began at 12, and I am sadly afraid he will be condemned; for an execution at this moment would be such an addition to our horrors! The 55th regiment, commanded by Major Chalmers, marched in to-day, and have had a dreadful and dangerous march across the island, on account of the torrents of rain that have fallen during the last few days.

I received a distressing letter, from one of our staff, whose history is a most unfortunate one. He has a young woman living with him, that he seduced in England, and brought over here. His remorse is great, and as she has behaved well, and he is still attached to her, I have advised his marrying her, without loss of time, and particularly for the sake of his two nice children; and also because the mother has been no further culpable than he has made her. Every thing is now arranged privately, through his friend, Colonel Irvine. General N. has promised a licence, and so a few days, will, I trust, put an end to his misery and remorse, and make all parties respectable as well as happy in future.

All the family dined at the mess to-day. General N. and I *tête-à-tête*, with the dear babes, as our greatest treat. – In the evening, before we went to bed, a despatch arrived from Antigua. – The French are still in the same position, as far as any intelligence can be obtained. Soon, however, our suspense must be at an end.

4th. At 12, the several forts and ships, in Port Royal harbour, fired a salute, in honour of the day.[1] Soon after, the garrison were drawn up in

[1] The King's birthday.

the square, in front of the King's House, and fired a *feu-de-joie*, and then passed General N. in the usual manner, as he and all the staff, with the new general officers, &c. stood in the portico. Then, General N. held a levee, which was very fully attended. – At 6, nearly two hundred people sat down to dinner, and at 12, all was over, to my great joy; for the dear children were so delighted with the noise and the music, that they would not be persuaded to go to bed, till all was quiet.

5*th*. The poor sergeant is condemned, and the wife came this morning, to petition me to save his life. She has six children, poor wretched creature. Write to Mr. Mitchell for his advice, and whether I should ask the favour, or not, from the Jamaica Government. He thinks the example would be so bad, that he must be left to his fate, and especially with St. Domingo before our eyes. I still do, however, hope, that some punishment, short of death, may be substituted for it. – Major Chalmers, and the officers of the 55th regiment, at dinner. – The poor man's sentence is solitary confinement for two years, and a fine of £4,000. As he is rich, the money is not of much consequence; but at sixty, in this climate, the confinement is almost as bad as death. However, it is a reprieve, and I trust, if he lives, he will come out of prison a better man.[1]

6*th*. Awoke before daylight by an express from England and the Windward Islands. The French force is detained in the harbour of Martinique, by a malignant and contagious fever, and the Minister informs General N. that he may soon expect a strong reinforcement in this part of the world. Our minds are more at ease, and I hope all may soon be well with us, and our suspense at an end.

7*th*. All the family writing; for we have English letters, as well as circulars, &c. to get ready. Much happier than usual towards evening, having obtained the pardon of twenty men, of the 85th, who were to have been punished to-morrow. – The staff dinner only; but a large evening party, and a dance, as it is Friday.

8*th*. Meredith very ill to-day, and all owing to his own imprudence. It is melancholy to think, how young men throw away their health in this country! The doctor says, however, that he will soon be well, with a little care and discipline. – A number of young officers at dinner, and in the evening more of them. – Don't feel comfortable myself, and fancy that I smell a fever. Dr. Rocket made me gargle my mouth with Madeira

---

[1] Two years later the sergeant, whose name was Thomas Roper, obtained a remission of the fine, claiming that while he was in gaol his business had gone to ruin.

wine, and go to bed at 9 o'clock. He says that fancies of that sort often lead to much evil.

13*th*. I was much amused this morning, with the account of poor Mrs. Brockmüller, who is not even allowed to sit down to table with her lord and master, the Ensign, but is obliged to wait behind his chair; and he has in fact married her to have a good servant, poor thing! – News of the French towards the middle of the day. Part of their force has proceeded south, and it is thought with the intention of attacking Trinidad. Soon, I trust, our fleet will arrive, to put an end to their depredations and our alarms.

15*th*. At 5, a dinner party, but I remained in my own room. Soon after, an express arrived from Lord Seaforth, &c. announcing to General N. that an additional French force had made its appearance, from Ferrol, and part of the squadron also from Brest had joined them, making in the whole about thirty sail of the line, and that a great number of troops was supposed to be on board. Lord Nelson arrived at Barbadoes, but was sent by a false report to Trinidad. However, an express has followed him, and shortly, it is to be hoped, we shall have some certain account of their destination and proceedings. In the mean time, all our suspense must continue, and our anxiety is cruelly renewed. For my own part, I feel really almost worn out, with watching and expectation, and my poor dear N. is so harassed with business, that I dread the effect upon his health.

All the house engaged to-day; and after all, the despatches could not be sent off till 12 at night. – In the evening, I received my company as usual, and the party was numerous, all wishing to hear, or to tell what they had heard; and, among other things, I have been told, by the few ladies who remain in Spanish Town, such horrid things of the savage ideas, &c. of the slaves, on the estates in the interior, that I am determined, if my dear N. is obliged to leave me to meet the enemy, that I will take my dear children on board a ship, or any where near the coast, from whence we may make our escape, rather than accept of the asylum offered me by Mr. Mitchell, &c. &c.

16*th*. The church shut up, on account of the heavy rains. – General N. engaged with despatches all day, to go by the *Staunch* brig, which sails for England to-morrow. – Just as we were going to dinner, heard of the arrival of a packet. All anxiety to hear the news, and General N. and I, in particular, to learn our fate. At half-past seven, came the public despatches. They are all that is comfortable. Sir Eyre Coote is to come out with a dormant commission, and to place himself under General N.'s command, till the alarms here are over, and the latter wishes to resign. This has raised our spirits very much, and if Lord Nelson can but send us a good account of the French fleet, we shall be happy indeed.

17*th*. A great deal of business still for my dear N., and the arrangements for Honduras, &c. are very troublesome.

18*th*. Another day of uncertainty and anxiety. An express from the Admiral, to say, that Lord Nelson, not having found the French fleet at Trinidad, had come on to Martinique as quick as possible; but we are still uncertain, whether the enemy remains there, or has come this way, as there are two accounts in a letter from St. Vincent's. The one states that the French had left Martinique, and, by the course they steered, it was supposed would have returned to Europe. The other, that the whole fleet was seen proceeding towards St. Domingo. Whichever may be the true report, our suspense must soon be at an end; but it is a painful state for us all, and a horseman does not come up quick to the door, day or night, but I tremble all over, and almost lose my breath from anxiety.

20*th*. Both my dear N. and I are out of spirits. – He says, that he cannot leave Jamaica till matters are a little more settled, and that he must wait Sir Eyre Coote's arrival. Yet, if the French leave these seas, he is anxious that I should go with the children to England, as soon as possible; but it will be a miserable separation to us both, and it will be a severe trial. – Only Berkeley and Lake in addition to our staff party to-day.

21*st*. General N. reviewed the 55th and 85th regiments, and the St. Catherine's militia, on the race-course, at daylight. I could not summon strength or spirits to go. How different I feel from what I did on my first arrival, and indeed for a long time after; then I had strength, spirits, and activity, for any thing. Now, all is an exertion beyond my strength, and probably my not sparing myself the first year or two, as well as the constant anxiety of late, have done as much as the climate, in wearing me out.

At 7, I met all the party from the review, at breakfast. Mr. Simon Taylor came soon after, to take leave of me; as he says he is now sure that all our alarms will be soon over, and that I must lose no time in going to England, for the sake of my health and that of the little ones. General N., he says, is a *rock*, and will stand any climate. In the course of his visit his expressions were so kind, and he seemed to feel so much, that I was as much surprised as affected by his manner, for he has the character of loving nothing but his money; and yet I have experienced such continued kindness from him, that he has shewn me almost the affection of a father. Indeed, I feel that I know him much better than the world does, and shall always feel gratefully affectionate towards him. – A Council of War held at 12 o'clock, and it was unanimously agreed that martial law should cease at 12 o'clock to-morrow night in case no further intelligence arrived to prevent it. – A meeting also of the Assembly to be called for the 2nd of July. – A large second breakfast, of the 55th and 85th officers.

At dinner, Colonel Pollock (St. Mary's), and Mr. Vaughan (Trelawny). Had a long conversation with the latter, on the subject of making Christians of the negroes, and of his experience of the advantages of teaching them their consequent duties, &c. – On his estate (Plumstead),[1] he has christened all his negroes, and has induced many of them to marry, and lead regular lives. He says, they have in consequence improved in all respects; are sober, quiet, and well behaved; and the last year twelve children were born of parents regularly married. The new negroes are attended to, the instant they arrive on the estate, and are taught their prayers most zealously, by the oldest black Christians, and those best instructed and most capable. How delightful this is! I wish to God it could be made general, and I am sure the benefits arising from it, in every point of view, would be incalculable. I gave Mr. Vaughan several of my catechisms, made for our black servants, and several good little books for their instruction, with which he seemed much pleased.

In the evening a very numerous party. I can't flatter myself that my departure is so much regretted, as they tell me, but still it is comfortable to feel that no one wishes me ill; and many indeed not only made strong professions of regard, but actually shed tears; but what was most gratifying to my feelings, were the very kind and handsome things said of my dear Nugent. They all agreed, that he was one of the most moral and able Governors they ever had, and wished us, a thousand times over, a happy meeting in our native land. All this I really felt very much, although I am not so vain as to take all the flattering things they said of myself, otherwise than as proceeding from their kindness, infinitely more than from any merits of my own. – We sat up longer than usual; for, after the 11 o'clock dancing, there was much to be said, in shaking hands, and bidding good night.

24*th*. At second breakfast, Mr. and Mrs. Woodham and their little girl.

[1] Probably a mistake for Flamstead, since the Vaughan properties were Flamstead and Vaughansfield, in St. James.

Immediately after, we all went to the chapel, where Harry and Eve's child was made a Christian, and now I shall not leave one, belonging to this house, unbaptized. – Continual visitors till 4 o'clock. Then, a deputation from all the *brown* people in the town, wishing to take leave of me. Received them immediately, and then shut myself up in my own room, to rest, and try to be equal to the further exertions of the evening. – At 6, a large party – King Mitchell, and Mr. and Mrs. James Mitchell, Messrs. Hinchliffe, Edwards, Bullock and Ricketts (Lord St. Vincent's heir), the commanding officers and our own staff; in all thirty persons.

25*th*. A long conversation in the evening with Colonel Drummond, about his affairs, &c. – Give him the best advice I can. General N. and I agreed to send off an express to the Admiral, with our excuses, as I am really unfit to undergo the fatigue of such a visit, nor has my dear N. spirits for it either.

26*th*. A long letter from the Admiral, who thinks we are quite right, not to encounter the fêtes which were intended to be given at Kingston, had we visited his Penn.

27*th*. Rise early. – All day the house is in more than usual bustle, and I am glad of it, for I can't sit down, or think comfortably of any thing, or write or read, or even interest myself much in my dear children, God bless them! – General Carmichael and several others at dinner. I left them early, and assembled all the servants in the chapel, and, after prayers, spoke to them on the subject of their future conduct every Christmas. I gave them each a catechism, with a certificate of their baptism; and deposited with old Phœbe a sum of money, to be divided among them. But to Cupid I gave a written character, and something to buy a keepsake. – Poor creatures, they were all in tears, and expressed the most affectionate regret, at the prospect of my departure. Before I went to bed, I received a message from the garrison, wishing to attend me on horseback, to the port where we embark. As it is twelve miles, I begged they would accept of my best thanks, for their kind intention, but not to risk so long a ride in this dreadfully hot weather. No news of the French, or of Lord Nelson, and to-morrow is fixed for the Fleet to sail![1]

28*th*. We never slept, and were in bed scarcely three hours. Poor dear

---

[1] By the middle of June the combined French and Spanish fleet was heading back to Europe with Nelson in its wake. The combined fleet had waited three weeks at Martinique for the Brest squadron, which had orders to join them there but failed to break out from Brest. They had achieved only the recapture of the Diamond Rock and the seizure of a small British convoy.

N. and I were both up and dressed, before 4 o'clock, though we had sat up so late writing and talking. Found all the servants assembled, and a large party of gentlemen on horseback at the door, who all insisted upon accompanying me, a few miles at least. – The parting with the poor blacks and them, with other friends on the road, was painful indeed. At 7, arrived at Old Harbour. A breakfast for all the staff, on board the *Augustus Cæsar*. Only my dearest N. remained afterwards. Sit on deck and can't talk of to-morrow; yet we can think of nothing else; and the thoughtless, playful innocence of the dear children, while we pretended to be amused with it, brought tears to our eyes, and it was difficult to restrain a burst of grief.

29th. Neither of us could rest, and we did nothing but complain of the smell of the sugar, and the dreadful heat of the cabin, all night, or rather for the few hours we were in the cabin, for at 2 o'clock we were both up, and remained conversing, and trying to make up our minds till 8, when, as we were nearly down the harbour, and the sea breeze was very strong, it was thought best that General N. should proceed no farther. God bless, and grant us a happy meeting once more.

The morning wretched. All sick, even the dear children. I believe that I was for a short time out of my senses, for I lay upon the cabin floor for several hours, in a most deplorable way. About 2 o'clock I went to bed, and before evening was tolerably composed, and the dear little ones were as merry as possible, only calling for papa, and it was difficult to pacify them, before they went to sleep.

30th. In the morning we were off Negril Harbour, the port of rendez-vous for the fleet.

July 1st. At 9, the *Theseus*, and the rest of our convoy, appeared in sight, and Captain Bell came to tell me it would be necessary for him to go on board the Commodore, for instructions, but that he would not be absent more than an hour. – The weather was beautiful when the boat was lowered down, and we watched him till he was safe on board the Commodore's deck. Soon after, a most sudden and dreadful squall came on. We were lying in the midst of the fleet, when our cable broke, and we were in the greatest danger of driving against a man-of-war, that threatened to fire into us. Fortunately, however, the mate was a good seaman, and he steered us safely through the ships, and quite out to sea, but we were, for some time, in a state of the greatest danger and alarm. They told me, afterwards, that I went to the helm, to give my assistance. I dare say, in my distraction, I might have done so; but I only recollect kneeling down, with my two children in my arms, and resting my head on the cabin floor, while they lay in dismay by me. As we stood out to sea, another danger presented itself, from the Spanish pirates, &c. One vessel, at no great distance from ours, was boarded. The crew escaped in their boats, but first set fire to her. Our mate, however, manœuvred us so well, that, towards evening, we had nearly got back to our former station, when the captain came on board, and declared he would never leave the ship again, till he saw me and the children safely landed in England.

2nd. About 10 o'clock, Captain Bell was so fortunate as to anchor the ship nearly in the very spot from which we had been driven yesterday, and to-day they hope to get up our lost anchor. – The dear little ones passed a quiet night, in spite of the great heat; and the maids, &c. seem well this morning. – I ought to mention my two fellow passengers, and who compose my family, Colonel Irvine and Dr. McNeil, with my three maids, and two dear little children.

All day watching the labour of the several vessels, in repairing the damage done by the storm. One ship is on shore near us, but they hope to get her off, and that she has not suffered much injury. – I had many visitors in the course of the day. Mr. Griffith, of St. Elizabeth's, came, and took charge of a letter for my dear N. Mr. Hylton arrived soon after, with one from him, and told me that a report had come on to Spanish Town, of our ship having gone on shore, and that we were in great distress. I therefore sent off another letter immediately, to set his mind at ease on our account. Captains Ross and Boger came to offer their services, and, at Captain Bell's request, I asked for two good helmsmen. Then came Captain Drury, to apologize for having scolded us so much, and threatened to fire into our ship, during the squall; but he said it was for our sake, more than his own; as, had we come in contact, his ship was so much stronger than ours we must have gone to the bottom. – The rest of the day passed quietly. The weather quite calm, and all well.

3rd. No alarm or incident during the night. At 6, this morning, a letter from my dear N., and I wrote to him in return, before I left my cabin. – The heat dreadful, and the smell of the sugar almost suffocating; so that we must live on deck very much. – About 10 o'clock, Captains Temple, Drury, Croft, Tucker, and Douglas, Messrs. Edwards and Griffith, Captain and Mrs. Dixon (Artillery), and young Berkeley, all came to see me, and stayed nearly two hours on board. – Little G. and L. much admired for their intelligence and great spirits, as well as pretty looks and engaging manners.

About 1, the signal was given, and we all weighed anchor for sea. This seemed to me like a second parting from my dear husband. Soon after we set sail, a heavy squall, with tremendous thunder and lightning, did not at all contribute to raising my spirits; but, before I went to my cabin for the night, the Commodore sent me a nice long letter, from General N., who is well, thank God! and promises to keep up his spirits, and take the greatest care of his health, with the hope of our meeting in happiness once more. – About 12 o'clock at night, we were fairly out to sea, and the ship tossing about very much, from the agitation occasioned by the late squalls. I could not rest, but sat looking at the fleet, and watching, for the greatest part of the night, the winds and the waves.

4th. The weather fine this morning, but the sea rough. However, all around me are well, and the little ones run about the cabin as if they were on shore; for having no shoes on, they don't slip about much. Only we are in constant fear of a sudden roll of the vessel doing them some mischief. The confinement alone seems irksome, and they are continually asking, when we shall go to the Penn, &c. My old maid, Johnson, is cross, and quarrelling with all around her. She has a most unfortunate and unhappy temper. – Dined at 4 in the round-house, with the two gentlemen and Captain Bell, and at 8, retired for the night.

5th. Heard this morning, by chance – for they did not intend I should know it – that the carpenter was found dead in the very act of putting up his tools, last night; and that some of the seamen are ill also, on account of getting wet, and striking in the prickly heat, during the heavy rain, the first night or two after we sailed. Tell Captain Bell to use all my stores, in any way that may be of service to the invalids. – See the Grand Caymanas, just before we went to dinner. It is inhabited by people who subsist by catching turtles, and procuring articles from vessels, that are unfortunately wrecked there. – A little rain in the evening, but the night calm and quiet; though the heat was so great, that the children could not rest, but were crying all night for water, which was so warm when they got it, that it would not allay their thirst, and only distressed them the more. Dear little L., in her impatience to drink, actually bit a piece of the glass fairly out, and it has cut her little lip and cheek a good deal.

6th. A calm this morning, and the ship rolling about with the swell of the sea, and very uncomfortable. The Grand Caymanas near us. It appears a very low miserable island. It is a dependency on Jamaica, and that gives it an interest with us, as being under the command of my dear Nugent. I look at it with a sort of melancholy pleasure, as something belonging to him, but as if we were again leaving him behind us. Soon after breakfast, Lake and Berkeley came, and brought the man Captain Temple had promised me, so now we are very tolerably off for steersmen. – A dead calm the whole day. – Little L. with a violent heat all over her, in addition to the prickly heat. The doctor says, their best diet for the present will be rice and arrowroot, and for George a little port wine.

16*th*. There has been a sad chasm in my journal; but, in spite of my present state of nervousness and weakness, I will try to fill it up. – In the night of the 8th, we were spoken to by the *Magicienne* frigate, to tell us, that the Havannah was clear, and no enemy in that quarter, or in the Gulf of Florida, so that we might steer our course, without any further fear. The Captain was anxious to know how we were, that he might tell General N. all about us, on his return to Port Royal. I was so anxious, for fear that Captain Bell would mention the illness on board, that I jumped out of bed, and ran to the cabin window, to say, all is well, and to beg Captain B. would tell the Captain of the *Magicienne* so. In an instant, I was struck, as with a great blow, or, rather, as if I had received a shot; and, from being in a profuse perspiration, and in a violent heat, I became instantly almost stiff with the cold. – Poor Clifford, who, in spite of her own illness, got up to see what was going on, got a blanket, and covered me up, but all would not do. I went up to breakfast, but was in such an odd way, that Dr. McNeil, who came to see how I was, ordered me to bed immediately. Vomitings then came on, and I was tortured with pains in every part of my body, as long as any recollection remained; but for twenty-four hours my head was in a sad state, and I knew nothing that had passed. Since that, my weakness has been dreadful, and the fever coming and going, so that I could scarcely move from my bed, even to have it put in order. – On Saturday, I was brought upon deck, and soon I hope to recover my strength. – On Wednesday, my sweet Louisa was seized with almost the same sort of fever, and for three days the darling little thing was in a sad stupid state, neither sleeping nor waking, nor taking notice of any thing. My own maid was also, on Wednesday, taken so ill with a fever, that she was put into bed and covered with blisters; and, to crown all, the doctor again took to his bed, on Thursday, with a fever. – Miss several poor sailors from the deck, since I was taken ill, but ask no questions, for I am afraid to hear sad tidings of them.

17*th*. Clifford is rather better to-day, but my dear little boy is feverish, and very complaining with his bowels. – He and Louisa are both ordered to have port wine and biscuit, at 11 o'clock, every day, and they take their little glass with great pleasure. Two of our best seamen were taken ill to-day, and their lives are despaired of. For my own part, I am so miserably low and weak, that I can scarcely support myself at all. However, I have made an effort to continue my journal for my dear N., in the usual cheerful strain, for his mind would be distracted, did he know our real situation. – We were obliged to lay to all night. To-morrow, however, I hope we shall get rid of this horrid Gulf of Florida, and be in a more open sea.

18*th*. My only attendant, since my illness, has been a tall old man, the steward of the ship, and he has thought of a plan for restoring my strength, which I have promised to adopt to-night. It is to take a piece of toasted bread, dipped in porter, and then sprinkled with sugar, just before I lie down to sleep. – Write my journal for General N., as now I must soon send it off; a midshipman was sent today by the Commodore to apprize me of this. – Still in the Gulf of Florida, and the ship obliged to lay to all night. The old steward will not resign his office, but still attends me, and to-night I shall take his prescription of toast and porter. His name is San Fiorenza, for he was born in a church of that name, during the great earthquake at Lisbon, and was immediately baptized by an officer, that happened to have taken refuge there with his mother, &c. He comes to my bedside every morning, and kneels down to take my orders, and the same at night, and never offers me any thing, when I am ill and in the cabin, without going down on one knee. His language is very curious; a mixture of English, French, Italian, and Portuguese. Altogether, he is quite a character.

19*th*. The sea calm this morning, but we are obliged to tack continually, on account of the shoals on the Florida shore, on one side, and the Bahama Keys on the other. Lake and Berkeley came and spent an hour this morning, and brought me a message from Captain Temple, to say that the schooner will leave us to-morrow evening, or Sunday morning, for Jamaica, and that my despatches must be ready by that time.

20*th*. Rise very early, and have the comfort of finding we are getting clear of the Gulf of Florida. – I must not omit to mention, that while I was ill one of my finest macaws flew overboard, and the same day my most intelligent parrot died. I wish we had no greater losses to lament; but, alas! many of the crew are missing, and have, I fear, also found a watery grave.[1] – Lat. 29, at 10 o'clock this morning. – Very light winds, but

---

[1] Perhaps Mrs. Nugent was not told at the time of the death of a fellow passenger, which was later reported in the *Dorchester and Sherborne Journal* as having occurred on

fair. – At 12 o'clock, sent my journal, for General N., on board the schooner.

26th. I forgot to mention, yesterday, the immense dolphin, that had been for several hours about our ship, was taken. Many of the sailors said, they had never seen so large a one. There were many smaller swimming about, and the men were much amused, with trying to harpoon them. The large one was brought upon the deck, and when it was dying, it looked beautifully; being green, blue, purple, yellow, with stripes and spots of mother of pearl, or silver; and the dear children were much astonished at the sight.

3 1*st.* I do indeed dread a long passage, for the smell of the sugar is so bad, it destroys every thing. All the cabin is covered with a sort of leaden surface, which comes off upon one's clothes, and even our skins seem to be dyed with it. I am shocked at the dingy, dirty appearance we make, but this is not the worst part of the business, for I constantly feel my throat and lungs affected by it. Every thing *tastes* of the *smell* of the sugar, and I am in continual apprehension, lest my dear babes should suffer in their health by it.

Here ends the month of July. – This evening, Captain Temple was so good as to take our madman (Gardiner) on board the *Theseus*, as he became mischievous, threw one of the turtles overboard, and threatened, every night, to get into the cabin, and to murder all the women and children, which, as we had no means of confining him, made our situation by no means pleasant. Many a sleepless hour has it cost me, since I have been on board.

August 1st. Young Berkeley came on board to dinner. He says that there are several of the ships missing. Some went on shore in the Gulf of Florida, and were lost; others are supposed to be taken; and some to have parted company in the heavy squalls we have had of late.

3rd. All our party are quite well, and the children are mending very fast; but the smell, and the dirt, occasioned by the sugar, seems to have increased with the damp weather. Every thing feels clammy, and if you touch the wainscot, it comes off like the marks of a black lead pencil, and no water can get the stain out. My nose seems always dirty.

July 19th: "Richard Meyler Esq., of Crawley House near Winchester, on board the *Augustus Caesar* West Indiaman, on his passage from Jamaica to this country." Richard Meyler was the proprietor of Meylersfield and other estates in Westmoreland, and his only son reputedly inherited a fortune of £35,000 a year. (*Caribbeana* vol. 2, p. 276).

7th. I really believe that the putrid steam of the sugar disorders my stomach; for it turns every thing of a dingy lead colour, and the maids complain of the continual nausea it occasions them.

8th. In the afternoon the tiller was put in order, and as it was necessary, for that purpose, to open the trap-doors in our cabin, the heat and intolerable stench from the sugar were indescribable. The vapour that arose from it blackened every thing, and was as hot as if it came from a boiling cauldron. The men, who went down, returned as if from a warm bath, and their faces all discoloured.

11th. A very calm night with a heavy swell. The ships unmanageable with the helm, in consequence, and we were obliged to tow ours out of the confusion. Almost all the fleet had their boats out, from two o'clock, and it is now eight in the morning, and they are obliged to continue the same mode of guiding them. The *Theseus* has two boats towing her, to keep her head the right way.

17th. We are now about two or three hundred miles from the banks of Newfoundland, and may look forward to seeing dear England in about three weeks, or perhaps sooner. Our voyage has been sadly tedious, with calms, squalls, and contrary winds; but now, I trust, we may look forward to more settled weather, and in three weeks, or a little more, we may leave this uncertain and tremendous element. – Spoke a ship from New Providence; Governor Cameron and his family quite well.

21st. Still a fair wind, and the fleet pretty well up, as the *Theseus* took a vessel in tow yesterday, and made several of the fast sailing merchant ships do the same. – I don't think I have ever mentioned how I pass the day on board ship. I will now detail the dull routine. As soon as I awake in the morning, the old steward comes into my cabin, with either a dish of ginger tea, or coffee, or sometimes a piece of a shaddock. I then have the children brought to me. They kiss papa's picture, and pray God to bless him. After playing with them a little time, I say my prayers, and then dress for breakfast; before which, I generally walk a short time with the gentlemen on deck. As soon as breakfast is over, I go down into the cabin, and see that the maids wash and dress my little ones, who come on deck with me; and the morning is spent, between reading, walking, and playing with the children. At 12, I always open my map, and mark on it the progress of my voyage. At 11, the children have each a biscuit, and some port wine and water. Louisa then goes to sleep, and George eats some chicken, or some thing or other, when we take our luncheon at 12. At 2, they have strong soup, either of mutton or chicken. At 3, I go to my cabin, read, and then dress for dinner. Soon after 4, we dine; and at half-past seven, I leave the gentlemen to smoke their cigars, and to drink their brandy and water. Soon after 8, I am always in bed, and the babes sound asleep. The old steward then comes to my bedside, with a large tumbler of porter and a toast in it. I eat the toast, drink the porter, and generally (when the sea and wind will permit) rest now tolerably well.

To-day we lay to, about half-past one o'clock, for the dull sailers, when Captain Bell went on board the *Theseus*, and I took the opportunity of sending some sweetmeats, half-a-dozen of Malmsey, and a nice little roasting pig, of the Chinese breed, to Mrs. Dixon. Captain Bell heard, from Mr. Lake, that they were all sadly off in the wardroom, for fresh meat and porter; so we made them a present of three or four pigs, a sheep, some poultry, and some porter, &c.

26*th*. Not much wind, and that little is against us; and, as it is at east, we feel it very cold; but I enjoy it, and the children don't seem to suffer the smallest inconvenience from it. – Lay to, the greatest part of the day, for the dull sailers, forty or fifty of our fleet being out of sight behind us.

27*th*. Rise early. – Not much wind, but it is fair, what there is of it; however, we are obliged to go back again, to collect some of our fleet, which have appeared in sight this morning, though at a great distance off. A captain of one of the merchant ships came on board, and brought two London newspapers; one as late as the 26th of July. I am quite out of spirits; Sir Eyre Coote had not left Cork on the 12th of July! Alas! I had flattered myself that my dear Nugent was already relieved, and on his way home. God bless and preserve him! – About 2 o'clock, a strange frigate, which proved to be *La Loire*, Captain Maitland, joined us from Cork; only six days out. This makes us feel ourselves near home. Soon after, the *Cerf*, Captain Chamberlayne, spoke us, and gave us an account of the naval engagement between Sir R. Calder, and the combined fleet from the West Indies, &c., with the promise of bringing us the papers as soon as possible; one as late as the 10th of August.

28*th*. Spoke the *Cerf* again, soon after 12, and sent on board for the newspapers. Sir R. Calder in disgrace, for not following up his advantage with the enemy. Sir John Orde superseded, for not following the Toulon squadron to the West Indies, and Lord Nelson is at Gibraltar. – Not a word in the papers about Sir Eyre Coote; so I hope and trust he sailed for Jamaica on the 13th of July, as the papers we had yesterday seemed to think the troops would leave Cork about that time. – Captain Chamberlayne came at 4 o'clock, and dined with us, and never in my life did I hear more scandal than he told us of the whole fleet. – Such quarrels, such discontents, and party business! I do indeed rejoice that I did not accept of the accommodation on board the *Theseus;* for Captain and Mrs. Dixon are perfectly detested and looked upon as the greatest incumbrances. What should I have been, with children and maid-servants, all sick, and of course unavoidably troublesome. – I sat up till near 9, and the gentlemen did not quit their cigars, &c. till near twelve.

29th. Captain C. has promised to get me some newspapers from the *Loire,* by which I hope to find out the exact time when Sir Eyre Coote sailed, that I may judge of the probable chance of my dear N.'s leaving Jamaica, before the season for another meeting of the Legislature there.

September 1*st.* The *Loire,* with the ships for Bristol and Liverpool, left us early in the night, and were out of sight this morning. Alas! one of my most beautiful Curaçoa birds died in the night, from the inclemency of the weather. He was very large, with a dark variegated plumage, and a purple tuft upon his head, or rather a lilac one; for it was too light a colour to be called purple. I examined it after death, and it appeared to be a hard sort of crumbling substance, like the inside of a bone. I am much afraid that I shall lose more of my birds, for, unfortunately, they are all moulting at present.

2*nd.* Towards the evening, very cold to *us Creoles.* Louisa did not seem to feel so much as George, who looked very grave at first, and then said his fingers were sore, which was a very natural idea for a child, who had never before known what cold was.

CHAPTER V

September 3rd. – Six o'clock in the morning. – The land just announced from the mast head, thank God! thank God! a thousand, and a thousand times! Dearest Nugent, soon I trust you will experience the same happiness, and complete ours, by your arrival in health and safety in dear old England. – About 2 o'clock, we were hailed by a small vessel, from Weymouth, offering to land us, if we were in a healthy state. The day was very wet, the rain incessant, and the wind high, so we kept the vessel alongside all night, to await our decision in the morning.

4th. The morning beautiful, and the wind directly fair, to take us into Weymouth. The fear of quarantine, and apprehension of falling in with some of the enemy's cruisers, and our convoy being very much scattered, decided us upon going on shore, and at 10 o'clock, we took our leave of the *Augustus Cæsar*, and good Captain Bell, and crowded all the sail our little vessel could carry. We had a sad, tedious time, till after 6 o'clock, when we came into Weymouth Harbour. There we were obliged to remain, for the health officer to examine us.

Before I describe our landing, I must mention our appearance. Colonel Irvine and Dr. McNeil were in old brown or pepper and salt clothes, that they had worn some years before in England. My three maids were in their best bonnets, &c. but the shape sadly old fashioned, as we soon found, and all their gowns and trimmings much tarnished, by the climate of the West Indies, and by the sun, air, &c. The children we put a second frock on, so as to supply the place of warm clothing; but their ankles, arms, and necks, were covered with beads; and for myself, in my hurry, and anxiety to get on shore, I forgot the dress prepared for me, and put on a full Lieutenant-General's uniform, that I had used as my dress of ceremony on the voyage. It was a scarlet habit, with embroidered fronts, and two large gold epaulettes on my shoulders. – In short, we made a most extraordinary appearance altogether.

Captain Bell was rather reluctant to our leaving the ship, at such a distance from the land, but provided us with sea stock, for a day or two, for fear of accidents; among which were, a large ham, and a large roasted turkey, which we immediately exchanged, with my captain of the fishing vessel, for some brown bread, butter, and fresh cheese, upon which we all feasted.

At 8, the health officer made his appearance. He told us that the Duke of Gloucester had just been buried, and the King and royal family, then at Weymouth, were all shut up; but he had been invited, by some of the attendants, to dinner, and this kept him so late. In fact, he appeared to be almost tipsy, but this was fortunate for us, as he was in high good humour, in consequence of the good cheer. My gentlemen, who, as well as myself, had been reading the rules respecting quarantine, on board the fishing vessel, began with assurances of our health, although they confessed we had been ill. This put me in a fright, and I ran to the side of the vessel, with the two children in my arms, making a most pathetic speech, about the hardship of our having got through all the dangers of foreign climates, and then to be left to die of the night air in sight of our native shore. This won the little man's heart; and, in his anxiety to be kind, and to tell us all about the quarantine regulations, &c. he jumped on board our little vessel; where, in a moment recollecting himself, he said, "Well, Madam, now it is all over, as, if you are to perform quarantine, I must perform it with you: so all we have to do is to remain quiet for a little while, and then keep our own secret after we land."

As it was getting darker every minute, we were soon in his boat, with our trunks, &c.; but I could not help laughing at his evident fear of the plague, notwithstanding all our assurances of all the party being in perfectly good health. The little light that remained, when he came on board, shewed him our sallow sickly faces, and I don't at all wonder at the poor man's alarm. During our short row to the shore, however, he resumed his spirits sufficiently to give us his whole history. First, he shed tears about his poor partner, whom he had laid under the sod, three years ago; but he smiled again, when he spoke of the daughter she had left him, now sixteen, apprenticed to a milliner, who was patronized by the princesses; all this would have made us laugh too, if we had not been expecting to land on our native shore every moment.

How shall I describe the instant when we left the little vessel! It was then so dark, that no one could see me, and my first movement was, like Columbus, to kneel down and kiss the earth, and return fervent thanks to Almighty God, for his mercy and goodness, in bringing us safe through all our perils and dangers. Then I embraced my dear children, and vented my feelings in tears and congratulations to all my fellow passengers. Our kind friend, the health officer, hurried us up some back lanes to our inn, where we were placed in confidence, under the care of his friend the landlord; and he also got some other friends, in the custom-house, to pass our baggage. All was done for a fee of five guineas, which I was directed to entrust him with, to pay all expenses, and keep all secret. My agreement with the captain of the sailing boat was twenty guineas, so I begin to think, that I shall not have money enough to take me to London. However, it was too late for the bank last night, and, though we can't leave Weymouth, on account of the review this morning, which will engage all the horses till 3, it is thought most advisable not to make ourselves known, till we have left the coast a little way. Nothing could exceed the attention of the people at the inn, except the delight of little George and Louisa, at the novelty of all around them. George seized upon the tongs with astonishment; and, before I could prevent her, Louisa had possession of the bell rope, and rung such a peal, that she brought up the waiters, &c. in a great hurry. In short, they were like little mad things, and it was late before they could be composed to sleep; and, even then, nothing but real fatigue induced them to close their dear little eyes. My gentlemen and I had a nice supper of partridges, and all went to bed happy and thankful.

6*th*. We left Weymouth before 4 o'clock, and, on our arrival at Dorchester, heard there were some officers in the house, that Sir Eyre Coote had not yet sailed, and that the time of his departure for Jamaica was quite uncertain. Then, upon examining the state of my purse, found that my Weymouth bill had sadly diminished its contents. I applied to the landlord, therefore, for money for a draft. He referred me to his wife, who was even more hard-hearted than himself, and dropped some hints, about *odd people* travelling about the country, &c. This set me on my mettle, and I collected all my gold pieces, and found I had sufficient to pay for a good dinner, apartments, &c.; and so I went to bed last night in good spirits; for I make no doubt the next stage I shall meet with kinder people. I must, however, say that there is some reason for the fear these poor people seem to have, about our being respectable, as I sent the landlady to a Colonel *somebody* in the house, last night, to ascertain the truth of General Nugent's being in Jamaica, &c., all of which was vouched for, but he had never heard that *General Nugent was married;* so no wonder the woman would not trust me – but I must dress, and be off with my dear little ones for Blandford.

7*th*. A nice breakfast at Blandford, yesterday morning, and the landlord in an instant ran over to the bank, to get me a hundred pounds for a draft upon Messrs. Drummond; and, on opening my desk, I found a letter of credit upon them, from General N., for any amount; and this, owing to my stupidity, I had never thought of since I landed. – Gave the children some dinner at Andover, and slept at this place, Hartford Bridge. – Now we are off for London, where we expect to be in time for the dear children's dinner to-day. – Drove to Berkeley Square, and found that the Russian Ambassador had taken possession of all the apartments at Thomas's Hotel. Then to Grosvenor Street, and find the house empty. My sister Fraser and all out of town. At Reddish's Hotel in St. James's Street, we got excellent apartments.

8*th*. Before 10, my dear sister Fraser from the country, &c. We went to St. George's church together. Delighted at being once more allowed to return thanks to God, for all his goodness and mercy. I wrote from Weymouth, to tell our dear friends at Stowe of our landing, and Dempsey was sent up to town to-day, to take charge of us down to Stowe. He brought a most kind and affectionate letter, from dear Lord Buckingham himself; offering even to come to town, if I could not immediately go to the country, and insisting upon my making Pall Mall my home, &c. and not going to an hotel. – Lord and Lady Westmeath, and their nice family, and, in short, abundance of friends, coming in every minute. Doctor Fraser spent an hour with me this evening, and thinks I had better remain a little while near him, as both the children and myself require a little care yet.

9*th*. Lord Westmeath came, to accompany me to Downing Street, where I had made an appointment with Mr. Cooke yesterday. He assured me that General N. would certainly be at home by Christmas, or very little after, and that Sir Eyre Coote would sail as soon as General N. would have time to take his passage, on board the November fleet, unless (alas!) some circumstances should arise, to prevent his giving up the command in Jamaica. He spoke to me about the anxious wish of General N.'s friends in the Government, that he should accept of a baronetage *now*, as giving him claims for the *ribbon*, which General N. prefers. – He stated that there are objections to his being made a Knight of the Bath at present, which makes all that espouse his interest, and the Duke of York in particular, anxious that he should accept of the favours now offered him. I will tell him all they say, and his judgment and feelings must decide the point. Our long conference ended with many praises bestowed upon my dear husband; and he does indeed deserve them, and I rejoice his conduct is so well understood and appreciated.

On my return to the hotel, Drs. Blair and McNeil. The former is going back to Jamaica. Mrs. Pye, also, was one of my visitors to-day, and made me almost fancy myself at the King's House again, she was so full of all the gossip of Spanish Town. Her brother is going to be married to a lady, with neither youth, beauty nor fortune, but she is well connected, sensible, and amiable; and so I trust he will be happy. Met Colonel Robinson in the street, who did not know me at all, at first; but says now, it is because *I am looking so well!* – Dined with Lord and Lady Westmeath to-day.

10*th*. See various people this morning, and hear a great deal of news, gossip, and scandal. Poor Captain (Jack) Murray would insist upon it, when we met in Jamaica, that Lord Temple was flirting with the Duchess of Rutland, and that our dear Lady Temple was very unhappy about it, in consequence. I denied the calumny stoutly, and it proved to be Lord Templetown; but I am sorry to say, that I find Lord Temple (alas!) a little changed too, for he has become a man of the world, and is now paying great attention to Lady Castlereagh. It may be a joke, but it is not right. Lady Lucan has forsaken her husband and family, and become quite abandoned. – How wretched! Poor Lady Frances Vandeleur is in a melancholy way, and so nervous as to alarm and distress all her friends very much. Sir Eyre Coote is married, I find, to one of the Misses Bagwell, who is to accompany him to Jamaica, and this accounts for his delays. D. Mackinnon is married to a Miss Rose Elliot, or going to be. She is a cousin of Lady Le Despencer and Lady Cosby. General Wellesley has arrived from India. I wonder if he will now renew his flirtation with Kitty Pakenham![1] All these little affairs I shall make news of, for the amusement of my dear N., whose mind I will try to distract from business, and divert as well as I can.

12*th*. A conversation to-day with Lord Westmeath, &c., and was advised to apply for the command in Ireland for my dear Nugent.

13*th*. Awoke early, and composed my letter to Mr. Cooke – *Private and confidential*. Then Mrs. F. took me another round of visits. I left my *grand* letter in Downing Street, or rather saw the servant deliver it, as we sat in the carriage.

14*th*. Drove out with Lord and Lady Westmeath, inspect my new

[1] While serving in Ireland, 1787–93, Arthur Wellesley (afterwards Duke of Wellington) became engaged to Catherine Pakenham, daughter of the second Baron Longford. Owing to the opposition of her family, and Wellesley's absence in India, they were not married until April 1806.

carriage, and see several houses, that I may report to my dear N. the one most likely to suit us, when he comes home. Settled my dear little party in Sloane Street.

16*th*. A begging letter from Admiral Smith. Another from a Mr. Nugent, and how I *am* to act with these sort of people! Drove with Mrs. Dixon to several shops, and then went to Spence, the dentist. He assures me I ought not to lose a tooth; that all are sound, and only require a little rubbing up. This he has done for me, and I came away smiling upon all, to shew my beautiful teeth. Dined at the Westmeaths'.

20*th*. Went to dine in Grosvenor Street at 6 o'clock. An agreeable surprise prepared for me, by dear sister Fraser. It was indeed joy to me, to find my dear sister Robinson and her good husband there; but it was mixed with regret, as I am to leave town to-morrow; as, having told Madame Du Pont that I shall be with her at dinner, I can't put it off.

21*st*. Before one, set off for Reading; but, as the children had not dined, stopped to refresh them, and so did not reach Reading till after Madame Du Pont had dined, for which I was very sorry, but it could not be helped. Left W. Fraser to run across the fields from Maidenhead to Eton. Put the dear children to bed, as soon as they had their supper. Madame Du Pont seemed much pleased with them, but little G. is still too unwell to appear to advantage.

27*th*. The children better, and I have decided upon going to Stowe to-morrow. Send my man Richard to arrange accordingly, as soon as we had dined. To bed at nine.

28*th*. Take leave of Madame Du Pont, soon after 8, and proceed as fast as possible to Lillies, where we arrived before 4, having given the little ones their dinners on the road. Dinner at 6, and as they had prepared for me, and insisted upon my remaining for the night, make up my mind, and put the children to bed at 8. There are now five generations in this house. Colonel Nugent, his mother, and grandmother, his daughter, and her daughter, all eating, drinking, and talking, and the old folks enjoying themselves, quite as much as the young ones.

29*th*. Set off for Stowe before eleven, quite in a fuss and agitation, to shew my children to my dear friends, and longing to see them all once more. Arrived at Stowe soon after 2 o'clock, and found all the dear party assembled. I found all looking well, but the growth of Lord George was beyond every thing. Lady Mary is now quite a woman, in size and appearance, and with a lovely face. Dearest little Lady Temple is wonderfully improved. Dear, dear Lord and Lady Buckingham are the same as when we went away, only a little older; and Lord Temple is as good humoured, kind, and handsome as ever, and the dear little man is grown tall and beautiful. Even Miss Mac appeared very handsome in my eyes, and the old Bishop of St. Pol de Leon and Doctor O'Connor more *interesting* than ever I thought them before. We had a hearty laugh before dinner; for on going up stairs, we found all the iron balustrades worked in and out, in a sort of net, for fear the children should fall through, and break their necks; as poor good William Smith of course concluded my children must be *mites*.

At dinner, we were surprised by the sudden and unexpected appearance of General (now Sir Arthur) Wellesley. He was greeted with the greatest friendship and delight, and placed on the other side of dear Lord Buckingham, who was anxious to learn all about his Indian campaigns, &c. as soon as possible; but he seemed more inclined to talk over his Aide-de-camp days, and to tell me all the tricks played by him, General N., &c.[1] – In short, the two people, from the east and west, both arriving the same day, afforded much mirth and amusement to the whole party, and it was 11 o'clock before we sat down to supper, and past 12 before we could think of going to bed. Only Major Moore here, in addition to the family party.

30th. My darlings much better, and amuse all the family very much, by their little funny talk, and Creole ideas and ways. – Obliged to write many letters, having myriads, from all parts of the country, to answer. – A talk with Sir Arthur Wellesley about Ireland, and Irish friends, and I think he still retains his old feelings. – Dine at 5. A most delightful evening. Music, and much agreeable conversation.

October 3rd. In the evening, had a long and very interesting conversation with Lord Buckingham, on the subject of General Nugent's affairs, and shall write, (please God) to-morrow, and detail all he says, as I am sure he is a real friend, and deeply interested for us all.

4th. In the evening, Lady B. said she was sure we all wanted exercise, and should walk over the house, and see my apartment in particular, as she had contrived so nicely for the little ones. Judge of my surprise, upon entering my own room, when she drew aside a curtain, and shewed me the bust of my dear Nugent, placed on a little cabinet, close behind the bed. It is an excellent likeness, and invaluable to me, and I kissed her most heartily for her kindness, and all the party seemed to share in my pleasure

[1] Wellesley and Nugent, who was twelve years senior to him, had both served as ADC to Lord Buckingham when he was Lord Lieutenant of Ireland.

and satisfaction. – The rest of the evening as usual, but many jokes, by Lord Temple, on their giving me a husband of marble, &c.

5*th*. Got a most delightful, long, and comfortable letter, from my dear, dear Nugent.

12*th*. In the evening, much talk about ghosts, and Lady B. projected a trick for the Duc de Serant, which succeeded famously; but he played us one in return, and sent us all pell-mell down stairs; but these events took up so much time, and made us all so merry, that we did not get to bed till after 1 o'clock.

13*th*. Write, &c. early. Evening church. Mr. and Mrs. W. Fremantle, and the Misses Harvey, just before dinner. Little L. made acquaintance with them immediately, and could scarcely be got away to bed. – The evening as usual.

14*th*. Drove with Miss E. Harvey, in the little pony phaeton. She is a worse whip than myself, if possible.

17*th*. Arrive in town soon after 4; found a letter from my dear N. waiting for me in Pall Mall. Sent to my sisters Fraser and Robinson, and they both came, and dined quietly with me.

18*th*. Read over General N.'s letter again, and then decide upon writing and consulting Lord B. upon the subject of the letters he has enclosed to me; one to Lord Camden, refusing the baronetage offered him, and the other to the Duke of York, respecting the red ribbon. – Still my mind too anxious, and too much occupied with my dear N.'s vexation about the baronetage, and his affairs, to think much of enjoying anything else.

19*th*. When I came home to dress, Mr. Birchall came to consult me, about Sir Eyre Coote's carriages. He appeared to be one of the stupidest men I ever met with, and will, I am sure, mismanage the whole thing. – I have promised, if possible, to find out some eligible party for Miss Coote to accompany to Jamaica. Some good gentleman-like steady family, if such there can be found leaving England in these times.

22*nd*. Lord B.'s letter all kindness. He has written to the Duke of York himself, and dictated a letter for me, to Lord Camden and the Duke. Employ myself until one, in copying the letters, and in doing all my writing business; then set off, with the Robinsons, and pass a delightful day at Blackheath, with our sister Fraser and the children.

30*th*. Dine with the dear Robinsons, to celebrate their wedding-day.

November 3*rd*. [Stowe] Go to church with dear Lady Temple. Lady Mary Grenville has a cold, and can't be of the party. – The rest of the ladies all Catholics.

4*th*. In the evening, Lady Buckingham invented a game, called "kiss the doctor," which sent us all to bed very merry. The old Bishop of St. Pol de Leon seemed to enjoy the fun as much as any of us.

7*th*. Great news! The combined fleet defeated off Cadiz, but Lord Nelson no more! I could not help being greatly affected by the whole account, and retired to my own room, to vent my feelings. I don't know why, but all these sort of things seem to have such a connection with my dear N. and his situation, that they appear as our own immediate concerns. – The whole day talking of the great event announced this morning. Various conjectures and ideas on the subject, but I hope it may bring about a peace.

8*th*. After a fidgety sort of night, have the comfort this morning of hearing that Sir Eyre Coote must certainly now be soon in Jamaica, as he left Cork on the 28th of October; and a packet is announced, so I shall soon have letters from my dear N.

18*th*. For some days I have been making up my mind to pass a few weeks at Bath, and this morning, at 7, I set off for Oxford. Found Lord G. Grenville expecting me there, and prepared to do the honours of *great Tom*, &c. to the children. – Lord G. took tea with me; after which he went to his rooms to dress, and returned to take me to the concert, given for the benefit of the widows and orphans of Trafalgar. Lord G. supped with me at the inn, and we talked till a late hour.

19*th*. Get to York House, in Bath, at 8 o'clock.

21*st*. Just as I was going to dinner, the Misses Kemble came, and I invited them to partake sans façon; so we had a nice sociable evening, working, and playing with the children, &c. First go with the children to the Pump-room, to give them each half a glass of Bath water, and took one myself. I hope this will strengthen us all, and set us up for the winter.

25*th*. After we had taken our glass of water, went with the little ones to Rosenberg's, and had them weighed. George was two stone and nine pounds, and Louisa two stone two pounds. I was six stone eight pounds. I spent the evening at Mrs. Dacres', to talk about the Admiral and Jamaica.

27*th*. Dined alone, and then took the Misses Kemble to a concert at the rooms, where an old gentleman seemed to take a particular fancy to our party, and shewed me especially much civility and attention, to the great amusement of us all.

29*th*. The dear little things more than usually lively and merry, this morning. The old gentleman, whose name I find is Morshead, who was so civil to our party last night, I met again, at the Pump-room to-day, and agreed to go to see the hospital with him, to which I have also subscribed. It is for indigent people, who come here for the benefit of the waters. – Dined alone, and then went, in the evening, to meet Mrs. Johnson, the Bayards, &c. at Mrs. Herring's. In the course of conversation, I happened to mention Mr. Morshead, and heard he was a dreadful character, and had been turned out of several lodging-houses, and indeed excluded society, for his conduct to women. So here the Misses Kemble and myself are in a fine scrape, and we must get rid of our acquaintance as well as we can! How lucky it is that my appointment with him was for a distant day; so I cut him the more easily.

December 2nd. Mr. W. Pitt at the Pump-room, and the little ones called out Billy Pitt so loud, that I was fearful he would hear them. He is very ill, only Lord Mulgrave with him; but all the company made a lane for him to go up to the Pump, and shewed him as much respect as if he were one of the Royal Family - to the great astonishment of some French generals, that are prisoners here, and were present. – In the evening was chaperon to the Misses Dacres and Kemble, to the rooms. A good ball, and pleasant evening altogether.

7th. The early part of the day as usual. Made a few visits. In the evening, with the Dacres, and heard again the praises of my dear N.; for old Mr. Deane knew his father and grandfather, and remembers him one of the finest looking and best bred men he ever saw.

15th. To church at the Abbey. Drink tea with Lady Belmore; Miss Kitty Fisher, the young Roscia, was there. I took her home in my chair, and was much amused with her conversation, and the secrets of the theatre which she divulged. She is certainly astonishing for her age, but I much doubt her turning out any thing very superior, by and by, as she speaks so much of the labour of learning her part, &c.[1]

18th. Arrive at Stowe about 7 o'clock.

24th. Write a long, and as consolatory letter as I can, to my poor sister R. whose husband is, alas! certainly going to Jamaica, and she is quite miserable about it.

30th. At 4 o'clock, the whole family party was dressed, and was ready

---

[1] True enough, she seems to have left no mark in theatrical history; she was evidently a female counterpart of "the young Roscius", the boy actor William Betty, who had recently been astounding London with his performances of Hamlet, etc., at the age of thirteen.

to receive the French Princes.[1] The band was placed in the gallery of the vestibule, or saloon. All the servants, in and out of livery, were arranged in the north hall. Then stood Lord and Lady Buckingham, with Lord George, at the top of the stairs, leading down to the Egyptian hall; for the weather was so bad, that the guests could not enter by the portico. All the party staying in the house were arranged in the saloon, and formed a sort of line, to where Lord and Lady B., &c. stood. I was desired to stand first, as representing Lady Temple, who, unfortunately, could not be there, on account of her illness.

Just as we were ready, the great people were announced. The band struck up, "God save the King," and we all made our bows and curtsies. – They were conducted to their apartments in great state, and then, after making a short toilette, returned to the library, and all went to dinner. My place was next to Monsieur, to my great annoyance, as I felt shy and uncomfortable, about speaking French, but dear Lady T.'s illness made it necessary, and so I did my best; and before dinner was over, felt greatly at ease, and much amused.

January 1st, 1806. After breakfast, there were prayers for Monsieur, &c. in the state dressing room. – Promised Monsieur, at dinner to-day, that he should see my little ones to-morrow; for, on account of their late colds and illness, I have never let them come down stairs since his arrival. He is anxious to see them, on account of their having been born in Jamaica, and has asked me thousands of questions respecting General N., &c. &c. The Duke de Berri admires Lady Mary Grenville, I think, very much, and the whole party seem exceedingly pleased and gratified with their Stowe visit, and the attention paid them by their host and hostess. – Music in the evening. – Blindman's buff, &c. and all very merry till half-past twelve o'clock.

2nd. Took the children down for a short time before dinner, to be shewn to Monsieur; both very much admired. Monsieur amused us much, by teasing me on the subject of their being so fair, &c. as he thought, being born among the blackies, they must have had a darker tinge. He would make me shew him General N.'s pictures, and made me a great many fine speeches. – In the evening, cards and music were pro-

---

[1] The Comte d'Artois ("Monsieur"), younger brother of the future King Louis XVIII of France, and Artois' son, the Duc de Berri. Lord Buckingham and his wife had been forward in giving assistance to French émigrés in England, and put Gosfield Hall, their house in Essex, at the disposal of the princes; who later moved to Hartwell, near Aylesbury.

posed, but the Duc de Berri begged so hard for blindman's buff again, that Lady B. consented, and a fine romp we all had. Poor Mrs. Cleaver got a sad tumble, and was pulled about by all the gentlemen most unmercifully; making her leap over benches, &c. Lady B. joined in the amusement, and in short it was rather a boisterous evening; but the French gentlemen were delighted, and it was altogether a very funny evening. Supper at 11 and to bed by one; Monsieur and all expressing their regret, that to-morrow they are to take their leave.

The Duc de Berri said, that it was always their fate, just as they became well acquainted, and found friends, they were obliged to be off; and in the present instance he felt it particularly. I thought he was really going to be very sentimental, and throw himself at Lady Mary Grenville's feet at once.

4th. Am amused to find that my old maid, Johnson, passed herself on the French valets de chambre for having been a maid of honour, in foreign parts, where, she assured them, I had been a queen! This accounts for poor nurse's anxiety, to be dressed smarter than usual every evening; for I suppose she passed for a maid of honour also.

13th. In the evening took profiles. General N.'s bust brought down from my room, and had a very good likeness taken from it.

14th. Awake early, in hopes of letters. Only one from Grandjean. General N.'s detained at the Horse Guards. Read old Grandjean's epistle half a dozen times, as he scarcely speaks of any thing but my dear N. and his kindness to him.

15th. Dined at Missenden, and got to Grosvenor Street in time to give my little ones their supper, and see them safe in bed and asleep.

17th. Announce myself to Admiral Nugent, and let Lady Gosford, &c. know I am in town.

21st. Dine again in Pall Mall. A sociable and agreeable, though a rather melancholy party, poor Mr. Pitt being at the point of death, and almost the sole subject of conversation. Came home, reflecting much upon the lives of politicians, and how absorbing politics are of every other feeling.

23rd. At Mrs. D.'s met Mrs. Charles Fox, who admired my children so much, that I could not help feeling very grateful, though I declined a regular introduction to her.[1]

30th. Sir T. Strange introduced to me. He is just from India, and going back again, and gave me a long account of dear Lady W. Bentinck. A

---

[1] In 1795 Fox married Mrs. Armistead, with whom he had lived for about ten years previously, but kept the marriage secret until 1802.

frigate has arrived, and brought an account of poor Lord Cornwallis's death!

February 5th. Dine in Pall Mall. All full of going to Court to-morrow, and am persuaded to be of the party; but, as this was not decided till about nine in the evening, am in a great fuss, having to get my dress ready. Send over for Mrs. Card, Lady B.'s dress-maker, and order all things.

6th. Mrs. Card sent home my dress before 1, and all the feathers, &c. were also ready; so I dressed, and joined the party in Pall Mall before 2, as Lady B. sent her chair for me. The dear little ones were with me while I dressed, and delighted with mamma's big petticoat. My dress was a blue satin robe, with white swan's down, white crape petticoat, on white satin, blue drapery with swan's down, to match the robe. Head dress, diamonds, pearls and white feathers. In short, all very smart. – The drawing room was crowded. Mr. Fox and all the new ministers there. The poor King and Queen tried to look pleased, but did not seem very comfortable. I could not but remark Mr. Fox's slovenly appearance; his stockings were loose about his legs, he had no bag on; and the joke in the newspapers the next day was, that he was not a *Bag Fox*.[1] Got home soon after 5. Take off my hoop, rest a little, and then meet a party at dinner, at Lord and Lady Carleton's. All in our Court plumes, and very gay, but feel very much fatigued indeed, before I get home at twelve.

7th. Have the good fortune of settling poor old Grandjean's affairs, (money matters) most comfortably, with Mr. Martin, and shall write and tell him all about it; for to-day I must close my West India despatches. Write to my dear N. constantly as usual, but hope he will not receive the journal, which I close for him this day, till he is safe in England.

10th. Dine with Mrs. Fraser, and then dress and go to the Duchess of Gordon's assembly, or rather concert; for the Misses Anguish, and Mr. T. Moore, sang the greatest part of the evening; there were also several professors there. Did not get home till near 3 o'clock, as I stayed to see the little dance after the concert.

12th. Remain at home all day, and only admitted Lady Gosford and

---

[1] A bag fox was one brought to the hunt in a bag and let loose before the hounds. In a bag wig, the queue or back hair was enclosed in a bag to keep the powder off the wearer's coat. When Pitt introduced a tax on hair powder in 1795 his Tory supporters loyally continued to use powder and so increase the revenue, but Fox urged his own supporters to give it up. Fox, detested by George III, was Foreign Secretary in the newly formed Ministry of which Lord Grenville was the nominal head. He died the same year.

Mrs. Kemble, the latter of whom has just arrived from Jamaica. Mrs. K. left my dear N. quite well, thank God! and preparing to embark.

13*th*. Have a great deal of talk with Lady B., on the subject of the *Peerage*. Lord B. thinks it is not the moment, but that it may be soon; and may then be pushed for. I don't care much about it, only as far as it will satisfy the world that my dear N.'s services have been properly appreciated.[1]

14*th*. Dined at *King Mitchell's*. The dinner was given to me, and all Jamaica was there. Upwards of twenty at dinner, and an immense crowd in the evening. I was so toadied and complimented, that I fancied myself again in the King's House, but looked for my dear N. in vain. In spite of what I have said, I was greatly pleased with my party, and stayed so late, that I could not join Lady Dungannon's *Beauty* party at supper, as I had promised; and perhaps it was good policy, as I should have entirely lost, by comparison, my little reputation of the sort, which they have given me.

19*th*. *Ash Wednesday*. To church with Mrs. Fraser. Then visit many Jamaica people, to have the happiness of hearing and answering enquiries about my dear N.

20*th*. Sup in Pall Mall. The party there, Sir Joseph, Lady, and Miss Banks, Lady Stanhope, and Lord Mahon, Dean Warburton, &c. Lady Temple and I were much amused, and behaved very ill, by laughing at Sir J. B. and his stick, Lady Stanhope's history, &c., but Lady Buckingham's affected gravity was the cause of all; and even Lord B. could not help laughing.

March 10*th*. General Merck came, and I really felt half afraid of him; he seemed so odd, and looked so like an assassin. Hear all he had to say, and promised I would detail it all to General N., &c. and then rejoice to see him depart.[2] On my way to dine in Pall Mall, I had a sad fright. I was late, and desired the coachman to drive fast; when, suddenly turning into Jermyn Street, I heard a scream, and found that we had driven over a poor child, about two or three years old. All the gentlemen from the clubs, &c. soon surrounded the carriage; but, fortunately, on examining

---

[1] Nugent had canvassed not for a peerage but for the honour of Knight of the Bath (cf. p. 188 n.) When he was made a Baronet in November 1806, Lord Buckingham remarked to his brother, Lord Grenville: "I think that George Nugent will be satisfied with his baronetage, but I see he is teased by his wife, who is very good but not very wise."

[2] For Merck, cf. p. 198 n. He claimed that Nugent had promised to recommend him in England for his services, but that after being shipped from Jamaica with the other French prisoners, he had been refused a commission in the British army.

the child, it was very little hurt, though the blood that flowed from its nose looked dreadful. The coachman was in great distress, but he was not to blame, as many people said. I desired a surgeon to take charge of the child, and to let me know in the morning all about it.

11*th*. The surgeon came, and brought the child and its mother; fortunately, it is not at all hurt, but, as she says she fears she will suffer seriously from the fright, make her a present, and give little G. and L. each half a guinea, to give to the child. All went away pleased, and I am thankful too.

15*th*. As I did not get my letters yesterday, I made up my mind in the night, that General N. would arrive to-day, and so rose very early, and got all the house up, the children dressed nicely, and every thing ready to receive their dear papa. Till 3 o'clock, in the greatest fuss and agitation, when General Grenville came, and told me, that he had seen a public letter from General N., and that now he would certainly not be here till towards May, as he is to sail in the next convoy; that is, this month or April. Receive my letters from the Secretary of State's office, and am much consoled by their contents. He is well, and writes in spirits, and I see he is right, in not coming away immediately; Sir Eyre Coote's appointment, to succeed him in the government, being merely provisional (that is to say, the commission runs, in case of his death, or absence from the island, *only*); so, of course, while there is any alarm, or prospect of an enemy, he would not leave his post; but thank God! all prospect of the French being in force in that part of the world has so far subsided, that there is scarcely a chance of his being detained beyond the April convoy. Dine quietly in Pall Mall, and go home immediately after supper.

21*st*. Lady Temple and I went to Mrs. Fremantle, in Stanhope Street. A large party and music. The Duke of Cambridge sang. Mrs. Billington, Madame Bianchi, &c.

April 9*th*. Set off for Gosfield. Arrived there at 7. Lord George, and Lady Mary with Miss Hernon, to meet me at the gate. A great deal of fun all the evening, and then some serious conversation with dear Lady B. before we went to bed.

I shall not keep a journal of days, or rather a diary, but speak of facts as they arise, during my stay in the country.

Went with dear Lady B. to visit the poor nuns; and, afterwards, to make the acquaintance of my dear Nugent's old friends in the village, who asked a great many questions, about *Master George*, and were much pleased to see his children.

21st. Took little G. to church for the first time in his life, and could not help reflecting very much upon the circumstance, of his being for the first time in the House of God, and seated directly over the remains of his grandfather, and great grandfather, whose monuments are in the pew, over the vault that contains their coffins. Lady B. talked to me most feelingly on the subject, when we went back to the house.[1]

On the evening of the 3rd of May, I received an express, just after dinner, to tell me that my dear N. had arrived at Plymouth. Set off early on the 4th, for town, and met my dearest N. on the road, near Chelmsford. I cannot describe the delight of our meeting, and the dear children partook of our joy, and seemed perfectly to recollect dear papa again; for they knew him the instant he appeared at the side of our carriage. We were both going as fast as four horses could take us, and were some distance past each other, before the horses could be stopped. General N. then jumped out of his carriage, and ran back to ours, and the little ones cried and laughed with joy, to see their dear father, so often prayed for, and about whom so much and such constant anxiety had been expressed. It was happiness indeed; and we all returned to town with hearts full of joy and thankfulness.

Lord and Lady B., and many friends, were soon assembled there, and we passed a delightful time till the 17th of June, when we left town for Cheltenham. But I ought first to mention, that General N. was pressed very much to go as Commander-in-Chief to India, to relieve Lord Lake; and I passed some days in anxiety and agitation, for fear he should be prevailed upon to accept the situation. However, he declined it, to my great joy, distinguished as the appointment was.

I must also mention, that we went to the King's birthday, at St. James's, which was particularly brilliant. Lady Temple and I had dresses just alike; lavender-colour satin robes, embroidered most richly in silver vine leaves, and bunches of grapes. Our petticoats white satin, with lavender crape and satin, rich embroidery, and the draperies looped up with a silver arrow. Head-dress, diamonds and feathers, mixed; the feathers, lavender and white. The Queen remarked our dresses, as we went up together, and said they were the prettiest she had seen.

---

[1] The pew, actually an enclosed compartment, in the parish church at Gosfield in Essex, contains a sculptured monument to John Knight, the second husband of Anne Craggs who afterwards married Robert, Earl Nugent. On the base of the monument are memorial inscriptions to Anne Craggs herself and to Earl Nugent, his sister Margaret, and his son Edmund (General Nugent's father).

PLATE 18

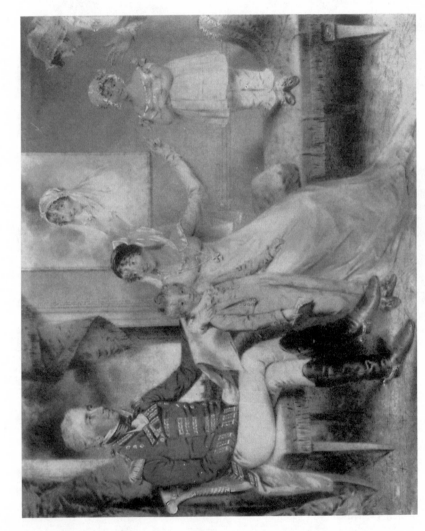

SIR GEORGE NUGENT AND FAMILY
From a painting by John Downman

Took possession of our house in the Barnfields, Exeter,[1] on the 9th of October, and on the 12th (Sunday) celebrated our dear little George's fourth birthday. General Phipps, and a large military party, met Lord and Lady Temple, &c. at dinner. – On the 17th we received letters, announcing the immediate dissolution of Parliament. Lord and Lady Temple had been spending a few days with us, but this has put us all to the rout. Lord Temple off instantly, and my dear N. will also be obliged to go in a few days.

On the 20th, General N. off Aylesbury, to canvass the Borough. He and Lord George Cavendish's son, the two Government members, and scarcely a doubt of their success.

November 2nd. Much discussion on the subject of the baronetage, which I think he will now accept.

9th. Expecting my dear N. every moment. He came at 3. He has succeeded in his election, or rather canvass, perfectly.

16th. We have given two grand dinners, to the Palks, Graves, Courtenays, and Rolles, &c. and divided the military and church militant among them, and so have made large and agreeable parties, for both days.

December 14th. The only event this week is our sitting to Mr. Downman for a family piece; which, if the likenesses are good, will be most interesting, to us at least. General N., the children, the nurse, and myself, are to be the group, and we shall see.[2]

Sunday, 21st. I have been looking back to several passages in my journal, and should this book be in existence, when my dear children grow up, they will perhaps think their little mamma, a very dissipated,

---

[1] In July Nugent had been appointed to the command of the Western Military District.

[2] John Downman, ARA, c. 1750–1824, exhibited regularly at the Royal Academy from 1779 to 1819. Among other family groups which he painted were those of Lord Buckingham (when he was still Earl Temple) and Kean Osborn, Speaker of the Jamaica Assembly. In 1806–7 Downman was living and working in Devonshire, where he had relatives.

The portraits of Sir George and Lady Nugent reproduced in the frontispiece and Plate I are from Downman's preliminary sketches for the complete group. His sketchbook (now in the British Museum) also contains a previous study of Maria Nugent which Downman annotated: "Lady Nugent, 1806. For the group. She sometimes wore very light hair as well as dark. This was after introduced as a picture in the group." There is also a portrait of Maria's sister, Mrs. Robinson, and one of the Nugents' infant son who died in 1807, "drawn after death, as an angel asleep in the church." Downman's portraits of Sir George and Lady Nugent were exhibited at the Royal Academy of 1810.

idle, and thoughtless woman. – I must therefore explain to them, that, notwithstanding all the gaieties and dissipation it records, her time was not all spent in amusement; but that the distressed and poor have never been forgotten, but have always been attended to; and not only part of her time, but part of their dear father's income, has been constantly devoted to their relief; as neither of us could be happy if it were not the case, nor should we deserve it to be so.

My ball on the 29th was particularly gay and brilliant, and Lady E. Palk was in all her diamonds, and Mr. and Mrs. Brummell came with the Graves' family. They were the only new people.

1807. *January 21st*. Left Exeter, and arrived at York House, Bath, between 4 and 5 o'clock on Thursday.

29th. Arrived in town, and found all the *world* (of *our* acquaintance) there before us.

On Tuesday, March 31st, General N. visited the 2nd battalion of his regiment (the 6th), at Ospringe barracks, Kent; and the 1st battalion the day following, at Deal, and returned to London, April the 3rd. On Tuesday, the 26th, General N. set off for Aylesbury, to begin his canvass. – On the following morning, I started for Stowe, with the little ones. We travelled with our own horses, and slept at Missenden, and did not reach Stowe till the 30th, in the evening. All Aylesbury in a bustle, as we passed through, and General N. had a hard battle to fight; but he was elected on the 9th of May, and Lord Temple for the county on Monday, the 11th. On Tuesday evening, the 12th, they returned triumphant to Stowe. All the house in green ribbons, but my poor deaf maid had a sad trick played upon her, and wore, as General N.'s colour, a *red bow;* and a sad quarrel was the consequence, with the ladies and gentlemen of the steward's room. – On Wednesday, the 13th, Mr. T. Grenville and Mr. R. Neville were elected for Buckingham, and we all attended them in the town to witness the ceremony.[1]

On the 19th, Mr. Robinson arrived from Jamaica, to our great joy, and I rejoiced with my dear sister, on his safe return, and without his health having suffered at all, apparently.

December 3rd. [Exeter] Sit to Downman for my picture a second time,

[1] This election, the second within six months, was due to the resignation of Lord Grenville's Ministry. Buckingham was a rotten borough where there were usually less than a dozen voters. In Aylesbury, following an unusually flagrant exercise of bribery (by a West India merchant) in 1802, the electorate was enlarged, and in 1806, 1470 votes were cast for the three candidates.

the first being no likeness at all; now it is thought it will be much better.

19*th*. I left off writing this day fortnight, and now resume my pen, with joy and thankfulness. A few minutes after 5 o'clock on that day, I felt slight pains, but I knew them to be decisive; I therefore quietly gave orders, for all things to be got ready, and tried to make up my mind to what was to follow. I had, however, but a short time to think of it; for the doctor and nurse could scarcely be with me, before my darling little fat Edmund made his *entrée* into the world of woe, as it is called by some, but may it be a world of happiness to him.

27*th*. With what different feelings, with what agony, do I resume my pen! God has taken my darling child from me! He is now no more. He breathed his last, yesterday, at half-past one o'clock.

1808. *January* 21*st*. Arrived this evening at Parrot's hotel, in Brook Street. – On Tuesday, we took possession of Lady Gosford's house, in Upper Harley Street. – On Friday, Mr. and Mrs. Robinson came to us, and spent a week, when they took apartments at an hotel, for the season. – General N., thank God, is looking better; but he has great fatigue, and has caught a severe cold in sitting on General Whitelocke's court martial.[1] I went with Ladies Buckingham and Temple, &c. to Chelsea, the last two days of the trial, and could not help pitying the wretched man, though he certainly fully deserves the sentence passed upon him.

July 8*th*. We are now going to begin a tour, as they say that nothing is so good as continual change of air to remove every vestige of the hooping cough, before winter. Arrange all our affairs in town accordingly, and General N. has obtained leave from the Duke of York, to be absent from his district till September.

11*th*. All set out for Stowe. Our party consisted of General N., myself, and the two children, Miss Vyse, my own maid (Johnson), nurse Hamilton, Monsieur Gênet, and Joshua our footman. The heat was great, and when we arrived at Stowe, poor General Grenville, &c. all panting and dying of it; the great amusement was, watching the state of the thermometer, which rose at one time as high as ninety-six. We remained there only a few days; and then set out on our tour, in spite of the sultry weather.

Little Miss O'Donnel and her maid were added to our party. I ought to observe, that the heat was so great, as we travelled, that many poor

---

[1] Gen. John Whitelocke was cashiered for his failure to retake Buenos Aires in 1807. Lord Lake, another member of the court martial, also caught a cold, which led to complications from which he died.

labourers dropped down dead, as they were working at the harvest.

We only spent two days in Dublin, to see Miss O'Donnel safe to her friends, and to see how the Dublin world were going on. The town was empty, however, and we only heard of all the Castle proceedings of the last season; among which, the disagreements between Sir A. and Lady Wellesley made the most prominent feature. We were only two days on our road to Belvoir, where we found all well, and my poor mother much better than we could possibly expect, after the sad accounts we had lately heard of the state of her health.

We remained ten days at Belvoir, the children being quite well of their cough, and quite happy with their cousins, and much liked and admired by all their relations and friends. Took rather a melancholy leave of the dear party, and crossed over to Port Patrick, from Donaghadee. Then through Ayr to Glasgow, where we were met by good old Colonel Murray. Stayed two days, to see the manufactories, &c.; all of which I explained to the dear children, as well as I could, and their early age would admit of. We then proceeded to Sir John Murray's (Lanerick Castle), where we were most hospitably entertained, and all their few neighbours invited, to do us honour. These were limited to a few of the MacGregor Clan, and Lord and Lady Doune. We were much amused with the clannish histories, &c.; and with hearing all the Jacobite feelings and prejudices descanted upon, just as if it was in the years 15 and 45. In the drawing room, and in Lady Murray's dressing room, there were portraits of Prince Charles; and General N., I am sure, shocked the whole party very much, by calling him the Pretender; for he was immediately corrected by the lady of the house, who said, "Prince Charles, if you please." I saw, too, a portrait of my dear father, among many others of the MacGregor Clan, and, although a wooden sort of painting, it is something of a likeness. We then set out again on our tour, accompanied by our kind and good friends, the Murrays, for Trinity Lodge, near Edinburgh, the seat of Colonel Murray. – Saw the Castle, Holyrood House, &c.; in short, all the lions of that beautiful city; and were fêted by all the MacGregors and their friends, for a week. – I must not omit to mention, that I saw my pedigree, both at Holyrood House, and at the Lord Advocate's library, and was desired to be proud of my descent.

We took leave of Edinburgh, and our hospitable friends, with the greatest regret; but had a delightful journey to London; seeing all that was worth seeing on the way. We were obliged to hurry away from Scotland, sooner than we wished, as my dear N. must be again in the west of England, early in September. The poor dear little things felt this leave taking almost as much as I did, and the next day, by way of getting rid of the painful impression, of dear papa's being gone for a long time, though not to the West Indies again, as dear little G. thought at first, I took them to see sights; and Mrs. Salmon's wax-work, in particular, was such an amusement, that it absorbed every other idea.

Soon after I came back to town, Mr. Scrope Bernard shewed me an advertisement of a place in Buckinghamshire, thirty miles from town, that seemed exactly to answer our purpose, as a *home*. Write to my dear N., who approved of the description, and wished me to go to see it. Mr. Scrope Bernard went to the lawyer, for all particulars, and I find it is for such immediate sale, and so many people about it, that I must make up my mind on the subject in twenty-four hours. So, not to be known, order a hack carriage, and with nurse and Georgy, go down to Marlow; where I arrived at about 8 o'clock in the evening. Mr. Scrope Bernard was there before me, and Mr. Hicks appointed to meet us, at 10 the next morning, at the house; to give me his opinion of the timber, and the value of the place altogether. Spend some hours with him (Mr. S. Bernard) at Westhorpe House, and then, by their advice, offer sixteen thousand pounds for the whole purchase, instead of acceding to the demand of twenty thousand pounds. – Am very nervous about it, but no time is to be lost, on account of the many people who wish to become the purchasers. Return to town that evening, see Mr. Robson, and deposit four thousand pounds. Then write to General N., full of anxiety about what I had done. Receive a most kind, affectionate, and comfortable answer, by return of post. He is quite sure he shall like it and be satisfied; at all events, that I have acted for the best, let it turn out what it may. On the second of November, I went down and took possession.

Fortunately, General N. was ordered to town, as one of the members of the Court of Inquiry, on the Cintra Convention, which is to sit on the 14th of this month.[1] He arrived on the evening of the 13th, and, as the Court was adjourned for three days, we made a visit to Westhorpe House; arriving there at 11 o'clock at night, on the 14th of November. We found great difficulty in making any body hear, to let us in, which kept us a considerable time at the gate, before we could gain admittance. We immediately went over the rooms, &c.; and early the next day inspected every

---

[1] The Convention of Cintra, signed by the British army chiefs in Portugal, permitted a defeated French army to return to France and provoked great indignation in Britain by the lenience of its terms.

thing else, and my mind was relieved from a load of anxiety, by his approving of every thing, and seeming perfectly satisfied with the purchase.

1809. Lay plans for a school, and mean to curtail my soup list; after this winter, to have only the sick and old people upon it. I intend that Saturday, May the 6th, shall be the last day for their receiving soup this year, or at least till next October or November.

May 1st. From this date, till June the 3rd, our time passed in receiving and making visits in the neighbourhood, and in regulations for our parish, and the poor, &c. &c. and in plans for the improvement of Westhorpe. Consult Mr. Bent, our builder, employed at the house in Brook Street, about stuccoing the house, as it is now a frightful, ugly, blue and red brick building, and all the window and door frames must be renewed, they are so ugly and worn out.

June 25th. After returning from our parish church, we gave many orders, for completing the preparations for our going to Exeter, and all was ready for Tuesday; when, on that morning, a letter came from the Commander-in-Chief, signifying his wish, that General N. should proceed, as soon as possible to Kent, and assume the command of that district, to replace Sir John Hope, and to regulate the embarkation of the troops, for the expedition to Walcheren.

July 10th. Off for Dover. All the hotels and inns were crowded, and our accommodation was very so so.

11th. Get a lodging house, but not very good.

18th. Set off for Deal, on our way to Ramsgate. – The embarkation, for the expedition, a most interesting and affecting sight. – Found Mr. and Mrs. Robinson at Ramsgate, and dined with them that day. He is Commissary-General, to the great armament, and she, poor soul! must be left behind.

21st. Went to Broadstairs, Kingsgate, &c. and then set off, in the evening, for Deal. Met Lady Wellesley, &c. there, and had a nice walk on the beach. The Downs full of ships, and the sight altogether magnificent. The poor fellows cheering as they embarked, and I don't know why, but I could scarcely refrain from shedding tears at their joy; it seemed, indeed, so thoughtless, when they were so soon to meet an enemy, &c. But soldiers, I believe, never think, and perhaps it is fortunate for them that they do not.

September 15th. Saturday, the Admiral's dinner, at Deal. – Sir Charles Paget, a judge of lace. – Am much amused with the gentlemen's bargains, made at Walcheren, for their wives, &c.

20th. My dear N. much harassed by the accounts from Walcheren. There is a dreadful fever among the troops, and the sufferers are beginning to come over, for a change of climate and medical care, &c. – All the morning, he has been on horseback along the coast, and giving orders, for every possible accommodation, &c. for the sick. – Unfortunately, we had another large party at dinner; Lord and Lady Temple, Lady –, &c. who all went with us to the ball. It was a later night than usual, and to mend the matter, there was an alarm of privateers near the shore, the night being very dark. One of them fired into the town, and Lord Temple's battalion guns turned out, to return the fire. We were in a great fuss for some hours.

21st. The accounts from Walcheren very bad, and General N. was off early for Deal, &c. We followed, a large party, in the middle of the day, and all dined at Ramsgate, with Sir Henry Dashwood, Lady Camden, the Ladies Pratt, &c. Mr. Mercer and music in the evening. A late supper. My dear N.'s mind more at ease, having to-day completed many arrangements, and given out his orders, for the accommodation and comfort of the poor invalids as they arrive, and the Archbishop of Canterbury is coming to consecrate a burying-ground, to receive those, who, alas! have no chance of recovery, the fever being of so malignant a nature.

22nd. The morning very busy, and we all dined again at Sir Henry Dashwood's. – The Duchess of Manchester, &c. Very amusing circumstances attending the arrangement of carriages, for the party to go to the ball, at Broadstairs. At last the Duchess and General N. went in a hack chaise, with the singing Mr. Mercer, as bodkin. The events of the ball equally amusing. Old Lady Nelson shocked at Lady John Campbell and the Duchess of Manchester, asking their own partners, &c. She assured me, that Lady J. Campbell must be mad, or worse; for she wore half boots, and had a dog called Devil. In short, we had a great deal of fun, and came back to Ramsgate very merry, in spite of all the anxieties of the morning, respecting the poor sick soldiers, &c.

23rd. General N., &c. on horseback early, along the coast. Lady T., Miss D., &c. walked on the pier, and how different the appearance of every thing, from what it was a short time ago, when Lord Chatham, and the Lords Manners (his Aides-de-camp), and so many gay and fine people, were parading about and troops embarking, and all in high spirits; and now we hear of nothing but sickness and disaster.

October 1st. My dear N.'s mind is most cruelly harassed, by the idea of the numberless sick, coming almost every moment from Walcheren, and almost the impossibility of making them at all comfortable.

3rd. A quiet day, and entirely given up to business by my dear N., who is heartily disgusted with all the reports from Walcheren.

6th. General N. determined to resign his command, and has written to be relieved.

9th. Before 5, we started for Canterbury, where we dined.

10th. A crowd of military coming, before we had finished our breakfast; and General N. issued his order, on resigning the command, which in fact, he has been induced to do, partly because his attendance on Parliament was required, and partly on account of the state of my health. We were most anxious, also, to settle ourselves in the country, and lead a quiet life, my confinement anywhere else being extremely inconvenient.

November 15th. [Westhorpe] My dear N. vexed, that he must attend a ball at Aylesbury to-morrow. The French Princes, and all the world, are to be there, as it is given to celebrate the fiftieth anniversary of our good old King's reign, as a jubilee. – He presides at it, as senior Member for the Borough, and Mr. Hussey assists, as the other Member for Aylesbury. But it can't be helped, and we only think that he may be back in time, to find me still out of bed, though I should rejoice if it were otherwise, and he should only have the joy of seeing the dear baby, without the anxiety of expecting it.

There is a chasm indeed in my journal, but I will try to recollect all the past, and fill it up as well as I can.

December 16th. Towards evening, my dearest N. returned. He was met by the shepherd, nearly a mile off, to tell him it was a *dawtre*, and to get the promised reward of a guinea.

27th. My time has been passed in taking care of my dear baby, and I have been a little nervous about her, as she certainly does not appear to have quite so strong a constitution as George and Louisa had at the same age; but Mr. Hickman still persists in his opinion, and so I shall try to be satisfied. Yesterday, the dear little soul was made a Christian, by the names of Maria Emilia.

1810. In the month of September, a sudden idea of our going to India occurred. It is a source of great anxiety to me – for my dear husband's sake, and for the future benefit of our dear children, I ought to wish it; as he thinks it is right not to remain without employment, and that he should now exert himself for them. But, for my own part, as I must give up the dear delight of being with them, I cannot make up my mind to wish it. But I will not talk of it at present. I am now too much interested in this parish, where we have established a school, and General N. has succeeded in securing a resident clergyman. On the 18th of this month, my sister and Mr. Robinson sailed for Canada, where he is appointed Commissary-General.

Of late I have had many anxieties, on various subjects; but the idea of going to India is uppermost.

In October, our good old King was seized with his former malady, and still continues in a sad state. Of course, a regency is in agitation. This has put all the political world in a bustle.

1811. *February* 18*th.* Since I closed my journal, in December, our good old King has been so much better, that it is thought he may yet be restored. But the Prince Regent appears to be going on quietly, and doing so well that it is a pity the reins should be taken out of his hands, till his good old father is able to resume them, with comfort to himself, and advantage to the country. He has, in fact, acted with the greatest prudence and consideration towards his parent; for, except giving to General Keppel the vacant regiment of General Craig, he does not mean to give anything away, but to leave all patronage for our good old King to decide upon, when he may recover.

Lord Wm. Bentinck, who has been for some time appointed Minister and Commander-in-Chief in Sicily, goes there soon, and she writes me, that she hopes to accompany him. Wherever they go, may they be happy and prosperous! – From some reports of late, I am in great hopes that General Brownrigg will be sent to India, instead of my dear Sir George.

My dear N. has had an audience of the Prince Regent, at Carlton House; he was most graciously received in his private apartment; but nothing new or satisfactory, about the Indian plan, was the result; so I am left to my hopes and fears still.

In March, the East India plan was decided upon, and my dear husband was unanimously and with acclamation appointed by the Court of Directors. All parties seem highly to approve of the appointment, and Lord Temple told me, to-day, that instead of feeling any regret I ought to be proud of such a testimony to his character, as it is that entirely that has gained him the appointment, not one of his friends being in power. But, alas! I cannot help thinking of my children; and, while I am going through all the bustle of dinners, to meet East Indians, &c. and while I am fatigued both in body and mind, with writing and various preparations, my whole heart is at Iver and at Westhorpe; for ten days ago, my dear little girls returned there, under the care of dear good Miss Dewey.

I am impatient to get out of town to them, but can't get rid of our engagements, till towards the last of the month . . .

On Wednesday, the 3rd, my dear N. was sworn in at the India House, and dined with the Court of Directors, and a large party, afterwards, at the London Tavern. Every thing went off most prosperously, and he has since settled a great deal of business. To-day, he saw Mr. Perceval, Mr. Yorke, &c. To-morrow night, after dining with the Nulli Secundus Club, to meet the Duke of York, &c., he means to set off, and hopes to be at home by 2 or 3 o'clock on Monday evening . . .

This book I shall seal up, and send to Westhorpe to be put into the desk, that is in the little breakfast room, where my dear children may find it, one of these days, should I not return; and along with it various little articles, as keepsakes, which they will value, I am sure, as relics of a father and mother, devoted to their interest and welfare. Now, may God Almighty bless, protect, and watch over, my beloved, my darling children, and may He, in his great mercy, permit us once more, in this world, the great and unspeakable happiness of seeing them again! My heart sinks within me, but I will not allow myself to think that there is anything of evil presentiment in the misery I feel; for I trust, oh my God! in thy mercy and goodness, for ordering whatever is best for us, here and hereafter.

May 29th, 1811.

APPENDIX

A. LETTER TO GENERAL NUGENT FROM THE MOSQUITO INDIAN CHIEF-
TAINS: from the Nugent papers in the Royal United Service Institution
Library.

General Nugent
Governour of Jamaica &c &c &c

Sir,

We beg leave to Acquaint you that we have had here a General meeting of the
greatest part of our Officers in Order to advise your Honour of our present Situation
and are very sorry that our King George the 2nd was assassinated in his house on the
10th August last by the people from Sandy Bay they robbed the House of all the Arms
and Amunition none of us to Leeward of this knew any thing of it, we have since
Elected his Br^r Stephen King for life we are in great want of a Supplie of Muskets
Mashets Powder Ball and Flints, falling Axes & small hatchets as we are afraid of an
Attack from the Spaniards as soon as the dry Season setts in which is soon and we
never liked the Spaniard and King George when alive allways looked up to the English
for Assistance in Arms and Amunition and we still look upon them as our Allies and
would be very happy they would return to live at Black River we will clear the Land
for them ourselves . . .

King Stephen is in great want of some Cloth and would be greatly obliged to his
Honour to send some such as Osnaburgs Checks and Platillas(?) a dozen pair of
Pistols and Swords. Notwithstanding we elected Stephen King we intirely leave it to
the determination of the British Government how to be directed for the Appointment
of One.

We beg leave to remain with the greatest Esteem and respects

Sir
Your most Sincere
Friends & most Obd^t F^{ful} Servt^s
General Marshall Wayatt his Mark +
General Robertson +
General Perkins +
Admiral Saint John his mark +
Major Jasper Hall ditto +
Capt. Thomas Pitts ditto +
Colonel Quaco ditto +
Captn. Smith +
Captn. Abraham +
Capt. Ross +

Cape Gratias a Dios Musquito Shore
8th Fibry. 1802

B. Two LETTERS FROM MRS. NUGENT TO ADMIRAL DUCKWORTH:
from the Nugent-Duckworth MS correspondence in the Library of
Rhodes House, Oxford.

1. An undated note evidently referring to the expedition to Stony Hill,
mentioned on p. 100 of the Journal.

How good you are My Dear Sir, to lay so comfortable a Plan for us – but I am
sorry to say that we cannot avail ourselves of your kind Intentions in our Favor, as
General Nugent is under the Necessity of visiting Stony Hill on Thursday having to
review the 85th Regiment. My *Aide de Camp*[1] was to have acquainted you with this
Manoeuvre today as he and I are to mount our Ponies and accompany Genl. Nugent –
our plan is to breakfast with Col. Gordon and then to pay our Respects to you at
Dinner – I have just been talking thro' the Keyhole to Mr. Duckworth upon this
Subject, as we are both in our Robes de Chambre preparing for Dinner – he says he
was just going to write – but as I do he will be satisfied this once with sending you
his best Love and Duty – General Nugent joins me in best Regards and good wishes –
in haste My Dear Sir your obliged and sincere

M. Nugent

2. A letter from the Decoy, referring to the incident at the Rio Magno.
The concluding part of this letter is reproduced in Plate 19.

Decoy, April 5th, 1803

I don't know whether I am not selfish enough my dear Sir, to rejoice that the last
Pacquet did not bring any Intelligence respecting your Fate although I am sufficiently
generous to feel for the unpleasant state of suspence you are kept in – however I hope
this Month will decide all & if you are to remain, we will then carry *our Plan*, with
regard to Miss Duckworth, into execution & look forward to a merry Party in a year
or two across the Atlantic & for the Time we remain here we will console ourselves
by being as jolly as possible –
We returned yesterday to this charming Place all in high Health & Spirits – The
Weather is now so fine and the Air so refreshing that I can almost fancy myself in dear
old England – My darling Boy is more improved than I can tell you – his little Cheeks
are now *couleur de Rose* & he has become most wonderfully *apprehensive* for his Age –
his *Acquirements* are indeed the astonishment of every one & I can scarcely make
People believe that he is not ten or twelve months old at least. I desire now that you
will not smile & think all this is nothing more than the mere *common Civilities* shewn
to the *Governor's Lady* –
The *Itinerant Staff* spent from Thursday 'till the following Wednesday with us at the
Ramble – all were in high Health & equally good Spirits. Your Son and his General
appeared upon the most comfortable Terms & I hear much of the activity & attention
of the former as a travelling A.D.C. &c &c –
You would be astonished at the Improvement of Mr. Baker[2] since he has been here –
he has lost his Deafness in a great Degree, has a very good appetite, looks quite fat
& rosy & keeps us constantly laughing with his odd Remarks & Drollery – I had no

[1] Lt. Duckworth, the Admiral's son.
[2] Lt. Henry Baker, RN, who was drowned the following year.

PLATE 19

CONCLUSION OF A LETTER FROM MARIA NUGENT TO ADMIRAL DUCKWORTH
(see opposite)

Idea of his possessing half the Spirits or Cleverness we have discovered in him & yet he never forgets for an instant the respect due to every One – I am requested by this Family, after presenting their best Compliments, good wishes &c &c to beg the Favor of Mr. Billi's[1] being permitted to visit the Decoy when Mr. Tyrrell[2] comes to escort me home – he is indeed a very fine Boy & I shall feel much obliged by your granting our Request. I have not yet fixed the Day of my Return, but as soon as I do, with your Permission, I will write to Mr. Tyrrell to arrange matters with Mr. Billi respecting his getting to Spanish Town &c & I think it will be about the 18th or 20th – We still talk of the *Rio Magno* – *Moses in the Bullrushes*, &c &c & I assure you your Health is drank in a *Bumper* of Madeira every Day – You cannot concieve my dear Sir, how grateful this good Family are for your attention respecting their Son – it is a constant Topic with them –

I hope by this Time Mr. Mitchell is in his usual Health – we regretted much to hear of his Illness, tho' I understand the Ladies of Kingston rejoiced at having the Thursday's Fête in Consequence of it –

    Adieu My dear Sir, believe me your
          much obliged & very sincere
          Maria Nugent

C. SOME KING'S HOUSE BILLS:
from the Nugent papers in the Institute of Jamaica. (Amounts are in Jamaica currency, of which £1 = about 14s. 3d. sterling).

His Honour Gen[l] Nugent
          Bought of Joshua Rouse
1801
Aug 7th   19 yds India Jean at 10/–   9. 10.
         a Green Silk Umbrella   2. 10.

                          £12.
     Rec'd Payment for J. Rouse
          (signed) Da[d] Clarke
     Entered

His Honor General Nugent
          Bo[t] of James Dunkerley
1801
Sept 9   A Plated Egg Frame   £4. 10.
     Received Payment for James Dunkerley
          (signed) J. Hammond
     Entered

[1] Lt. George Lawrence Billi, RN.
[2] John Tyrrell, the Governor's secretary.

Messrs Atkinsons Hanbury & Co.
1802
June 1st   Bt. of Stewart Bruce & Co.
                16 faths well Rope 50 lbs at 2/6   £6 5/-
                        General Nugent

His Honor Generall Nugent
                        To Thos Jones Dr
1802
Augt 21st   To 1 Superfine Blue Undress
                Coat Compleat   £20
                Received Payment of the above
                        (signed) Thos Jones

Mr Baptiste Vilno(?)
                        Bt of Jos. Johnson and Co.
1802
12 Dec.   4 Hams 73 lbs. . . . . 2/6   £9. 2. 0.
                Rec'd Payment
                        (signed) E. Johnson
                For the King's Ball

His Excellency General Nugent
                Bought of Munds and McIntosh
1802
Dec 29   1 Copy Hunter's diseases in Jamaica, calf-gilt 8vo   1. 5.
                1 do Lempriere's diseases in do do   2. 5.
                1 do Rumford's Essays, do   4. 10.
                                                                    _____
                                                                    £8

Gen¹ Nugent

D^r to Geo. Howard

1802

		£	s	d
Nov. 1	1 Milit^y Cock^d Hatt	5.	0.	0.
Dec. 20	4 prs. Hoby's Shoes¹	5.	0.	0.
	1 pr. d^o ½ Boots	3.	0.	0.
1803				
Feby 14	1 Brown and Green Hatt	2.	0.	0.

£16 [sic]

1802

Dec. 21	By cash rec^d of Messrs. Atkinsons	8. 13. 4.
22	By 3 prs. shoes returned	4.

12. 13. 4.

£3. 6. 8.

H: Ex: the Governor

to James Smith
Interpr^r C.V. Admlty D^r.

1803

Nov. 15	To Interpreter's fees on making a translation of a Letter from the Govr of Havana to the Gov. of Jamaica with certificates of descriptions of sundry Slaves. 6 pages at 25/–	£7. 10.
19	To Interpr^s fees on making a translation from the Spanish of a Letter from the Govr of Caracas to the Govr of Jamaica. 5 pa^s at 25/–	6. 5.

£13. 15.

---

¹ Geo. Hoby, of 163, Piccadilly, London; boot and shoemaker to Their Royal Highnesses the Dukes of Kent, Sussex and Cambridge.

Messrs. Atkinsons Hanbury and Co.,
      for Genl Nugent
         Bo^t of Hibbert Taylors and Markland

1803		
Novr 22^d	2 Pipes of Madeira Wine 235 G^s at £90 p^r 110 G^s	£192. 5. 5.

His Excelence General Nugent
        to Private Devis
          1st B^n 60th Regm^t

1804		
Aug 27th	to Reparering 2 Satles at 10^s Each	1. 0. 0.
	D^o 2 Pack Satles at 5^s Each	10.

£1. 10. 0.

       Philip Devis
Mr Atkinson will have the goodness to pay the above to
Mr. Myers and charge the amount to General Nugent.
                (signed) G. Rainy Lt Col.
                    1st/60 Reg^t

    M. Atkinson Esqr^e

        General Nugent
          Bou^t of John Munds

1804		
Sept 13th	a Magic Lantern with Slides	£12

His Honour Gen: George Nugent
        Bo^t of Joshua Rouse

Octr 1st	1 doz. Black Silk Hkfs. at 13/4	8.
	9 Leather Japan'd Hats for Servants at 26/8	12.

£20.

        Received payment
        (signed) J. P. Rayner

INDEX OF PERSONS

With biographical notes

Persons are listed with the rank or title which they held at the time when mentioned, including those junior naval and military officers to whom the author refers as "M1 . . . ." In the text of the Journal the author's spelling of names (which in previous editions was largely retained) has been emended where necessary to accord with the commonly accepted forms; except in cases where there is some confusion of identity, e.g. as between Messrs. Edwards and Edwardes, both of whom the author refers to as Edwards. In the Index the author's spelling, if substantially different from the norm, is added in brackets. Maiden names of married women, where known, are also given in brackets. Inevitably, some of the identifications are tentative.

"Justice" means a local lay magistrate, in which capacity the principal proprietors in each parish are listed in the contemporary Jamaica Almanacks. Names of properties are taken for the most part from the givings-in listed in the Almanacks from 1811 onwards, i.e. beginning

some years after the Journal was written. Comments in quotation marks are by General Nugent, mostly from a paper entitled "A sketch of the characters of the principal persons in office in Jamaica in 1806."

In this Index, a page reference such as 144–7 means that the person is mentioned on each of the intervening pages, and a reference such as 144–201 *passim* means that the person is mentioned frequently on the intervening pages, but not on every one.

Abbreviations used:

GN   General George Nugent
MA   Member of the Assembly
MC   Member of the Council
MN   Maria Nugent
MP   Member of Parliament
RA   Royal Artillery
RE   Royal Engineers
RN   Royal Navy
SD   Saint-Domingue
WIR   West India Regiment

1839, 2nd son of the 3rd Duke of Portland; Governor of Madras 1803–7, Minister and Commander-in Chief of British forces in Sicily 1811–14, Governor Gen. of Bengal 1827–33, of India 1833–5: 142, 277

Bentinck, Lady William (Mary Acheson), daughter of 1st Earl Gosford, 2, 142, 181, 264, 277

Berkeley, Frederick Augustus, 5th Earl, 188

Berkeley, Maurice Frederick Fitzhardinge, Midshipman, RN (later Admiral, Baron Fitzhardinge), 1788–1867, 2nd son of the 5th Earl Berkeley by an alleged private marriage whose validity was not admitted by the House of Lords, and grandson of the 4th Earl whose widow, Elizabeth Drax, became 3rd wife of Robert, Earl Nugent; 188, 203, 216, 218, 241, 245, 247–9

Bernard, Scrope, (later Sir Scrope Bernard Morland, 4th Bart.), son of Sir Francis Bernard, Bart., sometime Governor of New Jersey and of Massachusetts; MP Aylesbury 1790 and 1796: 273

Berri, Charles Ferdinand d'Artois, *Duc de*, 1778–1820, 2nd son of Charles, *Comte* d'Artois (*Monsieur*); assassinated in 1820: 263–4

Bessy, 164

Betty, William, "the young Roscius", 262n.

Bianchi, Madame, (*née* Jackson), singer, married to Francesco Bianchi, Italian composer: 267

Bigsby, Miss, d. 1804: 79, 203

Billi, Lt. George Lawrence, RN, 281

Billington, Mrs. (Elizabeth Weichsel), opera and concert soprano, at the height of her popularity 1801–11: 267

Birchall, Mr., agent to Sir Eyre Coote, 260

Bissett, James, Ensign, 69th Regt., 19

Black, Mr., from Ireland, 161

Blackburn, John, MA St. Thomas in the Vale 1802–5; of Wallens and New Works, St. Thomas in the Vale: 151

Blackwood, Sir James, 2

Blair, Mr., 145, 155–6

Blair, Mrs., 145, 148, 155–7

Blair, Lady Mary, mother of Mr. Blair, 145

Blair, Primrose, RN, Physician to the Fleet: 141, 171, 179, 186, 192, 257

Blake, Lt. W. W., 20th Light Dragoons, 44, 52

Blakeney, Lt. William Augustus, 85th Regt., d. 1802: 130

Bligh, Capt. (later Rear–Admiral) John, RN, cousin of Capt. William Bligh of the *Bounty*: 198n., 201

Boger, Capt. (later Rear–Admiral) Edmund, RN, 245

Bogle, Mr., of Bogle, Atkinsons and Co., Kingston, 29, 33, 60

Bogle, Mrs., 138

Boisdabert, *Mons.*, 52

Boss, Lt. L. de, 60th Regt., 221

Bourke, Jean Raymond Charles, 1772–1847, *Chef de Brigade*, of Irish descent, b. in France, served with French army in SD 1791–2 and 1802 (ADC to Gen. Leclerc), later in Europe, at Austerlitz, Wagram, etc; Baron of the Empire 1808, General 1813, Inspector General of Infantry 1817, Member of the Chamber of Peers 1826: 99, 118

Bouverie, Capt. (later Vice-Admiral)Hon. Duncombe Pleydell, RN, 233–4

Bowes (Bowles), Edward, d. 1805, "a very old inhabitant and one of the Masters in Ordinary": 204

Boyles, Capt. (later Vice–Admiral) Charles, RN, 102

Brent, Mr., 163, 166

Brisbane, Lt.–Col. Thomas Makdougall, 69th Regt., 1773–1860, in Jamaica 1800–3, Brigadier–Gen., Asst. Adjutant Gen. in the Peninsula 1812–13, Major–Gen., in Canada 1813, Governor of New South Wales 1821–5, after whom the river and city of Brisbane were named; an amateur astronomer, who established observatories at Paramatta near Sydney, and at Brisbane and Makerstoun in Scotland: 59–61, 101

Bristol, 51–2

Brockmuller, C.P., Ensign, Jamaica Garrison Company, formerly Quartermaster 60th Regt., "a very deserving old soldier": 238, 240

Brockmuller, Mrs. (*née* Cummins), 209, 238, 240

Brocksopp, Mr., father of Mrs. Horsford, 203

Brodbelt (Broadbelt), Dr. Francis Rigby, 1771–1827, medical practitioner in Spanish Town, MC 1798–?1812; "a diffident man, associating with but few persons, and generally silent in Council. He does not however want sense, and as he lives at the seat of government, is in so far a useful member." It was alleged that he had taken his seat on the Council on the strength of a writ intended for his father, a physician having the same names, who died 1795 (monument in Spanish Town Cathedral). In that year, F. R. Brodbelt junior, still a medical student in London, had been awarded a silver medal by the Medical Society of London for his paper on "A case of deposition of mercury upon the bones." For the Brodbelt family, see G. Mozley, *Letters to Jane from Jamaica,* Institute of Jamaica, 1939: 19, 117, 129, 160, 173

Brodbelt, Mrs. (Frances Millward), 173, 180

Brooke, Henry, Volunteer 1st Class (later Lt.), RN, 1792–1823 ("Little Brooke"): 3, 8, 9, 57, 59, 61, 63, 117, 148

Broome (Brown), Capt. Henry, 20th Light Dragoons, 102

Broughton, Mrs. (Phillis), m. (1) James Roper, of Roper, Cocker and Co., and (2) Henry Thomas Broughton, MA Port Royal 1803–9, "late clerk in the dockyard at Port Royal and brought into the Assembly, chiefly through the influence of the Admiral in the parish for want of a proper person to stand as candidate at the election – a perfectly insignificant character": 185

Browne, Henry, Ensign, 87th Regt., 144

Browne, 2nd Lt. (later Col.) Thomas Gore, RA, 1785–1854: brings presents from the Buckinghams, 57; considered as one of the family, 63n; affected

by death of brother officers, 123; very silly, 149; ill at King's House, 201; brings news from Port Royal, 225, 234; mentioned, 100, 112, 154, 175–6, 194, 209, 212, 221, 232

Brownrigg, Lt.–Gen. Robert, 277

Bruce, Mr., 63

Brummell, Mr. and Mrs., 270

Brunet, Jean Baptiste, 1763–1824, *Général de division*, in SD, effected the arrest of Toussaint 1802, commanded successively at the Mole, Port-au-Prince and Les Cayes, where he surrendered 1803; remained a prisoner until 1814, created *Chevalier de Saint Louis* at the restoration of the Bourbons, rallied to Napoleon 1815 and was thereafter retired: 180, 196, 198n.

Bryan, Charles, 1736–1810 ("the senior Mr. Bryan"), MA Portland 1792–1802, Custos 1802–10; of Bogg, in Portland, and Hertford, in St. Thomas in the East: 71–3

Bryan, William, son of Charles Bryan; of Pleasant Hill and Shotover, in Portland, and Muir Town, Reach, etc., in St. Thomas in the East: 71

Buckingham, George Nugent Temple Grenville, 1st Marquess of, 1753–1815, eldest surviving son of George Grenville, the Chancellor of Exchequer of Stamp Act fame; on the death of his father-in-law, Earl Nugent, in 1788, he inherited the latter's title and real estate worth some £14,000 a year, and adopted the names Nugent and Temple; Teller of the Exchequer (a sinecure office) 1764–1815, Lord Lieutenant of Ireland 1782–3 and 1787–9, Lord Lieutenant of Buckinghamshire 1782–1815; Cobbett's assertion that in half a century Lord Buckingham and his two brothers had derived some £900,000 from their various public offices, is thought to have been an exaggeration: patron of GN, xiii–xv; MN receives gifts from, 57, 220; GN writes to, 63n., 212; kind letter from, 256; godfather to George Edmund, 126; at Stowe, 258–9, 263; advises on GN's affairs, 259–60,

miral, 10th Baron Colville), 3–9, 40, 44
Colville, Mrs., 3
Commanding Officer of the Military, see Churchill, Gen. George
Commissary General, see Atkinson, Matthew
Conolly, Mr., proprietor of Porus, 96
Conolly, George Sloane, Ensign, 2nd WIR, 157
Cooke, Edward, Under-Secretary in the Colonial Department 1804–6: 256–7
Cookson, Major (Lt.-Col. in the army) Charles N., RA, 1756–1830, one of those Royal Artillery officers whom GN described as "useless. Their long residence in the country, and the connections they have formed, most certainly tend in a material degree to relax their attention to their duties.": 17, 38, 52, 63, 102, 122, 144, 157, 187, 192, 199; his Penn, visited, 39, 117, 164, 167
Cookson, Mrs., a perfect Creole, 52; mentioned, 128, 169
Coote, Lt.-Gen. Sir Eyre, 1762–1824, nephew of Gen. Sir Eyre Coote who served in India with Clive and Hastings; entered the army 1776, served in America, West Indies and Egypt 1776–1801, MP Queen's County, Ireland, 1802–5, Lt.-Governor and Commander in-Chief Jamaica 1806-8, 2nd in command Walcheren expedition 1809, General 1814, became mentally deranged and dismissed from the army 1815: xv, xxviii, 240–1, 251–2, 255–7, 260–1, 267
Coote, Miss, 260
Corbet, Edward, d. 1805, accompanied the British expedition to SD in 1793 "from motives of curiosity", Naval Officer and Deputy Receiver Gen. in SD 1794–8, British Agent in SD 1799–1801; while this was post was abeyance in the following years, GN employed him to report on troubles in Honduras Settlement and the Cayman Islands, to negotiate with Dessalines 1804, and finally to act as Collector of Customs in Kingston, and "uniformly experienced his intelligence, zeal and activity upon every occasion"; a sick man throughout these years, he died at sea on his

way to Britain: xxii, 33 and n., 34, 36, 51, 61, 99, 103–4, 107, 128, 132, 134, 194 and n., 195
Cornwallis, Gen. Charles, 1st Marquess, 2nd in command in the American War, surrendered at Yorktown 1782, Governor Gen. India 1786–93 and 1805, Lord Lieutenant Ireland 1798–1801: xiii, 1, 265
Correvont (Corovants), Mrs., d. 1817, ?wife of Capt. Lewis Correvont, 3rd WIR (on half pay), "an old officer and a Swiss by birth": 179
Correvont (Corovants), Miss, 179
Cosby, Lady (Anne Eliot), eldest daughter of Samuel Eliot of Antigua, wife of Lt.-Gen. Sir Henry Cosby, 257
Cosens, George Harrison, d. 1817, a Justice of St. Mary; of Sheerness and Markham, in St. Mary, Elysium, in St. George, and Shrewsbury and Fairy Hill, in Portland: 72
Cosens, Mrs. (Thomasina), d. 1811: 72
Cottrell, Capt. Frederick, RN, 162, 166
Courtenays, the, = William, 3rd Viscount Courtenay, and his sister, 269
Courvoisier, Capt., 173, 180
Coward, Mrs. (Milborough Scott), d. 1823, wife of George Fletcher Coward, Deputy Marshal for St. James, MA St. Ann 1816; of Islington and Whitehall, St. Ann: 89
Cowen, Hugh, Volunteer, 2nd WIR, 1783–1804, nephew of Gen. Carmichael: 177–8, 193
Cox, Captain, from the East Indies, 110
Cox, Mrs., 79
Crackley, Mrs., 128
Craggs, Anne, see Nugent, Mrs. Robert
Craig, Lt.-Gen. Sir James Henry, 277
Craskell, Thomas, Island Engineer, 11n.
Craskell, Capt. Thomas C., 9th WIR (on half-pay), Captain of Apostles Battery 1803; ? son of the preceding, and formerly Superintendent of Maroons at Trelawny Town: 166, 169, 180, 194
Craskell, Mrs., 180
Creyke (Criek), Lt. George Adey, RN, 40, 112
Croft, Mr. (? = the following), 201
Croft, Capt. (later Rear-Admiral) William,

GENERAL INDEX

Names of regiments and of ships are listed under those headings